A BOOK

A BOOK
by Desi Arnaz

WILLIAM MORROW AND COMPANY, INC.
NEW YORK   1976

Printed in the United States of America.

6 7 8 9 10   77 76

Library of Congress Cataloging in Publication Data

Arnaz, Desi (date)
  A book.

  Autobiography.
  1. Arnaz, Desi, 1917–
PN2287.A69A32   790.2′092′4   [B]   75-28040
ISBN 0-688-00342-7

Book design by Helen Roberts

For Lucie and Desi IV

A BOOK

1

I was born in Santiago de Cuba, on March 2, 1917. (I had to start someplace.) That makes me a Pisces, and there can't be a better place for a Pisces to be born than Cuba, surrounded by the Gulf of Mexico, the Straits of Florida, the Atlantic Ocean and the Caribbean Sea.

In 1869 the Queen of Spain appointed my great-grandfather, Don Manuel II, to be mayor of Santiago and gave his father, Don Manuel I, my great-great-grandfather, and his wife, Ventura, a nice chunk of Southern California.

In 1953, soon after Desi was born, I received a letter from the granddaughter of Don Manuel and Ventura. I talked with her and she told me that the land grant given to our ancestors by Queen Isabella included large sections of land in the areas known today as Ventura County, Beverly Hills and the Wilshire district in Los Angeles. Ventura Boulevard in the San Fernando Valley and Arnaz Drive in Beverly Hills were also named after them. When I told her I wished they could have hung on to those nice pieces of real estate, she answered, "You're telling me. Every time I go shopping at the Farmers' Market I could die."

My grandfather, Don Desiderio, was the Cuban doctor assigned to Teddy Roosevelt's Rough Riders when they went up San Juan Hill during the Spanish-American War, which gained Cuba her independence from Spain.

My father, Desiderio II, graduated from the Southern College of Pharmacy, in Atlanta, Georgia, in the class of 1912–1913. He married my mother, Dolores de Acha, in 1916, and in 1923 was elected mayor of Santiago. He was twenty-nine years old, the youngest mayor Cuba ever had.

My full name is Desiderio Alberto Arnaz y de Acha. When I became an American citizen while in the United States Army, the sergeant in charge of the swearing-in ceremony had a hell of a time pronouncing my name.

He politely told me, "You know, son, you could shorten your name a bit, that is if you want to, of course, on your citizenship certificate."

I said, "I guess I better, Sarge. Make it Desi Arnaz."

"You don't have to overdo it," he said. "Don't you want a middle initial or something?"

"No, thanks, Sarge. Just Desi Arnaz—period."

My son Desi's full name is Desiderio Alberto Arnaz y Ball. He quickly changed that to Desi Arnaz, Jr. But today he is called Desi Arnaz—period—and I, Desi Arnaz, Sr.

When my grandfather became very ill in 1929, I was attending a Jesuit school. We were all Catholics, but my grandfather was not a churchgoer. Knowing he was about to die, I talked him into seeing a priest friend of mine. Grandma Rosita had said to me, "Desiderio, if your grandpa knows the priest is a friend of yours, he will see him."

Father Gil was the priest's name. He used to teach mathematics at the Jesuit high school. So Father Gil came to see my grandfather. After they had talked for a while, Father Gil said to him, *"Ponga el Corazón con Dios."* (Keep your heart in God.)

My grandfather answered him with, *"Ponga el Corazón con Dios, y el Rabo tiezo."* (Keep your heart in God, and a stiff prick.)

The Spanish and Cuban people, as well as most other Latins, have the same kind of wakes the Irish do. They go on for two or three days and all the mourners do is drink a lot of booze and eat a lot of food. I was only twelve years old when my grandfather died, and I remember trying to get everyone out of the house. They were honoring him, but I couldn't understand why everyone should be having such a good time while my grandfather was in his coffin and the house smelled of death.

The funeral was one of the biggest funerals of all time in Santiago, not only because my father was the mayor and my father's brother, Manuel, was the chief of police, but also because of what my grandfather himself had done as a doctor. He was known and loved for his gratuitous services during the smallpox, yellow-fever and cholera epidemics in the latter part of the nineteenth century.

Don Desiderio and Grandma Rosita had seven children. When he died, my grandfather had been retired for quite a while, and he had spent most of his time at a little farm in El Caney, just outside Santiago, his Casa Chica. From there he still continued to treat all the poor people around at no charge. Casa Chica ("little house") is where his mistress lived with their seven or eight children. Whenever he heard that Grandma Rosita was coming, he said, "Everybody out!" And they would all hide in the barn until Grandma left. I am sure Grandma must have known, but she never said a word, and the mistress never got upset about having to get out and hide. As long as he continued to love each of them, and cared for their children equally, they were satisfied. Having two houses and two sets of children was very common among Latin men of means, and Latin women understood this and didn't make a fuss about it.

There was an article in the *Los Angeles Times* by David F. Belnap, datelined Santiago, Chile, October, 1973: "Chile's curfew is a boon for family life. It's done more for marital fidelity in a month than six months of hard-shell evangelism." The *Los Angeles Times* editor commented, "He was referring to the popular Chilean penchant for *'la casa chica'*—literally 'the little house' or, in bold terms, a mistress whom he sees two or three or more times each week."

So it seems that the custom of my grandfather's day is still going strong in Latin America. It is not, however, a way of life that you can safely carry on in this country. American girls do not seem to understand it.

Grandpa's big house, where he and Grandma lived, was directly across the street from us, and every afternoon when he came home from his little farm, all the grandchildren were there waiting for him. He would always have something for each of us—perhaps only a banana, an orange or a tangerine—but he always had something.

In the evenings after dinner, he enjoyed sitting with Grandma on their rocking chairs, facing each other by their large window next to the street, saying hello and gossiping with their friends as they went by. I used to love to go over and sit with them. Grandpa had a great sense of humor, and Grandma and I were his best audience. I remember one night when Grandma noticed one of their daughters and her husband approaching. She turned to him and said, "Here comes Miguelito and Rosita, and, by the way, your fly is open."

Grandpa smiled and answered, "That's all right, the bird doesn't fly anymore."

I was his only grandson, legitimately that is, and he would always tell me, "It is your duty and responsibility to see to it that the Arnaz name will continue."

"Don't worry, Grandpa, I'll give it a hell of a try."

* * *

On my mother's side of the family, my grandfather was Alberto de Acha, one of the founders of the Bacardí rum company. His wife, my grandmother, was Rosita Socias. Both my grandmothers had the same first name and the same build (5 by 5). I adored them both. We used to have lunch every Sunday at Grandpa Alberto's. They had twelve children, and the table would always be set for thirty people. Even so, many times the kids had to eat on the patio or in the kitchen or wherever they could find room. One of the things I miss a lot in this country is the family closeness of my youth. Relatives here seem to live so far apart, and even if they don't, they get together only on rare occasions.

Emilio Bacardí, for whom the rum was named, was a lover of good wine. He did not like the dark and heavy rum of Jamaica. So with a small still and equipment in a little back building he began experimenting with different mixtures until he came up with an excellent and light rum. Actually he was looking for a Scotch-type drink —sipping booze—and when friends were over at his house for dinner he always offered them a small glass of his concoction. Everybody raved about it and soon the guests were bringing empty Coca-Cola and beer bottles. Those bottles were always filled by Emilio before they left.

One day a French salesman, Enrique Schue, was having dinner at Emilio's house and he sampled the rum. He immediately became enthusiastic and told Emilio to stop giving it away. His drink was unique. Why not bottle it, label it "Bacardí" and sell it? It was done.

The Frenchman became the business manager and financier, Emilio made the rum, and Grandfather Alberto, who owned two mules, became the salesman. He would load the mules with as many bottles of rum as he could put into cardboard boxes and sell them in Santiago and the nearby countryside. When he died, he was a vice-president of the Bacardí Corporation. It is the best rum in the world.

My father, besides being the mayor, had three farms. On one of them he raised cattle. Another was a dairy farm. He was the first man to build a pasteurization plant in our province and also the first to use refrigerated trucks to deliver the milk. The third farm was used for poultry and pig raising and had a slaughterhouse where meat, sausages and all other products of this kind were processed and sold.

During school vacations there was always work for me at one of the farms. My father felt that if I wanted new oars for the boat or a motor overhaul or whatever, I should earn the money to pay for it. I didn't mind; it was fun.

I would get up at dawn with the other hands to start the day's chores. Every morning we had a contest to see who could fill a bucket with milk the quickest. Each of us would put up five cents and the one who could fill the bucket first would take the pot. I became pretty good at milking cows.

I also did whatever other cowboy chores the foremen would assign to me, but summers at the farm were not all work and no play. I was so young when I learned to ride, I can't even remember the first time I sat on a horse. My favorite was a beautiful Tennessee Walking pinto horse Father had given me on my tenth birthday, and which, being very inventive and original, I named Pinto.

There was also good fishing on the rambling river that passed behind our house at the dairy farm. Alongside the river were trees with extremely large leaves that we used to catch big river shrimp, and those are the most delicious.

My favorite place was our summer home on Cayo Smith, a small island in Santiago Bay, which is considered one of the three most beautiful bays in the world. Cayo Smith looks like a little mountain thrusting itself out of the water. There was a road cut all around the base of the island. It was just a narrow dirt road where no automobiles were allowed. We had bicycles, but it took only about forty-five minutes to walk around the island. However, my usual way was to swim around it. My teammates on our high school swimming team and I would swim halfway, visit a few friends and then continue to swim around to our homes. It was a good workout, particularly if we were preparing for a meet.

At the very top of the island was a little church and on Sunday the whole island population, of about three hundred to four hundred, at the height of the season, used to go to Mass there. On the hillside were the small houses of the fishermen and the people who would take care of our beach houses when we and the other vacationers left at the end of summer.

Our beach house was surrounded by garden terraces of tropical flowers and fruit trees—mangoes, pineapples, guavas, coconuts, bananas and many others. There was a 21-foot-wide covered veranda and railing that went all around the second story of the house.

The cook and the maid lived downstairs. So did Bombalé, a big, wonderful black man who cared for my dad's speedboat and who taught me all about boats and engines and how to handle them right. Nowadays when I'm in Baja California, trying to figure out these new, complicated engines and other gadgets, how I wish Bombalé was there with me!

There were four bedrooms, which were always occupied by our family, relatives and friends. Everybody loved Cayo Smith. Don't ask me why a little island in the middle of Santiago Bay should be named after Smith. I have never been able to find out.

Directly in front of the house was a 75-foot-long pier, extending out into the water. At the end of the pier was the boathouse, which was large enough to accommodate two boats—my dad's speedboat, which would take him back and forth to City Hall every day, and my first motorboat. It was an 18-foot Norwegian fishing skiff type, made of teak. One of the greatest thrills of my life was to see this boat being built right in front of my eyes, from the laying of the keel to the placing of the motor. Some of the best boats in Santiago Bay were built on that little island. Mine was powered by a one-cylinder Regal, and I got so that I could take it apart and put it back together blindfolded, thanks, of course, to Bombalé.

The Cayo Smith boathouse was designed so that each boat could be pulled up out of the water with pulleys, to clean the bottom and paint whenever necessary. It was also handy to pull them up level with the pier and make it possible for either one of my 5-by-5 grandmothers to get out of them when she came to visit. The boathouse was surrounded on three sides by a 10-foot-wide pier with a railing and was covered by a peaked tin roof. The boat entrance was, of course, on the open side. On the opposite side were two dressing rooms, one for men and one for women. One of the dressing rooms was the scene of a very important event. My first experience with sex.

The daughter of the cook was a cute twelve-year-old black girl. One day this girl and I, who was also at the wise old age of twelve, wound up in one of those dressing rooms. After locking the door, we began to experiment about how this thing was done. Neither of us had the slightest idea. This may sound unbelievable today, because I am sure that there are very few twelve-year-olds who don't know exactly what the whole deal is and how to go about it. I didn't have the first clue about where to put my little thing. And she wasn't much help. But I was obviously anxious and noticeably ready for action, and getting more and more frustrated by the minute. We had tried a number of ridiculous experiments and were working on a new one when there was a loud knock on the door. It was her mother, the cook, asking her to come out. I didn't have any trouble putting on my trunks in a hurry. The small proof of my anxiety had disappeared. I wish I could have done the same.

I was frantic. Looking around, I figured the only avenue of escape was through a high window which looked out over the water.

From the windowsill it was at least thirty feet down to the water and the pier around that side of the boathouse, as I said, was about 10 feet wide. But that was it!

I took a deep breath, dived from the window, cleared the pier, hit the water, headed for the bottom and swam underwater away from the scene of the crime. Underwater swimming was no problem. We used to stay under for at least two minutes. We had contests over who could stay underwater the longest. I came up for air at the next boathouse, about fifty yards from my start, but I still did not feel that was far enough away, so under I went again and on to the next one.

I arrived there and was getting my breath and trying to figure out my next move when I heard Salvador calling me. Salvador was my father's younger brother and one of my favorite uncles. He had a little soap factory in Santiago, didn't care about politics or getting a job in Dad's administration. And even though he wasn't making as much money as his brothers, I'm sure he was the happiest.

He was married to Willy May Reed, whom he had met while going to school in Atlanta. She was the first American girl I had ever met. She didn't speak a word of Spanish. When I saw her in Miami many years later, exiled with her daughter, Ampy, and her husband, she still wasn't doing much better with our language. I teased her about it and she answered, "If I were you, I wouldn't brag too much about the way you handle mine, either."

When I heard Salvador call me from the boat, I realized that I had forgotten I was going fishing with him that afternoon, an understandable lapse of memory. I was glad to see him. What a lucky break, I thought, a perfect alibi! If anyone brought up the subject of the boathouse incident, I would say, "I don't know what you are talking about. I was fishing with Uncle Salvador."

So I climbed aboard happily, took the oars and headed for the fishing grounds.

Salvador said, "Where do you want to go this afternoon?"

"Let's fish on top of the *Merrimac*."

"It'll take you an hour to row over there."

"I don't mind. It's a beautiful day and, at this time of year, it's the best spot on the bay." It was also the farthest away from my house.

The *Merrimac* was the ship the Americans had sunk during the Spanish-American War to block the very narrow entrance to Santiago's harbor, which prevented most of the Spanish fleet anchored there from getting out.

We always caught a lot of red snapper, bass and yellowtail and also lost a lot of hooks, weights and lines. If you weren't on your toes, once the fish knew he was hooked, he would head for the inside of the sunken hull, and if you allowed him to get into it, forget it. I had a habit of trying to picture where in the hull the fish might have gone. Maybe he was lying in a bunk and laughing at me after he had made sure my line was tangled in a porthole or something.

About halfway to the fishing ground, Uncle Salvador said, "I didn't know you were such a good underwater swimmer. It must be over one hundred yards from your boathouse to where I found you."

"I came up for air after the first fifty, and how do you know about this?"

"Well," he said, "I'll tell you. I was coming over to go fishing with you and, as I approached your house, I noticed a very interesting tableau. Your mother was on the front porch, looking very intently at the boathouse. I followed her gaze and saw and heard the cook knocking on the door and calling for her daughter to come out. A split second later, I saw you fly out of the window in a perfect swan dive into the bay."

"Holy Jesus, you mean my mother saw the whole action?"

"Yeah, and by the way she was standing on the porch, obviously waiting to see what would happen, I'm pretty sure it was she who sent the cook down to break up your clandestine operation."

"Ay! Ay! Ay! Ay! Ay!" said I.

"If it's any consolation," he continued, "I must say she was watching with a great deal of interest as you swam under the clean blue Caribbean water, all the way to the next boathouse. From her vantage point, it must have been a beautiful sight." Salvador had a wonderful sense of humor.

"What are we going to do now?"

"We're going to anchor on top of the *Merrimac* and fish."

"And then what?"

"Then *you* are going to go home and face the music!"

"But my father will be home and Mother will have told him the whole story."

I also told Salvador that nothing had really happened. "We couldn't figure out how to do it."

"Well, we'll do something about that later," he told me. "In the meantime, let's catch some fish and then you've got to go home."

So we fished, but I was too preoccupied with my predicament to enjoy it. I would have liked to stay above the *Merrimac* forever, but it was time to go. We rowed back, I went home, showered and changed. By that time my father had returned on his speedboat.

Mother hadn't said a word to me. At dinner the only thing Dad said was "Did you and Salvador catch any fish today?"

He really knew how to lay on the pressure. After dinner he went to his study just off the living room and called out, "Desi, come in here."

I thought, Oh, boy, here it comes.

I entered the room with much trepidation and he said, "Sit down. I want to talk to you."

He began, "Have you ever seen me insult your mother?"

"No, Dad."

"Have you ever seen me embarrass her or make her ashamed of me?"

"No, Dad."

"Then why did you do what you did this afternoon? I know what you were trying to do. You are a boy. But for God's sake, why were you so damned stupid? You could have picked a better spot than our own boathouse."

I could see his point.

Then he said, "Now you listen to me, young fellow, and listen good. Don't you ever insult your mother that way again or embarrass her as you did. Now get the hell out of here!"

And that was it!

My uncle Salvador, about three years later, and I'm sure under instructions from my father, took me to Casa Marina. I was then fifteen years old, the dangerous age, when you are no longer a child but still have quite a way to go before being considered a man.

The Casa Marina was the finest whorehouse in Santiago, and there I learned the whole deal. The ladies of that house were all young and clean and treated me very kindly, very nicely, very tenderly and very expertly. Sometimes I wonder if perhaps it is not better to educate a young boy like that instead of letting him get into a lot of trouble trying to find out for himself. If your father or mother or a close relative, as it was in my case, was willing to guide you and help you with this first inevitable and major problem of your teens, you would not be afraid or ashamed to go to him or her later with other problems.

2

In 1932 my father was still mayor while he was campaigning for election to the House of Representatives from our province of Oriente. We were living in a house on San Basilio Street, directly across from my grandma Rosita's home.

At one o'clock in the morning, June 1, my mother and I were asleep at home. A policeman, who was always on guard at our house, was in front by the door.

A loud kind of rumble woke me up. The house was shaking so hard the big beams in the open ceiling of that huge old house were dancing around like toothpicks. At the same time I heard what sounded like a train coming through the house. I jumped out of bed and went to my dad and mother's room, which was next to mine. Mother was kneeling by her bed praying and looking up at the crazy walls shaking and the old beams dancing.

Finally I realized that what sounded like a train coming through was a big bell from a train engine my dad had been given as a memento of the first train that traveled from Havana to Santiago. It was a valuable old relic mounted on a lovely solid mahogany base which he kept in his office at home.

An earthquake is the most scary thing in the world. There doesn't seem to be anything you can do and there are no warnings.

My father was at City Hill, still in his office, working on his Congressional campaign. He told us later that the first thing he heard was a low, ominous rumble which sounded as though it was coming from far, far away at first and then kept getting louder and louder. He said that it sounded as if the town were being rolled up toward him in a gigantic rug—the same sound that woke me up. Suddenly he was pinned against the wall by his desk. As he got away from there and ran outside to the courtyard, he remembered that this was no place to be because the courtyard was over a big water reservoir, so he ran to the park in front of City Hall. When he started to cross it in the direction of our house, he looked up at a gigantic statue of the archangel Gabriel and his trumpet which was swaying dangerously back and forth on top of the Cathedral. Hypnotized by this sight, he extended his arms toward the angel as if to catch the statue and prevent it from crashing to the street. When he realized what a ridiculous gesture that was, he continued running to our house.

On the other side of the plaza, to the right of City Hall, there was a hotel called Venus. It was a three-story building and it covered about half a square block. It was one of the two biggest hotels in Santiago. Thank God, there was nobody in the hotel, because it was being remodeled. The entire hotel crumbled to the ground. On the other side of the plaza, to the left of City Hall, was the Club San Carlos, a very exclusive for-men-only private club. In front of the club, overlooking the sidewalk and the plaza, were a few dozen rocking chairs where members, usually old politicians and businessmen, would come to sit and discuss the latest news or gossip, but mainly to watch all the pretty girls as they strolled around the plaza, clockwise, while the young men looked them over, going counterclockwise, and the municipal band played its nightly concert.

On the third floor of the Club San Carlos was a game room where a poker game always was in progress from 10 P.M. until dawn. When it finally finished shaking, the roof and four walls of that floor were completely demolished and the front wall facing the plaza had crashed down on the girl watchers' seating arrangement. But even though there had been a lot of people up there, they all got out without serious injury.

One of the guys playing poker that night was the husband of my father's sister, Maria Pepa, a fellow named Wasmer, who was of German descent. He was a compulsive gambler and always in financial trouble. They had three daughters and two sons. He had a good job, a nice house, but he was always in hock, always a loser and constantly borrowing from everyone, hoping for that one lucky night, and certain that it would come. Enrique, his older son, finally found him sitting in the plaza, cuts and bruises all over him, but still holding and staring at his poker hand, as if in shock. He was mumbling to himself, "Sonofabitch, the first time I've got aces full a fucking earthquake has to hit."

When Dad arrived home, after running six blocks and dodging falling walls, he was covered with stucco and was white from head to foot. He had on a white linen suit, his face was white, his hair was white and his shoes were white. He looked like a ghost.

"How is everybody?" he asked.

I said, "I'm fine and Mother's fine. The only one who got hurt was the cop on duty. If he'd stayed under the shelter of our portal he would have been okay, but he ran across the street, where a wall fell on him. He had a bad cut on his head. Salvador has already taken care of it."

My dad then went over to see if his mother and Willy May and her daughter, Ampy, were okay.

Everybody was fine.

Grandma's house, which she owned, and ours, which we were renting, were Spanish Colonial, very old but very strong, built during the days when Cuba was a Spanish colony, and they stood up well against the earthquake, except for one wall in my bedroom, the one behind my bed. When I went back to my room to get some clothes, I found my bed covered with bricks.

Dad came back from Grandma's and told us no one was hurt there. He had decided we would be safer out of the city, at our farm, El Cobre, only about twenty miles from town. He was concerned that if the shakes continued those old houses might not be able to take it. Worse yet, there was danger of fire, which had already started in many areas of the city, caused by high-voltage electric wires which had fallen down. He thought also of the very awesome possibility of a tidal wave.

He had found in the City Hall records that Don Manuel, his grandfather, who was the mayor during the quake of 1869, had evacuated everyone from the vicinity of the bay to the high ground inland, thus saving many lives from a pretty frightening tidal wave.

Dad told Salvador, "You and Desi take my mother with you. I'll take Lolita [my mother's nickname for Dolores], Ampy and Willy May. I will see that the rest of the family gets there in trucks or whatever." Not many people had cars in our town.

Salvador had an old Model T Ford coupe. We put Grandma in the middle, he was driving and I sat on the other side of her. He started for the ranch. We had to go very slowly because of the hot wires and the traffic. In addition, walls were falling down here and there; people were screaming and running all over the place. Houses were on fire, ambulances were going by and the police were trying their best to keep some kind of order. It was a mess.

Salvador was having a hell of a time getting out of town. My grandmother had been very quiet through all of this. Then we heard her say, "I have been in this car before, but I've never been as uncomfortable as I am now. Why is that?"

I looked to my left and only saw her feet. I looked up and broke out laughing. She looked down at me and said, "What are you laughing about?"

"Grandma, what are you doing, sitting up there?"

"I'm sitting where you put me."

As I was helping her down I realized that, in my rush to get her into the small car, I had somehow managed to push her onto the top of the backrest of the front seat, with the result that her back was pushing against the roof of the car and her feet were dangling in the air. Poor Grandma, who, as I mentioned, was 5 feet tall and weighed over two hundred pounds, was bent over like a fat pretzel. No wonder she was uncomfortable. As we got to the farm, everybody else began to arrive. Soon most of my relatives from both sides of the family were there. All my life I have wished I could have had brothers and sisters. I was an only child, but I did have a hell of a lot of cousins, I'll tell you.

All of the houses around that area were made of wood. I remember one of the neighbors coming over and telling us, "I was reading a novel when the earthquake hit and as I looked around, I could actually see the nails going in and out of the walls. I was fascinated by this unbelievable sight and all I could think of was: 'Please, God, let it stop when the nails are in.' "

Later I learned that during the quake a bus disappeared when the earth opened up, and it was never seen again. Thank God there were not too many passengers aboard at one o'clock in the morning.

Our biggest movie house was just a pile of bricks and mortar. All that was left was the big movie screen. It looked like a drive-in theater. A study was made later, which claimed there would have been at least ten thousand casualties if the earthquake had happened at 8 P.M. instead of 1 A.M. Actually, only thirty people were killed.

Cayo Smith also had wooden houses, no big buildings, and when the threat of a tidal wave had passed some of us went there and others stayed at the farm.

Dad was not able to spend much of that summer with us. He had a hell of a time getting the town rebuilt.

My dad's biggest project as mayor was Plan Arnaz, which had been approved more than a couple of years before by the City Council and the governor. It had been sitting in Havana since then waiting for the necessary federal approval and financing. It called for all streets to be paved; most were not, particularly where the blacks and poor people lived. Even the first house we lived in was on a dirt street. The plan also called for sewers and sidewalks, more and better equipped hospitals, more schools, an aqueduct to provide enough fresh and clean water, more firehouses, and better fire engines.

It was a plan that would not only convert the town into a very clean and modern city, but would also give the people much badly needed work. He fought for that plan for years and it broke his heart when it was finally turned down. As late as 1973 he was still saying that the only thing he wished he could have done was to have had that plan approved, and remodeled that town. After all those years he was still thinking of Santiago.

My high school at Colegio de Dolores was run by Jesuits and, boy, are they tough! Actually, all high schools in Cuba are tough. Nevertheless, in my freshman and sophomore years I did have top grades—all A's, even in English, believe it or not. But in my junior year I was in real trouble with my studies.

One of my best friends, Jack Cendoya, whose father owned a hardware store in town, was in the same boat. That third year of high school in Cuba is murder. Plane and solid geometry, trigonometry, Spanish literature, history of Spanish literature, logic, psychology and physics—all are required. In the United States these subjects are spread over two or three years.

We knew, as the old joke says, we had two chances to pass— slim and none. In geometry and trigonometry we had only one—none.

I went to my father and said, "Look, Dad, I don't think I'm going to be able to pass my final exams."

He looked up at me from his desk: "So? What do you want from me?"

I told him, "You have always said that anytime I was in trouble, I should come to you and nobody else. Well, I'm in trouble."

He nodded his head a few times, smiled and called his secretary to tell her he didn't want to be disturbed. He then said, "I'm glad that you came to me and told me the truth."

"I'm sorry, Dad, I don't know what happened."

"I know what happened," he said. "You discovered girls and from the report I got from my soap-making brother, you didn't have any trouble learning *that* subject."

I stuttered, "No, sir, I mean—"

"Never mind," he said, "there must be a way to get you over this hump."

He thought for a moment, pressed a button on his desk and said, "Have Sergeant Rojas come in."

He turned to me and said, "This sergeant, on the City Hall detail, is a whiz at mathematics."

"Well," I said, "if he can get me through geometry and trigonometry, I think I can get by with the others by cramming real hard for the next couple of months."

Dad said, "I tell you what I would do if I were in your spot. I would quit school as of now and use every hour to cram at home, because, at this late date, I am sure all the other guys in your classes will just be reviewing what they have previously studied, and according to what you've told me, you have nothing to review."

Sergeant Rojas came into the office and Dad explained the problem to him. He made a date to start the next morning at 8 A.M. at our house.

"Thanks a lot, Dad," I said, and started to leave.

He stopped me with "Listen, Desi, you better pass those finals because, if you don't, there will be no Cayo Smith for you this summer."

Little did he or anyone know that before the summer was over the course he had so carefully and lovingly charted for our lives to follow was to be torn to shreds.

3

My father was elected to Congress in November, 1932. I went to some of Santiago's precincts with him. There were no machines to count votes in those days. An official called them out and dropped them in the candidates' boxes. As I walked into one precinct the official was dropping some in Dad's box and calling, "*Arnaz—Arnaz uno más para el doctor* [dropping another into it]. *Desiderio—Desi— Desiderio—AY! Uno para el otro*," as he daintily dropped one in the other guy's box.

Dad went to Havana in January, 1933, to be sworn in as a Congressman. When he came back to Santiago to help turn over the City Hall to the new mayor, he was given a tremendous victory celebration parade. I saw him being carried by the largest Cuban flag I had ever seen. There must have been at least one hundred people holding him up and bouncing him up and down. He looked as if he were doing tricks on a trampoline. I thought, My God, they'll never get him here in one piece.

Mother and I were with the councilmen and the mayor, who were sponsoring the celebration party. Dad was laughing and waving to the crowd as they carried him all around the plaza to the steps of City Hall.

After the transfer of his administration to the new mayor, he went back to Havana to start serving his term in the House.

On March 2 I received a letter from Dad. It was my sixteenth birthday. It said that in his book that meant I was no longer a child, but a man. The rest of it, philosophizing about life in general, impressed me so much I framed it and hung it in my room. Mother also got a letter from him that day in which he told her he had found a wonderful house for us in El Vedado, a very nice residential section of Havana, the equivalent of Bel Air in Los Angeles. He also wrote that he would be home by the fifteenth of August and then we would all go to Cayo Smith until I had to go to finish high school in Havana. And I could hardly wait for the fall of '34 and Notre Dame.

Jack Cendoya and I, with the help of the sergeant's long hours of cramming, and by the grace of God, had managed to squeeze by the finals of our third year of high school. About three o'clock in the afternoon on August 12, I was at Jack's house, four or five blocks from our house, in Vista Alegre. Vista Alegre ("gay vista") was a residential suburb of Santiago. My dad had some nice property there and immediately after the earthquake he ordered a home built—all wood. Everyone who could afford it was moving away from Santiago and her old buildings. We had moved to Vista Alegre at the end of 1932.

Jack and I were playing penny-ante poker. I never got home before six o'clock, but about three o'clock in the afternoon I said to Jack, "I don't know why, but I feel I should go home."

"What do you mean, you should go home? Just because you're winning, eh?"

I said, "I'll be back in a little while."

As I got home, the phone was ringing. It was my mother's brother Eduardo, an up-and-coming lawyer who later became a judge. He sounded very excited:

"Get your mother out of the house, right away! They're coming after you."

"Who's coming after us?" I asked.

"Machado has fled the country and anyone who belonged to the Machado regime is in danger." (Machado was the President.)

"Will you calm down, Quiquín [that was his nickname]? What the hell are you talking about?"

"Listen to me, and listen carefully. All Machadistas are being arrested or killed. Their houses are being ransacked and burned."

I said, "Wait a minute! The people of Santiago just had this tremendous celebration party for Dad when he was elected to Congress. Why should they be coming after our house?"

He told me, "These are not the people of Santiago. These are just a bunch of anarchists and Bolsheviks [they weren't even called Communists in those days]. They have killed or wounded every policeman who has tried to stop them. Quartel Moncada [the largest army post in Santiago] is in flames! For God's sake don't waste any more time. Get out of there! Have Bombalé drive you to Bravo Correoso's house and I'll meet you there."

Antonio Bravo Correoso was my mother's uncle and one of the most famous criminal lawyers in Cuba. Some of his cases are still being used as textbooks at the University of Havana. He had also been a Senator. A brilliant man.

Just as I hung up, I heard a rumble. I looked out and I could not believe what I saw. About eight blocks away, just beginning to come over the top of the hill on our main boulevard, there was a mob of five hundred people or more carrying torches, pitchforks, guns and God knows what else.

Mother heard and saw this frightening mob.

"Oh, my God, what's that? What's happening?"

"Quiquín called and said they are anarchists who are destroying everything that belonged to any Machadista, and to get out right away and go to Bravo's house."

As I was helping her into her coat, I asked her, "Where's the petty cash that Father left?"

He had left about three or four hundred dollars for household expenditures. She took that and I grabbed a pearl-handled revolver Father had always kept in the drawer of his night table. I found Bombalé, who was driving for us because our regular chauffeur, Blanco, had gone with my father to Havana, out front shaking his head and looking at this crazy mob.

"They can't be coming here," he told me. "There are blacks in that mob."

What Bombalé meant was that the blacks had been Dad's greatest supporters. Without them he would never have been elected mayor three times. Most of the leaders of my father's political campaigns had been black. I never knew what racial prejudice was until I got to Florida. Instead of being prejudiced, we were proud of our black population.

Many of our War of Independence heroes, like Flor Crombet and Perito Perez, were blacks. José Maceo and Juan Gualberto Gomez, mulattoes, and, last but not least, the indomitable "Titan of Bronze," Antonio Maceo, who together with his white revolutionary brother

José Martí, became our greatest heroes and, indeed, liberators. Martí, our Simon Bolivar, and perhaps the most brilliant Cuban ever, wrote: "Man has no special rights because he belongs to a particular race. The soul emanates equal and eternal from bodies different in shape and color. It is sufficient to say 'Man' to comprehend therein all rights."

Our dances, for which we were as famous internationally as for our cigars, sugar and Bacardí rum, were mostly African: the conga, rumba and mambo. And our Cuban music, as Fernando Ortiz so lovingly put it, "derived from the love affair of an African drum and a Spanish guitar." (Changó, god of war, is the African god I sing to in "Babalu.")

Bombalé turned to my mother and said, "Señora Arnaz, please let me stay and protect your home."

Mother told him, "*Gracias,* Bombalé, but no. We need you. Please come and take us away."

Mother knew that if Bombalé had stayed there he could not have protected anything and would probably have been killed.

As we got into the car the police dog and Father's chihuahua were already inside; I guess they sensed something. Bombalé was trying to start the motor. It wouldn't start. Then I heard him say, "Oh, my God, I forgot that I took the battery to the garage this morning."

By this time the mob was almost there and a car skidded to a stop alongside our car. The guy driving was Emilio Lopez, one of the top men in the ABC, a group formed against Machado. He said, "Come on, Desi, and Lolita and Bombalé, get in here, and I'll take you to my home."

It's kind of ironic that the man who got us away from the mob, and perhaps saved our lives, was one of the heads of the opposition party. They had not foreseen that the fall of Machado would provide the anarchists and Bolsheviks with a perfect opportunity for mob violence.

We stayed at Emilio's home until dark. On the way to Bravo Correoso's we had to pass our house. That is, what was left of our house. The piano was smashed to pieces in the garden outside the living-room window. Our car, an Essex (that was bad enough), was upside down on the sidewalk with all the windows smashed and the tires gone. Scattered all around were tables, lamps, vases, chairs, paintings, glasses, plates, records, Victrola, radio, my bicycle (twisted and bent like a pretzel), a tennis racket, baseballs, footballs, Mother's clothes, Dad's clothes, my clothes—everything.

Some people were still going into or coming out of the house, looking for things to steal or perhaps just collecting souvenirs.

The last thing I saw was my guitar, the neck still smoldering away.

My mother said, "I can't believe that was our home just a couple of hours ago."

If you are reading this in the warmth and comfort of your home, surrounded by all the possessions you have accumulated during your lifetime—not just the valuable stuff, but all your personal things, all your mementos—try to imagine what it would be like if, within a few hours, it was all gone.

The things that my mother missed the most were the baby pictures, the baptism, first-communion and marriage certificates, wedding pictures, my father's first gift while he was courting her and other reminders of that sort. The value of these things at a hock shop would not bring a dollar, but they still are the things you value the most.

I remember, many years later, when Lucy and I were living at the ranch in Chatsworth and there was a big fire around us. Mother was coming home with us. The police at first wouldn't let us through. They were trying to keep everybody out of that area, but I explained that we had to get to our house and try to save, at least salvage, whatever we could. When we got there I went to the roof with a hose to keep it wet. Lucy was inside, deciding what to take out with her. Not knowing where to start, she asked my mother, "What do you take out first?"

"All the pictures, just take all your pictures and your private and personal documents and papers. Everything else can be replaced."

Lucy never forgot that, and when she told me what Mother had said, I was once again reminded that no matter how hard I'd tried, or how successful and wealthy I might get to be, there would always be certain things that money could never buy or replace.

Our house in Santiago wasn't the only one that was ransacked and burned. At least twenty or thirty more suffered the same fate. Some of them belonged to people who weren't even in the government, such as poor Salvador. Just because he was my father's brother, they burned down his stinking little soap factory. Grandma and Grandfather Alberto were almost blown to pieces by a bomb in front of their house. Thank God they were not sitting by the window in their rocking chairs. They were saved by being at the birthday party of one of their grandchildren in the inside patio. Grandpa had never even been in politics.

The actions of such a mob, incited and manipulated by those

who know how, are difficult to believe and frightening to witness. You could point a finger at someone and say, "He killed my brother!" and, without any regard to whether it was true or not, they would shoot him or, worse yet, tie a rope to his ankle and drag him through the streets. I saw such an incident. The poor bastard was bouncing from one sidewalk to the other as they dragged him all the way to the cemetery; and there, if by chance he was still alive and they had one ounce of pity left in them, they finally shot him as you would a crippled horse. By this time the soldiers and policemen were scared to death and outnumbered, so they became mere onlookers in the midst of the mob.

For the time being at least, my mother and I were safe at Bravo's house. He opposed the Machado regime and one of his sons, Tony, and Colonel Pujol, a son-in-law, were very prominent in the ABC, which was originally founded in 1931 by students and leaders of the opposition from the upper middle class. Their only goal was to get rid of Machado—but on middle-class terms. They were serious idealists, interested only in the regeneration of Cuban life.

The anarchist and Communist groups infiltrated the ABC in order to use that idealistic umbrella to put into effect their revolutionary methods of deliberately creating terror and thus causing a breakdown in government activities. When they succeeded and Machado was forced to leave, they grabbed the opportunity to destroy any semblance of authority, knowing that anarchy, chaos—the ideal conditions for their terrorist activities—would create such an intolerable situation that they could seize power and control the island with the promise of restoring law and order, which they had so skillfully previously destroyed.

Anarchy. I had heard it mentioned so many times that I asked Bravo, "What does it mean, *anarquia?*"

"*Gobierno sin Jefe,*" he explained. (Government without a chief.)

Tony Bravo and Colonel Pujol had been at Casa Marina since early morning, celebrating the fall of Machado. They didn't know our house had been ransacked and burned, or that Mother and I were hiding in their home until that evening, until someone came to the whorehouse carrying and showing around some of the "trophies" they had taken from our house. Among them was a group picture of their families and ours. That really dampened the party. When Tony called his father, he found out what had happened to us, and they both came to the house immediately.

My mother had been holding up pretty well, considering everything that had happened to her that day. The news of the following day, however, was more than she could take, and she became hysterical when we learned they had done the same thing to our three farms and to the beach house at Cayo Smith. They had also sunk Dad's speedboat and my little fishing boat. Worst of all, they had massacred most of the animals on the farms—cows, chickens, pigs, horses, goats. Bravo and Tony held Mother and me in a tight and long *abrazo*.

I asked Tony, "Did they kill the animals because they were hungry?"

"Hell, no, they just killed them and left them there to rot."

"But why—why the animals?"

"I don't know, Desi. I don't know why anybody would do such a thing. All I know is that they also let all the criminals out of jail, not just the political prisoners, but all the murderers, rapists and thieves. They have also broken into all the liquor stores. I have never seen so many drunks. It's just unbelievable how a well-trained group of agitators can turn what should be a peaceful and happy celebration into a barbaric orgy of killing and destruction."

For the next few days I walked around the house like a zombie. I ate and I slept, I took a bath, I talked and I thought. I thought a lot. The only thing I couldn't do was cry.

I could not understand what had happened. Dad had always been loved in that town. He was called *Alcalde Modelo* ("model mayor"). One of the last things he did as mayor was to convert a large area around the bay, which had been a disgraceful-looking ghetto where some of the blacks and poor lived, into a beautiful *malecón,* with parks and trees, two big swimming pools for the children, tennis and basketball courts and a baseball diamond. An example of what his Plan Arnaz would have done everywhere.

When it was finished, the union workers and leaders and the heads of commerce took up a collection, and at the entrance of the *malecón* they built a big tower. In it was a large clock and a bronze bust of my dad with ALCALDE MODELO imprinted underneath.

My father named the *malecón* Alameda Michaelson in honor of an American friend of Cuba. The clock and my father's bust are there now. They were restored a few years after they were torn down.

Later, when I saw Dad in prison at La Cabaña in Havana, I asked him, "How can something like this happen overnight?"

"It didn't happen overnight," he told me. "When so many people are hungry and don't have a decent place to live, medical care and good schools for their children, clean towns without flies and mosquitoes, without the continuous threat of typhoid, yellow fever and all the other maladies synonymous with dirt, they are apt to revolt.

"There was a lot of unrest, but nobody expected it would wind up like this, except the ones who were waiting to use it. Had I had the slightest suspicion I would have been in Santiago. I have to believe that not even Sumner Welles, the American Ambassador to Cuba at the time, realized what he was doing when he forced Machado's sudden flight. Everybody wanted to get rid of Machado. Even I was getting disenchanted with the man, and if Mr. Welles had not acted so stupidly everything should have been all right. He overlooked the fact that the country, suddenly left without a chief of state, would not have time to replace him in an orderly and lawful manner."

Dad compared it to what would happen if the main supporting wall of a building was rotten and had to be cut down and replaced. "Before you cut it down, you've got to make sure that all the other walls in that building are well shored and secured, because if they are not, and you just cut the rotten one down and throw it away, the whole building will collapse. And that, unfortunately, is what happened to Cuba."

We learned after a couple of days that Dad was safe at his sister's house in Havana, but every mayor, every governor, every chief of police, Senator, Representative and anyone else at all who had been in the Machado regime and could be found was being thrown in jail. The others, who had money stashed away outside Cuba and had not been caught, were getting out of the country as fast as they could.

I found out later that Dad had actually gone to the airport with the President and could have left with Machado when he went to Miami. Machado left in the early morning of the twelfth with five guys in pajamas. Each of them was carrying two or three sacks of gold, so Machado was going to be all right.

He told Dad, "You had better come with me, Desiderio, because after I've gone, it is going to be complete chaos."

Dad thanked him but said nothing was going to happen to him. "They're not going to bother with a little fish like me."

Machado answered, "Just mark my words, Desiderio, and don't take any chances. The people who are behind this whole thing are not the members of the opposition party as we have known it in the past, but the anarchists and Communists of today."

Santiago de Cuba had been the first town in the island in which a Communist had been thrown in jail, during my father's second term as mayor. That probably explains why they couldn't wait to destroy everything he had the minute they were able to do so. Dad decided to turn himself in at La Cabaña, where they had promised him protection until law and order could be restored.

Bravo Correoso's home was built around a beautiful patio, so large, and with so many flowers, trees, fountains and benches, it looked like a park. In the center of it was the most gorgeous cage filled with all kinds of birds, but it didn't even seem they were in a cage. It was at least a story and a half high and not less than 40 feet long by 30 feet wide. There was a huge shade tree in the middle, so actually the birds were happier being inside rather than outside. They had all the food and water they needed and all the beauties of nature. It was a haven for them and they bred like crazy in there.

Bravo knew that his son Tony was to drive us to Havana the following day. I remember him saying to Mother, as we walked around this patio, *"La vida es muy larga* [life is very long]. It is like a book with many chapters in it, and this is the first *golpe* in your life. [*Golpe,* according to Cassell's Spanish dictionary, means blow, knock, shock, hurt, wound—all very applicable to our first *golpe.*] And you will probably receive a few more. Life, it seems, is full of *golpes."*

Then he said: "I know you are not in the mood now to believe what I'm going to say next, but take my word for it, you will recover, you will go on, you will again have the things you have had and perhaps even more, but you will have to be strong; especially you, Desi, you're a very young boy and you have your whole life ahead of you. So let us pray that your future *golpes* will not be as hard and undeserving, or as incomprehensible to you as this one was."

Next day, Tony, my mother, her brother Eduardo, who was driving, and I started for Havana in Tony's car, which he had decorated with ABC flags. Anytime we got to a town or saw a mob of people he and I would get on the running board and shout *"Viva la Revolucion!"* until we safely arrived in Havana.

That whole week of August 12 had been like a horrible nightmare.

If I thought it was bad in Santiago and throughout the country, when we got to Havana it was much worse.

We got there after a day and a half of carefully traveling across the island and shouting *"Viva la Revolucion,"* and went directly to my aunt Amparo's house. She was my father's sister. That is when we learned Dad had already given himself up and was at La Cabaña prison.

As we got to my aunt's house, there was one goddamn idiot who, with an old-fashioned World War I open-cockpit plane and home-made bombs, was trying to bomb the new regime at the Palace. My aunt lived about three blocks from the Palace, a dangerous place to be because this asshole never came close to hitting the Palace. He hit everything around it though. At an outdoor café, a kid playing the maracas lost an arm. A couple on the beach, which was about three and a half blocks from the Palace, were killed. People coming out of the theater four blocks away were hit. The safest place to be in the whole town was *at* the Palace.

There was one sight I will never forget. A man's head stuck on a long pole and hung in front of his house. The rest of the body was hung two doors down in front of his father's house.

4

As I stepped down from the ferryboat that brought me from Cuba to the United States of America at Key West, it might not have been a giant step for mankind, but it was a big one for me.

While they were checking my tourist permit at the immigration office, I looked up and saw Dad laughing happily behind the glass partition.

When they let me through, I gave him the longest, biggest and tightest *abrazo* ever. He said, *"Bienvenido a Los Estados Unidos de Norte America,* and those will be the last Spanish words I will speak to you until you learn English."

I proudly reminded him that I had gotten A's in my last two years of English in high school.

He said, "That's right, so tell me in English."

"Okay." I tried but nothing too good came out.

"Well, it will take awhile for your ears to get used to it and for your tongue to handle it."

My ears eventually got used to it pretty well but my tongue has been fighting a losing battle ever since.

We got on the bus to Miami, and as we settled in our seats he offered me a cigarette. I had never smoked in front of him. "How did you know I had taken up smoking?"

"Oh, I just figured that sometime during the last nine months you probably had."

He had been in jail at La Cabaña in Havana for six months. We were finally able to get him out on a habeas corpus, which is a legal term for "Either shit or get off the pot."

I had read a newspaper account of a habeas corpus that had been successful, in favor of the governor of our province of Oriente, Barceló. They had nothing against him, no definite charges, no indictments, so they had to let him out.

I took the newspaper over to Bravo Correoso and said, "Wouldn't this work just as well for Dad? Nobody has accused him of any crime. He hasn't been indicted for anything."

He said, "Yeah, I don't see why not. Let me check with the courts in town and in Havana."

He checked and there was nothing against him. So he sent this newspaper clipping to my uncle Eduardo, the guy who called me when the crazy mob was coming to the house and who, as I said, was also a very fine lawyer. Eduardo took it to the courts and won the case, and Dad was freed. As soon as he was out, he was advised by Batista to go to Miami until Cuba could get back to normal.

There were still a lot of nuts running around loose, even though Batista by then had established some semblance of law and order. At least the courts were again operating.

"I'm sorry I was unable to have you join me sooner but you know I didn't have any money. To tell you the truth, I have very little now. I was able to borrow just a few hundred dollars."

"Don't worry about it, Dad, you've got a long way to go [he was only forty then]. We'll start all over again, and at least remember what happened to us in Cuba can never happen in the United States."

The room we had in the southwest part of Miami was in a rooming house and it wasn't much. I knew my father was ashamed of not being able to get us something better. But I didn't care and he shouldn't have. I was happy just to be there with him. All I wanted was to get going so we could send for my mother, who was in Santiago at her father's house, anxiously waiting to join us.

Next evening, he said, "Okay, you've got to start getting around on your own, so go and have dinner alone."

I walked around and found what looked like a modest restaurant but nice and clean. A real cute waitress brought me a menu. I looked up, said, "Thank you," and opened it. After looking it over, I began cursing the Jesuits. Not only had they failed to teach me how to understand or speak English, they had not even taught me how to read it. The waitress was standing by my side with pad and pencil. I looked at her and smiled again. She looked at me, smiled back and said something that sounded like "Areyouabouttoorderyourdinner now?"

That's the trouble with a foreign language, you see; nobody stops in between words. She could have said, "Areyougoingtositthere-allthefuckingnightorareyouabouttoorderyourdinneryousillylookingCu-ban?" And I wouldn't have known the difference. Anyway, not wanting to let her stand there any longer, I pointed to four different lines of the menu, and wound up with four different kinds of soups, which I ate or drank, or whatever the hell you call it, as if this were what I normally ordered for dinner. I thought she had looked kind of funny when I first pointed to the four different lines on the menu, and by the time she brought me the second plate of soup, I knew why. You must realize that in 1934 there were very few Cubans in Miami. The great avalanche of Cuban exiles that was about to descend on Miami during the next forty years had not yet started. The only ones who were there then were the exiles from the Machado regime. A week later I found one small restaurant with a sign which said, *"Se hable Español."* Today, with the half-million or more exiles in that same area of Miami, you are lucky if you can find one that says "English spoken."

My father told me he'd been afraid those A's from my English teacher, a Jesuit from Spain, weren't going to mean much when I got to this country. He had decided I would go to summer school at St. Leo's, about forty miles north of Tampa.

"We can't spend money for that," I protested.

He said it had all been arranged. A niece of ex-President Machado knew the schoolmaster through a friend of hers who had two sons there and they had given us a very good deal.

He then went to his suitcase and, as he was taking something out of it, he said, "Would you like to take this with you?"

It was the letter he had sent to me on my birthday the year before. The glass was broken and the frame was not in the best of shape.

"How did you ever get that?"

"Bombalé went back to the house after they had left you at Bravo's and sent it to me in prison. Read the note he sent with it. It's taped on the back."

Querido Doctor Arnaz:
   Siento mucho que no pude hacer nada. Pero pensé
que probablemente, Desi estaria contento de tener
esta carta que usted le mandó.
   Asi fué como la encontré en el patio atrás.
   Atentamente, su servidor y su amigo.

Bombalé

(Dear Doctor Arnaz:
   (I am sorry that I couldn't do anything. But I thought that prob-
ably Desi would like to have this letter that you sent him.
   (This is how I found it in the backyard.
   (Considerately, your servant and your friend.

(Bombalé)

I had a great time at St. Leo's that summer and hardly ever saw
the other two Cuban boys who were there. My father had instructed
the brothers to keep us apart so that I would have to speak only
English. My ears had not yet been able to decipher what the hell all
these words running together meant. It really sounded worse than
double-talk and it's annoying to listen to, particularly if someone is
trying to give you a long explanation about something. So if I did not
want to hear it, I pretended I understood and just said, "Yeah, yeah,
okay."

About three weeks after I arrived at St. Leo's, one of the
brothers who was in charge of athletics came to me with a long explanation about something or other. I said, "Yeah, yeah, okay."

The next evening I went to my boxing class and I noticed there
was a large crowd. Normally, there were just a few guys around, some
taking lessons, others just watching and kibitzing. This time there was
a packed house. The same brother was in the ring making some kind
of announcement and everybody was applauding and looking at me.
I knew something was screwy but couldn't figure out what.

The brother signaled for me to come up to the ring and then
helped me with the gloves. The boxing coach was already up there,
trunks and gloves on. The brother then took us to the center of the
ring, where I heard more double-talk. Made us shake hands and sent
us to our corners. The bell rang. (It never did for a lesson.) The first
time he hit me I knew damn well it was not a lesson. I landed right on
my ass. While on it, I was thinking, How the hell did I get into this?
I got up and started to dance a little. "Keep moving, keep moving," I
was telling myself. When I thought I saw an opening, I threw a right
and got hit with three combinations. Down on my ass again. The

rounds are two minutes, with one minute's rest, and let me tell you those are the longest two and the shortest one minute in the world.

I was mad and I was hurting and I wanted to quit but I didn't want to look like a coward—so we were at it again. But there was no way I could hit this guy. When I thought I had him and threw a punch, he ducks and *bim, bam, bummed* me three or four times, and I was right back on my you know what.

Well, it went like that for the whole three rounds. I never got such a beating in my life. I couldn't eat solid food for two weeks. What had happened was that when I said, "Yeah, yeah, okay," to the brother, I okayed an exhibition match, which those other two Cubans had told him that I, as the middleweight high-school champion of my town [not true], wanted to put on with the coach.

Hijos de puta! (Translation deleted.)

The coach, who, by the way, was the middleweight amateur champion of Florida, was very sorry about the incident and for the rest of the summer taught me a lot about taking care of myself. It has come in handy a few times. The first time was before the summer was over. I must admit I did not follow all the Marquis of Queensberry rules while "reasoning" with those two Cubans, one at a time.

At the end of the summer I went back to Miami and found that the ex-mayor of Santiago, the ex-governor of Santa Clara and the ex-governor of Camagüey had started a company to import building materials. The building boom was just beginning in Miami and Miami Beach. They imported roof tiles, bathroom tiles, kitchen tiles—all kinds of mosaics.

They called the company the Pan American Importing and Exporting Company, Incorporated, a hell of a name for a company with a capital of five hundred dollars. They would buy four hundred dollars' worth of tile from Mexico, and then they would have to wait until they had sold it to be able to order another shipment. They couldn't get any credit. They weren't even able to recuperate the breakage because they could not afford insurance.

The company headquarters was on Third Street, S.W., in Miami, one tiny little room with three desks for the executives. I was in charge of transportation, the one who used to go for coffee, go for sandwiches and go for tiles.

The warehouse, right in back of the office, had a pretty smooth cement floor and was a good-sized 40-by-40-foot room. It had a little can in the back and a washbasin.

One day while I was there counting and arranging the tiles, I saw Dad looking around and measuring a corner of it. I just knew what he was thinking, but he would never say it to me. So I said to him, "You know, Dad, I think we should stop paying five dollars a week to the lady in the boardinghouse. The food is lousy anyway, and we could close in a little piece of this area, right there behind the office, real easy. We could do it ourselves, with some cardboard and a few studs. We could put in a little chest of drawers, a couple of beds, a hanging closet in one of the corners. It would make a nice bedroom. We've got a john, we've got water and we really don't need all this room for the tiles. We'll get a two-burner, a couple of pots and pans, and we'll be in business."

He just kept looking at me. My father was a very proud man. I was his only son and he had given me everything a father can give a son ever since I was born.

He said, "I don't want my son living in a warehouse."

"That's silly, Dad, we can be more comfortable and eat better here than we do at the boardinghouse." It took me some time to convince my father, but I finally did.

I would get "home" from a date and find my dad, who had been the king of my hometown for ten years, a good-looking, still young, wonderful guy, going around with a fucking baseball bat trying to kill the rats before we could safely go to bed. We lived there for quite a while and made it sort of a game to see which one of us could come up with an idea to fix it up better and get rid of the rats.

We also used to go to the markets and look for food that was on special sale. One time, I remember, we found pork and beans selling for a really bargain price. We bought quite a few cartons, about sixty cans in all. After eating about half a dozen of them we tried the others with catsup, with garlic, with onions, with rice . . . we tried to disguise the pork and beans with every possible thing we could think of, but I'm telling you, you can't do it—they still come out pork and beans.

After a few transactions in the tile business the partners decided that, considering the breakage and all, this was not very profitable.

Importing bananas would be much better. "There is a much better turnover in bananas and a bigger return on your money," one of the partners said. "We could get the bananas real cheap from Puerto Rico and sell them here for at least five cents each. A very good business." So they started importing bananas.

With the first shipment they made a hell of a good profit, like 200 percent. So this was it. We were going to get rich with bananas.

When the next shipment arrived I went down to the ship to get the bananas. When I looked at them I started to laugh. They were all black. I mean every one of them was black, black, *rotten*. It was so tragic you couldn't do anything else but laugh. I picked up the phone and said, "Dad, I am sorry to tell you that the Pan American Import- ing and Exporting Company, Incorporated, just went out of business."

He said, "What are you talking about?"

"Every one of these bananas is as black as Bombalé."

"Oh, my God, are you sure?"

"Yeah, I'm sure, Pop, they are all rotten. I am sorry."

You would think this would have been the end of the P.A.I. & E.C., Inc. Not with my dad. The other two partners gave up, but not my father.

A few days later he and I were sitting back there in the frigging warehouse, and all that was left was a big pile of broken tiles from our previous business. Dad was looking at them and said, "There must be a way to make some money out of this big pile of broken tiles."

I said, "How? Glue them together?"

"Hey, wait a moment, that's a good idea."

"What's a good idea?"

"What you said—but not *glue* them together, *cement* them to- gether."

"Pop, I think you've blown your top."

"No, no," he said. "Listen, you know that fellow Goldstein, the one who's building that small apartment house in Miami Beach?"

"Yeah."

"Well, we are going to go over there and I'll bet you he'll be glad to buy this broken tile."

I asked him why.

"Just put a bunch of them in the back of the pickup and we'll drive out to the job." (During our banana prosperity we had bought an old pickup truck really cheap.)

When we got there, Dad told Mr. Goldstein he was going to let him in on something.

"Listen, there is a new style for tile work on fireplaces that's catching on real fast. It's the newest thing."

The man asked, "What? What is it?"

"Well, instead of using whole tiles, they break them up and put all the different little pieces together. It's very artistic."

Strangely enough, that became a big fad later on.

The builder said, "Hm. What will they think of next?"

"Yeah," I said, "how about that?" Dad just gave me a look.

The man asked him if he'd seen some work done that way.

"Oh, yes, the technique started in Cuba," my dad said. "We've got them all over our hacienda in Santiago."

"We learn something new every day, don't we?" said Goldstein.

"Ain't that the truth?" Dad said. "Desi, bring in a few of those tiles and we'll show him what it looks like."

I looked at him, trying to figure out how we were going to do this.

"Traelas para aquá. Coño," he said.

The man asked him what he had said.

"I was telling my son to bring only the ones that we had especially broken for this style. We'll do part of the fireplace and you can see."

We had never done any cement or tile work or anything else like that in our lives. So as I brought in the broken tiles, I said, "Dad, we don't know how to do this." In Spanish, of course.

"Never mind," he answered, in the same language, "we don't have to do the whole fireplace. We'll just do a little piece of the mantel top."

So we went ahead and started putting the little pieces together. We finished the whole top and, by God, it looked good! It took time, but who cared? We had nothing else to do.

The guy said, "Yeah, that looks good. Would you do all the fireplaces that way?"

Dad told him that we didn't have the time to do the actual work, but would be glad to show his mason how it should be done.

The builder said, "Fine, probably cheaper too, right?"

"Well, no," said Dad. "It costs a little more when it's done with broken tiles."

The builder asked, "Why?"

That explanation I had to hear also.

"Well, it's the labor, the cost of breaking the tiles."

I could hardly keep from laughing. We had a whole fucking mountain of broken tiles. But the man went for it, and believe it or not the broken-tile business kept us going for about a year. We did so well with it we ran out of broken tiles and had to start buying new ones and breaking them up. The labor cost of breaking them wasn't much. After picking up nice new ones I would find a real lousy back street with all kinds of holes and drive the little truck over them. Then I would dump the tiles hard on the concrete floor of the warehouse. After that there weren't so many more to break.

We were finally making enough money to eat good. By "good"

I mean we were eating. We were still living in the warehouse. By that time, however, it wasn't too bad. We had added an easy chair, a lamp, a radio, a few necessary pieces of china and silverware, even a tablecloth.

And we had won the battle of the rats.

5

I was nineteen and had not finished high school yet. Notre Dame, of course, was out of the question, but Dad wanted me to be a highschool graduate at least.

Father William Barry was the head of St. Patrick's High School in Miami Beach. When he saw my Jesuit high-school transcripts, which had been sent to him from Cuba, he told me that I had enough credits already to graduate.

"But," he said, "I strongly recommend that you take one year of English at least, and as long as the United States is the country you have chosen, a year of American history."

"That sounds great, Father Barry," I said, "but there is a problem. I have no money to pay tuition."

"That's all right, son," he said. "Your father has explained your situation. Maybe you can find some work in the morning and come to school in the afternoon for the two courses. You wouldn't have to be here until one-thirty, and you would be finished by three o'clock in the afternoon. In June you will graduate with the rest of the boys."

It was the easiest school year I ever had. I played basketball and swam on the school team. They didn't have soccer. My best friend was Al Capone, Jr.

I used to go to his house, which was on one of the most exclusive islands off Miami Beach, a magnificent home. His mother, May, always cooked nice lunches for us and gave us lemonade and cold drinks.

When we graduated, Sonny showed me a beautiful pocket watch with diamonds all around it.

"Sonny, that's beautiful," I said. "Who is it from?"

"It's from my dad," he answered.

I had never mentioned his dad to him. None of the kids ever did.

He said, "You know he's in Alcatraz?"

"Yes, I know, Sonny, but he didn't forget your graduation. He must love you very much."

"I love him too," he said.

Sometime after our graduation Capone got out of Alcatraz. One day when I called Sonny, he answered the phone and said, "Hello, hello." He had a very high voice, almost a soprano.

"May I speak to Sonny, please?" I asked.

"Who's this?"

"Who am I talking to?" I asked.

"This is Al, his father."

"Oh, Mr. Capone!" Jesus Christ, I was talking to Al Capone.

"Who is this?" he asked again.

"This is Desi."

"Oh, Desi. Yeah, yeah. May told me all about you and Sonny. Wait a minute, I'll get him."

I didn't know it then, but I heard later Sonny's father was in the early stages of general paresis (syphilis of the brain), which eventually killed him.

Another friend was Teddy Whitehouse. I had a big crush on his sister Lucy. Their mother was Cuban and their father American. Mr. Whitehouse had a hobby, canary breeding. He had so many canaries that he had converted his whole garage into a cage for them.

One day when I was visiting them, he told me he had figured out a way to make money with the canaries. He was going to buy about one hundred cages, put a canary in each cage, and then place them on consignment in drugstores around Miami, Miami Beach and Coral Gables, with a different price on each canary and its cage. If one cage was fancier and had a better canary than others, it would sell for $25.97. Others would sell for $15.98 or $12.99, never for $26.00, $16.00 or $13.00 (a good lesson in American salesmanship).

People would come into the store, see the pretty cage, hear the canary singing and chirping, read the book of instructions hanging on each cage on how to take care of them and the month's supply of special canary food. It made an attractive package deal.

As it turned out, my job was to go around, feed the canaries and clean the cages. I would start every morning in Coral Gables, then go to Miami and finish in Miami Beach. The last goddamn canary I took care of each day was the one closest to St. Patrick's, and that's where I had a little problem. I didn't want the kids from school to catch me at my job, so I spent a lot of time hiding behind piles of Kotex and Kleenex boxes.

I got fifteen dollars per week and my supper, and Mr. White-house sold all the canaries. It was a really good business, providing you had a garage full of canaries.

Those were great days in Miami Beach. On weekends a bunch of us, maybe six or seven guys, would put up a buck or so apiece and buy hot dogs, buns, Cokes and beer, and our dates would bring cakes and pies, blankets and pillows from their homes, and we would be in business.

The Roney Plaza Hotel was the last big building on the ocean-front in Miami Beach until you got all the way to the Deauville. Be-tween the two hotels was nothing but miles of gorgeous empty beach with beautiful white sand and tall coconut trees. We would set up a camp, go swimming, build a fire, have a drink, cook the hot dogs, play guitar and sing. I finally had managed to buy a five-dollar guitar in a hock shop. It was the corniest guitar I had ever seen. On the front of the guitar box someone had painted a whole panorama of palm trees and girls in hula skirts. But it played well enough.

I'll never forget those gorgeous nights on the beach, with the moon over Miami. We ate and drank, sang and played, and screwed and screwed. It was fantastic.

My career as a canary-cage cleaner ended when Mr. Whitehouse sold the canaries. My next job turned out to be my very first experi-ence in show business.

Alberto Barreras, the former president of the Cuban Senate, was also in exile, but he was in much better financial shape than Dad was. He had sent a lot of money to the United States before he had to get out of Cuba, and he now lived in a very lovely home in Biscayne Bay.

I had met his granddaughter, Gabriella, and they used to invite me to dinner often. The old man knew we were broke, but he was a good friend who sympathized with my father's misfortunes. Senator Barreras loved to play the numbers and that is why I got my first job in show business.

The guy who used to sell the numbers to him also had a little rumba band at the Roney Plaza. In those days they had two bands. Buddy Rogers led the main orchestra at the Roney, and this guy had a relief band called the Siboney Septet. I don't know why he called it a septet because, even after he added me, we were only five. One day he asked the Senator if he knew any Cuban who could play the guitar and sing. I had learned to play the guitar when I was a very young boy. In Cuba an integral part of romancing is serenading, and

Don Desiderio and grandma, Rosita, with the youngest mayor Cuba ever had.

It was one of the biggest funerals of all time in Santiago.

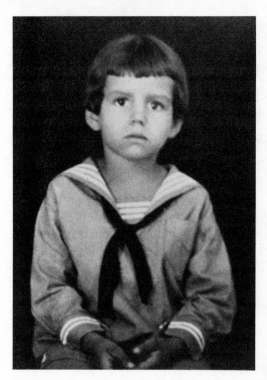

Desiderio Alberto Arnaz y de Acha at the age of four or five.

I was equally serious when I graduated from grammar school.

The clock tower that was built for the *Alcalde Modelo.*

This proves that my English was "outstanding," a talent
I must have left in Cuba.

INSTITUTO DE SEGUNDA ENSEÑANZA DE ORIENTE
Secretaría

ENSEÑANZA LIBRE

Curso de 193 1 a 193 2   Asignatura Inglés 2o. Curso

El Sr. *Desiderio Arnaz* ha sido examinado

en el día de hoy y obtenido la calificación de

Sobresaliente

Santiago de Cuba, *9* de *Junio* de 193 2

[signature]
Secretario del Tribunal.

Here I am at Saint Patrick's High School in Miami Beach looking over the right shoulder of Al Capone, Jr., who was my best friend there.

After I joined the Siboney Septet, we were only five. While I was in Cuba getting my residency papers, we added a bongo player.

for serenading the guitar is perfect. You would have a hell of a time carrying a piano.

The old man told him yes but he didn't know if the boy's father would let him do it, still thinking of that old family pride. In those days a musician came through the kitchen. Nevertheless, the next time I came to the house, the old man mentioned it to me.

"Great," I said. "What does it pay and when do you work?"

"They play seven nights a week and for tea dances on Sunday. You get five dollars a night and four dollars for the tea dance."

"That's thirty-nine dollars a week," I said. "How can I try to get it?"

"Go to this guy's house," he told me, "and audition. Take your guitar over there and sing him a couple of songs."

So I went over and sang him a couple of songs.

"That's great. You're hired," he said.

I then went to Dad and told him, "We're in business. I got a job which pays thirty-nine dollars a week."

"What business?

"I got a job with a band."

"Oh, no, my son is not going to be a goddamn musician."

"Come on, Dad. This is the United States of America, and besides, it can't be worse than cleaning birdcages."

Finally, the old Senator talked to my father and told him that he was being ridiculous.

"After all," he said, "the kid can make some money, buy new clothes, and what's wrong with that? He sings pretty good, and people are going to like him."

Dad finally said, "Okay."

I started in the winter of 1936. Our group was made up of my guitar, a maraca player, a bongo player, a piano player and the leader (the numbers seller), who played the *marimbula,* a wooden box with four metal strips above a hole in the middle. It takes the place of a bass. I also did all the vocals.

At that time very few people knew about the rumba. Hardly anyone knew how to dance it, and that's all we could play. While the Buddy Rogers orchestra was playing the dance floor would be full, but when they stopped for their ten-minute breaks everybody sat down. When we started playing nobody would get up to dance. I figured my job wasn't going to last very long if they kept doing that.

I went to Mr. Rogers and said, "Mr. Rogers, would you do us a favor?"

"What's that, son?"

"Well, when you quit and we get on, everybody sits down and we can't get them up again."

"It's just that they don't know how to dance to your music yet," he said.

"Yeah, I know, but if the last number you play in a set could be something we know, like 'The Peanut Vendor'—"

"Yeah."

"Well, after you start it, sneak your pianist out and we'll sneak our pianist in, and as the rest of your boys move out, our group will move in and we will continue the same number. The music will never stop and the people will still be dancing, but they'll be dancing to our band."

It worked, because all of a sudden the people realized they were dancing to a rumba and then decided it was not too tough after all, and they kept dancing.

One morning, during the first or second week that I was working at the Roney Plaza, Dad and I were at the warehouse, where we were still living, when we received a visit from an immigration officer. He told us that we had no right to be working in this country because we were not permanent residents and that we couldn't work until we got our papers straightened out. That was the law.

Dad asked the man, "What are we supposed to do?"

"Look, Dr. Arnaz, we know all about you and all you went through during the Revolution of Nineteen Thirty-three, so here's what we'll do. I won't go around the Roney Plaza for three months and I'll see that nobody from our department goes by there either, but three months from now I want you and your son to have your papers in order. Good luck to you both." And he left. It shows you that there are some nice people in this world.

We could not become permanent residents of the United States while we were in the country. We had to go to an American consulate outside of the United States to get our permanent-residency papers.

Dad found the cheapest way was to get to Puerto Rico (we didn't think Cuba was a safe bet for him yet). He came back in a couple of weeks and returned to his broken-tile business. I then went to Havana to get my papers.

When I returned I went back to work at the Roney Plaza. It had taken us only four weeks to get everything done. Shortly after that we sent for Mother.

6

My school chums did a very nice thing at the first tea dance after I came back. They all pretended not to pay any attention to Buddy Rogers and his orchestra. As soon as our little group started, they all began dancing. When I sang, they stopped, stood in front of the bandstand, looking up at me, and, as I finished, they all yelled and applauded. It made a good impression on the numbers seller and on somebody else who was standing right alongside the kids. I thought I had seen him someplace before.

I asked the piano player, "Who's the bald-headed guy there with the kids?"

"How long you been here, boy?" he answered. "That's Xavier Cugat."

Of course I'd seen his pictures many times. Cugie was the king of the rumba. Carlos Molina, Enrique Madriguera, Pancho and a few others were also popular, but there was no one close to Cugat.

When we finished playing that afternoon I had a hunch that Cugie was going to call me if I went by his table. I just knew it. I put my guitar in its case and started to leave, making sure my route would take me not too far from his table. Walking slowly, looking around nonchalantly, I got near his table. Nothing. Even with his table, I paused, not looking at him, and lit a cigarette. Nothing. By then I was saying to myself, "You asshole, why would he call you?" I started walking away and just as I reached the exit I heard, "Hey, Chico!"

My heart jumped. I turned, pretending I didn't know who was calling.

"You there with the guitar," he said. "Come over, please."

I went to this table. "Yes, sir?"

"I'm Xavier Cugat."

"Yes, I know."

He asked my name and told me I did a nice job up there.

"I've been thinking," he said. "Maybe I'll give you a chance in my orchestra. Will you come and audition?"

He had a rehearsal the next afternoon and wanted to know if I could come and do a couple of numbers with the band.

"Yes, *sir!*" I said. "I sure can."

So I went over to the Brook Club and did a couple of numbers with the band. Then he asked me if I knew "Para Vigo Me Voy" ("In Spain They Say *Sí Sí*").

"We don't do it in our group," I said, "but I think I know it pretty good."

"Okay, try it with me and the orchestra. What's your key?"

"I don't know."

He turned to the band and said, "The goddamn kid doesn't even know his fucking key. Try the arrangement we have. The verse first, you know it?"

"Yes, sir," I told him.

I was scared, but when that great band started the opening bars of the introduction leading to the verse, and when the rhythm section settled in the vamp with the kind of beat and excitement that I hadn't heard since I left Cuba, I was back in Santiago!

My Cuban blood was flowing. My hips were revolving, my feet were kicking, my arms were waving. It would have made Elvis Presley look as if he were standing still. I sang the shit out of that song.

I finished and the boys in the band were great. They all applauded. I was so goddamn excited I hardly heard Cugat say, "Say son, you got the job. When can you come to New York?"

"I can't come to New York until I graduate from high school."

"You haven't graduated from high school yet?" he asked.

I told him that I had lost three years because of the Revolution so I wouldn't graduate until next June.

"I see. Well, write to me then," he said.

I graduated from high school in June and I wrote him a letter. I figured I was not going to hear from him, but two weeks later he wrote to me. The offer was twenty-five dollars a week for two weeks, one-way bus transportation to New York, where I would rehearse with the band, and then I would open with them at Billy Rose's Aquacade in Cleveland, Ohio.

The letter also said, "This is just a tryout, but if you make good we'll talk business."

Dad thought I would be out of my mind to take the job.

"It's just like going to school, Dad. I don't know anything about the big-band business, and I can learn a lot from Cugat. Besides, I've never been anyplace but Miami."

Mother was on my side and, if it hadn't been for her help, I don't think Dad would have let me go.

The thing I remember most about New York was how little I felt. I arrived there in a bus with one small bag which contained everything my mother and dad had been able to scrounge for me. I had one good suit, a couple of shorts, a couple of shirts, a couple of socks, a pair of shoes—good shoes—one good tie and fifteen dollars in my pocket.

I was to report to Cugat at the Waldorf-Astoria. They were playing at the Starlight Roof. I had no idea where the Waldorf-Astoria was, but even before I could try to get there I had to find a place to stay. One of the porters at the bus station was a Puerto Rican. I told him this was my first time in New York and that I was looking for a cheap place to stay. He directed me to Forty-second or Forty-third Street, off Broadway. "You will find some cheap hotel there."

He was right. I found one, one dollar a night. I opened the blinds of the one window, expecting to look at a beautiful Broadway view, and found myself staring at a brick wall. However, I was so goddamn excited about being in New York that it really did not matter.

I unpacked, went down the hall to take a shower and shave, came back, put on my best shirt, my best pair of socks, my best tie and my one good suit, went down to the lobby and asked how to get to the Waldorf-Astoria. They told me that it was quite a ways, but I was so taken away with the sights that even if I had had the money for a cab, I would have walked anyway, which is what I did.

I entered through the Park Avenue entrance, walked through that magnificent lobby, finally reached the elevators and asked, "Starlight Roof, please."

Arriving at the Starlight Roof, I was met by the maître d'hôtel in white tie and tails. I said, "I am supposed to meet Mr. Cugat."

Being led to Cugat's table, where his wife, Carmen, was sitting, was almost too much for the son of the mayor of Santiago.

Carmen (a wonderful lady) understood this and tried to make me feel at home, which was not very easy while my mouth was wide open and my eyes were falling out of their sockets.

After Cugie finished conducting the set he joined us at the table, bought me dinner and a glass of wine, told me where the rehearsal would be the following day and that we would open at Billy Rose's Aquacade the following week.

The show that Billy Rose put on in Cleveland was really something. I had never seen anything like it in my life. A big dance floor covered a gorgeous man-made lake. The stage, scenery and entrance for the beautiful chorus was on the side opposite a tremendous grandstand for the audience. Showgirls, swimmers, fantastic costumes—and the stars were Johnny Weissmuller, Eleanor Holm, Buster Crabbe, Cugat, and the Cuban birdcage cleaner.

The water was filled with the most gorgeous aquamaids you've ever seen. I fell in love with a different one every other day.

Oh, man, what a summer!

Hell, I would have paid Cugat just to be there, if I'd had the money, that is. And I was happy because everybody said I was doing really well with the band.

At the end of the week I said to Cugat, "Everybody seems to like me real good. When do we talk business?"

"You're right, we talk business. I give you thirty dollars a week."

"That's the end of the business talk?"

"Yeah, that's it."

Well, what the hell, he could have cut me down to twenty dollars and I wouldn't have quit and left all those gorgeous aquamaids.

From Cleveland we went to Saratoga to play at the Arrowhead Inn, one of the finest gambling casinos in New York State at that time. It was a great thrill for me when Cugat decided that I should open the show with "Para Vigo Me Voy" before Veloz and Yolanda, who were the most famous dancing act in the world then, and of course the stars of the show, came on to do their act.

Saratoga, during the racing season, is always up to its ass with Vanderbilts, Whitneys and Du Ponts, plus an assortment of the top breeders, owners, trainers and jockeys of thoroughbred horses in America, and also stage, radio, and movie stars by the dozen.

One night the headwaiter came over to the bandstand a couple of times with a request for me to sing "Quiereme Mucho." (In English the song was called "Yours.") The third time he came over I heard him ask Cugat if it would be all right for me to sit with one of the guests. Cugat told him. "You know the rules." (Members of the band were not supposed to mingle with the guests then.) The headwaiter said that it would be okay. "It's Mr. Crosby."

As I approached the table and saw him I told the headwaiter, "What do you mean, Mr. Crosby? That's Bing Crosby!"

Bing stood up and greeted me with *"Mucho gusto, Señor."*

I answered, *"El gusto es todo mio, Señor Crosby."*

He then said, *"Como se llama usted?"*

"Desi Arnaz, *Señor.*"

"Sientese, por favor." He indicated a chair. *"Quiere un Scotch o quiere rum?"*

"Rum. Bacardí, por favor," I answered.

"Sí, como no."

A bottle of good old Añejo Bacardí was brought to the table. Mr. Crosby told me how much he loved Cuban music and that to celebrate meeting a native he would join me in the rum. After a couple he asked me, "How much is this Spaniard paying you?"

"Thirty a week," I told him.

"That cheap crook," he said. "Come on, let's talk to him."

"Hello, Bing," Cugat greeted him.

"Listen, you cheap Spaniard, what do you mean paying this fine Cuban singer thirty a week?"

"He's just starting, Bingo."

"Never mind the Bingo stuff. Give him a raise. One of these days you are going to be asking him for a job."

"Okay, okay. How about singing a song with the band, Bing?"

Bing said, "Will you give him a raise?"

"Of course."

Bing sang and the audience went wild. It was quite a feather in Cugat's cap to have Bing Crosby sing with his orchestra. He sang many songs, some of them with me. "Quiereme Mucho," his favorite, he sang in Spanish, which was pretty good, and then I sang it in English, which was pretty bad. The Añejo Bacardí helped a lot.

The next time I saw Bing was when I was a guest on his *Kraft Music Hall* radio show. It was the very first time I appeared on a national radio show.

The first thing he asked me was "Did you ever get that raise?"

"You bet. The following week he raised me to thirty-five, and the only thing extra I had to do was walk his dogs until they completed their business."

After we finished in Saratoga and before we opened at the Waldorf, Cugat had some theater dates to play. The band would travel by train but some of the boys used their own cars. Cugat didn't use a bus for the whole band as most of the orchestras did. He had to pay us for train transportation from one job to the next.

In those days you didn't have to belong to a union just to play bongos, the maracas or the conga drums, or to sing. There was no such thing as a minimum scale for this group.

One of the ways we used to save money was to have a car pool from one job to the other. One of the boys in the band, the maraca player, had a fairly decent car, so instead of going by train we chipped in for gas and other expenses, which would be enough for the owner to make a few bucks. With five men to the car we saved some of the train fare.

One day we were going from Detroit to Boston. Nico, the bongo player, was in the front seat. The boy who was driving was the maraca player. Nilo Melendez, Cugat's brilliant piano player and composer of the lifetime favorite "Green Eyes," myself and some other guy who played the guitar were in the back. It was raining, all the windows were up and everybody was smoking. I thought that the cigarettes smelled kind of funny and then I noticed that everybody was having a hell of a good time. They were all in a very happy mood and nobody seemed to care too much about the horrible weather, with the rain coming down and cars splashing water against the windows as they went by. Everybody was laughing.

Somebody would ask, "What time is it?"

A guy would say, "Three o'clock."

Then everybody would break up laughing. Pretty soon I found myself in the same mood. We were all having a hell of a time right in the middle of this terrible rainstorm.

Well, if you're not ahead of me, they were all smoking marijuana and, with all the windows closed, I didn't have to be smoking any, I got just as high as they were just by being in there.

I had been with Cugat for almost six months and I thought I had done a very good job. The audiences seemed to like me. I had been featured at the Waldorf; I had been the closing act in his theater show; but I was still getting only thirty-five dollars a week. To live on thirty-five dollars a week in New York, even in those days, was very difficult. Today, of course, it's impossible. Having to go through the Waldorf kitchen to get to the bandstand helped. I lifted all the celery, olives, carrots, pieces of bread, buns and butter and whatever else I could stash into my rumba shirt every time we came back through the kitchen for our ten-minute rest. Those wide, full sleeves with all the big ruffles were very useful.

I decided that six months was enough learning, and I did learn a lot from Cugat. He's a brilliant showman, but not only that, he is a very shrewd businessman, very commercial. He never fooled around trying to introduce something that hadn't been proven unless he was sure that it was very commercial.

During my internship with Cugie I learned not only about how the music should be played, how it should be presented, what the American people liked to dance to, but also how to handle the band, the rehearsals, the salaries, and all the angles of the band business.

One of the things Cugat was always very particular about and spent money on was how the band looked. He always had three or four people, usually a girl and two or three boys, dressed in big and colorful rumba shirts, who kept dancing and moving all the time. In every set the girl and one of the boys would dance on the stand so that the American people could see how that particular Latin dance number—samba, rumba or tango—was done.

We would usually finish about two or two-thirty in the morning and then have breakfast. One morning I asked if I could have breakfast with him and talk.

At breakfast I said, "I'm going back to Miami to see if I can get a small band together like that Siboney Septet you saw me with at the Roney. What the hell, I know just as much as that guy who was the leader—a lot more really, thanks to you—but I just can't make enough money with you."

"You won't have a chance," he said. 'There's not many people who know and like Latin music in this country yet. You'll have a tough time. You'll go hungry."

"Well, dammit, Cugie, I'm hungry now! Besides, my mother and father are there. Maybe I'll fall on my ass, but I've got to try it."

"Okay," he said, 'I'll tell you what I'll do to get you started. You can bill yourself as Desi Arnaz and his Xavier Cugat Orchestra direct from the Waldorf-Astoria Hotel in New York City."

"That's great! Marvelous! Thank you! But I want to pay you for the use of your name."

He looked up and said, "How much?"

"The same as you paid me when I started, twenty-five dollars a week, and if we do good we'll talk business."

Cugie had a great sense of humor. "All right, you goddamn Cuban, let's see what you can do."

7

Louis Nicoletti was Cugat's secretary and one of his jobs, which we often shared, was to take Carmen and Cugie's two Chihuahuas and a big police dog, Moro, for a walk around the Waldorf.

Nick asked me, "You're really quitting him?"

"I've already quit. I'm going to Miami. Cugat says I can use Desi Arnaz and his Xavier Cugat Orchestra, direct from the Waldorf-Astoria in New York City, if and when I get a job."

Nick then made a quick decision. "I'll quit too and come with you. I'll be the band manager."

"We haven't even got a band yet."

"We'll get something," he said, and he went to Cugie and told him, "I'm going with Desi."

"Okay, good luck to you guys," Cugie said. "If you connect, let me know and I'll send you a band."

When Nick and I left for Florida we had forty dollars between us. Nick had an old car, a broken-down something or other. We drove from New York to Miami in this thing and went to my parents' little house.

Dad was doing even better with his broken tiles and was also beginning to get into some small construction work with some other guys.

He and Mother had a tiny little house in Miami. In those days you could rent one extremely cheaply. You had to put newspapers in the cracks to stop the wind and cold from coming in, but at least it was a two-bedroom house with a bath, kitchen and living room, a hell of a lot better than the warehouse, and that's where Nick and I landed.

By the time we got there we had twenty dollars between us, plus one good suit each. It was early in December, and in those days the Miami and Miami Beach season didn't start until just before New Year's. We cased Miami and Miami Beach and found out that Bobby Kelly was going to open a new room in Miami Beach as an addition to the Park Central, one of the best restaurants on the beach. Bobby was the son of Mother Kelly (who, by the way, was his father, not his mother, but his bar was called Mother Kelly's, so everybody called him Mother). Bobby's room was going to have a bar, some booths and a little dance floor. It would seat two hundred or two hundred and fifty at the most. In the wall behind the bar, they had cut a hole and put a little stage there for whatever entertainment they would have.

We decided that this was our best chance because we had heard rumors that it might be done in a Latin motif. So one night we put on our best suits and with our twenty dollars went to Mother Kelly's.

The plan was for Nick to play the part of Cugat's band manager and say that Desi Arnaz, featured vocalist with Xavier Cugat, was here on vacation. He had been working very hard and very successfully at the Waldorf-Astoria and in theaters throughout the country, so Mr. Cugat had given him a leave of absence to come down here to get the sun and a rest before rejoining him in January at the Waldorf's Starlight Roof. He had assigned his band manager, Mr. Nicoletti, to look after his "precious treasure."

As we came in I said to Nick, "Order a bottle of champagne."

When the waiter came over to us, we asked, "You have champagne?"

"Yes, sir."

"Good. Do you have Cordon Rouge, Extra Dry?"

"Of course," answered the waiter.

"What year?" I asked.

He gave us the year, which really meant nothing to us, but we figured the question sounded good. The waiter seemed impressed.

Nick told him, "That's not a good year for Cordon Rouge. What else do you have?"

"We have Piper Heidsieck."

"What year?"

When he told us, I said, "That's a good year, Nick, very good."

We sat there with our champagne. I figured we'd already blown about ten or twelve bucks out of our twenty dollars. A few minutes later a girl came by with a little tray, chanting, "Cigarettes, cigars, candy." So we bought a package of cigarettes and gave her a dollar tip.

Pretty soon Mother Kelly came over to our table.

"Hello," he said. "Didn't you go to school here? Didn't you graduate from St. Patrick's with Sonny Capone and those boys?"

"Yes, sir. I sure did," I answered.

"I remember you kids came here on the graduation night."

"That's right, Mother. We were celebrating our graduation."

"Well, it's nice to see you again. How are you doing?"

"Well, I'm with Cugat. By the way, this is Mr. Louis Nicoletti, Mr. Cugat's manager."

Two how-do-you-do's later, I continued, "I've been starring in his show at the Starlight Roof and at theaters throughout the country and I'm a little beat, so Cugat was very kind to let me come down here for a couple of weeks."

Then Nick took over from there, telling him how great I was doing. He was a much better bullshitter than I.

Pretty soon Mother said, "I'd like Bobby to meet you."

"Who's Bobby?" As if we didn't know.

"My son."

Bobby came and sat down with us. "I'm opening a new room with a Latin motif. It's too bad you have to go back to the Waldorf because, boy, you'd be perfect for this place."

Bobby also remembered that I was there with Sonny Capone and all the kids when we graduated from St. Patrick's.

"Well," I said, "gee, you know, I love Miami and my parents and all my friends are here, but I'm under contract to Cugat and I have to open at the Starlight Roof in January."

Nick took over again and told Bobby that it was very nice of him to think of me and that I would be great.

"You should have seen him at the Waldorf with all the girls standing around. They wouldn't dance or anything. They just stood right there looking up at him." (Nobody stands around and looks up at anybody at the Waldorf!)

By this time Bobby was drooling. He asked Nick if there was any chance at all he could get me to appear at his place.

Nick told him, "There's no chance, Bobby, because even if we got Cugat's permission, your little room couldn't afford him."

I think that did it.

"Now wait a minute," Bobby said. "It's not a *little* room. We are going to run a high-type place and we can afford as much as anybody else can."

"Well, I'm glad to hear that, Bobby, but we still have a problem with Cugie letting him go," Nick told him.

Bobby wouldn't give up. "Give it a try. Tell him that it would be good for the kid to be on his own in Miami Beach and be the star of a new place. It could help Cugat's show in the future. Why don't you call him?"

Now he was begging us to go in there, and I was dying because I thought Nick was overdoing it a little. I kicked him under the table and said, *"Cuidado,"* when they started talking money.

I said, "Let's not talk money right now, Nick. You give Cugat a call and, if he says okay, you and Bobby can handle the financial details. I get embarrassed talking money, okay?"

"I understand, Desi," said Bobby. "Be sure to call me as soon as you hear, Nick."

I said to the waiter. "Would you bring me the check, please?"

"Oh, no, no," said Bobby. "It's on the house."

So we walked out of there minus only the price of a pack of cigarettes and the dollar I gave the girl.

"Nick," I said, "you are a hell of a con man. Let's call the god-damn Spaniard and see what he says."

"He told you he'd send you a band, didn't he?"

"Yeah."

We called Cugie and I told him, "You promised that if I got a

little job you would send me a band and that I could say 'Desi Arnaz
and his Xavier Cugat Orchestra direct from the Waldorf-Astoria in
New York City.' Is that correct?"

"Yeah," he said, "I did."

"Would you send me the band if I get this job set?" I asked.

"Sure, how many?"

"Well, I don't know yet because we haven't talked price to the
guy. I guess four or five. You know, just a small combo."

"All right," said Cugat, "you let me know what happens."

The next afternoon we went to Bobby's house and he started to
talk business with us again.

I said, "Bobby, I told you, I don't talk business. Nick is Cugat's
manager and he will handle the whole thing."

The con man, using reverse psychology, told him, "The only way
Cugat will let him do it is if you agree to say in all the ads 'Desi Arnaz
and his Xavier Cugat Orchestra direct from the Starlight Roof of the
Waldorf-Astoria Hotel in New York City.' I don't know if you want
to do that or not, but it's the only way he'll let Desi do it."

Bobby could hardly contain himself. "Oh, yeah, that's all right.
Sure, we can do that. Yeah, yeah. Let's see . . . a full-page ad. 'The
only typical Cuban band in Miami Beach! Desi Arnaz and his Xavier
Cugat Orchestra direct from the Starlight Roof of the Waldorf-Astoria
Hotel in New York City!' Yes, I'll agree to that."

Who wouldn't?

Nick and Bobby talked about money privately, and an hour
later Nick told me, "It's all set."

"What did you get?"

"Six hundred and fifty dollars a week for you and a five-piece
group for twelve weeks guaranteed."

That perhaps doesn't sound like much today, but in 1937 it was
a hell of a lot of money.

We would pay the musicians scale, which was about $70.00
plus transportation. So the band would cost us somewhere in the
neighborhood of $350.00 a week. We also had to send Cugat $25.00
a week for the use of his name as I had promised.

I asked Nick, "What do you think you should get?"

"Well, we are going to have to pay transportation, buy some
music, a tuxedo for you and other miscellaneous stuff. I was making
thirty-five dollars a week with Cugat, so put down about fifty dollars
for me, you take the rest and we'll see how we do."

We were going to stay at Dad's house so we didn't have many
living expenses, but we were already in trouble. It was a week before

the opening and we didn't have a band yet. Actually, Cugie had told me that I had a hell of a bad opening date. The one night of the year when every musician makes a lot of money is New Year's Eve, about triple the scale. Nobody wanted to go to Miami until after New Year's.

I explained to him that contracts were signed and Bobby was taking a full-page ad in the papers announcing the opening of "The only typical Cuban band in town, Desi Arnaz and his Xavier Cugat Orchestra direct from the Starlight Roof of the Waldorf-Astoria Hotel in New York City."

Then Nick told Cugat, "I told Bobby that was the only way you would let Desi do it, so you are going to be in as much trouble as we are if you don't send that band. The guy will sue us and he knows you've got the money, so he'll sue you too."

The truth was that Cugie was really having trouble getting musicians. Finally, he called the day before we were to open and said the guys were on the train. I asked him who he was sending us and he said, "Five guys—a bass, a drummer, a pianist, a saxophone and a violin."

I said, "What the hell kind of a Latin band is that? A saxophone and a violin? No trumpet, no accordion, no bongos?"

"They're the only ones I could get," he said.

"What are their names, Mr. Cugat?"

"How the hell would I know? Look for a short fat Italian carrying a bass."

"Great."

We had nothing but a few piano sheets, no special arrangements at all. We did have some standard publisher's arrangements, which are usually very good and easy to play for a standard combo, but very difficult to adapt to this unorthodox, crazy one we were getting. They were arriving at three o'clock in the afternoon, the day of the opening.

Nick and I rented a station wagon and went to the station in Miami. Quite a bunch of musicians got off the train at that time because, as I said, the season was just opening in Miami and Miami Beach. Some of them were with big, organized orchestras, such as those of Buddy Rogers and Lombardo.

Every time we saw a guy carrying an instrument we'd ask him who he was coming to play for. Finally, we saw this short fat Italian carrying a bass twice as big as he was.

Nick asked him, "Who are you working for?"

"Some guy by the name of Dizzy Arnazzy or something like that," he answered.

The bass player was Caesar De Franco and he helped us gather the other four guys. Now here's what we'd got for the only typical Cuban band in Miami Beach: an Italian for the bass player, a Spaniard for a drummer—and Spaniards can play nothing but *paso dobles;* they don't know or care for rumbas, tangos or sambas, just *paso dobles,* particularly the ones who were in this country in 1937. At the piano a Jewish boy—today the Jewish boys play Latin music as well or better than the Latins do, but in those days they didn't know anything about Latin music. On violin was another Italian fellow and on saxophone was another Jew.

That was my typical Cuban band. Well, that's what I got and that's what I had to work with. It was five in the afternoon and we were to open at ten that evening. We went to a rehearsal hall.

I asked the piano player, "Do you know any Latin music at all?"

"Well," he said, " 'The Peanut Vendor,' and—uh—uh—'Mama Inez,' and—uh—uh—I guess that's it."

"Oh, dear God," I said to myself.

"Okay, let's play those and see if the rest of the guys can fake them."

We struggled along but that Spaniard on the drums, no matter what we were playing, he was playing *paso dobles.*

I said to him, "What the hell are you doing? We are supposed to sound like a Latin band. We sound like we are playing for the fucking bull to come into the arena."

"Oi vay," said the pianist.

I also tried to get some kind of accompaniment for "Para Vigo Me Voy" and "Cachita" from the piano sheets.

At the end of the rehearsal, after trying everything we could, the entire music library we were taking to the job consisted of "Para Vigo Me Voy," "Cachita," "The Peanut Vendor," "Mama Inez," a couple of songs I had worked out with just piano and guitar, two or three stock arrangements we had adapted for the group (which wasn't easy) and one goddamn *paso doble* to please the Spaniard.

At 10 P.M. on the dot, December 30, 1937, I gave the down-beat to my first band.

We looked good. All the fellows wore the rumba shirts the ex-First Lady of Santiago had been sewing on for the past week. I wore black tuxedo pants, patent-leather shoes, white shirt with tiny ruffles, red bow tie under my white-linen summer tux jacket with wide lapels trimmed in white satin, and a tie-matching red handkerchief, care-lessly peeking out of my pocket.

After our first set we got out of the hole-in-the-wall and went down behind the bar. Bobby Kelly was waiting for me and said, "You're fired!"

I guess looks alone are not enough.

"That is the worst thing I've ever heard in my life," he said.

"You can't fire us. We've got a six-week engagement."

"I don't care what the hell you've got. This ain't a Latin band. This is ridiculous. You've got two Jewish people, two Italians and I don't know what the hell the guy on the drum is."

I gave the Spaniard a look and then started to laugh. I don't know why it is, but every time things are really terrible, I laugh.

"What are you laughing about?" Bobby asked.

By now all my "typical Cubanos" were pointing at each other and breaking up with laughter at the way they looked in their rumba shirts. It was the first time any one of them had ever worn one, and I had to agree with Bobby it was a ridiculous-looking group. I finally got hold of myself and said to him, "You're right, Bobby. I'm sorry, but by the time the fellows got here today it was much too late to be able to rehearse properly. When do you want us to leave?"

"Well, whether I like it or not, I have to keep you for at least two weeks. That's the union rule."

Thank God for Mr. Petrillo, the president of our American Federation of Musicians at that time.

"Okay, we'll try to do the best we can till then."

After the next set, which wasn't as bad but still far from even fair Latin music, Bobby came back and said, "You are going on the air tomorrow night as a feature on Ted Husing's radio show."

"What?" I said. "I thought you just fired me."

"I did and you're still fired. Ted Husing wants to put you on remote from here and have you sing a couple of songs, but just you and your guitar. Don't you dare let this whachamacallit group of yours play one note."

Ted Husing, one of the top radio announcers and sports commentators of the time, if not the top, was in the audience as Bobby's guest. While we were playing the second set Bobby had said to him, "I'm going to fire this group, Ted. I was sold a 'Xavier Cugat group from the Waldorf-Astoria' and I wind up with this bunch of crumbums. I'd have been better off hiring a Salvation Army band."

"I agree the band is not good," Ted told him, "but the Cuban kid has something. I don't know what, but something, and I'll tell you what I will do. I have a radio show from Miami every evening. I'll put him on for five minutes tomorrow night to sing a couple of songs from here."

"Not with that lousy group behind him," Bobby told him. "If you want him on your show, let him sing a couple of numbers just with his guitar."

I went over to Bobby's table, thanked Mr. Husing for his kind gesture and told him I would do a couple of numbers just with my guitar in the next set to see if he thought they were okay. After I did the numbers, I looked at Mr. Husing. He nodded his head and gave me the okay sign.

After that my whachamacallit group and I struggled with a few rumbas, but they didn't sound like rumbas, they didn't sound like anything. It was a pitiful sound. The boys weren't bad musicians but we had no arrangements, they had never played Latin music, and the instrumentation was all cockeyed for it. We needed a trumpet, bongos, maracas, conga drums. I had a conga drum with me because they're good to back up the rest of the percussion instruments and the drummer in all Latin rhythms, but you have to have a drummer and other percussion instruments that can play Latin rhythms. You can't do it all just with the conga drum . . . except . . . except . . .

And my mind did a flashback to the yearly carnivals in Santiago, when thousands of people in the streets form a conga line, and they go all over the town, singing and dancing for three days and nights to the beat of African conga drums. They also use frying pans, nailed to boards, bottom side up, which they beat with hard sticks, making a sharp *ding-ding-ding-ding it-ding it-ding-ding* sound, keeping tempo with the conga drum going *boom-boom-boom-BOOM*. It's a simple beat.

You can hear this sound approaching from ten blocks away and it keeps getting louder and louder and more exciting.

Alfonso Menencier was a very distinguished middle-aged black gentleman, and one of my dad's best friends and political campaign leaders. He always dressed elegantly in an impeccable white-linen suit, white shoes, white shirt and silk tie, expertly knotted, with a large diamond pin holding it in place just two inches below the knot. On his head he wore a wide-brimmed straw hat, which Chevalier would have been proud to wear, and was never without a silver-handled *bastón* (cane).

Menencier would stand on the steps of City Hall with Dad and his guests, listening for the start of this savage, sexy, primitive carnival rumble; and as it got closer, he would commence to criticize the custom.

"Here they come again. Every year they get full of rum and form this conga line, beating the drums and dancing frantically to their African beat."

His composure untouched, his dignity as yet unruffled, but if you looked closely, you would notice that his feet were having a tough time standing still.

The conga sound would get louder and louder as the hundreds of people in the conga line kept coming closer and closer.

"Oh, oh. They are coming this way. You can almost smell the rum."

At about this time one foot, probably unconsciously, would kick to the side on the last beat of the bar which accentuated the conga rhythm.

Now the conga line was visible coming around the corner of City Hall and beginning to circle the plaza in front of it. Hundreds of them kept pouring out of that corner. The beat of the drums, the incessant high-pitched sound of the frying pans accompanying their African leader's chant, which everybody else in the line shouted back in answer, kept building, almost monotonously, to an uncontrollable crescendo of frenzy.

He was watching them, fascinated now, as the leaders reached more than halfway around the plaza, and yet more and more kept pouring out of that corner. He started to perspire a little, the collar around his neck began to bother him. The cane was lightly keeping tempo with the beat on the steps of City Hall. His feet could no longer refrain from kicking just a little bit. He was having trouble keeping his composure and wanted to hold on to his dignity.

"My God—my God—my God—MY GOD!" The exclamation came out in conga rhythm.

They were coming right by where he was standing and were soon in front of him. They passed him and reached the end of the line of those still pouring out of that corner. Now they had encircled the whole plaza and continued to dance and shout around it. There were thousands of them. The drums were in the hundreds. The sound of the frying pans was like the sound of lightning, accompanying the thunder of drums. You could almost taste the rum. You could smell the sexes. It was like a wild orgy of feet kicking and arms flailing and hair twirling and asses and breasts and cocks. His heart and theirs were now pounding in unison. He could not control himself any longer, nobody could. His collar came open and his tie undone with one fuck-it-all yank. His straw hat landed on the back of his head and, with his cane high in the air, he joined them in ecstasy and so did everyone else standing on those steps, including the mayor and the American tourists and embassy guests of his.

8

The conga had never been done in the United States. I went to the bartender and said, "Give me a bottle of Bacardí rum."

Then I went backstage where the boys were.

"Okay, guys, you'd better have a few drinks because we're going to play a thing that I'm going to teach you, right here and now. So get loose."

That was the only time in my life I ever let a band drink while we were working.

"Listen carefully to what I play on this conga drum. It's four beats to the bar and the last beat a la Charleston, like this." And I hit *boom—boom—boom—BOOM*.

"Accentuate the last boom. The dance goes one—two—three—KICK. Now you goddamn Spaniard, you can do *boom—boom—boom—BOOM*, can't you?"

"*Sí, sí*, I can do that."

I told the pianist to play just four strong progressive chords with the same beat. The bass the same on the lower strings, the saxophonist to hit the bass drum with a soft mallet, also going *boom—boom—boom—BOOM*, and the violinist to play the frying pan. When I told him that, he looked at me as if I were crazy.

By the time I got back from the kitchen with the frying pan nailed to a board and two spoons to beat it with, the rum was almost gone and they were ready to try anything.

I then called Nick and told him what I was going to do, how to dance the conga and how to form a conga line. He was a good dancer and, being as desperate with our predicament as I was, happy to try anything.

We were ready to start. The violinist was looking at his frying pan and spoons, trying to figure out what to do with them.

"What's the matter?" I asked him.

"How do I go *boom-boom-boom-BOOM* with these?

"Oh, I'm sorry, I forgot to show you. You don't go *boom— boom—boom—BOOM*. You go *ding-ding-ding-ding it-ding it-ding- ding* as you hit the frying pan with the spoon, one on each hand."

Now he was sure I was crazy. *"Ding-ding-ding-ding it-ding it- ding-ding?"*

"That's right. Let's go!"

I hung the conga drum's large leather strap around my right shoulder and started to beat *boom—boom—boom—BOOM*. The band started to join me. It wasn't too difficult for them to go *boom— boom—boom—BOOM*. The people in the club didn't know what the hell was going on.

I told them, "This is a dance, folks, called la conga. It's very simple . . . one . . . two . . . three . . . KICK. One . . . two . . . three . . . KICK."

And I played and danced to the beat.

Nick was on the dance floor and he hollered, "Follow me, folks, I know how to do that—one . . . two . . . three . . . KICK. One . . . two . . . three . . . KICK. Get behind me. We'll form a conga line."

In a few minutes several couples got behind him. Then I jumped from the hole in the wall to the top of the bar. It was a long bar, about thirty feet, and I did the dance and beat the drum from one end to the other and back again. From there I jumped onto the dance floor and pretty soon we had the whole goddamn club doing this conga line.

And that was how it all began!

Since then I have always called the conga "My Dance of Desperation."

After that first time that night we had to do the conga line at least once in every set and about a week later the conga line had really caught on. You couldn't get into the club. It was jammed every night.

Soon I started leading the conga line from our dance floor out through the side door, around the corner and then left to the entrance of the Park Central, the restaurant which was adjoining, right through their supper crowd, into our room and back to our dance floor.

Bobby Kelly was ecstatic and told me to forget the two weeks' notice.

"Hey, Desi, how about calling the room Desi's Place?"

"No, call it La Conga."

Joe E. Lewis was appearing at The Continental around the corner from us. He visited La Conga, where he told me, "Hey, kid, you're doing great! You've started something different."

One night we had a real big group going. As we got into the street, I got carried away and chanted, "Let's—go—see—JOE! Let's—go—see—JOE!" And there we went! Around the corner into The Continental just as he was on the floor doing his midnight show. We all went around him a couple of times. The second time around, Joe joined the end of the line and congaed back to our club.

When I saw him there, I chanted to our group, "Let's go back, folks. Let's go back, folks." So we congaed Joe back to The Continental, left him in the center of the floor, exited and congaed back to our club without losing a beat.

Joe E. was not only a sensational entertainer but also a sweet, warm, lovable man. All of us who were fortunate enough to know him will always miss Joe E. Lewis.

All of Miami Beach was soon doing the conga. The reason it caught on so fast, I think, was because it is a very simple dance. Anybody can do it; one—two—three—KICK. Old people, young kids, anybody. Also it is a group dance and the rhythm, like the ocean, has a hypnotic quality.

One of our best customers and boosters at La Conga was Sonja Henie. She was in Miami at that time doing her extraordinary ice show, and she used to bring the whole group over. She loved to dance and she became a dear friend of mine, even tried to teach me to skate, but I kept falling on my Cuban ass. Harry Richman, another of the great entertainers of that era, was a regular customer. One night I kind of goofed a little and he came back and told me, "Now listen, you Cuban, you didn't go all out on that conga bit tonight. Don't you ever do that again. You don't know who might be sitting out there. You should do your best all the time, whatever you are doing."

He was right. From then on I tried not to goof again.

George Sanchez, the Cuban sugar king, was another good friend and booster even before La Conga, while I was still cleaning birdcages and picking up a few extra bucks with the Siboney Septet.

He had known my father and all of my family, particularly Grandpa Alberto. George was one of his best customers as he was always in need of large quantities of Bacardí for the big shindings at his sugar plantation, not too far from Santiago.

One night at La Conga he asked me if I would like to play the guitar and sing at a big luncheon he was giving at his home in Miami Beach.

"Seguro, Jorge."

"Well," he said, "I don't know if your father would like it, considering the guest of honor will be Batista, but you can make yourself one hundred dollars."

"My father has nothing against Batista. If it hadn't been for Batista getting the courts to operate again, Dad might still be in jail. Besides, one hundred dollars is one hundred dollars."

"I'm glad to hear that. See you Sunday around noon."

"Muchisimas gracias, Jorge."

After I sang a few Cuban songs I was escorted to Batista's table. He greeted me with *"Buenas tardes."*

"Buenas tardes, Señor." (I didn't know whether to call him Sargento, General, or Dictator, so I settled for Señor.)

"You have to be from Cuba. Correct?"

"Yes, sir."

"What part of Cuba?"

"Santiago de Cuba," proudly, as all Santiagueros always say it.

"Oh, Santiago's a wonderful city. What's your name?"

"Arnaz, Señor."

"Any relation to the mayor, Dr. Desiderio Arnaz?"

"Yes sir, he is my father."

"Well, now, how about that? *Como está su padre?"*

"He is fine, sir. Thank you, and thank you also for letting him out."

"He should have never been in. Give him my regards."

"Thank you, sir."

We finished our twelve weeks at La Conga and the season was over. In spite of that terrible beginning, we had been a big hit.

I said to Nick, "I'm going to go to Cuba and see if I can get a little more music. I also want to see my grandparents. I'll meet you in New York."

"Listen," said Nick, "do we have to send Cugat the twenty-five dollars for this last week? I'm broke, and I need it."

"Well, you'd better send it to him. I don't want that Spaniard having anything on us. I don't have a hell of a lot, but I can loan you fifty dollars."

"Thanks, Para Vigo. See you in New York in two weeks and we'll go job hunting."

He had started calling me Para Vigo when that was the only song I knew with Cugat's orchestra. I went to Havana and Nick was to pack the music, conga drum, rumba shirts, and all the rest of the stuff to take to New York.

At that time there was a lady in Miami called Louise, a fine lady, from one of the wealthiest Detroit families, a multimillionaire heiress. She was going with Pete Condoli, Bobby Kelly's friend and assistant. She had a great disposition and a wonderful sense of humor, and she was engaged to be married to Pete.

When Pete had to go to Chicago to buy some stock for the club, booze, which they could get cheaper in Chicago through some of their connections, he told Nick to take care of Louise while he was away. He said:

"Will you look after Louise, Nick? You know she loves to dance. So take her out dining and dancing. She knows you ain't got too much money but she wouldn't let you pay anyway. I'll only be gone a couple of days."

Nick answered, "Sure, I'd be glad to, I like her very much."

I had been in Havana three days when I got a call at eight o'clock in the morning. I picked the phone up, said, "Hello," and heard, "Hey, Para Vigo."

"Nick, where are you? In New York?"

"No, no, not in New York, I'm in Havana."

"In Havana? What the hell are you doing in Havana?"

He said, "I got the penthouse at the Plaza."

"Are you drunk?"

"No, I'm sober as a judge. I got the whole goddamn floor."

"Come on, Nick, what are you giving me? I just left you in Miami with fifty bucks, you were broke, you were going to New York. So what do you mean, you got the whole penthouse at the Plaza?"

He said, "I am telling you I am staying in the penthouse of the Plaza. I am on my honeymoon and I want you to join me for breakfast."

It suddenly dawned on me.

"You sonofabitch, you married Louise?"

"Yes, I sure did."

"Well, that's a nice way to take care of poor old Pete's girl friend . . . okay, I'll be over there in a little while."

I spent their honeymoon with them. We went to all the top nightclubs and to Varadero Beach. We lived like royalty for two weeks, and when they left I said, "Okay, Nick, good luck to you, she's a nice lady."

I still know her very well. She has a lovely home in Palm Springs, but poor Nick is dead.

I came back from "our" honeymoon to my aunt's house in Havana and found a letter from Cugat, with a contract already signed by him. He had heard about the big success we were at La Conga in spite of the lousy band.

The contract was for two hundred a week, fifty-two weeks, five years guaranteed. In this contract—and remember, this was 1938—he covered things that I had never dreamed of doing at that time. He covered radio shows, Broadway, motion pictures, vaudeville, and —believe it or not—television. He even had the right to change my name, if he felt it necessary. So, I thought, I better take this contract to a lawyer.

Mayito Mendoza and I used to swim on the same team while we were in school in Miami. (Ralph Flanagan, who eventually broke a lot of Johnny Weissmuller's records, was also on that team.) Mayito's father was Mario Mendoza, who had been one of the top lawyers in Cuba. I had been in their house in Miami many times.

I went to him and said, "Mr. Mendoza, would you mind reading this thing? It's already signed by Cugat, but before I do anything about it, I'd like you to give me your advice."

He said, "Okay, son, you leave it here and I'll look it over. When do you need it?"

"Well, I'd like to be able to make a decision as soon as possible, because I don't have a lot of money; in fact, I'm about broke. That's why I am tempted to sign this contract. It means a lot of security. But if I don't sign it, I want to get back to New York and see if I can get some other job there."

He said, "Okay, leave it here and come back tomorrow afternoon."

I came back the next day.

He said, "I read it, and the only thing that, according to this contract, Cugat cannot do to you is fuck you—and even that is debatable because I haven't really had time to read all the small print. So if you value your independence at all, don't sign this thing. If you do, you won't have any for the next five years."

"Thank you very much, Mr. Mendoza."

Two hundred dollars a week, fifty-two weeks every year, guaranteed for five years, was tough to turn down.

9

I was then twenty-one years old and, except for that little success I had in Miami Beach, I hadn't really done anything. I didn't know where I was going, or what I was going to do. The Miami Beach season lasted only three months a year. I knew I could come back there, but what the hell would I do for the other nine months?

I went back to New York and arrived there flat broke. First, I looked for Caesar De Franco, our bass player in Miami.

I found him at the Musicians Union. Everybody goes to the Union to find out about club dates, or who's looking for what and so forth. Caesar said, "Gee, we had a good time in Miami."

I said, "Yeah, we did."

Then he asked me if I had another job and I told him no, but was sure looking for something.

He said, "Well, why don't you come and stay with us? We got an extra room at the apartment in Brooklyn . . . Seventy-four Avenue O. My wife is a nice Italian woman and I'm sure she won't mind. You were nice to me and I had a wonderful time with you in Miami; you also gave me a job for twelve weeks. I'm sure you'll get something else soon, so don't you worry."

I said, "*Gracias,* Caesar, that's great."

His wife was a fine lady and I told Caesar, "Listen, I want to pay for staying here."

"Well, you eat here every night. She doesn't mind feeding two, three . . . same thing . . . particularly when we eat spaghetti most of the time, and when we get money we'll add meatballs."

I would pay them five dollars a week for room and board, when and if I could get the five, that is—if not, we marked it in the book.

But it was much more than just room and board. Mrs. De Franco washed my shirts and my socks, she pressed my clothes, she treated me like their son. They were both in their late fifties and had no children.

Downstairs was a barbershop and the manicurist was a very cute redhead. We started going together and I had a free manicure any-time I wanted. She also talked the barber into giving me a haircut when needed, on credit, of course.

One thing the De Francos always had was a jug of red wine; I don't know if they made it themselves or not. Some nights we'd have just bread, a hunk of cheese and wine. It was delicious.

We were having no luck getting any kind of a job. I remember one night I went to bed and prayed, "Please, God, I don't care what it is, I'll go back and clean canary cages . . . anything."

I'll tell you how broke we were. We used to get up at four in the morning and walk from Brooklyn to New York to save the nickel. The subway was a nickel then. And with the nickel we saved, we'd get two doughnuts and all the coffee we wanted. That was our lunch. It was a nice long walk across the Brooklyn Bridge.

One afternoon when we were in the Union looking for a club date or anything at all, we heard there was an orchestra leader who was looking for a guitar player for the weekend, starting that same evening. That meant, of course, a guitar player who could read music and play American music and all that stuff, which wasn't me!

Nevertheless I said to Caesar, "I'm going to take that job."

He said, "How can you do that? You can't read music."

"So what? We are broke, and by the time he finds out, it'll be too late."

I went to the leader and said, "I'm a guitar player."

The man said, "Oh, good, it's getting late. You got a tux?"

"Yes, sir."

He said, "Black?"

"Yes, sir, I got it."

I rented a black tux jacket to go with the pants, took my guitar and went where he told me. It was one of those German places up in the Eighties. They played a lot of German songs and they played American music, but they didn't play any Latin music at all.

I sat next to the drummer and they gave me all these arrangements. It was quite a nice orchestra, eight or nine pieces. I figured, sitting next to the drummer, maybe they wouldn't hear my guitar. I had a Spanish guitar and thought, "If I play it softly, perhaps nobody will notice."

We started, I was playing as softly as I could, but a couple of minutes later the bandleader turned around and motioned with his hand to bring it up a little. Before he gave the downbeat for the next number he said, "Listen, son, will you bring up the guitar a little bit? I can't hear you."

"Oh, I'm sorry, sir, I'll make sure to do that."

He gave the downbeat and I was still using my same feather touch, so again he gave me the hand business about bringing it up.

Well, I got by that one set. . . . As we were resting backstage in the musicians' room he came over and said, "Look, kid, I can't hear that guitar. Maybe you should sit up front. You know, you're right next to the drummer and with the saxophones in front of you I just can't hear the guitar at all. We'd do just as well without it."

I said, "Well, gee, I'm sorry. Let me try it right from where I am, but I tell you what—I'll use a pick. You see, I have been playing with my fingers. I'll use the pick like the American boys do and I think that will bring it up."

He said, "Yes, that's a good idea, use the pick, use the pick."

Now I was really dead. I'd better break a couple of strings, I was thinking. The next set I broke three.

He said, "What happened?"

I showed him the guitar with the broken strings.

"Well, fix them," he said.

I got off the bandstand and went backstage. I had an extra set of strings in my guitar case which I took out and put into my pants pocket.

He came back to the musicians' room and asked, "You got the guitar fixed?"

"No," I said, "I haven't got any strings."

"You mean to tell me you take a job and you don't bring a set of extra strings?"

I said, "Well, look, I've been flat broke. I mean, I didn't have a cent, it's really been rough."

He was a pretty nice fellow, and said, "I understand, we all go through that. What else can you do?"

I said, "I sing."

He said, "You sing?"

"Yeah, Latin numbers."

"Oh, dear God. Latin numbers?"

I said, "Don't you play any Latin numbers?"

"Well, we got a couple, like 'Peanut Vendor' and 'Mama Inez.' " (Aren't there any other Latin numbers these gringos know?)

"That's fine," I told him. "I'll get together with the pianist and see if we can fake a couple of those."

He said, "Okay, you got to do *something*."

I got together with the piano player, worked out the key and in the next set we did "The Peanut Vendor."

Backstage again the bandleader said, "I like that, gives us a variation. Are you doing anything for the next three or four weekends?"

I said, "No, nothing."

"Okay," he said, "I'll pay you now for tonight." Normally you get paid at the end of the weekend. "That way you can get a new set of strings and play the guitar with the orchestra besides singing."

"Well, look, you've been awfully nice to me but, to tell you the truth, I can't read music."

"You can't read music?"

"No, I can't. Those arrangements you gave me look like Chinese writing to me."

"Why, you sonofabitch," he said.

"I was hungry."

"Okay, okay, forget about the guitar."

"No, we don't have to forget about the guitar. When I sing those Spanish songs I can play the guitar and it'll make the band sound better. I've got a pair of maracas at home. I'll bring them and I'll teach one of the guys how to play them. We might even try to see how these Germans like the conga line."

"What the hell is that?"

"It's something we started in Miami."

The following weekend I brought the maracas and the conga drum and taught the rhythm to the band, and soon we had the Germans in a conga line. We stayed there for four weekends and before the job finally ended the Germans were congaing around the block.

It was really in this German place that the conga started in New York.

I was able to pay Caesar and his wife for my rent and we were having meatballs with the spaghetti again. But after that job finished, we had a long dry spell. Then one day I got a wire addressed to Desiderio Alberto Arnaz de Acha, 74 Avenue O, Brooklyn. It was signed "Tapps," and said that he had a possible job for me and my band for the coming summer at a place in Glens Falls, and asked if I would come in and talk to him about it.

I asked Caesar, "How come this guy knows my full name and where I live?"

At that time, nobody knew it. Anyone from Miami, for example, knew me as Desi Arnaz. That's the name I always used and everybody called me Desi. I remembered I had used my full name on my Musicians Union card because I had not yet changed my name legally.

"What the hell do you care how he knows it?" answered Caesar. "Let's go see the guy."

That day we spent a couple of nickels and took the subway. Tapps was a short, heavyset fellow with white hair. He didn't have a fancy office, not exactly like Lew Wasserman's at MCA in the Fifties, but not too bad. I introduced myself.

He said, "Well, I've got this little job during the summer and I may be able to swing it for you."

Before we went into the office, I had told Caesar, "Let me do the talking, you keep quiet."

I said nothing now either. I wanted Tapps to keep talking to see if I could find out how he got my full name and where he got it. I thought this would give me a clue as to where I stood.

Then he said, "These people are opening a road restaurant in Glens Falls, and they told me to look for a little rumba band from Miami. But they couldn't even remember your name, so I contacted the Union, found out and got your address."

That led me to think that somebody wanted me pretty bad to go to all this trouble. Of course, Mr. Tapps, who was a very good agent, was trying to make it sound like it wasn't that important.

"Well?" he asked.

"Sounds promising," I answered. "What is it all about?"

"You play there for probably two weeks, with some options, and if you're good, you might stay there for eight weeks."

"What does the job pay?" I asked.

"Four hundred dollars for you and the group you had in Miami."

"Oh. Well, thank you very much for going through all that trouble, Mr. Tapps, but there's no use wasting your time. I know you are a busy man."

"I'll take the time," he said. "Let's sit down and talk this over."

"Okay, but—a—a—"

"Now, look, maybe I can talk to them and get them to give you five hundred dollars, and of course transportation up there and back."

"What about the rooms and the food?"

"They have rooms there. I'll see that you get some."

"All right, what about the food?"

"Well, it's a roadside restaurant, I should be able to get you dinner. I'll try for lunch and dinner."

"That's a little better," I said, "but we're still way off in the price."

"I can't go any higher," he said. "Five, five-fifty. That's about the most."

"Thank you very much, Mr. Tapps, but that's not enough. Let's go, Caesar."

We started to leave.

"Wait a minute!" he called. "Wait a minute! Come back here!

What's the matter with you? Can't you spend a couple of minutes talking to me? How much did you have in mind?"

"As I see it, we'll be the only band. Right?"

"Right."

"And they want us to play both Latin and American music so I should add two more men, a trumpet player and an accordion. That'll be eight with me. Then we could play American music, tangos, rumbas, everything."

"Okay, okay. How much?"

"I'll tell you what, Mr. Tapps. If you get them to let me add the two men, transportation there and back, of course, plus board and room and a minimum of eight weeks, no options . . ."

"Yeah, yeah. How much?"

"I will cut our price down to a thousand dollars a week."

"You will cut it *down* to a thousand?" he asked.

"Yes, sir."

"Your mathematics are a little screwed up. You were getting $650 at La Conga for your five men, so two more men can only cost at the most $150 more. That would make it $800 total. So what do you mean, you'll cut it down to a thousand?"

Another lesson—agents can find out anything they want to know from the Union.

"Your figures are right, Mr. Tapps, but that was before we were a big hit, as we are now," I said, with a straight face.

From the corner of my eye, I saw Caesar surreptitiously making the sign of the cross.

"Well, there's no way I can get that," he said.

"I'm sorry, but we do appreciate your thinking of us. Come on, Caesar, let's go."

As we were going through the door Caesar was mumbling, "What's the matter? Don't you want to eat?" (Half in Italian, half in English.)

"Hey, come back here," we heard. "I don't think I can get you this deal. It's much more than they intended to pay. But I'll give it a try. Of course, you know that I get ten percent."

"Of my thousand?" I asked.

"Sure, all agents get ten percent."

"Then you'd better ask for eleven hundred dollars so you can get your hundred dollars."

"You're sure you're not Jewish?" he asked me.

He was representing Fan and Bill's but he also wanted 10 percent from me, which of course is par for the course. The owner of a club calls the agent and tells him what group he wants. Then the agent gets hold of the leader of that group and tells him, "Listen, I know of a place where I may be able to get you in."

The thing that tipped Mr. Tapps's hand was the wire addressed to my full name. He had to go to the Union to look for me. Also, he said they had called him to find "a little rumba band from Miami." Well, in those days I was the only little rumba band from Miami.

Anyway, Mr. Tapps said that he would call me the next day. On the way out, Caesar said, "I think you just blew the meatballs."

"I don't know, they were looking for us. Somebody must want us pretty bad to go to all this trouble."

Thank God I was right because the next day Mr. Tapps called and said we had the job.

The group I took to Fan and Bill's was the same one I had at La Conga. But by this time we had been working together for quite a while. The Spaniard had learned other rhythms besides *paso dobles,* and the trumpet and accordion we had added changed it into a pretty good combo.

We all had a great time at Lake George that summer. Fan and Bill were good to us, and it was they who, for the first time, put my name in lights—"Desi Arnaz and his Orchestra"—no Cugat anymore.

We played La Conga in Miami Beach again the following winter.

Toward the end of that season, a fellow by the name of Mario Torsatti came to the place and said he was opening a club in New York which he was also calling La Conga. He offered us a job, starting when we finished in Miami.

At La Conga in New York the other band was Pancho's. Pancho was famous for his tangos, which were very popular in those days. They also had a girl, Diosa Costello, a Puerto Rican singer and dancer who had an exciting act and fitted perfectly into my conga thing. She could shake her ass better and faster than anybody I had ever seen—a great performer.

New York's La Conga was an unbelievable success. Like the Charleston, the conga line became a national dance craze and soon afterward an international one.

The number-one debutante in New York was Brenda Frazier, and she came to La Conga to see what in hell all the noise was about. Her group used to stay on the East Side, at such places as the Stork Club, "21," The Versailles, and El Morocco. When Brenda came to La Conga, they all followed her. She was the leader and wherever she went all the other debutantes and their escorts went.

As Dorothy Kilgallen said in her column, "La Conga was the

first nightclub that brought the Eastside of New York to the Westside." La Conga was just off Broadway.

Brenda was, and I am sure still is, an extremely beautiful and striking girl. She was the first girl I ever saw who wore a very light, almost white makeup with hardly any lipstick at all. She had beautiful eyes, silky long dark hair, and the most provocative lips and smile. She was not what I presumed a spoiled New York society eighteen-year-old girl would be, not at all. We became good friends and she kept bringing all those people from the East Side over to La Conga. One of her escorts at that time was Peter Arno, the fellow who did all the *New Yorker* cartoons, one of the greatest cartoonists in the world—smart, very sharp, high class. Peter had one of those old Duesenberg racing cars and he and I used to drive it to Atlantic City for weekends once in a while. Atlantic City was really jumping in those days and Peter knew where the best "jumpers" were.

I made another good acquaintance at that time. One night, dancing in front of the bandstand, was one of the most gorgeous redheads I'd ever seen. She looked eighteen or nineteen. I couldn't stop looking at her and she seemed to be enjoying it in a very coquettish sort of way, which kind of perked up my curiosity a little further. After the set I asked Irving Zussman about her. Irving and Milton Rubin were the other two partners at La Conga and two of the best public-relations men in the business. Milton used to have breakfast with Winchell every morning and Walter started to come over to the place and gave me some great plugs in his column, which in those days were extremely valuable.

So I asked them who the redhead was.

Irving said, "Come on, I want you to meet her and the people she's with. I think they'll be very interesting for you to know."

He took me over to the table and said, "Mr. Arnaz, I would like you to meet a famous New York madam, Polly Adler and two of her very lovely young ladies."

I thought he had said "madame" and that probably she was the mother or aunt of the girls. She asked me to sit down with them. Polly had a very deep voice. She sounded like Bill Frawley with laryngitis. She introduced me to the redhead and the other, a beautiful brunette. Then she said, "Would you like to come and have breakfast with us after your last show?"

"Oh, that would be nice."

By this time I was really going crazy sitting next to this redhead. "Built like a brick shithouse" was a popular description in my time.

Polly Adler's house of ill repute in New York was really an

elegant place. The large living room was done in shades of red and white and furnished in luxurious seventeenth-century French style. The high ceiling supported a large Maria Theresa crystal chandelier. Her decorations were vases of fresh yellow roses, plus the most sensational-looking mulatto girl, dressed not as one of Hugh Hefner's bunnies but in a high-necked, white-silk evening gown—nothing else, a la Harlow—which hugged all the hills and valleys of her lovely body. I shouldn't have said "nothing else" because she also always wore high-heeled red shoes.

There was no open bar, but once this girl knew what you liked to drink, she made sure you never had to ask for it again. She seemed to have a sixth sense that told her when you were about to take your last sip. Before you had done so, a new drink would be there and the empty glass gone.

The bedrooms' main features were either four-posters with canopies or ultra-king-size beds with beautifully designed headboards. Large antique mirrors were hung in strategic places. Lit by candlelight only and scented with the fragrance of different fresh flowers to fit each room's particular color scheme, which in turn complemented the coloring of each occupant.

After we'd had a sumptuous breakfast of caviar, sturgeon, scrambled eggs, toast—the works—and nothing but the very best champagne to drink, Polly said, "You like the redhead, don't you?"

"Oh, yeah!"

But by now I had realized that I was in a very classy whorehouse and I was sure that, in this place, once-over-lightly had to be at least one hundred dollars.

So I said to her, "Mrs. Adler, I enjoyed your breakfast immensely. You have been a very gracious hostess, but I'm afraid the redhead is way beyond my means."

She looked at me, and with that wonderful, deep and hearty laugh of hers said, "That's all right, sonny, this one's on the house."

I started to protest, but she stopped me with "Go on now. She is waiting for you. You don't want her to think you don't like her, do you?"

"Of course not."

"Well, then, get going."

"What time is it?"

"Six-thirty."

"I have a rehearsal at two o'clock."

"I'll wake you up at noon. I hope she lets you sleep for a couple of hours."

Wow! I've had my share of delicious sex in my life, but that redhead was something else. If there was anything I had not learned at Casa Marina, she taught it to me then. She was insatiable. These girls who worked for Polly looked as good and as elegant and were just as refined as the society girls you found at El Morocco or "21." Polly really put them through school. Not only would a man go there to spend a couple of hours, but he also could take one of the girls out for the evening and *that* was five bills. Rich out-of-town businessmen didn't want to get in trouble with anybody or get into any romance deals. They could take these lovely young ladies anyplace, knowing they would always be well dressed and well mannered, and would never drink too much.

Polly also helped me a hell of a lot by instructing all her girls to take the men to La Conga whenever possible. Strange that my first best two girl friends in New York came from poles apart: Brenda Frazier, the number-one debutante and Polly Adler, the number-one madam. Between the two of them and from different sources, they sure brought a lot of people into La Conga.

I didn't know many motion-picture or theater people, but quite a few of them came to La Conga. One night after I'd finished the first show Mario called me into the office and said, "Do you know who wants to talk to you?"

"Who?"

"Rodgers and Hart."

"Who are they?" I really didn't know.

10

"Richard Rodgers and Larry Hart are the top musical-comedy writing team in America. They have all the big Broadway shows. That's who they are, you stupid Cuban!"

"I've never been to a Broadway show."

"Well, they're the greatest. They have hits all the time. I don't know what they want with you, but you'd better go talk to them and try to be your most charming self."

I met Dick Rodgers and Larry Hart. George Marion, Jr., was with them, and Mr. Hart explained to me that Mr. Marion had written a book called *Too Many Girls*. One of the characters in the story is a Latin boy, eighteen or nineteen, who is supposed to be the best football player ever to come out of Latin America. Anyone playing the role should be able to handle comedy, as well as sing and dance.

At that time the Latin type they were describing was not easy to find in this country. Today there are quite a few of them, and much better than I was. The only ones who were known then were the romantic Valentino types and the George Raft types, or the other extreme, the Crispin Martin lazy Mexican character or the Leo Carrillos.

Although I wasn't eighteen or nineteen, I looked a few years younger than I actually was.

Larry Hart said, "I saw you at La Conga in Miami."

"Oh, I didn't even know you were there, Mr. Hart."

"I know that. I saw you and I watched you. I told Dick and George about you. Can you act?"

"I don't know. I did a couple of parts in school plays when I was in Cuba and I used to be on the debating team. I can also recite 'La Marcha Triunfal de Rubén Darío.' "

"What the hell is that?" asked both Dick and Larry.

"That was my *pièce de résistance*. I started doing it when I was twelve."

"We'll never know until we try him, will we, Dick?" Mr. Marion said.

"I'll try anything," I threw in.

"Don't get too excited," Mr. Rodgers said. "We have to bring Mr. Abbott over here to take a look at you."

"Who's he?"

"You really don't know anything about the New York theater, do you?"

"I'm sorry."

"George Abbott is one of the top directors of the New York stage, and he's particularly good with inexperienced young people. He also happens to be the man who is going to direct this show, if we can ever cast it."

The next night, Larry Hart came back with George Abbott and he saw me do the conga line. As a matter of fact, Mr. Abbott joined it. Afterward he called me over and said, "I would like to have you come over to the theater and read a couple of scenes for me, day after tomorrow at nine A.M. Larry will tell you where it is."

Nine A.M. reminds me of Tommy Dorsey at MGM many years later. The assistant director told Tommy that he and his band were to be at Makeup at eight o'clock the next day, in order to be ready at nine. They were being featured in *DuBarry Was a Lady,* one of MGM's top musicals, with Lucy and Red Skelton costarring.

Dorsey asked the assistant, "You mean eight o'clock in the morning?"

"Of course," he was told.

"Jesus Christ," said Dorsey, "my boys don't even start vomiting till eleven."

Abbott left and Larry introduced Dr. Bender, a dentist who moonlighted as an agent.

Larry said, "Look, Abbott doesn't like anyone to see the script before reading it to him. Have you ever read a script for anyone?"

"I don't think so. What's a script?" I didn't even know what it meant.

"That's what I was afraid of. I'll tell you what I'll do. I'm going to bring you a script and we'll work with you before you read it for him. At least you'll have an idea of what it's supposed to be, but for God's sake, when you read for Abbott, the day after tomorrow, pretend it's the first time you've seen it. He would raise holy hell with us if he found out that we had given you a script before you went over there. He likes people to read cold for him."

This is one of the many things I learned from Mr. Abbott. While we were doing *I Love Lucy* even Lucy never saw a script until the first read-through on Monday morning, and neither did Bill or Vivian. I didn't want them to worry about what they would be doing the following week, while we were doing this week's show.

The part I was to read for was Manolito and he had some very important scenes. Larry and Doc Bender made me read them several times the next day. Later I practiced in front of a mirror, time and time again. I even threw in some gestures I thought appropriate.

I arrived at the audition, Abbott said, "You first sing something. Get with the piano player and we'll see how you sound in this theater without a microphone."

The audition, as I mentioned, was at nine in the morning, a rough time for me. I never finished at La Conga before 4:30 A.M. and of course I could never go to sleep right away. I had to relax. Usually I went over to Polly's and had breakfast—or something. I never went to sleep until seven or seven-thirty in the morning. On this particular day I knew that if I went to sleep I would never wake up in time to make the audition. So I didn't go to bed at all.

I got together with the piano player and sang one of Rodgers and

Hart's old songs; he didn't know any of my Latin numbers. It wasn't my type of song, or my time of day.

After I had finished, and I knew I had been pretty lousy, I overheard Abbott say to Dick Rodgers, who was sitting next to him, "Well, he's loud enough."

Next he handed me the script and asked me to read the scene he had marked. Manolito is trying to decide which college in the United States he will go to. He has many choices. All the colleges are after him, with offers of scholarships and all sorts of things. But there is only one thing Manolito wants to know in the scene. He says to one of the scouts, "All I'm interested in is going to a place where they have lots of pretty girls. In my life I have nine brothers, no sisters, ten uncles, no aunts. I'm eighteen years old and I have never had a girl. But I understand that here in the United States there are a lot of colleges with a lot of girls, who don't have to have chaperones or any of that stuff to worry about. So that's where I want to go."

The scout says, "You belong at Vassar."

"They got girls there?" Manolito asks.

"Yeah, they got girls—nothing else but," says the scout; "the only trouble is that they don't play football and they don't allow any men in there, either."

MANOLITO: Football is not the most important thing, I'd like to go to one where they played it, but it must have lots of girls."

SCOUT: You mean "coeducational."

MANOLITO: That's it—cooperational girls.

Manolito was a good character, simpatico. An American audience would sympathize with an eighteen-year-old kid who hasn't gotten laid yet.

Once I started saying the speech I was carried away with my acting and was waving my hands and doing all the gestures I had practiced in front of the mirror.

The script was all over the place, except in front of my eyes. Obviously, I wasn't reading it.

I finished, looked at Abbott—and he was looking at Dick Rodgers. Then I saw Larry Hart sneaking out of the theater.

Abbott also saw him and called out to him, "Larry! Where are you going?"

"Just to the—the—the john."

Abbott said, "You gave him the script, didn't you?"

"Who? Me? How? Why?"

"Because he hasn't looked at one goddamned word of that scene.

He did the whole thing like a big ham, emoting and waving all over the place. You taught him, didn't you? And, I may add, you did a bad job of it."

I felt terrible. I had put Larry in a very embarrassing position. After all, he had warned me about Abbott not liking anybody to see the script before an audition. Besides, as Mr. Abbott said, all those gestures and expressions I had added, in front of that goddamned mirror, were pretty bad. I had blown the audition for sure.

So, very quietly, I started to get off the stage. I was almost out of the theater when someone came and said that Mr. Abbott wanted to see me.

I went back and said, "I'm sorry, sir, it wasn't Mr. Hart's fault. He knew that I had never read from a script before. He was just trying to help me. I got carried away and added all those gestures and things."

"Okay, Dizzy."

"It's not Dizzy, sir, it's Desi."

"Okay, Desi, you seem to be the only one around who fits the part so if you don't mind working your ass off, we'll give it a try. Be back at one o'clock."

"You mean I've got the part?"

I don't think I even said, "Thank you." I couldn't believe it. I had never dreamed I would get a chance to be on the Broadway stage. That, to me, was way beyond my reach. I was making three hundred a week at La Conga in New York and, considering the previous five years, that was all the money in the world.

The press had been wonderful to me. Brenda Frazier, the number-one debutante in the country, was one of my biggest boosters. Polly Adler and her girls were my friends, and then some. I was having a ball.

The next day Mr. Abbott said, "We must work something out about your engagement at La Conga. How much longer does your contract call for there?"

"Well, I have to be there for at least three more months."

He said, "You can keep working there while we're in town. You won't have to rehearse at night, but after four weeks we will be out of town. We'll be in New Haven for a week or more and then we'll be in Boston for at least two weeks before our opening on Broadway. Do you think you could get a leave of absence from your contract?"

"I guess so."

I talked to Mario Torsatti, Irving Zussman and Milton Rubin, the partners in La Conga, and told them what Abbott had said about the leave of absence. Then I added, "Before you give me an answer, I must tell you I don't even know if I want it."

Mario said, "What do you mean, you don't know if you want it?"

"Well, I'm scared to death. I have never walked across a stage in my life, and this is Broadway, where all the big stars in the world appear. I haven't got the slightest idea what acting is. I don't even understand some of the jokes."

Mario answered, "Yeah, well, we understand how you feel, but George Abbott is the greatest director for inexperienced young people in the business and if he thinks you got a chance—you're crazy not to try."

"But suppose I just can't cut it? Suppose I'm a flop over there and then probably you guys won't have me back here, either."

"Look, if that's all that's worrying you, here's what we'll do. We will keep a nucleus of your band here while you're out of town. If the show is a flop, you will come back to La Conga at your same salary, and if the show is a big hit and you become a Broadway star, you will come back to La Conga for six months, not three, but also at the same salary."

"That's fair enough," I told them.

While we were rehearsing in New York, there was no problem because Mr. Abbott had the dancers rehearse at night in the numbers he didn't need me for and he always let me off at five or six o'clock at the latest, so that I had time enough to change and get ready for my dinner show at La Conga.

Of course all the kids from the show would come over to La Conga after rehearsals, so I had another group rooting for me and making the place jump.

George Marion, Jr., and George Abbott would be there often because they both loved to dance. Abbott is really a great rumba dancer. He would dance with Diosa all night between shows.

One night he said to me, "You know, the best thing you do is when you start doing the conga hollering and banging the hell out of that big drum of yours. We have to figure out how to work that into the show."

They changed the first-act finale so that the whole cast was doing the conga with me. Diosa was also given a part in the show. While I would bang the drum and lead the shouts, she would be shaking her nice Puerto Rican ass all over the place. All the chorus girls and boys, the whole cast, covering the entire stage at different levels, would get into this big conga line, answering the shouts, kicking their legs, throwing their arms up in the air while the drums kept getting louder and louder. It was really frantic. Robert Alton did a sensational job, choreographing this number.

Dick and Larry had written a great score. "I Didn't Know What Time It Was" was the number-one song on *The Hit Parade* for at least twelve straight weeks. Others were: "I Like to Recognize the Tune," "Give It Back to the Indians," "Love Never Went to College," "Spic and Spanish," "She Could Shake Her Maracas," "Too Many Girls," "Potowatamie" and "Harvard Look Out."

The last song became an interesting musical problem when we first tried to do it as a conga for the first-act finale. This number was right after we had won a big football game, in which Manolito had been the big hero, and a celebration was going on with all the guys on the team, the band, cheerleaders and the whole student body—just as at USC or UCLA after a big win.

The lyrics of "Harvard Look Out" continued with "Princeton look out, we shout, look out Yale, you're a ham, better scram Notre Dame, we'll make Williams wail, Navy you're through, Army you too, pooh, pooh, to Purdue."

It was a great rally song. The only problem was that Dick had written it as a march. Now the conga is very simple, but that one, two, three—kick; one, two, three—kick has to fit not only the melody but also the phrasing of the words. Otherwise you are thrown completely off and you can't dance to it or sing to it. You just can't do it at all.

When I tried to put the conga to this song, it just didn't fit. So I said to the pianist, the arranger and the conductor, who were all there, "Look, this cannot be done as a conga. The meter won't fit. The kids can do it straight, as it is, the first time they come out, but when I start playing the drum, we've got to change it."

Well, they got insulted.

The conductor said, *"You* are going to change a Dick Rodgers and Larry Hart song?"

"If they want to do the conga to this one, I'll have to. Otherwise I wouldn't be able to do it."

They said, "Forget it, boy. You are talking about Richard Rodgers and Lorenz Hart."

"I know that. As a matter of fact, I'm flabbergasted that I'm even in this thing at all. I'm scared stiff, but if they want me to do the conga to this song, we will have to put it in conga rhythm, otherwise we can't do it. Everybody in New York is doing the conga just the way they see us do it at the club. So if you want me to do it here, that's the way we'll have to do it, which is the right way."

Actually, it was the only way. You certainly can't dance a waltz to a tango, or a conga to a march.

"We can't change Rodgers' music" was their answer.

At this point I saw Rodgers coming down the aisle.

He said, "What's going on? What's the matter, Desi?"

"Well, Mr. Rodgers, I guess we have a problem and I—uh—uh—"

"Well, what is it?"

The conductor, echoed by the arranger, said, "Hiya, Dick, this kid here wants to change Larry's phrasing and your music to fit his goddamned conga drumbeat."

Dick said, "Let's see why. What's your problem, Desi?"

"Well, I can't sing 'Harvard look out, Princeton look out, we shout, look out Yale.' the way it is written, because I can't do the conga beat to that phrasing."

"How would you do it for a conga?"

"Well, it would have to go like: "Har—ar—ar—VARD! Look out, Prin—n—n—STON! Look out, we—e—e—EE! Shout, look out Ya—a—a—ALE!'·and so on."

Mr. Rodgers said, "Why not? What's the matter with you guys? We'll have the first chorus straight and then when Desi starts the conga beat, we'll change it to fit his thing. To tell you the truth, I like it better his way."

That is what Mr. Richard Rodgers, one of the greatest composers of this century, said and did. That is why I was so pleased and proud that I was asked to participate in a tribute to him a few years ago at the Tony Awards annual television extravaganza. Dick was there at the piano and I sang "She Could Shake Her Maracas," one of my solos from *Too Many Girls,* besides "Harvard Look Out" and the title song.

Dick came over afterward and kissed me. He said, "You're the first man I've ever kissed, Cuban."

"Dick, I love you. I've never forgotten what you did that day when we were trying to work out the conga music and all the other times you have helped me so much."

To think that I was just a kid who was lucky to have a job, didn't even know how to read music! All I knew was how to beat the hell out of a conga drum. And that, by the grace of God, starts some kind of craze all over the country, the world, eventually, and the only reason I had started doing it, I kept remembering, was because Cugat sent me a lousy band.

And now, probably the number-one music writer in the world was allowing me to change his music around to fit my "thing." Yeah, Dick Rodgers is quite a man, and I was a very lucky Cuban to have him and Larry and George Abbott helping me. Mr. Abbott is a genius when it comes to directing inexperienced young people. He just has a knack to make you feel comfortable, show you where to go, how to say it, when and how to react.

I didn't know anything about acting, much less about acting in a comedy, which is, as most actors would agree, much more difficult than drama. In all my long years in show business, I have found that an actor who is good at comedy can also be very good at drama, but not necessarily vice versa.

One of my biggest problems with comedy was that I did not understand some of the jokes, particularly the ones that depended on a funny play on words.

I used to go to Abbott and tell him, "I get a big laugh with this line and I don't know why."

He would get a kick out of that and then explain it to me. Also, at times Eddie Bracken, who had the comedy lead, would say something to me in the play and the audience would laugh like hell. Of course, I as Manolito had to react as if I knew what he had said and also laugh like hell. Many times I didn't know what we were all laughing about.

For instance:

BRACKEN (talking about a football game): The referee intercepted the pass and ran eighty yards for a touchdown.

MANOLITO: The referee?

BRACKEN: "Yeah, he was an old NYU back and had never been in the clear before—ha, ha, ha!

The first thing I didn't know about that one was what NYU meant.

One of the biggest jokes in the show was about a lot of girls at Potowatamie, wearing beanies on their heads. Beanies were round caps which covered the back of the girls' heads. All the guys were trying to find out if the beanies had any significance.

The scene started with Eddie Bracken onstage, alone, then I came in, followed by Hal LeRoy, a great dancer who also, in the play, played in the backfield on the team.

MANOLITO: I found out what beanies mean.

BRACKEN: What?

MANOLITO: Well, all the girls who wear beanies are . . . eh . . . virgins.

BRACKEN: Ah, come on, that couldn't be it.

MANOLITO: Yeah, that's it. One of the guys told us.

BRACKEN: He was kidding you, or something.

MANOLITO: No, no, he wasn't kidding me. The ones who wear beanies are all virgins.

BRACKEN: That's hard to believe.

MANOLITO: I know—there are so many of them.

Wow! What a laugh!

And I didn't know why. I first thought that it might be a religious joke. Well, I didn't get the connection at all until Abbott explained it to me.

The scene, by the way, continued with my date for the evening, Mary Jane Walsh, coming out to meet me. She stopped the show every night doing a great song, "Give It Back to the Indians."

MARY JANE (with a broad southern accent): Are you ready to go to the get-together?

MANOLITO: Oh yeah, how together do we get on these get-togethers?

MARY JANE: (with a meaningful, flirtatious smile): Well, you just come with me, you tall and handsome Cuban brute, and find out, you-all.

Manolito suddenly realizes that his cute, sexy date has no beanie on her head. He turns and looks back at Bracken and LeRoy, stage center, and points to her head. He then looks back at her again, "so the audience can really see your expression," as Abbott said, and taking her by the waist, with a big, big smile of anticipation on his face, he exits with her.

My only prior exposure to what I thought was American humor was based on observing a few American tourists who came to Santiago, and my reaction at that time was "What a bunch of silly characters." They all seemed to wear funny hats, tried to play the maracas or bongos and made asses of themselves, trying to rumba and laughing like hell at each other.

Sometimes one of them would tell you a joke in English and you would say, *"No sabe."* Then they would try to translate it into Spanish and, of course, then it would not make any sense at all, particularly the jokes that had to do with a play on words. So you would say to yourself, "What the hell kind of sense of humor do these characters have? They are really a bunch of silly people."

Later, when I got to this country and went to high school, and of course during the run of *Too Many Girls,* I learned differently. I could have gone to college for four years and not learned any more than I did in *Too Many Girls.* And when I learned about the American sense of humor and understood it, not only did I not think anymore that they were silly-ass people making fools of themselves and laughing at some idiotic joke, but I began to admire them for their sense of humor. I began to realize that they have a hell of a lot better sense of humor than we Latins have. The American people have the ability to laugh at themselves, to make fun not only of themselves but of their faults. It is one of the things that makes this country the great country that it is.

Too Many Girls opened out of town, in New Haven, Connecticut, on September 28, 1939.

New Haven was picked because it is a good college town, and our whole show was about college kids, football, and screwing. (Yes, in 1939 college kids did it too.) So it was a good town to try out the show. It was a big hit the very first night. By then I had learned more about what the jokes meant and I was enjoying playing my part, but I was a zombie that first night I walked out on that stage in front of a full house.

The first big laugh I got scared the hell out of me. I had never heard the sound of a full theater really laughing at a joke, a boffo. What a wonderful sound that is, and what a sensational feeling! I'll always remember New Haven as the place where I first got such a thrill.

On opening night we did the "Harvard Look Out" song, followed by the change in tempo for the conga number at the close of the first act. The first-act curtain came down to big applause. Then we heard the stage manager shout, "Places! ! !" So back we came and the curtain went up again. The people were still applauding, now standing up.

During the intermission Mr. Abbott stuck his head in our dressing room and said, "Hey, Desi, for an amateur you're doing great, kid. Keep it up."

Busy as he was on opening night, he took the time to come to the dressing room to say that. It meant the whole world to me.

Then Bracken said, "You know what we did just now?"

"What?" I asked.

"That was the end of the first act."

"I know that."

"I know you know that, but what you don't know is that the curtain doesn't go up at the end of the first act. The curtain comes down—end of the first act—and the people go out and they go across the street, get a couple of fast belts of booze and, when the bell rings, they come back for the second act. Nobody stops the show in the finale of the first act."

"Is that what we did?"

"Yah, that's what we did. We stopped the show with that conga thing of yours."

I figured he was just trying to make me feel good, but it really was the truth and it happened almost every night in New Haven, later in Boston, and even more so in New York.

We played one week in New Haven.

Next stop: Boston.

After the opening-night performance Mr. Abbott had quite a few notes for everyone in the cast. When he finished with us he turned to Larry Hart and said, "Larry, we need at least two more choruses for 'I Like to Recognize the Tune.' "

The number had stopped the show cold that night, and even though the cast were prepared with two extra choruses, which they sang, the audience still wanted more. Mary Jane Walsh, Eddie Bracken, Richard Kollmar and Marcy Westcott did that number.

Larry looked in his coat pocket and took out an envelope, put it on top of the rehearsal piano onstage, borrowed a pencil and started to write. That's how we left him as we went to a restaurant across the street from the theater for the party which Rodgers and Hart and George Abbott were giving for the cast and friends who had come up from New York.

In about a half-hour Larry came in, went to Mr. Abbott and Dick Rodgers and said, "What do you think of this?" as he handed them the envelope. He had written three more choruses as good as, if not better than, the ones he had written before. Unbelievable mind! Larry's lyrics always told a story so well and so completely that you could use some of them as the basis for a film. "It seemed we stood and talked like this before/We looked at each other in the same way then/But I can't remember where or when." It has happened to everybody. Sometimes you will be at a place and think, I've been here before; but you know you have never been, and yet . . . Another is: "I didn't know what time it was/Then I met you/Oh what a lovely time it was/How sublime it was too."

There is a definition of genius that I like very much. "A person who can do something different, extraordinary, which no other person has done before and especially something which would benefit mankind, or a person who does his or her job better than anyone else could do the same job."

Larry Hart must have been a genius. He qualifies in both categories.

11

On the train to Boston I felt one of my toes hurting really badly. It had been bothering me for a couple of days but I hadn't paid much attention to it. I took off my shoe and sock and looked at it. It was blue all over. One of the girls saw it and said, "You better show that to Mr. Abbott, Desi. That doesn't look good."

I went to Mr. Abbott and told him, "I hate to bother you with this, but some of the kids said I should show it to you."

He asked, "What's the matter?"

"Well, see the toe here . . ."

"Oh, boy, that's terrible! That looks like blood poisoning. How in the hell are you going to dance on that thing?"

"Well, maybe it'll go away by tomorrow."

"No, that thing doesn't go away by itself. You go to the hospital as soon as we arrive in Boston."

He put me in the hospital and the doctor said, "Yes, he has blood poisoning and it is spreading. Half of his foot is going to be that way by tonight. He has to stay here so we can control it."

I said, "I've gotta stay here? I can't, I'm opening tomorrow night in the show!"

The doctor said, with emphasis, "You ain't gonna open tomorrow night in no show, boy!"

My understudy, one of the dancers in the show, was Van Johnson. He was also understudying Richard Kollmar, Eddie Bracken and Hal LeRoy. I must say that Mr. Abbott was a little bit tight with the budget. He didn't carry one more person than he thought absolutely necessary.

When Van Johnson found out that it was I he might have to

understudy, he almost jumped off the balcony. "That's just my luck!" he shouted. "Bracken I can do, Kollmar I can do, LeRoy I can do. But how the hell am I gonna do this Cuban?"

As he was rambling on, dark wigs were being tried on him to see if he could be made to look Latin, which is kind of difficult to do with a tall, blue-eyed, freckled, redheaded, typical American type like Van.

The next day he came to the hospital to see me.

He said, "Talk!"

"About what?"

"Anything. Just talk. I have to do your accent tonight."

"You are going to play my part?"

"Yup, ain't that the shit? That's my lousy luck. It had to be you."

"Stick around. I'm going to talk to the doctor. He's on his way over here now."

The doctor came, and after he had looked at my foot I said to him, "Look, Doc, isn't there something you can do, something you can give me, to make the foot dead for two and a half hours?"

"Are you thinking of doing the show?"

"Well, if you can make this foot dead for that length of time, I can do it. Then I can come right back here so they can work on it all night."

What they'd been doing was putting hot compresses on the foot and then puncturing a little here and a little there. They were trying to see if they could get the infection out without having to do surgery.

The doctor said, "Okay, let's try it."

Van was tickled pink. "Thank God! Thank God!" he kept repeating.

So, for the first three nights in Boston, the doctor would deaden my foot, the ambulance would deliver me backstage—I had already dressed for my first scene—and I'd do the show. The ambulance would be there before we finished the last-act finale, and then would take me back to the hospital.

By that time it was beginning to "hoit," as they say in the old vaudeville joke. The minute I got back the nurses would be ready with the compresses and stuff. They'd work on the foot all night and all the next day, until it was time to deaden it again.

Three days and nights of that and they got it well. Four days later, the doctor said, "I want to see you. Will you come over here?"

I told him, "My foot is fine, Doc, you did a great job."

"Thanks, I'm glad to know that, but I still want to see you."

"But, Doc, we are rehearsing some new lyrics for the New York opening. It doesn't hurt anymore, believe me, and the color is natural and . . ."

"Yes, I know that, but as soon as you can, please come over."

"Okay, Doc."

I went to his office and noticed that he looked kind of somber and sad. We had gotten to be pretty good friends while he was helping me make those three nights in Boston.

He said, "Sit down, son."

I'm thinking, My God, what is it now?

"I hate to have to tell you this," he said, "but you have syphilis."

"I've got *what?*"

"Syphilis. You see, I had to test your blood because of the poison in your foot and the test showed that you have syphilis."

I was twenty-two years old. The show was a big hit, but it hadn't even gotten to Broadway yet. And this doctor was sitting there in front of me, telling me I had syphilis. In those days that was worse than death. There was no penicillin cure yet—nothing. Strange how many things go through your mind at a time like that: You are twenty-two, you've gone through five years of cleaning birdcages, gone hungry, worked at ratholes, the terrible things my father and mother had to go through in Cuba, and now I'm in a successful show, about to open on Broadway, a show which the newspapers say will be a big fat hit and it looks as if I'll be a hit too. A big fat hit on Broadway! And this man tells me I've got syphilis!

I went back to the hotel. My room was on the fifth floor. I couldn't stop thinking about the terrible news. I knew that a cure for syphilis was either nonexistent or extremely rare. I knew Al Capone had died from it.

I have never come so close to jumping out of a window in my life as I did that day. But I just couldn't believe what I had been told. I couldn't accept it.

I went back to the doctor and said, "Doctor, I just don't believe it. I have not been with that kind of girl. I don't know where I could have gotten something like that."

He said, "You could get it just by kissing somebody."

"Oh, my God, I have a scene where I kiss the girl about six times. You mean I could give it to her?"

"Well, if you have a cut on your lip and she happens to have a scratch on hers, yes, you could give it to her by kissing her."

"I guess I better not do the show anymore."

"But if you haven't any cut on your lips, it's all right."

"That's a hell of a thing to have to worry about. You know, Doc, I was ready to jump out of the goddamn window, but I just didn't believe it. I still don't believe it. I don't remember any bloody-lipped broad kissing me, and the girl's I've had affairs with—during the last six months or so—are all pretty nice. There ain't no way one of Polly's girls could have given it to me. They are the cleanest girls in New York."

"I am sorry, son. I know it is hard to believe."

"Doc, would you mind giving me another test?"

"Of course not, I'll take your blood right now."

"How long will it take for you to know?"

"Forty-eight hours."

"They will be the longest forty-eight hours in my life."

The doc said, "We'll say a prayer."

"Let's not be skimpy, Doc, we'll say a whole bunch of them."

I then asked him, "What shall I do about the show? If I have it, I don't want to give it to Lila." (She was the girl I did the kissing scene with.)

"Make sure that you check your lips."

Well, I didn't even dare smoke. I thought that maybe the paper would stick to my lip and I would rip it open. Every night, before that scene, I spent a long time in front of the mirror with a magnifying glass. It was a real cute scene for Manolito, in which he tells this coed, "I bet I can guess the kind of lipstick you are wearing." Of course the audience knows that he has already found out what kind she is wearing.

LILA: I bet you can't.

MANOLITO: If I kiss you, I can.

LILA: You can tell by the taste of my lips what kind of lipstick I'm using?

MANOLITO: Yeah.

Manolito then kisses, tastes his lips and says, "Chanel."

LILA: That's not it.

MANOLITO: Give me one more chance.

So he kisses her about six times before he tells her the right kind.

By that time Bracken is there saying, "Hey, you, what kind of racket do you have going here?"

That was the scene I was so worried about. I never did tell Lila. No use both of us worrying.

(Lila Ernst, if you read this book, please believe me—I was very careful!)

The result of the second test was NEGATIVE!

If I have ever thanked God in my life, I thanked Him then. What had happened (I found out later) was this. When they took a blood test in a hospital, if you were a bed patient, they brought a tray with a lot of little glass tubes on it, and the boys from the lab took the blood and put it in one of those tubes. Then they put the name of the patient on the tube. I was not in a private room. So they had also taken blood from the patient next to me, confused the tubes and put my name on his blood test. Then the doctor had to go out and find that poor bastard and tell him he had syphilis.

For the next year and a half I had a blood test taken every six months. I wouldn't trust any hospital. I would go right to the doctor and say, "You take the blood in front of me, you put it in that little glass tube in front of me, and I'm going to take it to the lab myself, or if someone else has to take it, I'll go with him."

12

Too Many Girls opened in New York on October 14, 1939, at the Imperial Theatre. I had never even seen a Broadway show, and here I was opening in one with a score by Rodgers and Hart, direction by George Abbott, book by George Marion, Jr., choreography by Robert Alton and costumes by Raoul Pène duBois.

In those days, for an opening such as this, the audience on the orchestra level, at least, always wore white tie and tails. I am sorry that today's generation hasn't had a chance to see what a beautiful sight that is. An audience listening to the overture, everyone in white tie and tails.

Bracken made me look through the peephole in the curtain. All the important critics and columnists were there: Walter Winchell, Dorothy Kilgallen, George Jean Nathan, Brooks Atkinson, Ed Sullivan, Louis Sobel, Danton Walker, Leonard Lyons, Earl Wilson and many others. Bracken was pointing them all out to me.

"Will you shut up?" I told him. "You are making me a nervous wreck."

The show was great. All the jokes got big laughs. Mary Jane

Walsh stopped the show. Hal LeRoy stopped the show; so did Marcy Westcott and Richard Kollmar with "I Didn't Know What Time It Was." Diosa Costello stopped the show. Bracken stopped the show. I got all my laughs, thank God, and the first-act finale really got a standing ovation. We all thought we had a big hit.

But as Bracken said, "You are never sure in New York until those reviews come out."

Well, I didn't have time to sit around Sardi's and wait for the reviews because I was opening at La Conga the same night. La Conga had taken a full-page advertisement in the theater program, telling the opening night crowd of *Too Many Girls* that Diosa Costello and I were opening at the club immediately after the last curtain, returning to the place of our New York debut.

As soon as I finished the title song, "Too Many Girls—Too Many Girls—But how can one man have Too Many Girls?" we did the finale and Diosa and I went to La Conga.

In later years Lucy would say, "*Too Many Girls* was not only the title of your first show, it is the story of your life."

She never missed a chance to come up with a crack like that.

By the time I arrived at La Conga it was full. A lot of people I had left at the Imperial were already there: Mr. and Mrs. Rodgers, Larry Hart, George Marion, Jr., and his wife, Mr. Abbott with our leading lady, Marcy Westcott, Brenda Frazier and Peter Arno, Richard Kollmar and Dorothy Kilgallen, Eddie Bracken, Hal LeRoy, Bob Alton and many, many more.

The joint was packed, with almost everyone in white tie and tails. La Conga looked beautiful. Soon after that night I started wearing white tie and tails in my show. I never wore a ready-made tie; I always tied it myself because I wanted to be able to yank it loose and let the collar fly open as I started banging on the drums.

We did our midnight show at one o'clock in the morning. By the time we got out of the theater, got there and said hello to everybody, we were late, but nobody minded.

The audience was great. Most of them had just seen us open on Broadway and the feeling was that *Too Many Girls* was a big fat hit. All the talk was "Congratulations, tremendous hit," etc.

Even Abbott said, "Don't worry."

Irving Zussman, Milton Rubin and Mario Torsatti, the partners in La Conga, were ecstatic. Nevertheless, we still had to wait for the reviews of Brooks Atkinson, George Jean Nathan and the others.

Everybody connected with the show had decided to come and wait for them at La Conga instead of Sardi's.

When we finished the last show, around 4 A.M., Diosa and I sat at the table with the Rodgerses, Larry Hart and his mother, George Abbott and Marcy, the George Marion, Jr.'s, Brenda and Peter and Dick Kollmar and Dorothy Kilgallen.

About half an hour later I saw Polly Adler heading for our table. She had all the newspapers in her hands, and as she approached, she hollered in that big, deep voice of hers, "Cuban, you are the biggest fucking hit in town!"

She shook up that table pretty good, including me, and I don't "shook-up" too easy. She grabbed me and kissed me, and after everyone had completed triple takes she passed the papers around and said, "There you are, folks, the reviews are great! Congratulations."

Then she said to me, "I'm going to buy you a bottle of champagne, Cuban. Come on."

"I'll be right with you, Mrs. Adler," I said, as properly as I could.

"Who is that lady?" Mrs. Rodgers asked me.

"She's just a friend of mine who did a lot to help me when I first started at La Conga. She's a—a— She's a—"

Peter Arno to the rescue: "She's Polly Adler, the greatest madam in the world and a very good friend of ours."

Brenda said, "Aha! So that's where you two spend the early hours of the morning."

I said, "Brenda, darling, we only go there because she serves a wonderful breakfast."

"Oh, sure!" And she hit Peter. He was closer.

By this time everybody else was so interested in reading the reviews that they forgot about Polly. The reviews were great. We were a big, fat hit. The biggest hit of that season so far, three and a half stars in the *Daily News,* more than any show since *Babes in Arms.*

I didn't want to just sit there any longer and ignore Polly, so I went over to her table. She had the champagne going and three of her girls were with her, my gorgeous redhead and a couple of others I hadn't met.

Polly introduced them to me and said, "How do you like our boy, eh? A big Cuban hit in a big American musical. We are going to celebrate, so keep the bubbly coming, Captain."

Then she turned to me. "What time is curtain tomorrow?"

"You know, same as always, eight-thirty," I told her.

"What are you planning to do between now and then?" she asked.

"Well, I'm going to hit the hay and get a good rest. I'm pooped."

She said, "You are right. You are going to bed but not before you have had your breakfast. Polly Adler's mansion shall be closed to all others until tomorrow night. My staff will feed you and relax you until you have to leave for *Too Many Girls*. What could be more appropriate?"

How could I say no?

Next night, at the end of the first act, Mr. Abbott came backstage and said to me, "What happened to you tonight?"

"What do you mean, Mr. Abbott?"

"Well, last night you tore this theater apart, but tonight you looked like you were half dead."

"Yeah. Well, I guess it was the excitement and all from the opening night."

I didn't dare tell him where I had spent the day.

"I assure you it will not happen again."

"I hope not. Make sure you get plenty of rest. Doubling here and at La Conga is not going to be easy for you. Don't fuck around."

"No, sir."

During the run of *Too Many Girls* Irving Pincus, who was the Twentieth Century-Fox man in charge of talent in New York, came backstage. He was very complimentary about my performance in the show and mentioned the fact that they were doing a picture, *Down Argentine Way*, with Alice Faye as the star; and he said that he was going to bring some people to New York to see if they'd like me well enough to star opposite Miss Faye in this picture.

When I told Abbott about it he said, "If you get the lead opposite Alice Faye in a musical at Fox, it would be a big break for you. How do you feel about it?"

"I feel that I don't know what I'm doing. If it hadn't been for you I wouldn't know how to walk across the stage. And if this is going to be my life's work, and you think that I have a good chance to succeed as an actor, I should learn how to be one. I didn't start driving that truck for my dad in Miami until I learned how to drive. Working under your direction on the stage seems to me like a very good way of learning how to act."

"Well, you're very sensible about it," he said. "We'd hate like hell to lose you, but I'm sure Dick and Larry would feel, as I do, that we shouldn't stand in your way for such a big break."

"Thank you very much," I said.

Pincus came back a week later and said, "The people have seen you and we're ready to make you an offer. We'd like you to costar with Alice Faye in this film. We'll start you out at fifteen hundred dollars a week for forty weeks. When can you leave for the Coast? What about your contract with the show?"

"Mr. Pincus," I said, "I talked to Mr. Abbott and he said they would not stand in my way. They'll let me go, even though they have a contract with me, and I'm sure the people at La Conga will also do the same. But I have decided against taking that job."

"What do you mean, you decided against taking the job?" he asked. "Have you decided against taking the lead opposite Alice Faye in one of the top Twentieth Century-Fox musical-comedy pictures of our program next year? Do you know what you are turning down?"

"Yes, more than I can afford to, but I can't do it."

"What do you mean, you can't do it? They'll let you go."

"Mr. Pincus, to tell you the truth, I don't even know what I'm doing up on that stage. I'm just doing what Mr. Abbott tells me to do."

"So what!" he said. "Not many actors know what the hell they're doing in Hollywood, either. They're all led by directors, just as you are by Abbott. And besides, it's a lot easier out there. They only do a couple of lines at a time. Here you have to sustain a performance for a whole evening."

He really couldn't believe that I was turning it down.

He said, "You want more money, that's it, eh?"

"No, really," I answered. "Your offer is incredible, and I thank you very much, but I cannot accept it."

Funny how things happened. Alice Faye became pregnant, Betty Grable got to do the picture, and the part they wanted me for went to Don Ameche. That became Betty's first big break in films and eventually she replaced Alice Faye as the queen of Twentieth Century-Fox musical films.

The romantic lead in *Too Many Girls* was Richard Kollmar, who was to marry Dorothy Kilgallen, the newspaper columnist of the *Journal-American*. Dorothy used to come to the theater at least twice a week to see the show—and Richard, of course. Every time she was in the audience, Richard, somewhere during the show, would go absolutely blank, and I mean blank. We used to take bets backstage on whether he'd blow up in the first act or the second act, in the first, second or third scene. It was like a fight pool—"Which round?"

In the show my first scene was with Richard. It was a scene which set the entire character of Manolito, the same one I did at my audition. A very important scene, because it established important story-line points, without which a lot of the later jokes wouldn't make any sense.

One night Dorothy was there. I had said only two lines and he answered with the *last* line of the scene: "You belong at Vassar." He had skipped four and three-quarter pages of dialogue. I just stood there and looked at him. I had had no experience at all for this kind of thing.

I said, "What did you say?" (Great ad lib, eh?)

"You belong at Vassar," he repeated.

I knew the first scene had won the pool.

It is a strange thing when someone goes blank like that. They don't realize it. They think it's the other guy who has forgotten his lines. They get stubborn about what they are saying.

By this time Jerry White, our stage manager, was dying in the wings, and the orchestra leader, Harry Levant, was getting ready for whatever.

Then I said, "That's what I thought you said, that I belong at Vassar." (Another fantastic ad lib.)

He looked at me as if I was nuts and answered strongly, "That's what I said!"

I couldn't get him out of it. I couldn't get him to give me the cue for what I was supposed to say, *had* to say.

So I started: "You mean because I had nine uncles and no aunts, et cetera, and because I don't care whether I play football for Harvard or Yale, et cetera, and because all I want is to go to someplace that has 'cooperational girls.' "

I did a whole monologue and he just stood there until I had said "cooperational girls." Then he woke up and said, "That's what I said, you belong at Vassar."

I damn near blurted out, "Yeah, you silly ass, but you said it four and three-quarter pages before you were supposed to say it."

When I came backstage, Mr. Abbott was there. He used to check the show every evening during the early part of the run. This was like the second or third week.

He looked at me and said, "Well, I'll tell you something, my Cuban friend, you graduated today."

We had a lot of great hit songs in the show. "I Didn't Know What Time It Was" was the biggest. In our show it was done first by the leading man, Richard, and the ingenue, Marcy. The setting was a campus park. The lovers were sitting on a little bench, with trees all around creating a very romantic mood. The song had two verses: one the boy sang, and the other the girl sang, after him.

One night Richard started his verse with "Once I was young, yesterday perhaps, danced with Jim and Paul and kissed some other chaps."

Backstage we said, "Oh migawd, he is singing Marcy's verse!" We knew Dorothy was in the theater again.

Naturally, the audience was hysterical, but Richard didn't have the slightest idea why they were laughing. Why, all of a sudden, "I Didn't Know What Time It Was" was getting so many laughs. He looked at Marcy and then out at the audience as if they were crazy, but he kept singing until he finished the entire girl's verse. Poor Marcy!

Afterward we asked her, "What were you thinking about?"

She answered, "I didn't know whether I should sing the boy's verse when my turn came, or what."

Finally she decided to repeat her own verse and let the audience know for sure what had happened.

What fun we had doing that show! The only time it was a little rough for me was on matinee days, Wednesday and Saturday. I would be at the theater at two in the afternoon for the matinee. Afterward, we would all go over to Dinty Moore's, which was just down the block, for dinner. Then everyone would rest until the evening show, but I had to go to La Conga for the dinner show at seven-thirty. Normally, the dinner show there was at eight-thirty, but during the run of *Too Many Girls* they agreed to let me do it earlier. As soon as I finished, a car would be waiting to take me to the theater for the evening show. Then, after I finished at the theater, I went back to La Conga for the midnight show, and when that was finished I still had to do the 2:30 A.M. show, which, thank God, was the last one. That made it five times in one day that I had to do the conga bit, which went on full blast for five minutes; but when you are young you can do a lot of things. I would drop dead today if I had to do it twice.

13

Nineteen thirty-nine was a wonderful year!

Except for one thing. My mother and father were divorced. I had no idea this was even a remote possibility. When Dad called me to explain the circumstances, it was such a shock to me that I hung up on him. Eventually, I came to realize it was just one more tragedy caused by the Revolution—having to be separated from Mother for such a long time, having to start a whole new life at forty years of age, broke and ashamed of not being able to take care of us. All these things were the basis of it.

He was only forty-six when they were divorced. He had been alone for a long time, except for my mother's visit to Miami. Ann, the woman he eventually married, was nice to him and kind. Her daughter Connie was then three years old, a doll, and she adored my father.

I finally called him and again we were very close until he passed away. It was really my mother who made me call him. She adored my father. She was only thirty-seven years old at the time of the Revolution and their forced separation, and only forty-three when they were divorced, but she has never married again. She still wears her wedding ring.

Once, in Cuba, I was very peeved at my dad for some childish reason and I said to my mother, "Who does he think he is? It's your fault, Mother. You always treat him as if he were a king."

I will never forget her answer: "That's the only way that I can be a queen."

My mother is not much of a prospect for Women's Lib.

In the early part of 1940 my mother came to New York and stayed with me at a beautiful penthouse I had sublet from Barney Ross, a great boxer of that era. It was at 60 Central Park West, directly across from the park, and really nice people lived there. One was Ethel Merman. The duplex was elegant, with huge glass windows facing the park.

Mother kept house there for me. Whenever she watched me bang the drums and lead the conga line, which was almost every night, she would tell me that I worked too hard.

"Why don't you just sing some pretty songs with your guitar?"

"They want to see me sweat, Mamá, and I don't mind. Besides, it's fun and keeps me in shape."

The only problem I had living with my mother was that I couldn't very well have a girl stay there with me, and I was having a very lovely and serious romance with the most astonishing woman I had ever met. Her love, her tenderness, her disposition were unbelievable. There isn't any doubt she was my first real love. We will call her "Freckles."

I had met her at La Conga one night when she came in with Brenda Frazier and Peter Arno. They were part of "the group from the Eastside," as Kilgallen, Winchell and others tagged them. Dorothy claimed that "they" came over to the Westside only to see a Broadway show or get into the conga line. Winchell called the conga line "The Desi Chain."

That night when I met Freckles I knew the meaning of Larry Hart's lyrics, "I took one look at you, that's all I meant to do, and then my heart stood still."

She was a jewel, a rare and unique find. We had the happiest, the most wonderful relationship. She had the understanding and the patience to put up with me, which I am sure wasn't an easy job at times. She never nagged, never argued. Even if she knew I had been with another girl during a short weekend detour, she'd pretend not to know and just ask me if I'd had a nice trip, which of course made me feel like a shit. I would decide positively right there and then I would never do it again. But at that age it was a hard promise to keep. Freckles knew it didn't mean a thing. She knew I loved *her* and that I had every intention of marrying her. All we were waiting for was her divorce.

She was part of a dance team, one of the most famous in the world, but she had been separated from her partner for some time and everybody knew why. He was terrible to her. He used to beat her up. Once she had to go onstage with a black eye covered with makeup. The only reason she had been loyal to him was because he had found her at a dancing school someplace when she was a teen-ager and he was a big star. He had taught her all she knew, but he had become possessive, a dictator. The whole Pygmalion bit is interesting until you think about the possibility of Henry Higgins' cruelty to Liza Doolittle over the years.

One night Freckles and I were going to her apartment at the Pierre to have some breakfast after I'd finished work, about four-thirty in the morning, and we found her husband waiting for us in the lobby. The man was at least twenty-five to thirty years older than I was, also smaller, so I wasn't worried about him. He got into the elevator with us, turned to the bellboy and said, "Son, I want you to meet my wife and her lover."

Of course the bellboy had seen me before but I don't think he knew there was a husband involved. So he looked at me kind of nervously, not knowing what to say. When we got to our floor, Mr. Husband got off with us.

I said to him, "What the hell are you here for?"

He answered, "I want to talk to you."

"Fine. As soon as I take her to her apartment, I'll be back."

Just before I let her in, she said, "Listen, Desi, please be careful. I know you are bigger and younger than he is, but, believe me, he is dangerous."

"Don't worry, darling, I can take care of myself."

"Just be on your guard every second. I've seen that crazy look in his eyes before. It won't be the first time he has tried to kill somebody."

"Okay, baby, I'll be careful. I promise."

I kissed her and went back to the nut. We went downstairs and out into the street, where he started putting on the gloves, leather gloves.

I said, "Look, I don't want to hurt you, but if you take one punch at me you are going to go right through that glass window behind you."

The feisty little bastard still took a punch at me. I ducked and grabbed him by the neck to hold him away. It was really kind of funny, he couldn't reach me, but he kept trying.

As I was holding him, I said, "I'll talk with you, but I don't want to fight with you."

"Okay, let me go and come to my apartment."

"Fine."

We walked to his apartment, which was about six blocks away. He lived on the seventeenth floor of a very nice building.

When we got inside his apartment, he opened the window and said, "Come over here and look at this view."

I said, "Look, Mister, are you by any chance flirting with the idea of pushing me out of that window?"

"What makes you think I'd try anything like that?" he asked.

"I don't know. It's just that we are standing here in the middle of the winter and all of a sudden you open the window, letting in the wind and snow, just so I can look at the view. I know the view—so close it!"

"I just wanted you to see . . ."

"Yeah, I know. Now close the fucking window before we both freeze to death."

He closed it, then he asked me, "Would you like some breakfast?"

"Yeah, that would be nice. That's what Freckles and I were about to do when you joined the party."

"How about bacon and eggs, toast and coffee?"

"Lovely, and while you're fixing it, would you mind telling me what you want from me?"

"I want you to ask her to come back and work with me."

"You've *got* to be out of your mind. You want *me* to go back there and tell that girl, after all you have done to her, that you want her to come back and work with you? How long has it been since you have worked together?"

"A few years," he said. "I need her. We can open at the Waldorf-Astoria at the height of the season. It would be our greatest comeback yet. You know we *were* the greatest."

"Yes, everybody knows that."

He went on for ten minutes about their act. "We performed before the King and Queen of England, the King of Spain. We are famous the world over. There is nobody like us."

"It's your fault that's no longer true," I said, eating the bacon and eggs.

"Tell her just this one engagement. That's all I want. I want to quit at the top. Then I will take the choreographer job in Hollywood which I have been offered. Don't you think she owes me that much?"

"How can she owe you anything?" I asked him.

"I took her when she was fifteen years old. I taught her everything she knows and I made her as big a star as I was—as I am. If it wasn't for me, she would still be a chorus girl . . . or God knows what."

"I'm sure she appreciates that," I said, "but all the abuse she took from you must go on her side of the ledger. I think she's paid up."

"Will you please ask her?" he insisted.

"I don't know. Thanks for the breakfast."

Freckles was waiting for me. "Thank God, you're back. I've been so worried. You've been gone for three hours. What happened?"

"Well, his first plan was to push me out of the window, but he then cooked a wonderful breakfast for me."

"*What?*"

"He told me his life story, including how he taught you everything you know."

"What does he want?"

"I think he's convinced you will never go back to him and he's willing to give you a divorce, but he wants you to work with him one more time."

"He's out of his mind," she said. "They'll put him away one of these days."

"You won't believe this, Freckles, but I feel sorry for him. Not that you owe him anything, and I told him so. He promised me you would have different dressing rooms, and that he would never lay a hand on you again. All he wants is this last engagement, to quit on top. Then he'll be able to accept this choreographer job in Hollywood and give you the divorce without a fight."

"What do you think, Desi?"

"I don't know, darling, I can't tell you what to do. You will have to decide, and whatever you do will be fine with me."

"Well, if that's the only way I can get a divorce . . ."

"Don't let that sway you. I don't want you to do it just because you want to get a divorce. You'll get it, one way or the other. He's just using that."

They did go back together for that one engagement. Their opening night at the Waldorf was the greatest event in a long, long time in New York café-society history. I had never seen them dance before.

She danced with such a devilish abandon it seemed as if the sound of music made her weightless and she was teasing her partner as she ran and jumped and pirouetted through the air. Every once in a while she'd steal a look and give me a naughty-girl wink. They were fantastic.

Lex Thompson was a multimillionaire and we had met at "21." He had the most beautiful motor home, magnificently decorated and all built to his specifications. It must have been the first of its kind. In front of the motor home, completely shut off from the living quarters, was a place for the chauffeur and a waiter. Whenever you needed them you just rang a bell and the waiter came. In the rear was a living room, a bar, a kitchen and a big, gorgeous bedroom. Above the driver's seat was a large porch, all glass-enclosed, with a built-in couch along the wall, facing the front.

Sunday was the only day that neither Freckles nor I had to work, so Lex, who had become a good friend of ours, would arrange for the motor home to pick us up at La Conga after I had finished the last show on Saturday. We'd get in and tell the driver to drive to the country, upper New York. We would stay away all day Sunday and all day Monday, getting back just in time for our shows.

We would find a stream and fish, go up into the mountains and look around, take a lot of pictures and walk in the woods. The driver would sometimes ask us where we wanted to go and I'd say, "Surprise us. Take us someplace we haven't been before."

That same year Betty Grable was a sensation in Ethel Merman's Broadway show, *DuBarry Was a Lady*. She was gorgeous—what a figure and what legs! Her skin was magnificent and so smooth she looked like a peach all over.

Our theaters were next to each other. We all had the same matinee days so we started having dinner together at Dinty Moore's between shows. She would join our table and it was impossible to sit next to Betty and not want to know her a little better.

I invited her to La Conga to see our show. She would come, we would dance and she would wait for me until I'd finished. Then we would go bowling or something. Betty was the longest-lasting detour I took during the time I was with Freckles, who again knew and understood. She was something else. She realized that I was a young guy in his first big hit on Broadway, enjoying every minute of life and drinking everything that was sweet to drink.

RKO bought the motion-picture rights to *Too Many Girls* and I was signed for the film. When the show closed in New York, I was to report to the studio in Hollywood. I didn't have to be there for two weeks, so I decided to see a bit of the country on the way to the Coast, where Freckles would meet me.

I stopped in Detroit to visit the Bansfields. Mr. Bansfield had quite a nice business. His company made the upholstery for all General Motors automobiles. I went with Pat, his daughter, in Miami, while I was at La Conga there. When they came to New York to see me in *Too Many Girls,* Mr. Bansfield told me, "Anytime you want a car, Desi, come to Detroit and I'll get you one, wholesale."

That was the year the Buick Roadmaster convertible came out. I bought one which was light gray with a black top, black upholstery and whitewall tires. It was terrific, one of the best cars I have ever owned.

Richard, my valet, and I spent a delightful week in Detroit as guests of the Bansfields. Richard was a dresser during the run of *Too Many Girls.* He was assigned to Bracken, LeRoy and me. All three of us used to dress in the same dressing room. He was in his sixties but that guy could help all three of us make a thirty-second change with ease. He had everything so prepared, timed and ready. Another great thing I remember about Richard was that anytime one of us had a headache or a hangover, he was the greatest to have around. He had big strong hands and he would press your temples just as hard as he could with them. Then he would ease the pressure very slowly and repeat the whole routine about three times, and even if you had the worst hangover-headache in your life, when he finished his manipulation it was gone. It was unbelievable and, in those days, we needed Richard quite often.

So when we finished the show, I asked him if he would like to be my valet and see Hollywood. Richard had never been out of New York, New Haven and Boston. He was always with a show because he had the reputation of being one of the best dressers in the theater. Any show was lucky to get Richard. So was I. Freckles had insisted we drive across the United States and see the country and that she would take the train and meet us in Hollywood. I told Richard that whenever he wanted to get back to the Broadway stage, which was the life he loved, just to let me know.

Mother had gone to Cuba to get her permanent-resident papers, not because she was going to work, but just so she wouldn't have to renew her visitor's permit every six months.

Richard and I got the maps, set a route and—California, here we come! We would start driving at dawn, stop for lunch for an hour or so, then drive until it was almost dark. We'd spend the night at a roadside motel, get up before daylight, have breakfast and start driving again. It was a very nice, leisurely trip. We both enjoyed it immensely because we had never seen the United States, at least not from Detroit to Hollywood. It was the only way to go if you wanted to take it easy and enjoy all the beautiful countryside.

We drove all the way without any trouble until we got to Pasadena. We arrived there about 6 P.M. and we didn't get to Hollywood until about ten o'clock that night. I just couldn't get out of Pasadena.

I still don't know how to get to Hollywood from Pasadena. A sign would say "HOLLYWOOD" that way, and you would follow the arrow. You then drove around for a while and just when you thought you should be getting there, you saw a sign which said "PASADENA."

We wanted to get to the Hollywood Roosevelt Hotel, where we had reservations. Finally, after we'd tried many times to get out of Pasadena, a cop stopped us and wanted to know what we were doing, driving around and around. We explained that we had come all the way from Detroit without any difficulty whatsoever until we got to this goddamn place Pasadena, and now it seemed that we were trapped.

"We are only trying to go to Hollywood, but we can't seem to get there."

The cop laughed like hell and then was nice enough to show us the way.

We finally got there and checked in. There was no objection to

Richard's staying there, which we had been worrying about, because he was black, even though as we traveled across the country nobody gave us trouble about staying in the same place or eating in the same restaurant. I guess if we had gone through the South we would have had some problems.

We were to report to the Casting Department at RKO Studios at nine-thirty the next morning. I asked the desk clerk how to get there.

The man said, "Go down Sunset Boulevard to Gower, then turn right until you see the sign. You can't miss it."

We drove down to Sunset, went to Gower and turned right, and I spotted this big building and the sign, "RKO." There was a big gate so I turned into it. A man was standing there and I said, "Good morning."

He answered, "Good morning."

"I'm supposed to report to Casting. Where is it?"

"Casting?"

"Yes."

"I think you are in the wrong place."

"What do you mean? They told me Sunset to Gower, turn right. This is Gower and that sign says RKO."

"Well, no. This place is adjacent to RKO. This is Beth Olam, a cemetery, and I think you are a little early for this place."

Richard asked, "How do we get out of here?"

The man answered, "Back up, keep going down to Melrose and then turn left. When you get to the first corner, it's just a little street there, turn left again, but that's not it. I mean that the studio you see in front of you is not RKO. That is Paramount, but you're almost there. Look left and you will see the RKO gate, and that's where you want to go."

I thanked him. Richard was a little shook up.

"I hope we ain't supposed to report here for a while."

"Don't worry, neither you nor I am likely to report here, ever. It's a Jewish cemetery."

We finally arrived at the entrance gate of RKO Studios.

14

I was about to drive through the gate of one of the most famous motion-picture studios in the world to costar in a film. I had to pinch myself to believe it.

I blew the horn and a cop came out of a little glass-enclosed cage. A chain stretched across the entrance.

Richard was dressed in his brand-new uniform, black cap and all. And I looked pretty sharp too, in a sports outfit, Panama hat and scarf.

The cop said, "Yes, sir?"

I answered, "Desi Arnaz from New York. I have an appointment here at nine-thirty. Take the chain down, please."

"Who did you say you were?"

"Desi Arnaz from New York. Take the goddamn chain down, I'm late!"

"Yes, sir. Right away!"

He didn't know if I was the head of RKO in New York or who I was. But Richard and I looked pretty impressive. I drove through and parked in front of the administration building. (About seventeen years later my own offices were there, by the pretty little park.)

I saw a free parking space, so I eased into it and told Richard, "You stay here and I'll go and find out where this casting place is."

I asked the people in the administration building how to get to Casting, that I was Desi Arnaz reporting for *Too Many Girls*.

The girl said, "Oh, fine, they're at the Little Theatre. Mr. Abbott was already asking about you."

She showed me the way to go and I thanked her. We drove to the Little Theatre and parked in front of it. Later on, I found out that everyone was wondering who the hell was this guy with the chauffeur, because very few people were allowed to drive into the studio— Fred Astaire, Ginger Rogers, Carole Lombard, Katharine Hepburn, the president and maybe a couple of vice-presidents and that was about it. I didn't know, so we drove all over the place and parked wherever it was most convenient.

All the kids were at the Little Theatre. We met Richard Carlson, who was to play Richard Kollmar's part; Ann Miller, who was to play Diosa's part—don't ask me why; same reason as Van Johnson being my understudy, I guess. He too was there. Also Frances Langford, who was to play Mary Jane's part, plus all the boys and girls from the Broadway chorus.

I admired Ann Miller and Frances Langford very much indeed, but why did they have Annie trying to play Diosa's part, accent and all? Also, why replace Mary Jane Walsh, who for a year on Broadway never failed to stop the show at least once or twice nightly?

"That's the way they do things in Hollywood," people would say when you asked them. As if they were saying, "That's the way God created the universe."

The only person who was not at the Little Theatre was Lucille Ball, who was to play Marcy's part of the ingenue.

I don't know if this generation digs the image of what an ingenue was in those days. She was usually a very delicate, blond, blue-eyed girl with an innocent, virginal quality about her.

Marcy Westcott was the prototype of the ingenue and she had been playing that part for fifteen years. I don't think George Abbott ever did a show in which Marcy was not the ingenue. She was a lovely girl, but no one would ever think about going to bed with her without wedding bells and all the trimmings. Larry Hart used to say to me, "I bet she pisses ice water." Very much like Larry, and probably very unlike Marcy, but she did have the image.

So we were expecting that image to walk in, and in walks Lucille Ball, whom I didn't recognize. Miss Ball had just come from a stage where she had been filming *Dance, Girl, Dance* with Maureen O'Hara, in which they both played burlesque queens. She had just finished a scene with Miss O'Hara in which they had been in a big fight. She looked like a two-dollar whore who had been badly beaten by her pimp, with her hair all over her face and a black eye, and she was dressed in a cheap costume. She had just stopped by to say hello to George.

After she left, I asked Mr. Abbott, "Who the hell was that?"

He answered, "That's the girl who is going to play Marcy's part. That's Lucille Ball."

"That's Lucille Ball and she's gonna do the ingenue thing? You gotta be kidding."

"Well, now, wait a minute. She was in makeup for something else."

"I think you've blown your top, George. There is no way they can change her back to look like an ingenue."

We broke for lunch. We were to be back there at five that afternoon to go over the music with the new people, the arranger, the pianist and the whole cast. Richard and I drove all around, looking for the commissary, which turned out to be right next to the Little Theatre. We parked and Richard said he wasn't hungry. He stood by the car as if he owned the studio. We had now parked in every place where you were not supposed to park.

Five o'clock and we were back going over the music. I was doing "She Could Shake the Maracas" with the piano player when I saw this girl come in. She was dressed in a pair of tight-fitting beige slacks and a yellow sweater, with beautiful blond hair and big blue eyes.

I said to the piano player, "Man, that is a hunk of woman!"

He answered, "You met her today."

"No, I never met her. I've never seen her before."

"That's Lucille Ball," he said.

"That's Lucille Ball? She sure doesn't look anything like she did this morning."

"Hello," she said as she walked up to me.

I asked, "Miss Ball?" Like I wasn't sure I had met her before.

"Why don't you call me Lucille and I'll call you Dizzy."

"Okay, Lucille, but it's not Dizzy."

"Oh? How do you say it? Daisy?"

"No, Daisy is a flower, it's Desi—D E S I."

The next few lines I used were the oldest in history—and the corniest. "Do you know how to rumba, Lucille?"

"No, I've never learned."

"Would you like me to teach you how to rumba?"

A pretty impressive approach, eh? I don't know why she ever went out with me after that one.

I continued this brilliant repartee with "It may come in handy for your part in the picture."

I said this even though her part didn't call for a rumba, but she didn't know that yet.

I went on, "We are all going down to El Zarape, which they tell me is a swinging Mexican restaurant on Sunset, almost downtown, over a market. All the kids from New York are going there for dinner. I hear they have a great little Latin group there and I thought perhaps you'd like to come along and get to know the kids a little better, if you don't have anything else to do."

She said, "I 'dunt' have 'anythin' else and I'd love to."

I told Richard to take the night off, and Lucille and I joined the rest of the group at El Zarape. We danced all night, had dinner, and everybody got loaded.

I took her home, she thanked me for a lovely evening and we said good night. That could have been the end of the Lucy story. As it turned out, it wasn't even the beginning.

Freckles arrived Saturday on the Chief. I picked her up at the Union Station in Los Angeles; I didn't dare to go to Pasadena again. We had a wonderful reunion. On Sunday we drove out to Eddie Bracken's house at Malibu. He and Connie, his wife, had invited all the kids to come out and spend the day at the beach. They had rented a real nice house, and the Broadway group plus the Hollywood group were all there.

They had a beautiful layout. Everyone was in bathing suits and having a ball. As I walked down to the beach, I saw Lucille.

"Hi! How's my rumba teacher?" she said.

I laughed and said, "Hello."

"I had a wonderful time at El Zarape," she said, looking right through me with those damned big beautiful blue eyes.

"Thank you, so did I."

She patted the sand and said, "Sit down."

I sat down and never went back to Freckles.

I was told later that evening that Freckles had left with somebody else. She never said a word, never asked me what the hell was going on. I did not go back to the Hollywood Roosevelt. I went to Lucille's apartment and that was our first night together.

The next day she called Al Hall, her fiancé, and told him, "I'm moving out, Al. I'll send somebody to pick up my clothes. I'll explain it to you another time."

I called Freckles and told her, "I don't know what made me do what I did—and to you of all people. You know I was in love with you."

"Yes, but you're not now, are you?"

"Freckles, I don't know how a thing like this can happen. It's not natural, it has no reason."

All she said was "Everything that happens in life is natural and has a reason. Good luck, Desi."

I've met many women in my life, but no one as unselfish and understanding as Freckles. And even though I might have done some bad things in my life, none of them could have been as bad as what I did to her.

Lucy and I used to take my car, the Roadmaster that I had bought in Detroit, put the top down and drive to Palm Springs over the weekends. In those days you could find some very nice and lonely roads which went on for miles that way. I was very proud of that

Bing sang and the
audience went wild.

I learned a lot from Xavier Cugat, and so did Louis Nicoletti (right).

Here is the band Cugat sent me, but when this picture was taken we had been working together for quite a while.

Here is our football hero, Manolito, with Diosa Costello (left) and Mary Jane Walsh.

Mother came to New York to
keep house for me.

Leila Ernst, D.A., Diosa Costello,
Richard Kollmar, Marcy Westcott,
Hal LeRoy, and Mary Jane Walsh.

RKO's *Too Many Girls* was not as good. The football players are (left to right) Richard Carlson, D.A., Hal LeRoy, and Eddie Bracken.

"Do you know how to rumba, Lucille?"

Roadmaster, it drove beautifully, and I would go over one hundred miles an hour on the straightaway, which scared the hell out of Lucy. She thought I was nuts. When she got enough confidence in my driving and knew that I wouldn't take stupid chances, she would relax and then start sceraming at the top of her lungs, which in turn scared the hell out of me.

"What's wrong?" I'd shout over her screaming.

"Nothing, go ahead," she'd shout back. "Katharine Hepburn told me I should lower my voice."

"So?" I'd shout back.

"The best way to lower your voice is to scream at the top of your lungs when you are driving in an open car."

"Okay. You scream and I'll drive."

If a cop had seen us and heard us, he would have locked us up.

RKO's *Too Many Girls* was not as good as Broadway's *Too Many Girls,* but I don't think that we ever made another picture in which everyone had so much fun as we did on that one. One of the things I mentioned before was that Van Johnson was one of the chorus boys who was brought out to do the picture. And this brings me to the question of what makes a star.

I don't think anyone can tell what it is that makes a star. It's just somebody who jumps out of the screen at you—you are the audience, and you make the star. Van was a perfect example.

At the previews of a new picture, the studios always have those little white cards in the lobby which ask the audience to answer such questions as, How did you like the picture in general? How was the music? How about the performance of so and so? What part of it did you like the most? What part of it did you like the least? Toward the end they ask, Any more comments?

An unbelievable number of these cards from our previews came back asking who the tall, redheaded fellow was, standing behind Desi, or Ann Miller, or whoever. They meant Van. And he had no speaking lines or anything. They picked him out of the background. The audience made Van a star.

After the picture was finished I had to go to Chicago to do my part in *Too Many Girls* on the stage and Van played the lead. Richard Kollmar had by then married Dorothy Kilgallen, who couldn't leave New York because of her column in the paper. I think they had also started their early morning radio show, *Dorothy and Dick.* So he couldn't leave New York, and Abbott gave Van the chance to play the lead.

Lucy came to Chicago, and from that day in Chicago to November 30, 1940, the obstacles, the problems, the fights we went through would have been enough to discourage anyone from getting married. We would love furiously and fight furiously.

I had started calling her Lucy shortly after we met; I didn't like the name Lucille. That name had been used by other men. "Lucy" was mine alone. That's how, eventually, our television show was called *I Love Lucy,* not *I Love Lucille.*

Lucy's ancestors are Irish, Scottish, and French. Mine are Spanish, Irish, and French, with a touch of Cuban. She was born in Jamestown, New York, and I in Santiago de Cuba.

It's really amazing that two people from such different backgrounds and geographical origins ever got together. That was perhaps part of the attraction, and also, I am sure, the cause of many of our arguments, fights and other problems. I had a different concept of things. She was brought up differently from me.

She could stay in Chicago only a couple of days because she had to finish a picture in Hollywood which she was doing for Harold Lloyd called *A Girl, a Guy and a Gob*. Edmond O'Brien and George Murphy were costars.

When I finished the run of the play in Chicago, I went to the University of Tennessee and a few other colleges, plugging *Too Many Girls,* the motion picture, which was about to be released. We had contests in each town to pick out co-eds who could dance the rumba, which was still kind of new in those days, and the best co-ed rumba dancer would appear with me that night at the show and get some prizes, and we would put on a rumba exhibition. It was fun and the kids enjoyed it. At the end of that tour I opened at The Versailles in New York. By then I did not have the band with me anymore. I was doing a single. My old friends from La Conga didn't have to go across town anymore. It was a good step up the ladder in my nightclub career, all the way from a Broadway cellar to the high-class Versailles. The Hartmans, the famous acrobatic comedy dance team, were my costars.

After Versailles I opened at the Roxy in New York on the first of November. I was there four weeks and I had a very successful engagement. I was lucky to have a very good picture with me. I think it was *Alexander's Ragtime Band.* It was a good break for me because all the box-office figures in *Variety* were great. The show business bible headlined "Arnaz On Stage, Roxy Theatre, WOW!"

During all this period Lucy and I were separated, except the weekend that Harold let her come to Chicago. But the telephone conversations back and forth during that time, the bills for them—Jesus, we could have bought half of AT & T. I would call her and say, "Where were you when I called you last time? I know you weren't at the studio. Who the hell were you having dinner with?" I was extremely jealous, and she was no better, perhaps even worse.

Then she would say, "Well, I was here and there."

And I couldn't find out where the hell she was, so I'd get mad and hang up with "Well, the hell with you, that's all, forget it. I can't trust you, you're a this and that."

Then either she would call back a few minutes later, or I would call her back and apologize, or she would call me another time, just before the matinee, and say, "You Cuban sonofabitch, where were you all last night? What are you trying to do, lay every goddamned one of those chorus girls in *Too Many Girls?* No wonder they picked you for the show!" Then she'd hang up on me.

This went on all the time through this period. She went to Milwaukee to promote *Dance, Girl, Dance,* and I saw a picture of the mayor. He was a good-looking young sonofabitch. She was only supposed to stay there for two days, but she stayed a week.

The next call was from me. "I know why you're staying in Milwaukee, you crumbum, you're screwing the mayor." And she would accuse me of screwing every broad in every town I was in.

How the hell we survived this period after all this and still had the guts to get married, I'll never understand.

When we got married, nobody gave it more than two weeks. There were bets all over the country, with astronomical odds against us.

She finally finished her Milwaukee deal and came to New York. I was wrong about her screwing the mayor—I think—and I was madly in love with her, and I knew she was in love with me.

Lucy got to New York on Friday, the twenty-ninth of November. I was still at the Roxy but I went over to the Pierre, where she had a suite, between shows.

She was giving an interview to a lady magazine writer and Lucy was telling her all the reasons why she and I should not get married. She was telling the writer that she had just come to New York to say hello, and was promoting her picture, *Dance, Girl, Dance.* Also she was glad that I was in New York at the same time. We would certainly see each other, but there was no way we were going to get married, because of too many different difficulties between us. Our characters were completely apart. I had to live a certain kind of life on the road, nightclubs and theater work, and she was more or less committed to Hollywood.

Finally the lady left.

We hadn't seen each other for a long time so we kissed and we apologized for all the nasty things we had said to each other over the telephone. We kissed again and made love in a hurry, because I had to go back to the Roxy and do the next show.

As I was leaving, I told Lucy, "This girl is going to have a hell of a time with that story."

"Why?"

"Because I have everything arranged to marry you tomorrow morning, if you would like to marry me."

She said, "Where?"

"In Connecticut," I answered.

"You're kidding, right?"

"No, I'm not kidding. I want to marry you and I want to marry you tomorrow."

"Why couldn't we just live together?" she asked. She was way ahead of her generation.

I answered, "No, I don't want to just live together. I want to marry you and I want to have some children with you and I want to have a home. I am not like the image you have of me. Now, do you want to marry me, or not?"

"Of course I want to marry you, you idiot, but aren't we supposed to wait three days for a permit or something?"

"I got the whole thing straightened out. I've already got a permit, and the judge to give us an exemption."

"Well, how are we going to . . . don't you have to work at the Roxy tomorrow?"

"Yes, but my first show tomorrow is not until eleven o'clock."

She asked, "You mean we are going to drive over to Connecticut, get married and come back, then go to the Roxy to your dressing room . . . for a honeymoon?"

"That's it for a week or so."

"I knew when I met you things weren't going to be normal," she said.

"You love me, don't you?"

"I love you very much."

"Well, I love you very much too. So what the hell else is there? I've got to go now, I'll be back after the next show."

When I came back, George Schaeffer was there with her. He was the president of RKO. She hadn't told him yet that we were getting married because I had said, "Don't tell anybody anything. If the Roxy finds out they're liable to get nervous about me getting back in time for the show."

Mr. Schaeffer knew me, of course, and as I came into the room he was pointing furiously at me and trying to do it without Lucy noticing. I couldn't figure out what the hell he was trying to tell me. Finally, Lucy noticed it.

She said, "Dear . . ."

"Yes?"

"Mr. Schaeffer is trying to tell you that your fly is open."

I had changed my stage clothes in such a hurry that I had forgotten not only the zipper, but also my shorts.

I said, "Oh, my God!" (After all, my bird could fly.)

She turned to Mr. Schaeffer and said, "He believes in advertising."

That was a hectic day. I had one more show to do. I think I had a quick sandwich and a glass of milk, which Lucy had ordered from room service, and she went back with me to the Roxy.

I did the last show. We went back to her suite and I said, "We better get to bed. We are going to have to sleep real fast."

At 6 A.M. we got out of a nice warm bed and drove to Greenwich, Connecticut, to get married.

15

Probate Judge Harold L. Nape waived the five-day wait required by Connecticut law, and Justice of the Peace John P. O'Brien performed the ceremony at the Byran River Beagle Club at noon on Saturday, November 30, 1940.

I'd forgotten to buy a wedding ring and I didn't know we had to get a Wassermann test. That was the one thing the judge couldn't waive. While Lucy and I went to get the test, Deke Magaziner, my business manager, and Doc Bender, the friend of Larry Hart's who was my theatrical agent, went to get a ring. All the jewelry stores were closed because it was Saturday, so they came back with one from the five-and-dime store.

"That's terrible," I told them.

Lucy overheard us and asked, "What's the matter?"

I told her what had happened and showed her the ring.

She said, "I love it!"

It got greener and skinnier as the years went by, but she never took it off. Even after I gave her a real nice one in our church wedding in 1949, she insisted on keeping the five-and-dime green one on also.

I looked at the time and it was obvious that there was no way I could make the first show. I called the manager's office at the Roxy. When he answered, he presumed I was backstage because it was just about an hour before show time and he knew I liked to get there early to warm up my drum. I had to put a light inside it to get the head tight and I never trusted anyone else to do that. I also had to check my guitar and see that the strings weren't broken.

He said, "Oh, hi, Desi, how's everything back there?"

"I'm not back there."

"Oh, you're not in the theater yet?"

"No, I'm not in the theater."

"Where are you?"

"I'm in Greenwich, Connecticut."

"You're in Greenwich, Connecticut?" he screamed. "We've got a full house and we've got a line that goes all around the block. There is no way you can make the eleven o'clock show!"

"I know that. That's why I am calling you."

"What am I going to do with all these people? What am I going to tell them?" he asked.

"Well, I think if you tell them the truth," I said. "they'll forgive us and I'll be there for the second show. I promise you."

"What are you doing in Greenwich, Connecticut, if you don't mind telling me about it?"

"I'm getting married."

"You're getting married?"

The last thing anyone in New York expected me to do was get married.

"Who are you marrying?"

"I'm marrying Lucy, Lucille Ball, the girl who was in the picture with me."

"That's wonderful!" he said.

"Judge O'Brien has arranged for a motorcycle escort to take us back to the Roxy. I promise you I'll be there for the second show. I'll even bring Lucy onstage and tell the audience what happened."

"Well, there's nothing I can do but say good luck to both of you and congratulations."

Justice O'Brien then told us, "Look, I don't want to marry you here in my office. Let's go over to the Byram River Beagle Club."

"What's that?" I asked.

"Well, it's a club we have here, a country club. It's a very nice place."

It really was the most lovely setting. A rambling river going by, beautiful flowers and trees, the mountains in the background. There was a glass-enclosed area in back where the ceremony took place. The judge had called ahead and had them cool some champagne and put flowers all over the place. The view Lucy and I looked at during the wedding was a Christmas card.

We thanked Justice of the Peace O'Brien for taking us there. It's something neither of us ever forgot, and we corresponded with him for many years until he passed away.

By the time we got back to New York, the *Journal-American* had a headline about it; and photographers and movie fans, most of whom knew Lucy better than they knew me, plus the ones who knew me from Broadway, La Conga and of course the Roxy, made up quite a mob. The stage manager was a nervous wreck.

"Desi, you got fifteen minutes . . . twelve minutes you got . . . you got to change."

Finally I said, "Kids, sorry, I got to go. You know I missed the first show already."

They were all laughing and congratulating us. They were really very nice, not a clothes-tearing mob but friendly and happy.

Lucy went upstairs with me and of course, as soon as we got to my dressing room, I had to do it. The first threshold I carried her over was the one at its door.

They had a beautiful bucket of Mumm's Extra Dry in the dressing room and flowers for Lucy. The management really went all the way.

I never had such an ovation in my life as when I went onstage. The theater was just packed. Very few people had left after the announcement during the first show, and many more had to be let in from the street, the ones who had been waiting in line. The management even had to get permission from the fire department so the people could stand in the aisles, at least until they saw Lucy and me.

After thanking the audience for their wonderful reception I said, "I'd like you to meet my very lovely bride of just an hour." And I brought out Lucy.

The Roxy had many tiers, four or five going higher and higher, and the management had sent out for small packages of rice. Everyone in that theater had one of these little packages. It looked like a snowstorm when they put the spotlights on and we saw this cascade of rice coming down from way up in the last tier onto the stage. I don't know how long it took them to clean out the mess, but it was really a sight.

We kissed and we cried and we threw kisses at them and they got up and shouted and screamed and threw rice at us.

I had arranged a wedding party at El Morocco that night, white tie and tails only, and all our friends in New York came: Brenda Frazier, Peter Arno, Rodgers and Hart, George Abbott, George Marion, Jr., Dorothy Kilgallen and Richard, everybody from La Conga (I skipped Polly that night; I thought it was prudent), everybody from *Too Many Girls,* George Schaeffer, the RKO president, and all of Lucy's friends from there, Caesar and his wife, some of the other boys in the band, the people from the Roxy and God knows how many more.

They had the whole place decorated with flowers and wedding cakes and the band played "The Wedding March" as we came in. We danced to "I Love You Truly," then they played all the songs from *Too Many Girls* and songs that had been in Lucy's other pictures. It was a beautiful night—exhausting, but beautiful.

RKO was paying for Lucy's lovely big suite at the Pierre while she promoted her picture in New York. Luckily the next day was Sunday, so my first show at the Roxy wouldn't start until 1 P.M. We didn't get to bed until six in the morning. We'd been drinking champagne all day long, from the Byram River Beagle Club, throughout all the shows at the Roxy, and at the whole Morocco party. I woke up in the middle of the night, very thirsty. So I spanked her on the fanny and said, "Get me some water, will you? I'm thirsty."

She mumbled, "Huh?"

"Get me some water, I'm thirsty."

She got up, half asleep, and went through the living room, which looked like a snowstorm because she had left the windows open. That was one of our main problems always. She kept opening the windows, I kept closing them. I like it hot, she likes it cold. She went into the kitchen, got me a big glass of water, put some ice in it, brought it to me and said, "Here you are, sweetheart," and fell back to sleep.

About 11 A.M. she sat up in bed, shook me and said, "Hey, hey!"

"What? What's the matter?" I asked.

"Listen, you. The next time you want a glass of water, get up and get it yourself. I just realized what you made me do."

"I'm sorry, honey," I said. "I'll tell you what, from now on just make sure there's a pitcher of water on my bed table before I go to bed because I get thirsty, particularly if I am drinking, I get awful thirsty. And as long as we're awake, I might as well tell you to keep the goddamn window closed. I just about froze to death trying to go to the can a minute ago."

We got off to a beautiful start, but we made good use of it. It became one of the *I Love Lucy* episodes.

She stayed with me until I finished my engagement at the Roxy and then we had a lovely trip to California. By that time I had received word from Lew Wasserman, who had since become my agent (MCA had bought out Doc Bender), that RKO had given me a contract to make three pictures in the next two years for ten thousand dollars a picture. It wasn't a lot of money but to me it was fine. I was going to be able to stay where Lucy was going to be. We were extremely happy when we boarded the Chief.

We had gotten two bedrooms and we opened the center partition, which made the space into a beautiful compartment. It looked romantic and gay with all the red and white carnations, her favorite flowers, I had ordered placed there.

For three days we made love, we ate, we rested, we had a wonderful trip. I had my guitar with me and the first day and part of the night I kept strumming the guitar and mumbling to myself. She told me later, "I was getting a little nervous with you and that guitar of yours in a corner, mumbling to yourself. I thought, My God, he's already tired of me."

What I was doing was writing a song for her: "When I looked into your eyes/ And then you softly said 'I do'/ I suddenly realized I had a new world/ A world with you/ A world where life is worth living/ A world that is so new to me/ A world of taking and giving/ Like God meant the world to be/ Where good times will find two to greet/ Where hard times will find two to beat/ I found my new world with you, darling/ When you said, softly, 'I do.' "

Lucy was very pleased. It became a ritual that at each of our anniversaries in the future I sang that song and also sent her red and white carnations. To this day, after fifteen years of being divorced, I send her red and white carnations on our anniversary.

When we arrived in Hollywood, we had a wonderful reception by the press, the studio, the family—everybody. We went back to Lucy's apartment—we didn't have a house yet—and there she began to learn about my cooking. She learned all about the Cuban dishes: the rice, black beans and *picadillo, arroz con pollo* (chicken and rice) and others. She loved them all and learned to cook them well.

We had some wonderful intimate parties in the apartment with just a few friends and plenty of music, of course. Where I am, there's got to be music. We always had a few guitar players. Carmen Miranda would come with her group. Bakaleinikoff would bring some new soloist from the RKO orchestra and some good Russian vodka and caviar. We had great times in that apartment.

We wanted to get a place of our own, however, a house with a yard and trees, a little ranch if possible. Lucy had known Jack Oakie for a long time and had made some pictures with him. Jack lived in the Valley in a house which was originally owned by Barbara Stanwyck, in Northridge.

One evening when we were visiting Jack, he said, "Why don't you take a look around the San Fernando Valley? It's an area that is just beginning to grow. I know this fellow, Bill Sesnon, whose family has owned this acreage for years and years, some in the hills and some on the flatlands in the Valley, which he is starting to develop. He has taken five-acre plots and built small, rambling ranch houses, colonial types, put a nice little pool on each one and planted about two hundred orange trees in front and back of each house. He has also enclosed the entire five acres with three-rail white fences."

You cannot visualize exactly what five acres are until you see them enclosed in their pretty white three-rail fence, with a nice big gate in front. When we saw the two hundred orange trees, the little road leading to the house, and the swimming pool in back, we thought it was just perfect. It was about three blocks down from where Jack lived, on the same street, Devonshire Boulevard. We fell in love with the place immediately.

"Hey, inside that fence is our land. That could be our little place. We could have chickens, cows, a vegetable garden and all kinds of things."

Neither of us was making too much money at the time. Lucy was under contract to RKO and I was going to make the three pictures, but I had not been able to save much, and she had always taken care of her family—her grandfather, her mother, her brother and her cousin Cleo—until she married. She had bought a little house for them and had been supporting them all her life, since she first got a job.

Lucy and I used to talk about our first jobs, how broke we were, and how we got started in show business. She told me she once was a soda jerk in a New York drugstore, and she was fired because she always forgot to put the bananas in the banana splits. She told me about being broke and hungry and how she concocted this scheme to have free breakfast. She would go to one of those two-doughnuts-and-coffee places (the same kind Caesar and I went to) and try to spot "a one-doughnut man"—the type who is always in a hurry, swallows one doughnut and his coffee in five seconds flat, looks at his watch, takes one quick last bite of the other doughnut and puts a nickel tip on the counter before running out. Once Lucy spotted a one-doughnut man she would wait close by, not seated yet, and the minute he took off she would slide onto his stool, grab the nickel and the leftover doughnut, call the attendant and say, putting the nickel on the counter, "I would like two more doughnuts and a fresh cup of coffee, please."

When she came to Hollywood, Lucy was a Goldwyn Girl, making fifty dollars a week. Neither of us had been able to build a savings account or buy bonds and stocks or things like that.

We asked Mr. Sesnon what he wanted, and you won't believe it in this day and age—$14,500 for the five acres, the house, the pool, the trees, everything, and right on the corner of Corbin and Devonshire.

Bill Sesnon was very smart. He was trying to get some people who were fairly well-known to buy in his new development in order to attract other people and raise the value of his property. But we didn't have the $14,500.

When we told him so, he said, "Don't worry about that. What can you put down?"

"Maybe fifteen hundred dollars or something like that."

"That's fine," he said. "You put down the fifteen hundred dollars and take as long as you want to pay the rest. Would ten years be okay?"

We called Andy Hickox, Lucy's business manager, and said, "We'd like to do this very much. We want our own little place and saw one we love. Mr. Sesnon has offered us a wonderful deal."

We told him what it was and he said, "I think you might be able to handle that if you kids will watch it. I'll put you on an allowance, Lucy, and that's all you'll get. I'll talk to your business manager, Magaziner, and you'll be put on an allowance too, Cuban."

"Okay, okay," we agreed.

It was really a lovely place. I fell in love with the kitchen immediately. It had big glass windows on one side, facing north toward the gate, the driveway in front of the house and the orange grove. Another big window opposite looked toward the backyard and pool area. From the kitchen there was a swinging door to a nice big room, the dining room and living room combined, with 16 feet of glass windows from ceiling to floor on the north side, and on the south side an 18-foot rectangular glass-enclosed corner with a padded seat.

From the master bedroom you looked through another ceiling-to-floor 16-foot glass window at the grove of orange trees, the mountains and countryside. In those days it was breathtaking because there were no houses in that direction. The only one fairly close to us was west of us, the home of Bill Henry, the distinguished *Los Angeles Times* columnist. Now it's a big housing development and everybody's right on top of each other.

It was really a sensational buy and Lucy had a ball decorating the place in beautiful white organdy, ruffled curtains and chintzes, which looked great with the living-room wallpaper of big red roses and green leaves. She did it little by little. My mother, her mother and Cleo all helped to make the curtains and hang them.

All our friends gave us a big shower and brought us pots and pans, silverware and plates, glasses and vases, even napkins and toilet paper. We didn't furnish it with any kinds of expensive stuff, just nice comfortable things, Early American. "Early Northridge, if you please," Lucy would correct me.

We wanted a name for our beautiful five acres. We had heard of Pickfair, Mary Pickford and Douglas Fairbanks' elegant million-dollar estate, so why shouldn't we have one? Our place looked like a million to us. We tried Arnaball (no good), Ballarnaz (ugh), Lucy's Des (no), Desi's Ball (definitely not), Ludesi (not quite), Desilu—BINGO!

First time I'd gotten top billing, but she didn't mind. Thornton Wilder later told me Desilu sounded like the past participle of a French verb.

16

Soon after we bought the ranchito I started filming another picture at RKO, *Four Jacks and a Jill,* which I hope nobody remembers. I wish I could forget it myself. Good title and it didn't have a bad cast, really: Ray Bolger was in it, also Eddie Foy, Jr., and Ann Shirley.

But we had a director, no use mentioning his name. I don't think he's around anymore, and if he is nobody knows where. Maybe he's been hiding ever since. He was originally an editor. Strangely enough, most of the directors who came from the editing department usually made darn good directors. For one thing, they're practical and they know film. But this guy was something else. I learned two things from him. I mean I learned how *not* to do them.

First of all, I played a dual role: prince and taxicab driver. It was *supposed* to be a musical comedy. The prince would have the cab driver wear his clothes and go in his place to supper at the Waldorf, or to talk to some big dignitaries or such. I didn't think the audience was going to know whether it was the prince at these functions or the taxicab driver passing himself off as the prince. It wasn't clear to me, so how could it be clear to an audience?

I said to the director, "I think if the audience knows for sure that he is the taxicab driver, a boozer and a character, trying to pass as the prince with the dignity and pomp of royalty, it will be funny. If the audience doesn't know that he is the prince, then it won't work. What the hell is funny about that? That's the way the prince *should* carry on."

So he said to me, "I hope you're right. That will keep the audience guessing. It will keep them in suspense."

"Wait a minute," I said, "I don't get that. What the hell are we doing, a comedy or a mystery? Are we doing Hitchcock or are we doing Lubitsch?"

"Don't worry about that, boy. I hope you're right, boy. That'll be great, boy."

The more he called me "boy" the more I disliked the asshole. But it was my first picture after *Too Many Girls* and I was tickled pink that I had these other three pictures contracted for, so I didn't want to make any waves.

I was happy just to be with Lucy in our own little place and do what I was told, but I knew the guy was wrong. He had to be wrong. Common sense would tell you that. You've got to let the audience know what the situation is, maybe even let them be ahead of you. It's good if they say, "Wait, wait until you see what's going to happen." As sometimes our *I Love Lucy* audience reacted, "Oh, boy, wait until Ricky gets home. She's going to be in a lot of trouble."

That's fine. It's good for the audience to be anticipating you. Then when it does happen, they say, "See, I told you so. I told you she was going to get it."

Once in a while you throw them a curve, which is all right too, if it is a funny curve. Of course it was years before *I Love Lucy,* so I wasn't 100 percent sure I was right. But after the picture came out and the audience, on the preview cards, told us the same thing—that they didn't know what the hell was going on, who was who and what was what—I knew I'd been right. I never forgot the lesson I learned from that director: "How Not to Do Comedy."

He should have seen how much detail and care George Abbott used in establishing a story-line point so that the jokes would work. And how much patience and understanding he had directing the cast.

Lou Holtz, one of the top comedians in vaudeville—in the same class with George Burns, Jack Benny, Milton Berle, Henny Young-man and Bob Hope—a man who was getting top money in night-clubs and theaters, was appearing for the first time in a motion picture as a guest star in a cameo role in *Four Jacks and a Jill*.

In his big scene he had a very long speech, a monologue. It had not been written by Mr. Holtz or his writers. It was not one of his famous vaudeville routines, and not particularly in his style.

We got to the day we were going to film the scene and our direc-tor (no one could miss the fact he was the director—a large-lettered sign on the back of his canvas chair said so) told the cast, "All right, let's try this thing."

He rehearsed it once and Mr. Holtz made a couple of mistakes, but the director, without rehearsing it again, said, "Okay, let's try a take."

It was a very warm day. They didn't have air conditioning on the stages in those days and the lights were very hot, a lot hotter than they are today. When you were on a small set, and this was a very small café set, crowded with all the principals and extras and filled with smoke, it was pretty uncomfortable even for us young people.

Mr. Holtz was in his fifties and we all thought he was doing fine. He is a very funny man with a wonderful puss. On this first take he stumbled a bit and made a mistake.

"Cut, cut, cut, cut! Fix the makeup, he's perspiring."

They fixed the makeup. "Okay, let's try it again. Roll 'em. Camera. Action."

Mr. Holtz got to the same spot and he stumbled again on the same line. And it was almost three-fourths of the way toward the end of the speech. He only had a few more sentences left, but the director again said, "Okay. Cut, cut, cut! Now, Mr. Holtz, it's not that difficult, get hold of yourself, will you? Fix the makeup, he's sweating again. It's going to look lousy on the screen."

The director could have done several things. He could have used all the stuff up to that point, changed the camera angle a little and picked it up a couple of lines before the end. He knew he was not going to stay on that same angle all through that long speech. He was going to have to use two or three angles for close-ups of Mr. Holtz and other people's reactions. But no, he wanted to get this one crummy "master shot" in one take.

A man like John Ford would have said, "That's wonderful, Mr. Holtz, perfect. Print that. Bring the camera over here for a close-up of Mr. Holtz. It was beautiful up to that point, Lou. People would think you've been in pictures all your life."

That's the way you should do it. That's the way a good director does it. It makes a man feel great and chances are the next time he will not stumble over that same line. But this goddamn idiot made Lou feel like a broken-down amateur and embarrassed the hell out of him in a room full of extras and all the other actresses and actors in the picture. The whole cast was in that scene.

So back they went again. Well, he made this poor man go over this thing ten or more times. By then they had to change his shirt and tie three different times. They'd fixed his makeup several times. Poor Lou didn't have a prayer of ever getting this whole long speech in one take. Once you get a mental block at a particular spot, you are dead. Worse yet, by now he had lost all the good stuff he had had up to that point.

So Lou said, "Mr. Director, I'm sure that if I could change that line just a little bit and mean actually the same thing, I wouldn't have any more trouble."

It was such a slight change that it really didn't make a darn bit of difference. It didn't change the joke, the sense of it, the logic, any-thing. It was just that he knew he had a mental block with this one particular phrase, and if he could say it his own way he would lose the mental block.

Here's what this director did. He got up out of his chair and in front of the whole cast and extras said, "Well, Mr. Holtz, I didn't know you wanted to direct this picture. Please sit in my chair and direct it."

Lou started shaking. He couldn't talk. You couldn't tell the angry tears from the sweat. Then he turned his back on us, walked out of the set, out of the stage, out of the studio and never came back.

I grabbed the director by the shirt and told him, "You sonofa-bitch. You broken-down bum. You have never done a goddamn thing but a five- and-ten-cent budget piece of shit like this. You stupid asshole. Who the fuck told you you could direct?"

Part of that was probably in Spanish. They had to pull me away from him. I guess my Latin temper couldn't take it. It blows up pretty fast, but it goes down just as fast. Maybe that's why you seldom hear of ulcers in Latin America.

After that one we did a picture called *Father Takes a Wife* with Adolphe Menjou and Gloria Swanson. Menjou had a wonderful sense of humor and knew every trick of the trade. We were doing a scene in a taxicab and were supposed to get out of the cab to go into a hotel. As we got out of the taxicab, Menjou first and me second, I was supposed to be saying a line. We did it and the director yelled, "Cut!"

This wasn't the same director, thank Christ, it was somebody else.

"Let's do it again," he said, "but, Desi, when you get out of the taxicab, clear yourself from behind Menjou so that the camera can see you."

"Okay," I said.

We did it again. Menjou came out of the taxicab with that great flair he had—and I was covered again as I spoke the line.

"Cut!"

I had a lot of respect for Mr. Menjou. I admired him very much in all his pictures. I knew he'd been in pictures for a long, long time and that he was one of the best character actors in the business, so I didn't dare say anything.

The director told me, "Desi, you were covered again."

"Well, I'm having a little trouble clearing myself. Mr. Menjou takes up most of the room when we come out of there."

"Adolphe will take it all if he can get away with it. Just don't let him."

"Okay, I'll give it another try."

We did it again, and again I failed.

"Cut!"

Back in the taxicab.

I said, "Mr. Menjou, you've got to help me out a little bit because the director is giving me hell. He wants me to clear myself from behind you when we come out of the taxicab so he can see my face when I say my line. I've tried to clear myself five times now and I haven't been very successful."

He answered, "Every actor for himself!"

"Every actor for himself?" I asked.

"That's right."

The next time we came out of the cab, I gave him a real shove and he almost went on his ass.

"Cut!"

Back inside the cab.

"That's going a little overboard to clear yourself, isn't it?" asked Adolphe.

"Well, every actor for himself, Mr. Menjou."

He laughed. "You'll do fine out here, you learn fast."

In the next take we didn't have any trouble and he was very helpful to me for the rest of the picture; he helped me with my lines, how to do the comedy bits, my reactions. He was a lovely man.

While doing this picture I learned something else about how they do things in Hollywood. Charlie Koerner, who was now president of RKO and a great guy, had been present when I sang "Perfidia" at a benefit in San Francisco. He liked the song and the way I sang it, just with my guitar. So he instructed his people to buy the film rights and have me sing it in this picture with Menjou and Swanson.

"Perfidia" was a lovely Latin ballad in slow tempo, a *son*. The part I was playing in the picture was that of an operatic tenor. So even though the studio had bought it because their president liked the way I sang it, the producer of the picture decided that I should sing it as an operatic aria with a big orchestra which, one, my voice was not equipped to do, and two, it was not the way it should be done.

So "Perfidia," bought by Mr. Koerner to be sung by me, simply to my guitar accompaniment and in my own perhaps not too good but typical Latin way, wound up being sung in the picture by an Italian tenor, dubbing my voice in the style of an operatic aria, accompanied by a symphony orchestra.

Later I received letters from Latin America, Spain, and especially Cuba, asking me, "What the hell were you trying to do to 'Perfidia,' and where did you pick up that Italian accent?"

After *Father Takes a Wife* RKO did not have another picture for me to do, so I went off salary. I had made twenty thousand dollars in a short time, but my career as a motion-picture actor had not been benefited. Both pictures were lemons.

I went with Lucy to Taos, New Mexico, where she was costarring in a picture with James Craig called *Valley of the Sun*. There were a lot of Indians in the movie and, having nothing else to do, I took one of their drums and showed them the conga beat. Soon I had the whole Indian tribe doing the conga all over their village.

After *Valley of the Sun* Lucy's next picture was to be *Big Street* with Henry Fonda, based on Damon Runyon's *Little Pinks*. It was a heavy drama in which she played a cripple in a wheelchair—a mean, bitchy cripple at that.

She told Charles Laughton, who was also at RKO at the time, that she was worried about the part. It was the first time I'd seen her afraid to tackle a role. Laughton told her, "Lucy, darling, if you are going to play a bitch, play the bitchiest bitch who ever lived or don't play the part at all."

Mr. Laughton also tried to get me in a picture he was going to make with Carole Lombard, my favorite comedienne. Carole had a quality which is rare; you can count the women who have had it on the fingers of one hand. Carole, while doing the wild antics of a clown, disheveled, rain-soaked, disregarding how she looked even with mud all over her, could make you laugh, and yet at the same time make you want to go to bed with her. Lucy has that same quality.

In spite of Mr. Laughton's arguments with the RKO hierarchy that I would be perfect for the part of the young man in the picture, which later became *The Most Happy Fella* on Broadway as a Frank Loesser musical, they did not want me for the part because of my accent.

They were willing to pay for an elocution coach to see if I could get rid of it. I took lessons for three months and at the end of the three months they tested me in the part. My accent came from the sound track as thick and as Cuban as ever.

Meanwhile, back at the ranch, I went to work on the vegetable garden. I built a barbecue and a *bohío* (thatched-roof native Cuban hut) at one end of the pool. At the other end I started to build a bathhouse.

We had an elderly man from Chatsworth, Mr. Conlin, who worked part time for us and helped me with these projects. At the farthest corner of the five acres we also built two horse stalls, just to be ready if I ever got some again, and a large wooden incubator. We filled the incubator with a hundred eggs, which were soon to bring our first batch of baby chicks.

One day Lucy, Mr. Conlin and I were in the kitchen eating lunch when we noticed through the large glass windows that the entire yard was in shadow, but there hadn't been a cloud in the sky. It turned out to be a large swarm of bees. Mr. Conlin told me to bring my conga drum out in the yard and play it.

"What do you mean?"

"Just bring it out, stand in the center of the yard and keep a steady monotonous beat. They will gather in a bunch on one of the trees and then we can catch them and you'll have your own honey. I'll go home and bring a beehive while you're playing the drum for them."

He left as if he had just given me a very simple, everyday chore.

Lucy said, "Go on, you heard the man."

As I stood there beating a steady beat on my drum those thousands of bees were all over me, including my face and my hair. Lucy was safely behind the screen on the porch. I told her, with as little facial movement as possible, "I have played this drum for a lot of people but never for a bunch of bees."

She was laughing so hard she was crying.

Mr. Conlin was right. They did not sting me once, and eventually they all gathered on a big olive tree right in front of the porch. He put them in a box and we had our own honey for quite a while.

Another good helper I had on these ranch projects was Lucy's grandfather, Fred C. Hunt, a real character. I met him for the first time after we'd been married and had gone to Palm Springs for about three weeks, at their home on Ogden Drive, the one Lucy had bought for her family.

When I get in the sun I get very tanned. You can't tell me from the native fishermen in Hawaii or Mexico. It was then he first saw his granddaughter's husband.

After meeting me he called Lucy aside and told her, "He seems like a nice fellow, but he doesn't speak so good and he's a little dark, isn't he?"

He was in his early seventies and, though retired, he could still make beautiful furniture in his garage shop. One of the few good, old-fashioned woodturners left. When RKO heard about him, they talked Lucy into letting Grandpa work, at least for a few hours a day, in their carpentry and furniture-making department. At the end of three days of working there he had talked the entire department into a strike against RKO, demanding better wages. As a result he was fired, of course, and Lucy almost got fired right along with him.

Grandpa Hunt was a great fan and follower of Eugene V. Debs's Socialist ideals, and also a daily reader of the *People's World,* a Socialist-Communist newspaper in Los Angeles. He would capture anybody who walked into that house and read the editorials for as long as he could hold them there. Lucy's mother, DeeDee, Grandpa's daughter, had a hell of a time keeping even a part-time maid or cook. He would go into the kitchen, talk to them and comment on what lousy wages they were getting, and soon the maid or cook would quit.

He was so much for the underdog he was considered a rebel. Today he would be a conservative.

He was helping me with the roof of the bathhouse late one afternoon. It was hot and I asked him, "Grandpa, would you like a cold beer or a nice tall gin fizz?"

"No, no, I don't touch the stuff anymore," he said.

"You don't drink at all?"

"No, not for a long, long time."

"How come? What happened?"

"I used to be a pretty good drinker," he explained. "What happened was that the last time I got drunk was on Thanksgiving. When I sobered up it was New Year's Day, and I couldn't remember what happened in between. That's the time I thought I'd better quit, and went to take the cure."

DeeDee gave him an allowance of five dollars a week. He didn't have any expenses, of course; he had a home, food and anything he wanted. The five dollars was just for pocket money. Grandpa would go to the corner of Sunset and Fairfax, near their house. It was a hangout for streetwalkers, who sat on the bench there, pretending to be waiting for the bus while trying to pick up somebody. If Grandpa liked one of the girls he'd give her his five-dollar allowance and say to her, "Look, honey, why don't you take the night off?"

There were some beautiful trees in front of 1344 North Ogden Drive between the sidewalk and the street, all up and down the block. Grandpa liked to sit on the porch and look at the people and traffic go by. One big tree loused up his view. He kept saying, "That goddamn tree is blocking our view. I think we should take it down."

Anyone who heard him say that would tell him, "Grandpa, you better not. That belongs to the city. You can get us in a lot of trouble. That's not our tree."

He would say, "It's going to fall down anyway. It's old and not too healthy and the next time a good rain and wind comes, that thing is going to go."

Cleo is Lucy's first cousin, but they were brought up as sisters and they're that close. Grandpa Hunt was also Cleo's grandfather. She was married at that time to Artie Auerbach, a very good radio performer who was quite famous as Mr. Kitzel on *The Jack Benny Show*.

Artie told me that one night late and dark, he found that Grandpa had removed the sod around the tree in squares so he could put them back, as they transfer lawns, and was sawing the roots. He was making sure his prophecy would come true when the rains came.

After Artie told me he asked, "What do you think we should do?"

"Forget it, Artie. Let him alone. So what if the tree falls down."

Unfortunately, when the rains came and the tree fell down, it fell right on top of Lucy's brand-new convertible.

A couple of years later Cleo divorced Artie and married Kenny

Morgan, who later became head of public relations at Desilu Productions. Kenny was a captain in the Army during the war and came home on leave. Cleo told Grandpa, "You remember my husband, Kenny, don't you?"

Grandpa said, "Whatever happened to Artie?"

After Pearl Harbor, Grandpa wanted to do something for the war effort and he was made the air-raid warden of his block. Grandpa had a double hernia, so he had to wear a double truss. He also couldn't see without his glasses. Whenever the practice air-raid alert sounded, DeeDee and Cleo had to get up, find his double truss, his glasses, and his air-raid warden hard hat before they could get him out of the house. They couldn't do any of these things in the dark. The only house in the whole block that had the lights on during the blackout was the air-raid warden's house. Usually, by the time they had gotten him ready to go outside, the all-clear signal had sounded.

I loved Grandpa Hunt. He was right out of *You Can't Take It With You,* a lovable, loony character.

With the help of Mr. Conlin and Grandpa and Lucy herself, when she wasn't working on a picture, I had gotten our Desilu ranch in great shape. The chickens were hatched, all good and healthy, and we had a chicken coop full of them. The vegetable garden was doing fine. We had wonderful corn, beautiful artichokes and potatoes. I have never tasted such good potatoes in my life. It's amazing how different they taste when you get them right out of the ground. We had carrots and radishes, which grew all over the place; you couldn't stop them from growing.

A friend gave us two calves. One of them died, the other one was very sick, and Lucy and I stayed up all night long with her. She had a high fever and we held her, wrapped up in blankets, and gave her the stuff which the vet had told us to give her. Finally, she got over the illness and lived. We both felt good and proud of our triumph to have this beautiful little white-and-black calf we called The Duchess of Devonshire live through the efforts of our nursing. She was a white-faced Holstein.

Eventually she got to be twenty-two hundred pounds. She fell in love with me and would come to our bedroom window in the middle of the night and moo, moo, moo. Lucy would wake up and say, "There's your goddamn girl friend trying to get into the bedroom. You better go and do something before she comes right through the window."

We had been given the calf to fatten up and eventually butcher, but there was no way we could have butchered The Duchess. We finally paid somebody for her room and board until she died a natural death.

Everything and everybody seemed to be doing well, except me and my career. It wasn't going anywhere, and I was not happy about that. Lucy was doing fine. She was not a star of Ginger Rogers' magnitude, but she had become the undisputed queen of RKO's "B" pictures. I would have settled for some "C" picture assignments.

My accent was not helping me any. It narrowed down the number of roles they might even consider me for. One night I dressed to the teeth, hoping some producer would see me and think of me for something, and I took Lucy to an RKO premiere at the Pantages Theatre in my beautiful Buick Roadmaster, which I had spent half the day cleaning and polishing. I must say we made a fine, handsome couple.

At the end of a premiere an usher with a microphone calls the cars of the stars to be brought to the front by either your chauffeur or the uniformed parking attendant. As the names are called, the spotlights hit that couple, and the movie fans, crowding the stands especially erected for the occasion and all over the sidewalks and street, go wild applauding and shouting at their favorites.

As our turn came the usher looked at us, smiled, nodded and then called, "Lucille Ball's car, please!" The car was brought to the front, I helped her in, went around to the driver's side, got in behind the wheel and got out of there.

A block away, and I don't know how I forced myself to wait that long, I said to Lucy, "That does it!"

"What do you mean?"

"I'm getting out of this goddamn town and get a job."

"You have to be patient. I'm sure you'll get something soon. You don't know how many people come up to me and say you should be the next Rudolph Valentino."

"Well, thank you, sweetheart, I appreciate your trying to make me feel better."

"Now listen to me, honey," she said. "Just now Perry Lieber [the publicity director of RKO] gave me this article which appeared all over the country datelined Hollywood, June twenty-second, a syndicated news releases. Let me read it to you."

She turned on the car reading light, and while we drove home she read:

> "If Desi Arnaz, handsome, olive-tinted, black hair, smoldering eyes, Cuban chap who Abbott saw at La Conga, cast him in *Too*

Many Girls and became a matinee idol, can now repeat on the screen, he may well cause movie producers to search for Latins as they did following Valentino's rise. It was Valentino in whom the Latin type reached its finest hour. So great was the vogue for that type then that men, not even Latins, essayed the roles. Warner Baxter in *In Old Arizona,* Wallace Beery in *Viva Villa,* Ricardo Cortez, although not a Latin, capitalized on his sultry looks by adopting a professional name to fit. But that hour is no longer here. Desi Arnaz, the newcomer, may be just what the doctor ordered for the revival of the Latin craze following Valentino's success, the blade to carve out such a revival."

I answered her, "Well, that's very nice, but I guess I was a few years too late and obviously my blade was not sharp enough. I've also read in many other Hollywood and New York columns that I was to play opposite Ginger Rogers in a top musical, that I was to play opposite Maureen O'Hara in another RKO extravaganza, et cetera, and all I have done so far are three lousy pictures and now I'm out of a job. There's no way I'm going to stay here and become Mr. Ball!"

The next morning I called Caesar and told him to pick up the same type of band we had at La Conga in New York or Fan and Bill's. We hadn't worked together since La Conga and I hadn't seen him since our wedding party. He was glad to get back into action.

I then called MCA and told them I was going to New York to rehearse with the band and to get a job someplace. I packed my clothes, took my guitar and my drum and left, not mad or after a fight with Lucy, just discouraged and pissed off.

The job MCA got was at the Rumba Casino, a new place just being opened up by Tom Cassara, the man who ran The Continental when Joe E. Lewis was there and I was at La Conga.

During the end of that engagement the State Department asked me if I would join a group of artists and movie stars who were being sent to Mexico to kick off President Roosevelt's Good Neighbor Policy. I was flattered to be asked and wouldn't have missed it for the world.

The Good Neighbor Policy was a wonderful idea and meant to get the people of North America, especially those who lived in the United States, a little closer to the people who lived below the Rio Grande, not just in Mexico but in all Latin American countries. The Rockefeller Foundation was also involved in the promotion of this project for the President.

The kickoff consisted of three DC-3 planes, loaded with stars from Hollywood going to Mexico City. When I say planeloads full of stars, I mean full of stars like Mickey Rooney, Norma Shearer, James Cagney, Clark Gable, Robert Taylor, Bing Crosby—the top of the top!

I was on the trip not because I was in that same class. The only reason I was sent there is because they wanted me to get a reaction from the Mexican people about Mr. Roosevelt's Good Neighbor Policy. I was tickled pink that I was going to go, for whatever reason.

The great romance during the trip was that of Mickey Rooney and Norma Shearer. They looked kind of funny together, Miss Shearer always elegant in long organdy dresses with a parasol, and Mickey trotting alongside her through the Presidential Gardens of Chapultepec Park. When they stopped to talk and faced each other, if you weren't close, it looked as though Mickey was talking to her knockers.

It was quite a deal down there. We went only to Mexico City and stayed there for three days, but we had mobs of people greeting and following us all over the place. We played five, six or seven theaters every day and were royally treated.

Years before, Lee Tracy, a great character actor, went to Mexico as the guest of the Mexican government in celebration of the Cinco de Mayo, which is for them like the Fourth of July for us. Lee used to live it up pretty good. He happened to be pissing off a balcony just as the parade was going by. Of course, he was loaded at the time, but the Mexican people were not only mad at Lee, they were mad at the United States. It became a big international incident and it actually ruined Mr. Tracy's career.

When we were there in 1941, anytime one of the American actors stepped out on the balcony, you could see the mob dispersing. They were thinking, The crazy goddamn Americans are going to piss on us again!

The most important thing about this trip was the reaction of the Mexican people to Mr. Roosevelt's Good Neighbor Policy. As I mentioned, the only reason I went was because I spoke Spanish and they wanted me to report to the Roosevelt people and to the Rockefeller Foundation.

When we came back, I met with them and they asked, "What was their reaction?"

I told them, "They are suspicious."

"What do you mean, they're suspicious?"

"They don't get it. They don't get this, all of a sudden, Good Neighbor Policy deal."

"Didn't you tell them we meant . . ."

"I told them President Roosevelt has a wonderful idea and it's about time, but I guess I must tell you how one Mexican put it to me, because I think he put it very well, when I asked him why he was suspicious of this policy. I said to him, exactly the following, 'I know that President Roosevelt means it, I know he wants to strengthen the relations between the United States and Latin America. So why are you suspicious?'

"He said, 'Well, that might be all true and that's fine and dandy, but let me tell you something, Desi. If you lived next door to somebody for twenty years, and he never said good morning to you, never invited you for a drink, never remembered your wife's birthday, Christmas, or anything and he's been your neighbor for twenty years, but never had anything to do with you at all; then all of a sudden one day he says good morning, sends your wife flowers and asks you over for dinner. What's your reaction? It's got to be "What the hell does the sonofabitch want?" ' "

That was the exact reaction of the Mexican people to the Good Neighbor Policy. "What is this all of a sudden? We've been here for a hundred and fifty years, nobody paid a goddamn bit of attention to us. All of a sudden they say, 'I want to be your friend.' What do they want? Take the rest of Mexico? They already have taken a big chunk. What is it that they want now?"

Of course, that is one of our biggest problems. We turn it on too strongly and too suddenly. They do not understand our foreign policy. As far as Latin America is concerned, it has always been a poor, poor policy.

We keep goofing all the time. We just don't know what the hell we're doing down there. Part of the reason is that—and I don't understand why we do this—our ambassadors down there, most of them anyway, don't even speak the language. I am sure we have enough people in this country from all over Latin America, from Argentina, Mexico, Brazil, Chile, Colombia, Peru, etc., etc., who are now American citizens and can speak both languages perfectly. So why don't we pick some of those guys to be our ambassadors down there, instead of sending a Sumner Welles, who sat in the goddamn lobby of the National Hotel reading poetry while Batista was killing off all the generals?

17

December 7, 1941. Lucy and I were in New York City staying at a lovely penthouse apartment which a friend of mine had loaned us. She had come to New York to be with me after my meeting with the people of the Rockefeller Foundation and it was there that we heard the word about the Japanese bombing Pearl Harbor. We knew that they had badly crippled our Navy and everybody presumed they would follow it up by attacking California or some other spot on the Pacific Coast.

We made arrangements to fly to Los Angeles immediately and be with our families. Within a week Cuba had also declared war on Japan, and shortly after the first of the year I received a commission as a lieutenant in the Cuban Army. Everybody in Hollywood was either joining or being drafted. I decided to resign my commission in the Cuban Army and join the U.S. Navy. I loved the ocean, had been around boats all my life, could navigate pretty well, at least by dead reckoning, so the Navy was it!

I had met Captain Jackson Tate of the Navy through Ed Sedgwick, a director at MGM for most of the Buster Keaton pictures, and a very good friend of Lucy's. We learned a lot about slapstick comedy from Mr. Sedgwick.

Captain Tate was in command of an aircraft carrier at the time. He had been the first man to land an aircraft on a carrier in the U.S. Navy. He told me, "If the Navy accepts you, you can start as an assistant navigator."

I told him I knew how to navigate ships by dead reckoning, but I didn't know much about celestial navigation.

"Don't worry about that," he said, "because the way we do it now on our navigational tables, move a couple of rulers this way and the other and you've got it. It's really very simple. You can learn the whole thing in a very short time."

I was really exicted about it, but when I went to the Navy recruiting station to join, to my utter disbelief I found I could not. There is a law that if you're not a citizen of the United States you cannot volunteer. You can be drafted, but you cannot volunteer, which is kind of a ridiculous law. If you are good enough to be drafted, why aren't you good enough to join?

Captain Tate tried to help. He even went all the way to the Secretary of the Navy trying to get me in, but they told him it would take an act of Congress to change the law. I had already applied for my citizenship papers a couple of years before. It became a race between receiving my final American citizenship papers or "Greetings from Uncle Sam." As it turned out, after several months Uncle Sam won.

In the meantime I did the last picture on my RKO contract, *The Navy Comes Through.* It was directed by Edward Sutherland, a fine director. He was the complete opposite of the jerk who did *Four Jacks and a Jill.* This was a man who really knew his business, and a fine man besides; he had started as an actor.

In the cast were Pat O'Brien, George Murphy, Carl Esmond (who played a great German "heavy" in this picture), Frank Jenkins, Max Baer and Jackie Cooper (playing the epitome of a young hero sailor), plus Ray Collins, Lee Bonnell and others. The only girl in the picture was Jane Wyatt, as a nurse.

It was based on a magazine story by Borden Chase. The picture got very good reviews and I got my first good one as a film actor. It said: "Also reveals a superior character delineation by Desi Arnaz and Frank Jenkins." It was the only good one out of the three I did at RKO. Nevertheless, they dropped my option. That means I was fired.

I had met Max Baer in Miami just before he became the heavyweight champion of the world. Max was the gentlest, kindest man I'd ever met. How he ever got into the boxing business I'll never know. He didn't have the disposition, the necessary killer instinct. When he fought Primo Carnera for the title, I was at ringside. Carnera was already in the ring. He was a giant. As Max came down the aisle he saw me, stopped for a second, looked up at Carnera in the ring and then said to me in a high-pitched woman's voice and with a very funny "gay" delivery: "He's a big one, isn't he?" Then he climbed into the ring, knocked Carnera out in the first round and became the heavyweight champion of the world.

After we finished *The Navy Comes Through,* I toured the country during April and May of 1942, for the Army and Navy Relief, to raise funds for the widows and families of our soldiers and sailors killed overseas. A private train of seventeen cars transported twenty-two of the biggest stars in Hollywood, plus seven gorgeous starlets and musicians and technical people, around the country.

It was the Hollywood Victory Caravan.

Mark Sandrich, a brilliant producer-director at Paramount, put the show together. Alfred Newman, a top music director at Twentieth Century-Fox, conducted an orchestra of thirty musicians. If that train had been wrecked, Hollywood would have been out of business.

One newspaper carried a story that it would cost more than $4 million a night to put on that show, which doesn't seem too far-fetched when you consider who was in it.

As usual, when there are so many stars involved, the billing was alphabetical. Thanks to the *A*, Desi Arnaz got top billing, but, believe me, that was the one and only reason; the others were Joan Bennett, Joan Blondell, Charles Boyer, James Cagney, Jerry Colonna, Clau-dette Colbert, Olivia de Havilland, Cary Grant, Charlotte Greenwood, Bob Hope, Bert Lahr, Frances Langford, Laurel and Hardy, Groucho Marx, Frank McHugh, Ray Middleton, Pat O'Brien, Merle Oberon, Eleanor Powell and Rise Stevens. Bing Crosby joined us in Minne-apolis.

Big hits on the tour with everybody they met were seven beauti-ful starlets of that year: Alma Carroll, Marie MacDonald, Frances Gifford, Elyse Knox, Fay MacKenzie, Juanita Stark and Arleen Whelan.

We had only two days' rehearsal before the opening, on April 30, at the Capital Theatre in Washington, D.C. Writers who con-tributed material included George S. Kaufman, Moss Hart, Marc Connelly, Jerome Kern and Alan Scott.

Mrs. Roosevelt gave a tea party at the White House on the afternoon of our opening night at the Capital Theatre. She was at the head of the receiving line and every time anybody came up to her she would say something very personal and very intimate before let-ting them go by. I knew she knew Cary Grant, Charles Boyer, James Cagney, Bob Hope, and all the other big stars, but how did she know me and some of the girls who were just starlets? But she treated us all as though we were also big stars. She spent just as much time with us and asked about our private lives.

When she came to me, she said, "Hello, Desi. How is Lucille?" I was really nobody in those days. So I was thinking, How in hell can she do this? There were at least forty or fifty people going by. How can she possibly remember each one, who they are married to, and say something personal to each of them? Even James Farley couldn't have done it, and he had the reputation of being the best at that sort of thing.

I finally spotted a fellow standing behind her. Let's suppose that

Cagney was in front of me and she was shaking hands with him. The guy behind Mrs. Roosevelt would whisper, "Desi Arnaz, married to Lucille Ball, he's a Cuban."

I learned how to use that in later years when I went into the big-band business. In every town we visited there would be four or five people very important to us for that engagement: the theater manager, the most popular disk jockey, and the local newspaper guys. In each town we would spend the whole week with these people and become very friendly with them. Then we would go to the next town and find another group of the same type of people. And so it would go on and on.

The next time I would come back to Omaha, for instance, it would be impossible for me to remember the names of that group. That's when I would use Mrs. Roosevelt's technique.

Lucy's brother, Freddie, was working for me and I had quite a problem trying to find out what the hell Freddie could do. I thought this might be the answer.

I told him, "Okay, Freddie, here's the only thing you have to do: Every time we hit a town I want you to take a picture of these few important guys. Then I want you to put them in a book, with their names right under their pictures, and just keep a record of it, so that when we come back to this same town six months from now, and I get off the train and the disk jockey comes up to me, you stand behind my ear and just say Bill, or John, or Mike, and I'll take it from there."

That's what makes a very good headwaiter, by the way—remembering people's names.

Thinking about headwaiters: Lopez at the Copacabana was the greatest. We worked there with the big band in 1946, a hell of a run, eighteen weeks, tying Joe E. Lewis's record.

The bar was upstairs, on the first floor. Lopez would greet people coming downstairs.

"May we have a table?" they'd ask.

He'd say, "I don't know for sure."

He would always have one hand behind his back, with open palm, as he was looking over the room. If he felt something in the palm, he would say, "Perhaps I can find you a table."

I kept watching this routine and wondering how he knew how much it was that had been put into his palm. It's all paper, right? A $1 bill is the same size and weight as a $100 bill, or $20, or $10, or $5. So how does he know what it is? Or where to put the guy who fills that empty palm of his? A $100 bill would get you ringside, or even an extra table on the floor, but if it's $1, he'd kick you out of the club. So how does he know?

I finally asked him, and he said, "It's the feeling, it's the way they put it there."

18

After we got back to Hollywood I was really floundering. Ken Murray was doing a show called *Ken Murray's Blackouts,* and he called me to ask if I would go into this thing with him. The show had been running for quite a while and it was a big hit. I was glad to have a job.

One night after the show, Mr. Louis B. Mayer came backstage; he had been in the audience that night. Of course I knew who Mr. Mayer was but I had never met him.

He said, "I'd like to talk to you. Will you come to my office at MGM tomorrow? I don't want you to bring any agent. You just come and talk to me."

"That's fine, Mr. Mayer," I said.

I was so excited, I thought maybe, finally, a good Hollywood break. I went to his office, a magnificent one in the Thalberg Building at MGM. MGM in those days was THE place . . .Gable and Turner, Tracy and Hepburn, Taylor and Garbo, Judy Garland, James Stewart, the Barrymores, Joan Crawford, Mickey Rooney—"More Stars Than There Are In Heaven" was its slogan.

God knows, I was impressed.

Mr. Mayer sat me down and said, "When I saw your show last night, you reminded me of Busher."

I had always been a great race fan. I didn't have any horses of my own at that time, but I knew that Busher was one of Mr. Mayer's great racehorses, possibly his greatest. So I knew that somehow he must have meant it as a compliment.

"I'm sure that what you said must be complimentary," I said, "because I know Busher is one of the top stars in your racing stable, but how do I remind you of Busher, if you don't mind?"

"Well, Busher looks very common when he's around the barn, but when they put a saddle on him, and he goes out onto the track, you know he's a champion. The same thing happens to you when you hang that drum around your shoulder. Up to that point you're just another Mexican."

"Not Mexican, sir, Cuban."

"Well, one of those Latin fellows. I want to see what we can do with you around here."

He then pressed a button and said, "Have Lana come in."

As soon as Miss Turner arrived, he said, "Will you stand next to her, then turn her around and look at her, up and down, then turn her around again, hold her in your arms and kiss her?"

What a sweet job this was going to be!

I did what he told me and then he said to Lana, "Go back to the set."

I escorted her to the door and said, "Thank you."

She said, "My pleasure," and left.

The button again. "Have Judy come in."

Judy Garland came in and he made me go through the same thing with her. By this time my bird really wanted to fly.

He then said, "You know this is the best studio in the world, and we make stars here, a lot of stars. I think you have a chance to be a star."

"Mr. Mayer, that's the nicest compliment I've had since I started in this business."

"We'll start you at five hundred dollars a week."

"Mr. Mayer," I said, "you know I like to live well. I like to eat at Chasen's; I'm married and I'm supporting my mother and I like to wear good clothes; five hundred dollars a week won't do it."

"Son, that's a pretty good deal. You haven't done much in pictures. You made three of them at RKO, which were not so good. . . ."

"I can't argue with you on that, sir. They didn't even pick up my option."

"I appreciate your honesty, but five hundred dollars is not bad to start at."

"I'll tell you what. I can't bluff you; I'm not in a position to bluff and I do want to be under contract to you. The biggest break of my career was that you happened to go to the *Blackouts* the other night and saw me and liked what I did. So, if you insist, I will sign for five hundred dollars, but I'll be a lot happier if you give me six hundred and fifty dollars."

He just looked at me for a while, laughed and said, "You sonofabitch, how can I say no? You got six hundred and fifty dollars."

After I signed the contract, the USO wanted me to go to the

Caribbean to entertain in that area, where there were many Cubans, Puerto Ricans and other Latin boys with our American troops.

Mr. Mayer said, "Go ahead. I think I have a good picture for you coming up, but it is not ready quite yet. As soon as it is we'll get the USO to send you back."

First stop: Guantánamo Bay in my native Cuba!

There were only three performers in this group—Billy Gilbert, that wonderful comedian with the trained sneeze; his wife, Lolly; Fay MacKenzie, his niece, a very pretty girl and a good singer and dancer; and myself.

We went through all the different bases in the Caribbean. We weren't big stars, but we gave them a good show. We worked with whatever the boys had. Sometimes a trio, other times just a piano player. Most of the bases had no stages, so we used the back of a truck for the stage. For lights we used the headlights of two other trucks and for curtains we used Army blankets or whatever else was around. If we wanted a girl dancing chorus, we would get six guys from the troops, dress them as girls, put a couple halves of coconuts on their chests and let them prance around. The troops liked this bit so well we did it at every base.

While we were in Guantánamo Bay, which is close to my old hometown, I asked the base commander, "Is there any way that I could get to Santiago, at least for a couple of hours, to see my grandparents?"

"How long has it been," he asked, "since you saw them last?"

"About six or seven years. I only have two grandparents left and this might be my last chance. They're getting pretty old."

"Well, you aren't scheduled to do anything until tomorrow night. I'll get one of the boys to fly you over there and back."

"That would be wonderful. Thank you so much."

The next morning a Navy ensign came to me and took me to their landing strip.

He said, "You don't mind flying in this plane, do you?"

"What plane?" I asked.

He pointed it out to me and said, "We call it *The Yellow Peril.* It's the one we use to train the boys."

It was yellow all right, a two-seater, open cockpit.

"Well?" he asked.

"Let's go, man!"

We took off and landed at Santiago. We got a car and drove over to my grandfather's house. Nobody knew that I was even in the country, and when my grandfather and grandmother saw this U.S.

Navy ensign in his uniform and realized that the Navy had flown me there just to see them, they were really impressed. They figured I must be a pretty big shot in the United States. And, of course, we hadn't been there for half an hour before the whole town knew about it. There are twelve brothers and sisters in my mother's family and seven in my father's. With their husbands and wives, children and cousins, all of a sudden there were 150 people around the house.

By this time it was about three o'clock in the afternoon. I saw big, heavy clouds going past in the sky and moving pretty fast. In our country these tropical storms come up quickly. So I turned to the ensign with "I think we better get the hell out of here because this is gonna get pretty rough."

My grandfather looked up and said, *"Sí, vete pronto."* He didn't understand English but he understood those clouds and knew what I was worrying about.

We had come over the hills, which is the short way, but by the time we got to the airport and into the plane, it was so bad that there was no way we could go back over the hills. The ensign said, "How else could we get to Guantánamo from here?"

"Across the bay," I answered.

"Yes," he said, "but there are high mountains surrounding Santiago Bay and the entrance is awfully narrow."

"I know, but I can thread a needle through that bay."

"Okay," he said, "you direct me and we'll fly a hundred feet above water."

He figured that if he got out of the bay and straight out to sea, we'd be okay. A storm of that kind may be concentrated in a very small area.

I saw my old fishing grounds and told him, "Go over the *Merrimac,* which is there, keep straight on that course, and you'll go right through the entrance."

"Desi, don't let your parachute get wet," he said.

"What?" I asked.

"Don't let your parachute get wet, because if it does it won't work."

"This is a hell of a time to tell me—it's soaked now!"

"Oh migawd, I should have told you to sit on it."

We cleared the entrance and five minutes later cleared the storm. It was like going through a door into the most beautiful tropical climate. The sun was shining, the fish were jumping, the water was blue and calm; and just on the left, so close you could almost touch it, a black, scary mass where all hell was breaking loose.

That is the way those tropical storms are.

We had been going south to clear the storm, then east and parallel to it, but we had to turn north to get to Guantánamo.

Halfway there the ensign said, "You know, the only trouble is that we're going to get to Guantánamo in about fifteen minutes and this little plane is not going to be able to go through that wall."

By now it had really closed in.

A few minutes later he said, "We're about even with the bay, we should now be turning north, but it's impossible to get through that."

As we were talking on the intercom, that solid black storm wall suddenly opened up slightly, and there was Guantánamo Bay.

As we got out of the plane, we both looked up and said, "Thank you, Sir."

When we got to St. Thomas, the commanding officer told me to get ready to fly to Puerto Rico, where I would be put on a plane to Hollywood. MGM was starting *Bataan*. This picture was the story of a handful of men who defended a bridge to allow General Mac-Arthur's escape from the Philippines.

In the film every man in our platoon knew he wasn't going to get out of there. It was just when and how we were all going to be killed. An interesting thing about this kind of picture is that when you read the script you can almost tell how important your part is by figuring out in which reel you are going to die. If you are killed in the first reel you haven't much of a part.

We had a great cast: Robert Taylor, George Murphy, Robert Walker, Sr., Thomas Mitchell, Lloyd Nolan, Lee Bowman, Barry Nelson and Phil Terry, who later married Joan Crawford. It was Robert Walker's first picture and he was sensational in it.

Robert Taylor was the sergeant in charge and, of course, died last. It was a very good experience for me, watching everybody trying to die differently, and how many ways are there to die when you're shot? Jimmy Cagney was the guy who died most beautifully in all his films. He would fall, crawl around, turn back to the camera, kneel down, get up again, try to climb some stairs or something, turn back toward the camera and finally die. He was the master.

Murphy and I had the only different death scenes. He took his plane up, full of dynamite, and then, in a great act of heroism, crashed it on the bridge. I died slowly of malaria, shaking like hell. I think I died about three-quarters of the way through the picture, so it was a pretty good part. When we rehearsed my death scene I was inside

a mosquito net while Robert Taylor was sitting outside the net. Whatever words I had were in Spanish. So I said to Tay Garnett, our director, "I haven't got a prayer in this scene. You've got Robert Taylor
outside the net. Is there any way you could take this mosquito net
away?"

"Okay," he said, "we'll take the net out."

"Another thing," I said, "when he is about to die, let him kind
of go back to his childhood and recite the *Mea Culpa,* not in Spanish
or English, but in Latin, as we did it when I was a kid in Jesuit
school."

He loved the suggestion, and when he checked it out with Bob
Taylor, he was told by him, "I think it's great."

Bataan was one of the top World War II films. As a matter of
fact, it was selected to be kept at the Motion Picture Museum of Art
for posterity, and it also got me recognition as an actor—the Photo-
play Award for the best performance of the month—because of the
death scene, I'm sure. It wasn't the Academy Award but damn good
enough for me.

19

I received my "Greetings from Uncle Sam" in May, 1943.

I applied for the Air Force. I had passed all the tests and was set
to go to bombardier school on a Monday.

Sunday, the day before I was to leave, I was playing in a baseball
game at the Arlington Reception Center near Riverside, California.
I swung at the ball, missed it and tore the cartilage in my remaining
good knee. I had torn the other playing soccer in Cuba. I wound up
in the hospital for three months. A cast was put on my leg, which I
learned later was the wrong thing to do. When the cast was taken
off, my leg was stiff.

They wanted to operate on my knee. I had gone to a specialist
in New York about the torn cartilage in my other knee and I'd learned
from him that, in those years, a knee operation was not always successful. When I explained about this, the Army doctor said, "Let's try
something else first. Every morning, sit on the side of your bed and
stick out your leg [it was just like a 2-by-4 piece of wood], and do it
two or three more times during the day. An hour each time."

One day it bent about half an inch, then, little by little, it kept dropping more and more, and then I began to be able to bend it back some; but to this day I cannot bend it back far enough to touch my ass.

After I was discharged from the hospital I was, of course, sent to the infantry.

As a bombardier all I would have had to do was sit down, look through the sights, study them, press the button and drop the bombs. But I could not pass the physical for the Air Force, so I was assigned to the infantry, and that's a nice place to be with two goddamn torn cartilages.

To make things worse, I was a little better known by then and everyone knew I was married to Lucille Ball, so naturally all some of those guys could think about was that anyone who came from Hollywood was a glamour boy or a fag or something. I had a few fights and wound up in the compound a couple of times. I also spent a lot of time doing latrine duty and peeling potatoes, but I just couldn't let anybody get away with that shit.

Eventually it all squared off. I went through the last basic-training exercises, the obstacle course and the ten-mile hike with full pack. Some of the guys were dropping all over the place, fainting, exhausted or just faking. I wouldn't have stopped unless I dropped dead. When we came back from the hike my knee was as big as a ham again. I was put back into the hospital and later classified for limited service.

I wound up in another camp as an instructor of illiterates. I was there for about six months. I didn't know how many illiterates were drafted into the Army. I really didn't think there were that many illiterates in the whole country.

While I was at that camp the commander had said to me, "You know, everybody is worried about entertaining the troops outside of the United States. But one of our biggest needs is to entertain these kids who have just been drafted. They're going through a tremendous change in their lives. It's the first time, for most of them, that they have been away from home, and if there's anything you can do about getting some entertainment for them, it would be a wonderful thing."

Nobody cared about entertaining in illiterate camps. It was more glamorous to go with Bob Hope to where the real action was. However, psychologically, these boys needed it just as much. There were many kids in these camps who were really mixed up.

"I'll do the best I can," I told him.

Lucy was a tremendous help. She got a lot of people to come. We had Ann Sheridan, Lucille Ball, Lana Turner, Tommy Dorsey and his orchestra, Mickey Rooney, Lena Horne, Martha Raye and many more. We put on the biggest shows anyplace around, thanks to Lucy. She just phoned them and told them they had to come.

The Army woke up one day and asked, "How come this little training camp of illiterates is getting all of these big stars? What is going on?"

In the early part of 1944 I was transferred to Birmingham Hospital in the San Fernando Valley. This hospital was almost completed and ready to take all the casualties from the South Pacific.

Because of what I had done at the illiterate place their staff assigned me to the psychological section. By then I was a corporal. A few months later I became a staff sergeant. My job was to see that these men, who came directly from their ships to Birmingham, had something to distract their minds the minute their ship anchored. These were boys with major injuries, many basket cases, many with combat fatigue who went right into the psychiatry wards. We had been getting the hell kicked out of us in the Pacific, so we had a lot of major casualties.

Lucy again helped out a lot. Whenever a ship arrived she'd bring twenty or thirty young girls from the studios, stars and starlets. It didn't matter, just so they were beautiful girls to serve the boys cold milk. We had found out that if you asked any of them what he wanted first, he'd say, "A glass of cold milk."

We had trucks loaded with cold milk, and these gorgeous girls to pour it as they disembarked. Some of these guys would drink four quarts, one after another, before leaving for the hospital.

B'nai B'rith was a great help to us also. Irving Briskin, who was then an executive at Columbia Studios, and this wonderful organization were always there when we needed them. The way the Army does things is sometimes a little strange. They would build a hospital and tell you to entertain the guys. But we didn't have any facilities to do that. Through Lucy, Irving and a lot of other people we eventually got a swimming pool and a bowling alley, and the Army built a theater with a projection machine. But the seating arrangements were terrible —wooden benches without backs.

Many of the patients at the hospital were not in shape to sit on those benches for a couple of hours. Even I couldn't sit on one of them and look at a whole movie, so how could those poor guys do it?

What made it more ridiculous was that even if we could raise the money we still couldn't get regular theater seats. These seats were classified "Triple A" priority and to get that you had to go through the Ninth Service Command in San Francisco, they had to okay it, it had to be sent to the Pentagon in Washington for final approval, then back to the Ninth Service Command before it finally got back to us.

I figured that if we had to go through all this damn red tape, the war would be over before the three hundred seats arrived. There must be another way to get them, I thought. So I called Irving Briskin at Columbia. "Irving, do you think B'nai B'rith would be willing to donate three hundred theater seats to Birmingham Hospital?"

"I think so, but you need a 'Triple A' priority to get them. I know this because we can't even get them for our own theaters."

"I understand," I said, "but suppose I can get the priority? Then would the B'nai B'rith be able to buy the seats?"

"I'll call you back in a couple of hours."

He called back. "You've got the money, just get the priority and you've got the seats. Nice, good seats, padded, with armrests and everything."

"That's just beautiful," I said, and thanked him.

While trying to figure out how to get around all the Army red tape I found out that, eventually, all the papers came from a girl secretary at our post, who, after you had shown her your authority from the Ninth Service Command, would make out and sign the "Triple A."

I began to get friendly with her, not mentioning anything whatsoever about the theater seats. I took her out dining and dancing a couple of times, and bought her a few drinks. I knew that the theater seats were probably coming in soon. I hadn't done a darn thing about the priority, because I knew we didn't have a prayer of getting it in time.

The following week Briskin called me and said, "Okay, we've got the seat. Do you have the 'Triple A' priority?"

"Yes, sir," I said. "You bet! Do you have the people to install them?"

"Yes, we'll do the whole thing for you. When do you want them? This afternoon? Tomorrow?"

"Tomorrow afternoon," I answered.

"Fine. They will be out there tomorrow."

"Wonderful. Tell them to come to the Administration Building. My office is right next to the entrance. Turn right two offices down the hall."

The guys came out with the seats and I directed them to the theater and said, "Go ahead and start putting them in."

I then called the girl who had to give the "Triple A" deal and said, "Hi, honey! You have my priority thing for the theater seats, right?"

"What?" she said.

"The priority, my 'Triple A' priority for the seats for the theater!"

"I don't know what you're talking about," she said.

"Come on, don't tell me you forgot. I told you a month ago. We went through the whole shebang about this thing."

"I haven't any orders from anybody," she said.

"Didn't I give you the letter from the Ninth Service Command with the approval from the Pentagon?"

"You sure as hell didn't. You didn't give me anything."

"Oh, my God, I'm sorry," I said. "I've been doing so darn many things I forgot. The guys are putting the seats in now, so please make out the 'Triple A.' I'm sorry I forgot to give you the papers, honey, but I'll bring them to you right away. I am just going to go and see that they're putting them in right and as soon as I check the theater, I'll come over and give you the authority."

"Okay, Desi, I'll start making it out now, but please bring me the papers okaying it."

"I'll bring them to you right after I go over to the theater."

By now the guys were nearly finished putting the seats down. The foreman in charge said, "Sergeant, where's the priority?"

"The *what?*" I asked.

"I was told we were not supposed to install these seats without a priority."

"Oh, that's right," I said. "Wait a minute and I'll go get it right away."

Now I was getting it from both sides. The guy putting in the seats was asking for the "Triple A" and the girl who was supposed to give it to me was asking for the authority to issue it.

I went to the girl and asked, "You got that thing made out?"

"Yeah, here it is," she said. "Where's the authority?"

I grabbed the "Triple A" from her, thanked her, searched in all my pockets for her authority and finally said, "Goddamn it, I left it at the office. Listen, that sonofabitch won't finish the job until he has this. Why don't you walk over to my office and I'll meet you there after I give this to him. Then I'll come right over and give you the papers."

"You sure you got them?" she asked.

"Of course. Are you kidding? Why would I say I do if I don't?"

"All right," she said, "I'll meet you in your office."

I gave the guy the "Triple A" priority; she met me at my office and, of course, I couldn't find the papers there either.

"Well, they were here a couple of minutes ago," I said. "I don't know what could have happened to them."

By this time I knew she knew I didn't have anything.

"You sure you wrote to anybody about this?" she asked.

I said, "Now look . . . do you want to see those boys sitting on hard benches, without their arms, without their legs, with broken backs, broken necks and broken assholes? It's not even confortable for you or me."

"You never did get the authority, did you?" she asked.

"Answer me, do you want to see those guys sitting in there on those hard benches? Yes or no?"

"Well, no. But we're liable to get into a hell of a lot of trouble. What are we going to tell the colonel?"

"He doesn't know anything about it. We have the seats. The guy got his 'Triple A' priority and B'nai B'rith paid for them. By the time the Army finds out about this deal the war will be over and nobody will know what happened. Some poor sonofabitch Army clerk, a few years from now, will still be trying to find out how we got these damn seats. You know the way they do things. They send you seven copies of an order, all in different colors, telling you how to save paper."

"Okay," she said, "I won't say anything if you won't."

About three days later the colonel asked me to come to his office. "Sergeant, I hear that there's some kind of controversy about how we got the seats for the theater. Nobody seems to know exactly whether we owe money for them or whether we got a priority or if we did, how we got it. The only thing I know is that the theater looks fine, the seats are very comfortable and the boys are enjoying it a lot more than before. Even the missus and I enjoyed them last night. So what's the story?"

"Well, first of all, Colonel, sir, we didn't pay for the seats. B'nai B'rith donated them through the good graces of Irving Briskin of Columbia Pictures. Now, if you want me to tell you how I got the 'Triple A' priority, I will, but it's quite a long story and I know you're a very busy man. But if you want me to, I will."

He looked at me questioningly and I looked back innocently.

"No, Sergeant," he said, "I have a hunch that I don't want to hear it. God knows where the Ninth Service Command may decide to send you, and I don't think I would like it there."

"As you wish, Colonel, sir." And I saluted and walked out of his office.

They're probably still trying to find out how we got the "Triple A" priority for those seats.

Most of my legitimate duties were with the critically wounded and the mentally disturbed patients. The doctors had told us not to let these patients know we felt sorry for them but to be as rough with them as we could. It wasn't easy to do.

I remember one kid very well. I followed him all the way from the time he got off the ship. He was a good-looking, 6-foot, 2-inch college-football hero from Texas and he had lost a leg. When he got off the ship he didn't want to talk to the pretty girls we always had waiting at the disembarkation point; he didn't even want any cold milk when I brought him some.

"Get away from me, you shit!" was what he told me.

When he got to the hospital and was put to bed, he didn't want to eat. He just lay there and gave the attendants and the nurses nothing but trouble. Not having been shot at or gone through what he had, I felt like what he called me when I had to bawl him out.

"Why the hell are you feeling so goddamn sorry for yourself?" I asked him. "You lost one leg. Okay. Would you like me to show you other guys who have lost two? Others without arms also? You are lucky. So you don't want to eat? Fine, die of hunger, but stop bothering everybody with your complaints."

You don't feel too good about saying that to anyone who looks at you and says, "Well, you shit, you haven't been shot up so what the fuck do you know? You're here in this goddamn hospital having a ball. You never went overseas or nothing!"

"No, I didn't," I admitted.

I really liked this kid. He became a personal challenge. What we were trying to do was to have something different for them to do every day and night. For those who could swim, we had a swimming pool; for those who could walk and bowl, we had a bowling alley. We had the theater and all the Hollywood studios sent us movies and were very cooperative in many other areas.

We also had our own show, a stage show in which we used to do a lot of old-fashioned blackouts. Eddie LeBaron, the orchestra leader, was in our group. Cully Richards, who used to work with Ben Blue, was also there. We would use some of the guys as chorus girls in dresses, as we did in the Caribbean, and we had a band.

We put on a pretty good show with our own personnel and with the patients who could do something. But sooner or later we ran out of things to do. We were trying to figure out what else we could do, on Tuesday, for instance. So we settled for Bingo, but not just ordinary Bingo. Again Lucy and her pals in Hollywood came through.

I said to her, "I want thirty good-looking young girls here every Tuesday."

We would put three guys and one or two of these cute gals at each table to play Bingo. The stores in the San Fernando Valley were also cooperative and gave us belts, watches, wallets, shirts and all kinds of other things for prizes. The patients didn't have to put up anything to win, but they always bought the girls soft drinks and candy on their own.

The prizes were not the main attraction. It was the fact that thirty or forty good-looking girls were sitting around talking and kidding with the guys. That Bingo night was the biggest hit of all. They couldn't wait to get there and sit around with these gorgeous broads, but I really felt like an asshole, sitting up there with all these guys who had all kinds of medals, decorations and combat experience, going "B7, A2, D4."

This Texas buddy of mine was such a nasty sonofabitch he never came to the Bingo games. I had asked him many times, "Why don't you come one night? There are some real good-looking gals down there. Cute chicks."

"Fuck Bingo!" he answered. "Why the hell should I play Bingo, you silly-ass fucking sergeant?"

He always managed to call me exactly what I felt like.

I said, "All right, drop dead. Who gives a damn?"

About three weeks later we were doing this Bingo bit and I saw him coming down the aisle in his wheelchair. They hadn't yet fitted him with an artificial leg and he was looking right at me with a kind of fed-up expression on his face.

I thought, "Oh migawd, now he's really gonna do it."

He came right down in front of the stage, looked up at me and waited until I had finished calling the game.

Then he said, "Hey, Sarge!"

"What do you want?" I asked.

"I want to talk to you."

"All right, I'll be down in a minute. Got to find out who won the last game. We're checking it."

We figured out the winner, gave him the prize, then I turned to LeBaron. "Call out the next game, will you?"

I came down from the stage and said, "Are you going to fuck up this Bingo deal now?"

"I want to call the numbers," he said.

"You want to do what?"

"I want to go up there and call the numbers like you do."

"You can't call the numbers. You wouldn't know how. You have to have experience for that; you have to know what line and what numbers and things like that. Take a look over there on your left. See the blonde and the redhead? Why don't you let me call the numbers and you go over there with those two and play, huh?"

"Sarge, I think you got the right idea," he said.

And that was it! He was fine from then on and eventually learned to use his artificial leg as if it were his own.

Some of our patients were in even worse shape than this fellow. I remember one boy who came out of his stupor—battle fatigue— while Eddie Cantor was singing in his ward. We had a piano on rollers, which we moved around from ward to ward. Right in the middle of one of Eddie's songs, this kid, who didn't know who the hell he was, where he came from, wouldn't or couldn't talk at all, for the first time spoke. "Eddie Cantor!" He was on his way to recovery.

I also was the editor of the *Birmingham Reporter*. I had made a deal with the *Hollywood Reporter* and it was published in the same format—same paper, same style. Billy Wilkerson, the editor-publisher of the trade paper, printed it for us for nothing.

I don't know whether people have given enough credit to those like Eddie Cantor, Joe E. Brown, Bing Crosby, Al Jolson, Betty Hutton, Bob Hope, Martha Raye and many thousands more who, through the USO, did such wonderful things for these boys.

20

Sometime during the latter part of September in 1944, I got a call at Birmingham from Lucy's lawyer, advising me that she was divorcing me. And in fact she went ahead and got an interlocutory decree in October of 1944. I began writing this chapter in November of 1974. I could clearly recollect the year and the month and what happened the day and night before her appearance in court, and also what happened immediately following her being granted the interlocutory decree. But I'll be damned if I could remember why she divorced me. Now it was thirty years later. So I called her.

"Why did you divorce me in nineteen forty-four?"

"Don't give me that," she said. "You know why. You were screwing everybody at Birmingham Hospital."

"Who?" I asked. "Cully Richards? Eddie LeBaron? I would have been court-martialed if I'd fooled around with the nurses. So who?"

"You know darn well who, the Bingo girls, the milk girls, and the worst part of it was that it was me who supplied them to you."

"Well, you were completely mistaken. I would never have done such a thing."

"Ha! [a la Lucy in the show] You would never do such a 'thin'? Ha!"

"Well, honey, you were wrong."

If she had caught me in bed with a girl, unless it was right in the middle of the act, I would have jumped out and demanded to know how that girl got in there. Thank God she never did, or I wouldn't be writing about it today.

"Besides," she said, "why are you bringing this up? It was thirty years ago and the shortest-lived interlocutory in the history of the California courts."

She was right. The day before I knew she was to appear in court seeking the decree—I wasn't going to contest it—I called her. "How are you?"

"I'm fine," she answered.

"What are you doing tonight?" I asked.

"Nothing particular. You know I'm divorcing you tomorrow morning."

"Yeah, I know that, but what are you doing tonight?"

"Nothing special."

"Well, would you like to have dinner with me?"

"All right," she said, and gave me the address of an apartment in Beverly Hills someplace.

I got a pass, picked her up and we went to dinner. After dinner we went back to the apartment and went to bed together. We had a beautiful night. At seven thirty in the morning she got up and said, "Oh, my God, I'm late. I've got to go."

"What do you mean?" I asked. "Where are you going?"

"I told you I'm divorcing you this morning."

"Yeah, I know you told me but you're not going to go through with it now, are you?"

"I gotta go through with it," she answered. "All the newspaper people are down there. I got a new suit and a new hat. I gotta go."

"You're crazy," I said.

"Well, I can't disappoint the press."

So she got dressed in her new suit and her new hat, kissed me and said, "I won't say too many nasty things about you. I'll be back as soon as I can."

"Hurry back, you gorgeous nut. I'll be waiting for you right here."

She went to court, got the divorce, came right back and joined me in bed. This, of course, annulled the divorce immediately because in California in those days there was a one-year waiting period between the interlocutory and the final, and if during that period the principals got together and had an affair, the divorce was automatically null and void.

We both went back to the ranchito in Chatsworth. The chickens were getting older and The Duchess of Devonshire was really getting big. The following day I went back to Birmingham but I was able to go home quite often after work, when I didn't have night duty, plus some weekends. The hospital was only about fifteen minutes from our ranch.

I will never forget the day when I was sitting in my office at Birmingham, looked out of the window and saw the flag flying at half-mast. I didn't know why at first, and then I found out that President Roosevelt had died. April 12, 1945.

That was a very sad day and quite a shock for everybody. Nobody knew Mr. Truman and I guess nobody thought much about the kind of President he would be. I know most of us thought we would now be in the Army forever. As it turned out, Harry S. Truman will go down in history as one of the greatest Presidents the U.S.A. has ever had.

In 1948, when Truman was running against Dewey, I had been out of the Army for almost three years. I got a call from the chairman of the Democratic Party in California. He told me that the President was coming to Los Angeles and he was going to be at the Biltmore Hotel. They wanted to have some Hollywood stars join him for dinner.

He asked, "Would you and Lucy have dinner with the President and Mrs. Truman?"

"Of course," I said. "We'll be honored. Thank you very much. When is it?"

He told me and then he said, "I want you to do something else for me. Do you think you could get some other stars to have dinner with them?"

"What do you mean?" I asked.

"Well, you know, everybody in Hollywood is for Dewey and nobody wants to come to Truman's dinner."

"That sounds ridiculous," I said. "Even if you are for Dewey, Truman is *now* the President of the United States. How much greater an honor can you have than to be invited to have dinner with him and the First Lady?"

"I'm telling you," he said, "I'm having a hell of a time getting anybody to come. You're the first one who has said yes and I've called a lot of people. It's amazing; it's unbelievable."

"I'll try to do the best I can," I said.

Eventually, it became Lucy and me, Humphrey Bogart and Lauren Bacall, Alan Ladd and his wife, Sue Carol, and George Jessel, who was afraid he would be fired because he was working for Twentieth Century-Fox Studios and Darryl Zanuck at the time. Zanuck had the whole studio campaigning for Dewey.

We met downstairs in the bar before we went up to the Presidential Suite. There weren't enough people to hold the dinner in one of the hotel's big dining rooms, so we had it in his suite.

I can't think of any other stars who were at that dinner. Some prominent California Democrats were there, of course, but not more than thirty people in all. Because there were so few, the President was able to have different couples sit on each side of him during the dinner. For example, Bogart and Betty for the soup course, Jessel and his date for the fish course, Alan and Sue for the main course, and Lucy and I for coffee and brandy.

I couldn't help telling the President how well he looked. I said to him, "Mr. President, I have been going around the country doing one-nighters with my band and I think I'm quite a bit younger than you are, and yet those things just about kill me. They're tough. I know what you've been doing on your whistle-stop campaign and you look wonderful, so healthy and with such a beautiful suntan. How do you do it?"

He looked right at me—he was an unbelievable man, so honest, so direct—and said, "Well, I'll tell you something, son. I love a good fight and you mark my words [hitting the table with his right fist to accent each word], *I am going to win it!*"

I didn't have the slightest doubt at that moment that this man was going to win, even though everybody was saying he didn't have a chance and all the polls were against him.

The night of the election I was playing with my band at the Palace Hotel in San Francisco, which was the Republican head-quarters. All the early and even late returns we were getting were for Dewey. Everybody figured it was going to be a landslide for him. I kept remembering Mr. Truman pounding the table and saying, *"I am going to win it!"* I kept taking bets, and as the odds kept getting bigger and bigger, I even got some bets at 10 to 1.

Everybody knows the story of the *Chicago Daily Tribune*'s head-line: DEWEY DEFEATS TRUMAN.

Everyone who was at that Biltmore dinner got a special invita-tion from him to his inauguration. Lucy couldn't make it, but I did and sat in his box at the Washington Armory victory party. I told him I had made a lot of money on the election.

"Good for you," he said.

One of the bands playing at that party was Cugat's. At one time during the evening I saw Cugie down on the floor below the Presi-dent's box trying to get my attention.

I looked down and said, "What do you want, peasant?"

The President turned to me and said, "What does that fellow want?"

"I used to work for that fellow," I said. "I'm just kidding him now."

We finally brought him up into the box and the President signed his program. After he left I told the President that the first job Cugat gave me only paid twenty-five dollars a week.

"Why, the crook!" the President said.

"That's exactly what Bing Crosby told him, but I learned a lot from him."

Years later I had an idea for a television show—a top American statesman talking to young people from all over the world. One of the things that gave me this idea was knowing that a lot of Latin Ameri-can people didn't quite understand certain things Americans did in their foreign policy toward Latin America. Working from that, I thought it would be great if the former President did it. He would have a forum with about five or six youngsters from such different coun-tries as Russia, Japan, Mexico, Cuba, Germany and France. They would ask the President, "Why did you do this? Why does America do that?" And he would answer them from the American point of view.

I went to Independence, Missouri. He received me in his office in the Truman Library and showed me all his mementos and every-thing. It's quite a place.

At one point he said, "Oh, here . . . I want to show you a picture of God. That's him."

I looked and it was General MacArthur.

He continued, "At least he thought he was God."

It was getting to be around twelve-thirty so he said, "Let's go have lunch."

We walked out of the library and over to his car. I didn't see any chauffeur around so I started opening the back door for him.

He said, "No, no. Come on. Sit in front. I'm driving."

He got into the driver's seat and I sat next to him. Just the two of us, not even a Secret Service man. He drove pretty flamboyantly and talked very colorfully. Such as: "Get out of the way, you sonofabitch [sticking his head out of the window]. What are you doing with that truck?"

The truck driver recognized him, laughed like hell and shouted, "Okay, Harry." He was just like anyone else, so natural.

When we got to the center of town he parked the car at a parking space he found, then we walked about a block and a half down to the hotel where we were going to have lunch. He had lunch there every day. That was a regular routine with him.

As we walked everybody was saying, "Hello, Harry, how are you?" And he: "Hi, Joe—Bill—Ed."

He knew everybody in town and everybody loved him. We went upstairs to the suite where he always had lunch with four or five of his cronies.

"Would you like to have a drink before lunch?" he asked me.

"Are you going to have something, Mr. President?"

"Oh, yes, I always do. What would you like?"

"I'll have Scotch and water, please." I had switched from rum to Scotch.

"Scotch?" he asked. "That's funny. I would have sworn you'd be a bourbon drinker."

"Is that a point against me?" I asked.

"No," he said, "it's just that I didn't figure you for a Scotch drinker."

The waiter knew what he drank, two fingers of bourbon before lunch, so he brought him that, me the Scotch and the other gentlemen whatever they drank. Then he ordered lunch, a big lunch, and during all this we kept talking about the TV show.

"I like your idea," he said. "I like working with young people. I think it's a very good idea."

"Mr. President," I said, "what would you say to a boy from

Japan if he asked you what made you drop the bomb on Hiroshima?"

"That would be a tough one, wouldn't it?"

"That would be the toughest one of all," I answered. "That's why I wanted to bring it up."

"Well, I would tell him the truth. I would tell him that it was the biggest and most difficult decision I ever had to make in my whole life, and the reason I finally decided it was right was because I felt that we could save a million lives, both Japanese and American. If we'd had to invade Japan with the infantry and paratroopers, certainly half a million Japanese or more would have been killed, plus the same number or perhaps even more of our boys. Eventually, I'm sure we could have won it that way, but by dropping the bomb we saved many lives. That's what finally made me decide."

All this time I had been addressing him as Mr. President.

He said, "Let me ask you something. Why do you keep calling me Mr. President? I'm not the President anymore. At the most formal I am Mr. Truman. Most people call me Harry. So why do you keep calling me Mr. President?"

I really didn't know. I had never thought about it. It's just a habit, I guess. If somebody has been governor, you keep calling him Governor, and if President, you always say Mr. President. But he was such a down-to-earth man, I knew that I had to think of an honest answer because this was the kind of man you don't bullshit. You better tell him the truth.

I said to him, "I don't know. Let me think about it a moment."

I really thought about it and all of a sudden I knew.

"I know why I call you Mr. President."

"Why?" he asked.

"Because it makes me a bigger man. I'm talking to the President so it raises my level."

"That's in my book," he said. "You read it."

"No, sir, I didn't read it. You just gave me your book. You just autographed it to me an hour ago and then I drove down here with you and I've been with you all the time, so I haven't had time to read it yet."

"Well, when you read it, you'll see it."

And it is in his book—that people still address them as Mr. President after they are out of office, because it makes them bigger. It's true.

The television deal was about set and he liked the idea.

Then I said, "There's only one thing about this show that I hope you agree with me on. It cannot be political; it cannot be partisan. It has to be an American statesman talking with people from foreign countries and, whether Democrat or Republican, he cannot use the show for the political advancement of any candidates of either party."

"There's no way I could ever do that," he said. "There's no way I could keep myself from taking advantage of this for political reasons."

"Mr. President, I mean Mr. Truman, it wouldn't work that way."

He wasn't upset or anything. He had another bourbon before lunch arrived, bought me another drink and ate all his lunch. I had a nice lunch too. Then he said, "After lunch I go to bed and sleep for two or three hours. I'm sorry that what you had in mind didn't work out, but I have enjoyed being with you."

"Thank you, Mr. Truman."

I can't tell you how wonderful this man was.

Number 392-956-43 was discharged from the Army on November 16, 1945. I had been told I would get out a month before. All I had to do was go back to MGM and say, "Here I am."

While you're in the Army the studios didn't pay you but your raises took effect anyway. I had started at $650 per week, the second year took it up to $750, the third year to $850, etc. So by the time I got out of the Army my contract was up to $1,000 a week, for forty weeks. Not bad—$40,000 in 1945.

I knew MGM was making a musical with Esther Williams. It sounded like a perfect setup for me. I was under contract to them; they had been pleased with my job on *Bataan*, so I figured I'd just go over and tell them I was getting out of the Army.

I went to the studio and told Jack Cummings, who was to produce the picture, "Jack, I'm going to be out in about a month and you're doing a picture with Esther Williams and her romantic interest is a Latin fellow. I wanted you to know I'll be available. I'm perfect for the part."

"I'm glad you're getting out," he said, "but I've already got somebody else."

"Who?" I asked.

"Ricardo Montalban," he answered.

"Ricardo who?"

"Montalban," he said. "A Mexican actor we have signed. He's going to play the lead opposite Esther in the picture."

"I have been in the Army for two and a half years," I told him. "This is a perfect part for me and you are going to give it to someone else who's not even under contract to the studio?"

"It's already done," he said.

It was quite a heartbreaker for me. I was sure I was a cinch to start with that film. But I also realized Jack Cummings, a top producer of musicals, was very much sold on Montalban and I worried about how many parts were going to come up for that type of lead. If he was that sold on Montalban, I was going to be there playing second fiddle and doing whatever they didn't want him to do.

I guess it was out of sight, out of mind. I had been gone two and a half years and they had forgotten what they had hired me for . . . musical comedies.

I was still pretty young and during my life, when I had a crisis of this kind, I always turned back to music, to the band business. So I figured I had to get the hell out of there and get a band organized.

The problem was that I didn't think Mr. Mayer would give me a release. He was proud of his record as a star maker. I was his personal find and he himself had hired me.

I owed thirty thousand dollars when I was released from the Army, most of it to the Internal Revenue Service. If I had stayed at MGM I would have had the forty thousand dollars, guaranteed for at least one year. But there are times when you have to look at your life and where you're at. You've got to say to yourself, "This is all right for now, but what's going to happen in the future if I stay in this direction?" I've always been a gambler anyway.

So when I found out Mr. Mayer was going to Newmarket, England, to buy some horses, I knew I had a better chance of getting my release. Benny Thau would be the man to decide. He was in the players' contract end of things.

Before I went to talk to Mr. Thau I went to a very good friend of mine who was the head of General Artists Corporation in California, a man named Milton Krasny, and explained the situation to him.

"I know exactly the kind of orchestra I want, Milton. Latin American music in this country has had a basic fault. When a band like Machito in New York plays Latin music, the rhythm is great but the sound is not melodically good enough—it's tinny. On the other hand, when Kostelanetz plays "Amor," it's lush but it has no balls. My idea is to combine the Latin rhythms of Machito with the lushness of Kostelanetz."

Krasny said, "It's a good idea. Let's go talk to H. D. Hover. He is reopening Ciro's soon."

He told Hover, "Desi's getting out of the Army; he's got a hell of an orchestra and they'll be perfect for Ciro's."

We didn't have the orchestra yet, we didn't have any arrangements—we had nothing. It reminded me of the La Conga days in Miami. Mr. Krasny's quite an agent. When we left Mr. Hover's office we had a contract for eight weeks, guaranteed. We would open at Ciro's with a twenty-two-piece orchestra. I had told Krasny that's what I wanted to get the sound I had in mind.

Krasny asked me, "How are you going to organize it?"

"I don't know," I told him. "Can your agency loan me some money?"

He called Mr. Tommy Rockwell, the president of GAC in New York, and they loaned me $8,000. We needed arrangements, uniforms, a rehearsal hall and copyists. You just can't open at Ciro's with stock arrangements.

When I had everything set, I went to Benny Thau. I was in good shape at that time, but I wanted to look real lousy when I went into his office so that I wouldn't have much trouble getting out of my contract. I borrowed a uniform that was too tight for me, put a little pillow on my belly, plastered my hair down flat, which doesn't flatter my round face any, and the night before I stayed out drinking all night.

The minute I walked into Thau's office and saw the way he looked at me, I was sure I wasn't going to have any trouble getting out of the deal.

"Mr. Thau," I said, "I am about to get out of the Army and I am convinced that I'll never get anywhere in the picture business. I would like my release so that I can get a little rumba band together and start all over again."

He said, "You sure you know what you're doing? You've got a thousand dollars a week coming, the day you get out of the Army, for at least forty weeks. You're giving up a hell of a lot."

"I know," I said, "but I just feel that I have to take a new direction."

Anyway, after being kind enough to try to talk me out of it, he said, "Okay, if that's what you want."

I knew I owed MGM fifteen hundred dollars, which they had loaned me during the time I was in the Army.

"I hate to mention this," he said, "but you owe the studio fifteen hundred dollars, which we would have taken out of your salary at about a hundred dollars a week if you had stayed here, but if I give you your release . . ."

"I know, Mr. Thau." I reached into my back pocket and laid fifteen hundred-dollar bills on his desk.

He looked at me kind of surprised and said, "I guess you were prepared for this pretty well."

"I'd like you to meet my very lovely bride."

Lucy's grandfather, Fred C. Hunt.

There was no way we could have butchered The Duchess.

In *Bataan*, I died about three-quarters of
the way through the picture.

I also spent a lot of time doing
latrine duty and peeling potatoes.

The way the Army does things is
sometimes a little strange.

Our "little rumba band" opened at Ciro's.

Ken, Cleo, Lucy, DeeDee, D.A., and Lolita at Ciro's.

"I knew I owed you money, Mr. Thau, and I wasn't going to ask you to forget it or to carry me."

"Good luck," he said.

We opened at Ciro's two weeks later. It was the first black-tie opening since the end of the war. Hover and I had agreed to make it black tie only.

The band consisted of three trumpets, two trombones, four saxophones, who also doubled on clarinets and flutes, four violins, a guitar, a piano, bass, drums, bongos, maracas, congas and two girls—an American girl, Amanda Lane, and a Latin girl, Dulcina.

We started playing dance music at eight o'clock and then around nine o'clock we put on the first show. Benny Thau had a ringside table and he had brought a lot of MGM stars with him.

After we had finished playing our first set of dance music, Mr. Thau called me over to his table and said, "Listen, you Cuban, is that 'the little rumba band' you wanted to start your career all over with?"

"Well, Mr. Thau, it just kept getting larger and larger as we went along."

"It sounds good, very good, and you look a little different from when you came into my office two weeks ago. You look great!"

"I've been on a diet."

"Uh huh . . . you sure put on a hell of an act in my office. Anyway, good luck and congratulations."

"Thank you, Mr. Thau."

Ciro's was really jammed, thanks to the efforts of Lucy, Krasny, H. D. Hover and, as I said, Benny Thau himself.

We opened with a real fast orchestra instrumental. Then I introduced Dulcina, who was cute, had a hell of a figure, and the same kind of rear action Diosa has.

After Dulcina, I introduced, in his first professional engagement, a young man by the name of Larry Storch. Hedda Hopper had called and told me she had seen this young man while he was in the Navy in one of the shows she had done with Bob Hope and that he was very good, did good imitations, and was very funny. Larry was not only good, he was great! I'm sure by now most everyone knows the name of Larry Storch.

For a change of pace, Amanda Lane, the American singer, a very beautiful and sexy gal, came on and did an upbeat jazz number. Then she did the verse to "Cuban Pete," which actually introduced me.

After "Pete" I just said hello to the audience and thanked them for being there. I didn't try to do any jokes, mostly because I didn't know any. Then we finished with "Babalu," as a conga number with the drum. It was the first time I did "Babalu."

The show was a success. The audience seemed to like everyone in it and we got good reviews. In between sets I sat with Bogart, Errol Flynn, Bruce Cabot and some of my other boosters from La Conga in New York.

I remember Bogie looking over the place and commenting how beautiful all the girls looked and how handsome the men were. Then he said to me, "No wonder they all fuck each other."

21

While I was playing at Ciro's, Howard Welsh, one of the executive producers at Universal Studios, and Jonie Tapps, in charge of music at Columbia and the son of the New York agent who got us into Glens Falls, approached me about doing a low-budget musical picture to be called *Cuban Pete*. It was to be a "B-minus" picture. They had seen me at Ciro's and thought they could make a little picture about a fellow called Desi Arnaz and his band, and maybe cash in on their growing popularity.

I accepted the offer to do the picture because I hadn't done a picture for three years. I would be playing myself and it was certainly good publicity for my orchestra. Most important of all, the Internal Revenue Service was very happy about the money. It would only take me twelve days to do the film and make ten thousand dollars. The IRS would get five thousand. I had made a deal with them to settle my debt by paying them one-half of my earnings after I got out of the Army.

After we finished the picture, the IRS man in Los Angeles came to see me and said, "Hey, can't we get any more of these pictures? This was a pretty good deal. You get a few more of those and you won't owe us a penny."

"If you want to become my agent and hustle some more of them, it's all right with me."

I think *Cuban Pete* served its purpose. By the time I started going around with the band, doing theater tours, at least the people had seen us; and that could do nothing but help our box office. It also introduced our orchestra to Latin America and, I am sure, contributed a lot to the success of our first album for RCA Victor.

Monte Proser's Copacabana was *the* place in New York at the time. Only the biggest names in the country played there: Joe E. Lewis, Jimmie Durante, Lena Horne, Frank Sinatra, Dean Martin and Jerry Lewis. I was thrilled when Milton Krasny told me we were to open at the Copacabana immediately following our engagement at Ciro's.

The Copa always did a big business, and that's easy to understand with the type of entertainers they always had. *And* they also had the Copa Girls—six or eight of the most gorgeous gals you have ever seen on a nightclub floor in your life. I mean, they were really something! You had a hell of a time deciding which one to go after.

Jane Froman was the star of the show when we opened there. When her engagement finished, Monte brought in Peter Lind Hayes to costar with me. I couldn't have been happier.

Peter had just gotten out of the Army also and we had been friends since I first came to Hollywood. Peter's mother, Grace Hayes, had a club in the San Fernando Valley called Grace Hayes' Lodge. She was married to Charlie Foy, the oldest kid of the famous Foy family of vaudeville. Charlie worked there and so did Joe Frisco, one of the top old-time vaudevillians and a great natural wit.

I remember one night when we had a weekend pass and Peter, Cully Richards and I went over to Grace's place. She was always wonderful to us, treated us to big steak dinners. On our Army salaries, steaks were kind of hard to come by.

One night the three of us were sitting at our table, discussing who was the richest man in the world. What else would we talk about, with only thirty bucks a month to spend?

One of us said Rockefeller, another said Ford. I said, "Maybe Du Pont."

Frisco was listening to this discussion and he said, in his stuttering way, "Hold it, f-f-fellas, you're all wr-wr-wrong. The richest man in the world is Andrew M-M-Mellon. He owns M-M-Mellon oil, M-M-Mellon railroad; he owns all the honeydew m-m-melons and he owns half of that song, 'Come to M-M-Me M-M-My M-M-Melancholy B-B-Baby.' "

That was Joe on the spur of the moment. Always original and he never had a writer. One day, as he showed Peter and me a letter from the Internal Revenue Service telling him to appear at the IRS office in Los Angeles, he asked us, "Do you think I should g-g-go?"

"You better, Joe," we told him. "You don't fool around with the federal government."

Joe was always broke. He loved the horses. One of the greatest routines he did in his act was about handicapping horses. He'd do half an hour about how to pick a horse, with the racing form and all the scratch sheets, newspapers, tip sheets, etc. It was hilarious. Anyway, he went down to the IRS. In the anteroom he met Pat Rooney Jr., whose father was also one of the all-time greats in vaudeville.

Frisco asked him, "Wh-wh-what are you doing here, k-k-kid?"

"Well, they tell me that I owe four hundred and seventy-five dollars, or something like that, in taxes and I haven't got a cent."

"Oh, I s-s-see."

Joe's name was called and he went into the office of the man they were both there to see. Joe had never made an income tax report.

He always said, "It's b-b-better not to g-g-get st-st-started."

"Mr. Frisco," the IRS man said, "you owe the government twenty-two thousand, five hundred and seventy-five dollars and fifteen cents. Have you got the money to pay this?"

"Are you k-k-kidding? If I had that m-m-money I'd b-b-be at Hollywood Park." He never stuttered saying Hollywood Park, which is our very beautiful and famous racetrack.

"That's very humorous, Mr. Frisco, but this is a serious matter. We're going to have to attach your salary."

"You're t-t-too late," said Joe. "Three guys have d-d-done that already."

Joe had no property—he never owned a house or anything else. He either lived at the Plaza Hotel in Hollywood, which was managed by an old show-business friend of his, or he moved in with Charlie Foy.

In any event, there was not a hell of a lot the IRS could do about it because there was nothing they could find to take or attach. As for his salary, he was right. There were always three or four guys trying to get to it for room or groceries, but mostly for money he owed the bookies.

So the IRS man had to let him go. On his way out he again saw young Pat, who was still sitting there, looking very worried.

Joe remembered that the kid had said they had him for $475. So he went back to the IRS man he had just left and said to him, "M-M-Mister, there's a nice k-k-kid sitting out there. He owes you $475. Just p-p-put it on my t-t-tab."

Bing Crosby loved Frisco. He used him on the *Kraft Music Hall* radio show as many times as he possibly could. Bing was the first one to tell me about Frisco's policy when borrowing money at the track. If Joe knew you were just getting by, he'd borrow five dollars, maybe. If you got a break in a feature film, he'd borrow twenty dollars. If you became a star, he'd hit you for fifty dollars.

I knew Bing was right, because when I was at Ciro's he would only ask me for ten dollars, but when my records of "Babalu" and "Cuban Pete" started selling, he went up to twenty-five dollars, and when *I Love Lucy* became number one he hit me for fifty.

Crosby he hit for a hundred—he was a superstar. And Bing usually gave it to him.

One day, Bing told me, he had sprung for one hundred dollars and then about three races later he heard that Frisco had put the C-Note on a long shot and was now loaded with money, big bills sticking out of every pocket in his coat, buying drinks for everybody at the Turf Club bar. That's the first thing he always did when he got lucky.

Bing said to himself, "Just for the hell of it, I'm going to see if I can get my hundred back."

He went over to Joe at the bar, which was really crowded, and tapped him on the shoulder. Frisco looked back at him and asked, "What is it, k-k-kid?"

Bing told him, "What about the hundred, Joe?"

"All right, k-k-kid. Hold it, f-f-folks, k-k-keep it quiet."

He then turned to Bing, gave him a hundred-dollar bill and said, "Give us a ch-ch-chorus of 'Wh-Wh-White Chr-Chr-Christmas.' "

As part of his act at the Copa, Peter used to tell quite a few Joe Frisco stories, especially the ones about Frisco in New York. I remember one in which Joe was walking down Sixth Avenue.

Joe stopped at the edge of a deep hole they were digging, looked down and asked one of the workers, "What are you d-d-doing down there?"

"We're building a subway," the man shouted back at him.

"How long b-b-before it'll b-b-be ready?" Joe shouted back.

"About two years," said the man.

"Oh, I b-b-better take a t-t-taxi."

We did three shows a night at the Copa—8:30, midnight, and 2:30 A.M. Sometimes it would get kind of noisy on the last one. The people would have had their dinner and/or late after-theater supper and by now would be boozing it up pretty good. So there were always a few drunks and at times a few hecklers.

Joe E. Lewis was the master of taking care of hecklers and drunks. He could handle them better than anybody else. I wasn't that well learned about what to do with them.

One night Joe E. saw me struggling, and after the show he said, "Desi, I'll give you a tip. When these bums get loaded and loud, you get soft, and they'll shut up. If they can hear you with one ear and talk to and hear the girl next to them with the other, they'll keep talking. But if by talking they can't hear you, they will shut up because they're afraid they might be missing something."

I tried it. Whenever the audience got noisy, I did "Tabu," which is a very soft Afro-Cuban number with no drums and no band, just me and my guitar. I would sing it, even without a mike, walking among the crowd. So if they wanted to hear it, they had to shut up. It really worked. Joe's suggestion was perfect.

One night, though, right in the middle of "Tabu," I heard some coins hit the floor and I tell you, they sounded like cymbal crashes because this heckler had picked that time when I had the audience nice and quiet to throw a handful of pennies at me. I looked and saw those pennies on the floor and was really embarrassed.

I finished the song and then took my time picking up every single one of the pennies. While I was doing this, it got *real* quiet. The audience didn't know if I had spotted the guy who had thrown the pennies, and if I had, whether I was going over there and punch him in the nose, or what. What they also didn't know was that I didn't know what I was going to do either.

Joe E. would have had quite a few beautiful remarks to make and they would all have been very funny, I am sure. But me—I was just standing there. Then I started to flip one of the pennies up into the air, like George Raft used to do with half-dollars in his film. I kept doing this in order to stall until I could think of something. Then, finally, I thought about The Rat Hole bar in Miami.

"You know, ladies and gentlemen, I've been very fortunate in this country. I've had a lot of wonderful breaks. Years ago, when I was in Miami and didn't have any money at all, I used to play my guitar at a place called The Rat Hole for a dollar a night and tips. It looked just like the name implies, a rathole, and the clientele there was certainly not the kind of clientele we usually get here at the Copa, far from it. They were not well educated. They had not the slightest idea of what good manners meant. They were just a bunch of poor drunken bums. But if they gave you a penny or two or three, as a tip, it was quite flattering because they couldn't afford much more. So I'm very happy to know that one of my old fans from The Rat Hole is here at the Copa tonight."

Monte Proser was a great showman. I think he's retired now. His number-one man and manager was Jack Entratter, a big, strong man, 6 feet, 4 inches tall, who could take a punch on the chin and look right back at you without blinking an eye. Not that I ever tried it, but I saw a drunk do it one night and when he saw Jack just staring back at him, he got petrified, sobered up in a hurry and got the hell out of the club. Jack was the man who in later years made The Sands Hotel in Las Vegas such a fabulous success. Unfortunately he has since passed away. He was my best man when I married Edie, my second wife, and a very dear friend.

Nick Kelly was Jack's assistant, a jolly, fat, kind man. Everybody in the business knew that Monte did not own the Copa. Frank Costello, Lucky Luciano, and their "boys" did. Kelly used to brag all the time about his days with Capone, and how he could handle a machine gun. He wanted you to think he was one of the big, bad boys during the Prohibition era. But, in reality, everyone knew that Nick never was any such thing. He was a pussycat. He'd never been able to kill a fly.

When Jack went to The Sands, Nick went with him; and he never missed one of *The Untouchables* shows, which Desilu produced. Nick used to call me now and then to tell me that the show had been good, but that "the Purple Gang didn't pull that job, *we* did."

I would answer him, "What do you guys want? Screen credit?"

They were a fine group of men to work for and they all were very proud of the Copa. The shows they put on were the best shows in New York.

Every new show had original choreography, original music and lyrics written for it, new costumes, new lighting—just as they would do for a Broadway revue.

For my show they had a very lovely Latin motif throughout. The costumes were Carmen Mirandaish. Julie Wilson, a gorgeous gal, did all the production numbers and sang the new lyrics. The big hit of our show, written specifically for our engagement, was "They've Got an Awful Lot of Coffee in Brazil," which Julie and the Copa Girls did and then, later on, I would do a reprise of it.

They were also very proud of their clientele. They did have a very good clientele, except once in a while there'd be one like the guy who threw pennies at me. But that can't be helped in a nightclub. At the Copa there weren't really that many of them, because Monte, Jack, Nick and Lopez, our maître d', kept their eyes on things and saw to it that people behaved. One other time, though, we got the king of the hecklers. He was a multimillionaire socialite from Canada. It would not add anything to this incident to mention the man's name, so I won't.

The advice Joe E. Lewis gave me about singing softly when the

crowd got noisy, to quiet them, worked fine most of the time. Unfortunately, it also gave one of these occasional hecklers a chance to
be heard. The guy who threw the pennies didn't say anything, he just
threw the pennies, then he was thrown out. But this other man from
Canada was sitting ringside, and he was really a lush, one of the
worst drunks I have ever met in all my years in nightclubs.

While I was doing "Tabu," he kept talking to me all the way
through the number. I kept trying to smile and ignore him but he
kept at it and at it and at it. I saw Monte getting up from his table
and watching him. Then the man said, "How may Copa Girls have
you laid already?"

That did it!

Monte, who was a small man, came down to this obnoxious guy's
table, which was right in front of one of the palm trees we had at the
Copa. The palm trees were made of cement, painted white with green
fake leaves.

As he got to the table, Monte said, "Get up, you sonofabitch, I'm
going to punch you right in the nose."

As this was going on I was still trying to finish my soft version
of "Tabu." Monte took his glasses off. He couldn't see a foot in front
of him without his glasses. He took a swing at the guy, missed him
by more than a foot, hit the palm tree and broke his hand.

Entratter, Kelly and Lopez were there within seconds. Lopez
took Monte to the hospital to get his hand fixed, Entratter and Kelly
each picked up an arm of the chair in which this bastard was sitting,
picked up the chair with him in it, took him off the ringside, up the
stairs to the second floor of the Copa, through the hall, out to the
entrance, sat him on the sidewalk and called for his limousine. When
the limousine arrived in front of the Copa, they opened the door,
tipped the chair and threw the guy head first onto the floor of his
limousine. That was another guy who never came back to the Copa.
Monte barred him forever.

Peter Lind Hayes was a big hit at the Copa. Besides doing all
the Frisco stories, he did some of his own material. One special
routine he did was a characterization of a punch-drunk fighter. He
used to call it Punchy Callahan. He would use just a cap but he really
transformed himself into this fighter. The routine had a lot of laughs,
it also had a lot of pathos and a story. It was a classic.

I did the same show I had done at Ciro's. That's where Monte
had seen me and the reason he booked me into the Copa was because
he liked the show I had done there.

So I did a fast opening number with our orchestra, "Cuban Pete," which the Copa Girls introduced, and the guitar number; and finished with the drum and "Babalu."

Monte suggested that Peter and I close the show doing something together.

Peter wrote a parody on "Gallagher and Shean." The gist of it was that he would address me as "Mr. Arnaz, oh, Mr. Arnaz," and then he would say what a nice racket I had. Just putting that big, elongated drum over my shoulder, shouting and banging the hell out of it and stopping the show by doing so.

Then I would say to him, "Oh, Mr. Hayes, I don't know why you should squawk so. All you do is tell a bunch of Joe Frisco stories and then you do this Punchy Callahan bit and you bring the house down."

"Is that so, Mr. Arnaz?"

"Yes, that is so, Mr. Hayes."

"Well, Mr. Arnaz, would you like to try to do my act?"

"Mr. Hayes, it would be a cinch."

"Would you like to do Punchy Callahan?"

"Sure, there's nothing to it."

He would then give me the cap, I would put it on and I would try to do Punchy Callahan the way he did it. Of course I would be lousy.

Then he would say, "That will never do, Mr. Arnaz."

"Perhaps you're right, Mr. Hayes. Would you like to try to do my act?"

He'd say, "You mean just put that big elongated drum over my shoulder, shout and bang the hell out of it?"

I'd say, "Yes, Mr. Hayes."

He'd say, "Mr. Arnaz, anybody can do that."

"Please be my guest, Mr. Hayes."

I would then hang the drum on his shoulder, he would shout "Babalu, Babalu," and then the first time he hit the drum he would fall right on his ass, drum and all, which of course brought the house down. I would help him up and take the drum off his shoulder, and then he would say, "Mr. Arnaz?"

I would say, "Yes, Mr. Hayes."

"I think you'd better continue to bang on your big drum and do your 'Babalu' and your shouts."

"Thank you, Mr. Hayes, and I think it would be better if you continue to do the Frisco stories and Punchy Callahan."

"Thank you, Mr. Arnaz."

"You are welcome, Mr. Hayes."

Peter would then say, "Would you care to dance, Mr. Arnaz?"

"I would love to, Mr. Hayes."

Then we would get into a dancing position, dance all around the floor and up the steps and disappear into our dressing rooms.

I forget who did the leading.

The audience liked that finish very much because I think that it showed that these two young people, who were for the first time costarring at this famous place, were not trying to outdo each other, that they were friends and enjoyed working together. We were both glad Monte had suggested it.

Damon Runyon, one of America's most famous and beloved writers, visited the Copa often and became one of my biggest boosters. Vincent X. Flaherty, who was for many years the famed sports editor of the *Los Angeles Times,* wrote his whole column one day about me based on a letter from Mr. Runyon. In his story, which must have appeared in the sports section, he bawled the hell out of Hollywood for not recognizing my talents. God bless his soul!

Since organizing the big band we had played the top nightclub in Hollywood and the top nightclub in New York. We had also recorded our first album, plus some singles. You could not have asked for a better entrance into the big time of show business.

Between the two places and my record contract, plus some radio guests shots in New York, I had cleared over $100,000. At that point I was very glad that Metro had signed Montalban.

My professional life was doing good and getting better all the time, but my personal life was doing no good and getting worse all the time.

22

Long separations had always brought Lucy and me much unhappiness, even before we were married. The Army years created even longer separations at times. Those actually led to that first divorce in 1944, which happily was not consummated. And now it seemed that our conflicting careers would continue to hamper our lives and create a much-less-than-ideal marital situation. Add to that the fact that we were both extremely jealous and temperamental and we had a real problem, a problem we both tried to overcome as much as we could.

But Lucy's film career was doing very well, which kept her in Hollywood, while unfortunately the film capital of the world didn't seem to be interested in me at all.

I could have stayed home and been kept by my wife, which would have really completed the image most Americans had of us Latins, especially in those days. But if I had done that I wouldn't have been able to live with myself. So I had no choice but to accept such engagements as the Copacabana in New York and the many other nightclubs and theater tours that would follow.

I tried to book the band in Hollywood for as long as I could, but even during the first long engagement at Ciro's, before the Copa, Lucy and I were unable to spend much time together.

Most of the time we would meet at the top of Coldwater Canyon as she was driving to work at MGM—it was a forty-five-minute drive from our ranch to the studio—and the girls who were starring or costarring in a picture always had to report to the studio hairdressing department at six in the morning. On the other hand, I never finished at Ciro's before four o'clock in the morning, and by the time I had unwound and had a bite to eat, I would be driving home about five o'clock in the morning.

So we would meet at the top of Coldwater Canyon about five thirty. If she was late, we just waved at each other. If she had a few moments to spare, we would sit in her car, talk a little while, steal a couple of kisses, and then she'd go to work and I'd go home and go to bed.

Most days we would meet again that same evening at around seven o'clock, as she was coming home from work—she never finished before six o'clock and I had to start at Ciro's at eight—and the same scene would take place at the top of Coldwater Canyon again.

When she had a late call at the studio the following day, or perhaps no call at all, she would come to Ciro's with me, have dinner and stay there until I had finished, and then we would drive home together.

And while I was at the Copa, if she had a week or two off, she would fly to New York and be with me. She was there for our opening and was able to stay a couple of weeks.

But those were the rare occasions. The rest of the time, in particular when we were geographically far apart, AT & T continued to increase their profits from our long-distance and interminable telephone conversations, frequently three or four a day, most of them ending in some terrible argument, in which we'd accuse each other of all kinds of things, because of our jealous natures.

Some of the newspaper columnists didn't help us any in this situation, but, to be fair to the columnists, a lot of the items that they printed were sent to them by the press agent of whatever place I was working at. These press agents had decided to keep building me up as a playboy and a ladies' man, which they considered would be good for business.

One of the items Lucy had read was about the drunken bum from Canada, the altercation at the Copa and what he had asked me about the Copa Girls. Lucy, having seen the Copa Girls and not trusting me at all, wanted to know if I had ever told the man how many of them. I would then get awfully mad at her for accusing me of something based on some remark by this obnoxious character. I would protest that I never fooled around with people I was working with. To which she would answer, "Hah!" But it was true, most of the time, anyway.

Another item that started a beaut of a row appeared in one of the top New York papers by one of the most famous columnists. He wrote that "Desi's pals advised him 'You should be more discreet.' " To which I answered, according to this columnist, "That is the same thing they told King Edward VIII during his courtship of Mrs. Simpson and the king replied by saying 'Discretion is not a quality I particularly admire.' I guess I don't either, fellows." The article went even further and said that, in spite of my answer to my pals, I had tried to heed their advice, but that the next girl I had an affair with rushed to a magazine editor and sold him her story. At which point, this columnist wrote, I had lamented, as he put it, "I can't win."

There were other items concerning Lucy which I would read. For example: Lucille Ball had been seen the previous night in such and such nightclub having a very cozy tête-à-tête with the costar of her current film. This would make me start the argument on the next telephone conversation by telling her that, while she was always accusing me of laying every goddamn broad I ever worked with, she seemed to be having a ball with every costar in her films. She would then get mad, call me a few none-too-flattering names and try to explain that, even though she didn't like it, she had to appear, for publicity's sake, at some public functions and parties. To which I would answer, "Well, then, quit the fucking film business and just be my wife. I don't like you being seen around town with any other man than me. I have not become *that* Americanized yet!"

I must admit that I was an old-fashioned Latin, raised observing and believing in the classic double standard. Your wife is your wife and you want to know that you can trust her and be secure in that knowledge. Your fooling around can in no way affect your love for her. That relationship is sacred and a few peccadilloes mean nothing. Lucy knew this.

I was pleased to read her very honest answer to Laura Bergquist in an interview with her for *Look* magazine. Miss Bergquist asked her, "Was that the conflict? The double standard, the so-called 'machismo'? Machismo is that which supposedly all Latins are constantly trying to prove, that they are good studs, that their sexual capabilities are extraordinary." Which is also a lot of bullshit.

When this lady asked Lucy this question she answered, "No, the 'machismo' didn't bother me. I like to play games, too."

I'm convinced that the reason we survived this constant arguing, fighting and accusations for so many years was because we had something extra-special going for us. We were very much in love with each other, and when we were able to be together, our sexual relationship was heavenly. Also, and perhaps even more important, we had a good sense of humor. We were able to laugh at ourselves and at our sometimes absurd and stupid arguments.

Most of those conversations on the telephone would end with either her hanging up on me or me hanging up on her. Then we would sit there at our respective ends of the country, thinking about what we had just said to each other, and realize how terrible we had been and what ridiculous things we had accused each other of. We would start to laugh, and within five minutes one of us would pick up the phone and call the other to apologize for what we had said, make up and finally be able to go to sleep.

One night, after a particularly nasty telephone argument, neither of us called the other. I was staying at the Warwick Hotel in New York. The New York hotel telephone operators listened to everything that went on, particularly if they knew you. They all knew Lucy and they all knew me. They were in the habit of listening to all our arguments, and were accustomed to the fact that after one of us had hung up on the other, five minutes later there would be another call, either from me to her on the Coast or from her to me at the Warwick.

On this particular night, in which this did not happen or at least hadn't happened yet, the operator herself, bless her soul, called Lucy and said, "Why haven't you called him back? I know he's in his room feeling miserable, waiting for you to call him. He didn't mean any of the things he said and I'm sure you didn't either, so why don't you call him back and make up with him? He's just a baby."

That, of course, broke Lucy up and she couldn't wait to call me back and tell me about the operator calling her and saying I was "just a baby," which led to making up again.

23

After the Copacabana we started on our first theater tour. I had played theaters in the Forties before I went into the Army. I was playing the Roxy when I married Lucy, but then I was only doing a single and was paid a salary—period. These band tours in the theaters were something completely different. The deal was that the theater would provide all the facilities and employees, plus a film. The band leader would provide the stage show and split 50–50 with the theater owner. Because the theater had to pay for the film that would be shown during the engagement, it always booked the cheapest ones it could find—such gems as Monogram's *Who Killed Tilly in the Mountains and the Valley?*

My nut was in the neighborhood of five thousand dollars a week or more. Therefore, if it was a lousy week, I could lose money. Our first three theaters were the Chicago Theatre in Chicago, the Riverside Theatre in Milwaukee, and the Orpheum Theatre in Omaha. I was concerned that my type of entertainment would not do well in the Midwest. What would Omaha, Nebraska, think of "Babalu"?

As it turned out, we had a $65,000 week in Chicago and a bigger gross the second week. We broke Tommy Dorsey's record in Milwaukee and tied it in Omaha.

While we were in Omaha, I got a call from Lucy, telling me that she had been talking to Bob Hope about how well I had been doing on our theater tour. She had showed him all the copies of *Variety* with the reviews and box-office figures, and had asked him if he would consider me and my orchestra for his radio show, which would start in October sometime. She made a darn good agent and of course was also trying to do all she could to keep us together.

We had one problem. By the time Lucy had conned Bob into it and the agents had gotten together, we had about two days to get from Omaha to Hollywood to start rehearsals for Mr. Hope's opening show of the season, and we couldn't get reservations for the whole band and myself, plus the cargo—our large trunks of music, costumes, bandstands, instruments, etc.—on a regularly scheduled airline to make it in time to Los Angeles. You must remember that in those days there weren't that many airlines and they didn't have those big planes either. They had DC-3s.

I asked Fred Ball, who was acting as band manager on the road, to charter a plane.

We finished the last show on the last day at the Orpheum in Omaha. We had packed all we could during the day, but we still had to pack all the instruments, the costumes and everything else we used in the last show. By the time we had done all that and gotten to the airport, it was four o'clock in the morning. We couldn't see our hands in front of our eyes, it was so foggy. We couldn't even find the plane we had chartered. After looking all over the airport, Fred thought he spotted it, and as we came close enough to be able to see it, I saw a big sign on the side of the plane which read: MID-WEST VEGETABLE CO., INC.

I said, "What the hell kind of a thing did you get for us? This guy goes around flying vegetables in the Midwest."

Fred said, "Don't worry about it. I checked the pilot. He's a very good pilot, very well recommended. You know DC-3s are good planes, and besides, this is all I could get."

Well, if that was all we could get, that was all we could get.

As we started loading I recognized it as an old DC-3 Army Transport, which doesn't have regular seats, just bucket seats along both sides. We also bumped into a few heads of lettuce and cabbages and such, still rolling around in there.

We were ready to take off, but the tower would not let the pilot do so until the fog lifted. We sat inside that thing for two and a half hours. Finally they gave him the okay to take off, and we did.

Alberto Marrero, who was my drummer—a Puerto Rican fellow —was sitting right next to me. He hated flying and had never done so before.

This time I said to him, "You've got to fly because there's no way we can make it to the Hope engagement unless we fly. So come on, goddamn it!"

I sat right next to him to keep him calm. He was a mulatto. We were about an hour out of Omaha when he nudged me and said, "Is that supposed to be that way?" pointing to the propeller on our side of the plane. I looked at it and realized that it was not propelling. It was just standing there—dead.

I said, "No, not quite."

I went up to the pilot's cabin and just as I got there he was making a turn.

"What's cooking?" I asked.

"We lost an engine and I think our best chance is to go back to Omaha. That's my headquarters and we can get the plane fixed there. Besides, I don't know any other airport around here at which we can land before losing too much altitude."

"Do you think we can make it back to Omaha?"

"Well, we're not that far away and these DC-3s fly pretty good on one engine. We'll be losing altitude all the time, but I think we'll make it."

I went back and told the boys, "Don't worry about anything. We've got to go back to Omaha to fix the engine, but there's no danger. Just relax, everything will be all right."

I sat down next to Marrero again. Relaxing was out of the question for him.

"How the hell did you let Fred Ball find a plane to take us to California?" he asked. "For Crissake, he couldn't find the address of the right wife to send her trunk to."

Marrero had three "open marriages" simultaneously—one in Los Angeles, one in Chicago and one in New York—and he was referring to the time Fred had made a mistake and sent the trunk which was supposed to go to Marrero's woman in Los Angeles to his woman in Chicago. Marrero's Chicago woman, a Puerto Rican with a fiery temper, realized that these were not her clothes; and when Marrero got there for our Chicago engagement, she went after him with a kitchen knife, aiming to cut his balls off. Marrero turned just in time or he would have been a gelding. She got him in the ass instead, a gash that required fifteen stitches and made him have to stand all the way through that Chicago engagement while playing the drums.

Now in the plane these bucket seats weren't helping his disposition or his ass any.

We finally got the plane fixed and took off again from Omaha. As we were approaching Los Angeles I heard a ring from the pilot's cabin, which meant that the pilot wanted to see me. I went to his cabin. We were just past Palm Springs or in that neighborhood, and we were all pretty happy we were almost there after all the troubles we had had.

As I arrived at the cabin, the pilot said to me, "Where's Los Angeles?"

"What the hell kind of question is that? Where is Los Angeles?"

"Well, I've only flown around the Midwest and I don't know where it is."

He didn't have any navigator or copilot.

"I suggest you put the radio on," I told him, "and try to reach the International Airport in Los Angeles and tell them what your problem is, because I can't guide you there. I'm not a pilot. I've flown in there lots of times, but just sitting in the back talking to the pretty stewardesses, having a drink and relaxing."

He put on the radio. I thought I'd better listen to this conversation between him and the Los Angeles tower. I sat down in the co-pilot seat and put on the other pair of earphones. What I heard was more or less as follows:

The Los Angeles tower asked him to identify himself. Our pilot gave them the plane number or license number, whatever you call it. The tower acknowledged recognition and then asked, "What's the problem?"

"I don't know where Los Angeles is," he answered.

TOWER: Please repeat your last transmission. I don't think I heard you correctly. For some reason or other all I thought I heard was that you are flying into Los Angeles but that you don't know where Los Angeles is.

PILOT: That's correct.

TOWER: Where did your flight originate?

PILOT: Omaha, Nebraska.

TOWER: And you don't know where Los Angeles is, or at which airport you are supposed to land?

PILOT: That is also correct.

TOWER: Do you have any passengers on your plane?

PILOT: Yes, we have quite a few. We have Desi Arnaz and his whole orchestra, a couple of girl singers, the orchestra manager and the band boy. All together, besides me, we've got twenty-four people.

TOWER: Do you know where you are now? Could you perhaps find that out?

PILOT: Wait a minute. [He then turned to me and asked, "Where do you think we are now? More or less, I mean." I told him, "I know we just passed Palm Springs." I had flown over there so many times that I could identify the Palm Springs lights.]

PILOT: We just passed Palm Springs.

TOWER: Could you possibly be a little more specific? Could you give us your latitude, longitude, altitude and your present compass reading, the course you are flying now?

PILOT: Wait a minute. [He really was a good pilot but he had never flown any other place but the Midwest. He called the tower back.]

PILOT: I can give you our altitude and our course. [Which he did.]

TOWER: All right, I've got your problem now. First of all, go up two thousand feet. There are mountains in that neighborhood. And for now, stay on your present course. By the way, what's your air speed?

PILOT: One hundred and twenty miles per hour.

TOWER: Okay, steady on that course, keep the higher altitude, keep calm and we will contact you soon.

TOWER: [a couple of minutes later] The pilot of an airline plane, on his way to Los Angeles International Airport, which just passed you on your left called us, trying to identify who you were. He could not read your plane number. Then, using his high-powered binoculars, reported that this plane had a big sign on its side. MIDWEST VEGE-TABLE CO., INC. Is that you?

PILOT: That's us, all right.

TOWER: Okay, now we know exactly where you are. Keep the same altitude, make a five-degree turn to the right. In a short time you should be able to see the lights of Los Angeles Airport. As you do, start a holding pattern.

PILOT: You mean, just go around and around on top of the airport?

TOWER: You got it. That's right.

PILOT: Okay, we'll do that.

TOWER: There are a few other planes coming in to land which are also in a holding pattern at different altitudes. So just make sure you stay at the same altitude at which you are now and as soon as we can we will assist you in bringing you down to land. We will tell you what course to get on for the right approach, which runway, etc.

This the tower did, very calmly, very efficiently, and we finally landed.

During all this time I was not able to keep Marrero in his seat. He wanted to be up front with me to know what was going on, and by now his complexion, which was pretty dark, had turned much lighter than Lucy's very fair one.

24

Since my arrival in the United States in 1934, even though I was only able to finish high school and never got to college, I had been learning all the time. I learned a lot in those first years in Miami, while struggling just for survival, by observing my father's fortitude.

The time I spent with Cugat was better than going to school to learn the big-band business. George Abbott's tutelage was invaluable. The lousy pictures I made taught me a few things about the film business. You can learn by learning what *not* to do. Staging my own show at Ciro's, the Copacabana, and the theaters we played before arriving in Los Angeles to join Mr. Hope's radio show all contributed to my education in show business.

Now I was going to the best college anyone could find to learn the art of comedy as taught by its leading professor, Mr. Robert Hope, the master showman.

As musical director of his show I would have to attend his first meeting with his writers (I think he had ten or twelve at the time) to find out what music, bridges or background he needed, and whether he wanted a particular number for me to sing with the band or not, who the guest stars were going to be and what type of song they should sing. He might not want a slow ballad in a certain spot that week. He might want an upbeat tune.

Those writers' conferences were very instructive. Each one of the writers wrote a complete half-hour radio show. Then, and I've seen him do this, Bob would go into a large office, spread all these ten or twelve different versions of that week's show on the floor, and crawl on his hands and knees from one script to the other, followed by one secretary with a pair of scissors, another one with Scotch tape.

He had read all of them already, but now he was editing what he considered the best of all the versions, what would be more topical for that week, which jokes would be funnier or fit his style better, and what sketch or sketches would be right for the guest star and the cast. That was quite a long and arduous session for him, but when he finished it, he would have one script out of those ten or twelve versions and that would be the one they would retype and make copies of for that week's show.

During the day before the broadcast he would rehearse the entire show, supervise the music, the costumes, the props, the sets (he always did his show in front of an audience) and rehearse the sketches with the guest stars and the regulars—Jerry Colonna, Vera Vague, and sometimes me. Frances Langford was not with him anymore, so we had to find a new girl every week.

I would audition a lot of them for Bob. One of the girls we auditioned was Doris Day. She was a doll, and I liked the way she sang, but I wasn't sure I should recommend her to Bob because he had been used to Frances, who really belted out a song. But as Doris finished collecting her music, thanked me and the band, and walked away from us, I said, "That's it!"

Her sexy figure from that angle had a delightful action. She became one of the singers on our shows. Shortly after that she was doing so great in pictures she couldn't find time for radio anymore.

Forgetting Doris for now, which is not easy to do, I'll go back to my education during this period. I watched Bob work every week on all the things I mentioned—supervising every facet of that show, actually producing and directing it himself, which he still does.

On the night we did the show he would walk on that stage to the strains of "Thanks for the Memory," with his chin up high, taking those long strides he takes, switching from side to side, looking a bit like a fag, which I personally can assure you he is not, and then arrive at the microphone by the footlights at stage center and take over that audience, as no one else but Bob can.

His delivery is always so great. He tells the big punch line to a joke, one he knows darn well is going to get a big laugh, as if he weren't aware it was going to get such a laugh. Other comedians pause after the punch line, and if the laugh does not come they wind up with egg all over their faces.

One other thing I learned from Bob, and perhaps the most important one, was how to conserve energy. He could let go anytime at all. When he had to do something, he would do it, unplug and relax, like turning a motor off. It's a great gift.

In the car en route to the next benefit appearance, he would ask me, "What's the routine for this one?" I would tell him and if he liked it he'd say, "That's fine."

He would then put his head on the back of the seat and go to sleep, in spite of the goddamn sirens and the car going through traffic at seventy-five or eighty miles an hour. I would just be hanging on, but he'd sleep until we got to where we were going, then go straight to his dressing room, wash his face and relax until we were set up and ready onstage. The minute he heard the strains of "Thanks for the Memory," he would come out there full of pep and vigor.

The ability to do that is what makes it possible for Bob to do the many shows, the benefits and those long, frantic, sometimes even dangerous tours all over the world.

It is one thing that, unfortunately, Lucy has never learned. She cannot suddenly put on those mental and physical brakes.

Al Jolson was one of the greatest entertainers who ever lived. He was a great hero of mine. He could also walk out in front of an audience and, just by his presence, have them in the palm of his hand.

Jolson did a lot of Broadway shows. At times he would come out before the second act and tell the people, "Look, to hell with the second act. It's not that good anyway. I told everybody in the cast to go home and I'm gonna sit down here on this apron and sing to you for as long as you want me to."

The audience would love it. I haven't heard of anyone else who has been able to do that on a Broadway theater stage.

There was a period in Jolson's life in which he was forgotten. He had said he was going to retire, which he might have meant at the time, but after a few years, when he wanted to come back, nobody seemed to want him anymore.

Then Columbia Pictures decided to do *The Jolson Story*. It was sold to them by an old friend of his, Sidney Skolsky, a very well-known New York and Hollywood columnist. Larry Parks played Jolson, but Al sang the songs. If you were around in the late Forties, you will remember it. If you weren't, you've probably seen it on television many times.

The film was such a tremendous success they did a sequel, *Jolson Sings Again,* and Al was bigger than he had ever been.

Anytime he would appear in person in front of an audience, the reaction was just unbelievable. It was a standing ovation every time, every place. And it wasn't like an audience just applauding his singing or his performance; it was more than that. It was as if they were saying to him, "We love you, we missed you, we're glad you're back." There was a lot of emotion in those ovations.

When Al was to be our next guest star we were doing Bob's radio show from the El Capitan Theatre in Hollywood, the same place I worked in *Ken Murray's Blackouts* and where Mr. Mayer saw me.

Bob, being a very astute showman, knew the audience would

give Al an ovation the minute he introduced him and that it would keep going as long as Al wanted it to keep going. Not having more than a half-hour—actually less, allowing for the commercials—Bob wanted to have Jolson and the great contribution he would make to the show that week; at the same time, he didn't want to waste too much time on the ovation or Bob would be forced to cut a lot of jokes.

He wanted Jolson to start singing the minute he introduced him, and, while the applause was going on at the end of the number, he wanted to come out, join Mr. Jolson and do the jokes. So as he was going over the music with me, he said, "Listen, Cuban, the minute I finish my introduction of Al with 'And here he is, Al Jolson!' start the music right away."

"All right."

Shortly after that, and only a few minutes before we were to go on the air, Jolson came up to me and said, "Maestro?"

"Yes, Mr. Jolson," I said.

"Do not start my music before I turn around and bow to you."

The orchestra was behind the singers, who used front and center microphones.

"Mr. Jolson," I said, "those are not my instructions."

"That's what I figured," he said, "but don't start the music because I ain't gonna start singin' until I turn around to you and say, 'Maestro?' "

When Bob said, "And here he is—Al Jolson!" Jolson walked on to the stage to an earsplitting ovation.

Mr. Jolson knew how to milk such an ovation. He would look at the theater and divide it into sections—three sections on the main floor, three sections on the upper floor. When the ovation began he would bow to the center section of the main floor, then he would bow to the center section of the upper floor, followed by a bow to the left section of the main floor and by another one to the right section of the main floor. If the people on the upper floor were beginning to let up a bit, he would look up at the center section of that floor, to the right of it and to the left of it, which would make them all come up again. By this time the main floor might be dying down. So he'd look right at their faces and up they would come again.

He could keep it going forever. Quite a technique. I, with my baton raised, was hypnotized watching it. I could also see Bob out of the corner of my eye, standing in the wings and pointing at me, calling me all kinds of dirty names. I did not have to be a great lip-reader to understand them.

Jolson finally turned to me and said, "Maestro?" And I gave the downbeat.

After the show, Bob couldn't wait to talk to me.

"You sonofabitch, you goddamn Cuban bastard!"

"What's the matter?" I asked. "What did I do?"

"I told you to start the music the minute I said, 'And here he is, Al Jolson!' "

"Yes, sir, Mr. Hope, but if I had started the music, wouldn't that have stopped the applause that Mr. Jolson was getting?"

Bob looked at me with that beautiful, humorous, sarcastic expression of his and said, "R-e-a-l-l-y?"

Then he started walking off the stage and, as he reached the wings, turned back toward me and said, very sweetly, "You shit!"

25

During the last couple of months of that season with Bob Hope, we did his radio shows from many different cities around the country —Detroit, Toledo, Atlanta, Philadelphia, New York, Washington and others. At some places we just stopped to do a benefit, as at Boys Ranch in Amarillo, Texas. We finished the season with his Washington broadcast on June 10, 1947.

On June 12, the orchestra and I started on our own tour at the Midwest Summer Music Festival in Omaha. We then went to the Chicago Theatre for a return engagement there. After the Chicago Theatre we were booked into the Palace Hotel in San Francisco for twelve weeks, and from there we had a remote radio broadcast every night. It was very important for an orchestra to have that in those days. It kept you in front of the public and it helped your record sales.

After one of my shows at the Palace Hotel, the maître d' brought me a note which said, "Mr. Maurice Chevalier would like you to join him at his table." I didn't know that Mr. Chevalier was in the audience that night. I later learned he had been doing a concert tour of the U.S.A. and was then appearing at one of the theaters in San Francisco.

If Jolson was one of my heroes, Chevalier was certainly the

other one. I used a straw hat in a lot of my numbers, "Cuban Pete," "Cuban Cabby," "The Straw Hat Song" and others.

The straw hat is the typical hat Cubans use, as the felt hat is to New Yorkers. It's cool and keeps the sun away from your face. You can see a sea of straw hats in most any town in Cuba. So when I used the straw hat in these Cuban numbers I was not trying to be like Chevalier. Nobody could anyway. It was just the typical Latin thing to use.

"Cuban Cabby" is the story of a fellow who drives a horse and carriage in Havana and who, as he sings, tells the people how much better that is than a taxicab, how much more romantic, so why not ride with him and he'll show you the town. During the number I would walk around the tables, pick a girl at ringside, kneel down in front of her, sing her a love song, kiss her hand and then continue on among the crowd to the end of the song, while glancing back at her, as I went along.

The note from Mr. Chevalier was a big thrill and I could hardly wait to finish the show and get to his table. When I got there he introduced himself (as if he had to) and then said, referring to the straw hat and "Cuban Cabby," "You know, that is very good, what you do. How you throw the hat to the back, catch it with one hand and then push it down over your eyes. How do you that?"

I said, "Now wait a minute, Mr. Chevalier, don't put me on, please. You use the straw hat better than anybody in the world. You are the master, you're identified with it. What do you mean, how do I do that?"

"No, no, no," he said in that charming French accent, "I'm not putting you on. I just don't know how you do it so that it doesn't fall off."

He was the epitome of charm. Then he said, "Something else you do is very good and not easy to get away with. Do you know what it is?"

"What?"

"When you go around the tables and pick out a couple at ringside, you make love to the girl, but the man who is with her does not get mad at you. That's good—very good. I do the same thing."

Years later Lucy and I went to Paris and were guests at his home, about twenty minutes outside Paris. There was a circular staircase that led to his study and bedroom on the second floor. As you went up the stairs there was a series of pictures on the wall showing Chevalier from the time he was a child to the present. At the very top of the stairs the last picture on that wall was a picture of Lucy, me and himself. I am sure that the last picture on that wall at the top of those stairs was changed according to who his guests were at that particular time.

He loved his house. It was not large, but very charming, and the grounds around it were magnificent. He even had an outdoor stage built at one end of the lawn, and there he would help the young French performers put on their amateur productions and then invite a lot of his friends, directors and producers to come and watch these young performers.

At that time he had already done a show with us, on the *Lucy-Desi Comedy Hour*. He was then more than eighty years old.

On his eightieth birthday a newspaperman asked him, "How does it feel to be eighty years old, Mr. Chevalier?"

He answered, "Well, considering the alternative, it feels pretty good."

Maurice also had the wonderful gift of conserving energy, as Bob has. When he did the show with us he would say to me, "Let me know when everything is ready and you want me to do it."

I would then rehearse his numbers with the band, set up which way he should walk, position the cameras, etc. I would act as his stand-in. When I thought everything was right, I'd say, "Okay, Maurice, now I need you."

Then it was just as if someone had plugged him in. He would look thirty years younger and do the number with that inimitable charm, that lovable, flirtatious personality.

When I had what I wanted on film, I would say, "Cut! *Bien magnifique!*"

He would then, like Bob, unplug, go to his dressing room or just sit in a chair in a corner of the stage and go to sleep.

Being able to work with and observe these great showmen that I have mentioned so far, and with the many others that it was to be my good fortune to work with in the future, was an invaluable experience. A great help to me.

After the Palace Hotel in San Francisco Lucy and I had two of the worst years we had ever had. Not because we wanted them to be that way but circumstances made them that way. It seemed that the more our own conflicting careers did well the more problems they created in our personal lives.

She was able to come to the Palace for a weekend, which was wonderful, but again we had a tempestuous time. We'd either make love like mad or fight like hell.

At the Palace I had Carole Richards, a new, young, sexy, exciting gal, as my American singer. Dulcina was still my Latin girl.

"What the hell is this?" said Lucy. "Every time I see you, you have a new girl. The only one who seems to please you enough to keep is Dulcina."

It's true we had many different ones.

"Now wait a minute. I will try to explain."

"Yeah, go ahead and 'splain.' "

"It's very difficult to find the kind of girl I need. She has to sing American songs, plus Latin songs, and have sex and excitement for the type of things I want to do."

"Yeah, well, all the ones you've had had plenty of sex and excitement, for the type of things you want to do."

Whatever made her think I would fool around with these gals I would never know. Besides, her brother Fred usually got to them first.

After the Palace and for the next couple of years, we hardly saw each other and AT&T kept getting richer. The orchestra was booked in every darn theater in the country, with split weeks or one-nighters in between. And Lucy was doing one film after another and also traveling throughout the country with her first stage play, *Dream Girl*, in which she was magnificent and which made some producers wake up to the fact that she was a hell of a comedienne.

We played Oakland after the Palace, then Indianapolis, Milwaukee, Omaha, Chicago again and the Paramount Theatre in New York. The Paramount was where the whole screaming-and-fainting bit started with Frank Sinatra. I was in the Army then, so I wasn't too aware of what had happened and how it sounded.

After the kids got into the screaming bit for Frank, it became a habit, the thing to do. It didn't have to be Frank anymore; anyone they liked who was up there on the stage would bring on the screaming.

The first time I heard this thing, while doing "Cuban Pete," I thought somebody had had a heart attack. I stopped singing right then and there and asked, "What's the matter? Somebody hurt? Should we get a doctor?"

Bob Weitman, who was the theater manager, came up to me and explained that this was par for the course. The kids did it all the time and got their kicks that way.

These youngsters would line up outside the theater at 7 A.M. in order to get seats in the front rows and then sit there through three or four shows. The theaters didn't have all the food concessions they have now for hot dogs, popcorn, candy, soda pop, etc., and the kids had been there since very early in the morning. They hadn't even eaten all day. So I used to make a deal with them.

"I'll tell you what I'll do. If you promise me you'll go home after the next show, I'll send out and get some doughnuts, candy and some other goodies. You've probably skipped school, and if you don't get home soon you are going to get into an awful lot of trouble."

"Okay, Desi, okay. We'll do that," they'd shout at me.

We'd send the band boy and a couple of ushers to get the stuff and distribute it among the kids' own personal fifteen or twenty rows. They'd have their goodies and see the third show. By now it was about 4 P.M. Then, "Thanks, Desi, see you soon," and away they'd go.

During one of the trips from one theater to another we had a terrible tragedy. Our bus, carrying the entire orchestra and the show, collided with a truck on U.S. Highway 20, just outside Rolling Prairie, Indiana. We had just finished playing a split week in Madison, Wisconsin, and were to open in Akron, Ohio, the following day.

Ten members of the orchestra were badly injured. Five of them were taken to a hospital in La Porte, Indiana, and five were taken to Michigan City Hospital. Among those injured were Bobby Jones, my first trumpet player, who used to be Glenn Miller's first trumpet player; Charlie Harris, violinist and concertmaster; Joe Miller, saxophone section and top flutist; Ralph Felices, our band boy, who once in a while doubled on the maracas; and Roger Holler, another one of the saxophone men.

In Michigan City Hospital were Marco Rizo, our pianist; Joe Guttierrez, first trombone, whom I had stolen from Cugat; Fred Dutierrez, another saxophone player; Jack Pickering, one of our top arrangers and second trombone player; and Jack Baker, another one from the saxophone section. That whole sax section was about wiped out.

Our bus driver fell asleep while going about eighty-five miles an hour, and drove right into this big, heavy truck in front of him. The front half of our bus was completely demolished. The boys were lucky to get out of that bus alive, because soon after the crash the whole thing caught fire. If it hadn't been for the driver of the truck our bus had run into, and his very quick action and help, they would have been burned to death. There was only one exit door on that bus and it had been jammed by the crash. The truck driver, using a hatchet, opened a hole big enough for them to escape.

I had always traveled with the orchestra in that bus. This time, however, Lucy was in Detroit, doing *Dream Girl,* which I hadn't seen yet and which I very much wanted to see. I told Charlie Harris, my concertmaster, to take over for me on this trip, make sure there was enough cold beer and sandwiches on the bus for everybody, supervise the stage setup at Akron, and so forth, so that I could fly to Detroit, see the show, spend the night with Lucy and fly back in time for our first show in Akron.

Charlie saw to it that they had everything they needed on the bus before they left Madison and then sat where I always sat, which was the worst seat he could have picked. He was the most seriously hurt. A broken leg, a broken arm, bad head cuts and, worst of all, he lost an eye.

If Lucy hadn't been in Detroit and I hadn't wanted to go and see her, I would have been in that seat. *Que será, será.*

We sued the company which rented us the bus and won the suit, and they had to pay Charlie more than $100,000 cash, plus all his doctor and hospital expenses—still not enough compensation for the loss of an eye.

The accident happened at one o'clock in the morning of the day we were to open in Akron.

I got a call shortly after that at the hotel in Detroit where I was spending the night with Lucy. When the phone rang, disturbing us, I bawled the hell out of the operator. I had given strict instructions that we were not to be disturbed until 7 A.M., which would give me enough time to catch the plane for Akron.

That was a precious evening, after all the months of separation, which I had managed to steal, and I was in no mood to have anyone fuck it up. During my tirade this kind and patient lady managed to get in one line: "Your entire orchestra is in the hospital. Do you want to hear where and why or not?"

I am sure I was unable to apologize to her for my irascible temper. Nevertheless, she helped me find a plane to charter and fly to the scene of the accident within the next hour.

Some of the boys were in no shape at all to fulfill our engagement that day. A few of the others, even though they were not in too good shape, with stitches on cuts, bandages on their heads, plaster casts on legs and arms, still wanted to go ahead and do so.

I didn't see how we could put on our show and play our arrangements halfway decently with some of our top guys missing.

I was just about to give up when I got a call from General Artists Corporation in New York, telling me that Tommy had heard about the accident and was sending me two Dorsey trombone players, Duke Ellington was sending a couple of his saxophone players, and Cugat was sending a maraca player. They all got there in time and we were able to fulfill our engagement.

No one should ever argue with me about people in show business being kind of nice.

26

In 1949 I asked Lucy if she would consent to be married in the Catholic Church. We had been married only by the justice of the peace in Connecticut.

I said, "You know, I just don't feel like I'm married yet."

Maybe that sounds a little corny and non sequitur (I didn't even think I knew that word until I wrote it). But I thought that perhaps, after all the troubles we had had in the past, this might prove to her that I really loved her very much and that I wanted to anchor our marriage down in all ways.

Lucy wasn't a Catholic and didn't have to become one, but she happily took all the necessary instructions to understand what it was all about and she agreed that, if we ever had children, they would be raised in the Catholic Church.

On June 19, in front of the altar of Our Lady of the Valley, a very charming little church in Chatsworth, Father Michael Hurley married us again. This time with God's blessings.

It wasn't a big deal, just our families and intimate friends. We had been married for nine years but when I saw her coming down the aisle with her bouquet and wedding dress and hat, I got as much of a thrill as the first time, perhaps even more. The church and all made it seem so much more real. Lucy looked lovely, with those big blue eyes looking straight at me.

One of our dearest friends, Ed Sedgwick, gave the bride away. Ed was a director at MGM and had been like a father to Lucy for many years. He had directed Buster Keaton pictures, Tom Mix westerns and many of the Keystone cops' hilarious chases and slapstick routines while he was under contract to Hal Roach.

Captain Kenny Morgan, married to Lucy's cousin Cleo, flew out from his duty at the Pentagon in Washington to be my best man.

My mother was Lucy's matron of honor. Groucho Marx sent us a telegram: "WHAT'S NEW?"

The reason we hadn't had a child was not because we weren't trying. We were doing everything humanly possible to have one. I'll never forget the day I had an appointment with one doctor. Maybe it was my fault, I thought.

"I have to have your semen count," he told me, "so go into the bathroom back there, take this little bottle and put your semen in it."

"Wait a minute," I said. "How?"

"Masturbate, and when the orgasm comes make sure it flows into this bottle here."

"I'm getting a little too old for that, Doc. Couldn't one of the nurses help?"

"Never mind," he said, "you're on your own."

I went into the bathroom and told myself, "Well, you gotta do it, so do it."

Fire engines and police sirens going by on the street below did not help my chore any. The result was that there was no physical reason why I couldn't be a father. Lucy had already been examined and there was nothing wrong with her either.

Six months after our wedding in the Catholic Church, Lucy was pregnant. I felt sure God had rewarded us.

One evening at the ranch she suddenly started screaming, "Oh, my God, my God! Honey, I'm bleeding!" She was in her third month.

I put her in the car immediately and started driving from Chatsworth to the Cedars of Lebanon Hospital in Los Angeles, about thirty miles away. I was breaking every speed law in the state when I saw a motorcycle cop chasing us. I paid no attention to him so he speeded up and came alongside, waving his arms and pointing to the curb.

I shouted, "Cedars of Lebanon, *please!*"

He didn't ask why or anything. He just got in front of us and led us all the way to the hospital.

Red Krone, the doctor in charge, and his staff fought for three days to save our baby. I don't think it's possible to experience a more unhappy time than we did.

Lucy was completely shattered. She felt unfit, unable. It was heartbreaking.

The next morning after she had lost the baby, Dr. Krone came to her room and told us, "I know how you two feel, but this is the best thing that could have happened."

I almost hit him. "How in hell can you say that to us, Red?"

"Now wait a minute, Desi," he said. "Let me explain it to you.

When after so many years of marriage the first pregnancy winds up as a miscarriage it means that the pregnancy was not right. This is what nature does to straighten things out. I'll bet you a dinner at Chasen's she will soon be pregnant again and won't have one bit of trouble."

My Favorite Husband was a radio show on CBS that Lucy had been doing for a few years. Richard Denning played the husband. It was a very good half-hour situation comedy, sponsored by Jell-O, and always near the top of the national ratings.

During the early part of 1950 CBS had begun to talk to Lucy about transferring *My Favorite Husband* to television as a series. Lucy said she would do it, but "only if Desi plays the husband." Her husband on the radio show was a typical American guy, second vice-president of a bank and a tall, blue-eyed blond. There was no way I could be believed in that role.

However, that's when the idea that perhaps we could work together on television began to take root. Not by doing *My Favorite Husband,* but a husband-and-wife situation comedy, with the husband character written so that I could play it and be believable in it. However, the network, the agencies, everybody involved said nobody was going to believe that a Latin bandleader with a Cuban Pete conga-drum Babalu image could ever be married to a typical red-headed American girl. (By now she was a redhead.)

"It just doesn't make sense," they all said.

Lucy didn't give up. She said to me, "Why don't we try it?"

"Look, honey, maybe they're right," I said. "Maybe you and I don't make any sense playing husband and wife. As a matter of fact, lots of people said it didn't make any sense for us to get married in the first place. Maybe it's not good for your career, or for mine either."

At that time she was doing pretty well with her radio and motion-picture careers, and I wasn't doing too badly either. By now I was netting way over $100,000 a year, which ain't hay.

By going into television we would have to give up what we had for sure, to take a chance on something that everybody told us didn't have a chance at all. But I have always been a great believer in the wisdom of an audience. The American people are the ones who decide what and who are right and what and who aren't. The great George M. Cohan said something like this: "Each individual in an audience most probably doesn't have the savvy to know why they like something or why they don't, but as a group they are geniuses."

And if you present something someplace and that particular audience likes it, laughs at it, cries at it or whatever else you are trying to make them do, another audience, someplace else, 99 percent of the time will react the same way.

Believing this from my vaudeville and theater experiences, I said, "Okay, let's try it this way: We'll get an act together, and this summer you come with me on my theater tour and let's see what the American people think of us working as a team."

I had a very dear friend named Pepito, who used to go fishing with me. He's retired now but he was one of the world's greatest clowns. His billing was "Pepito, the Spanish Clown." He headlined at the Hippodrome for years during the time that theater was *the* place in New York. He also had done command performances for the Queen of England and the King of Spain. A brilliant clown.

While we were fishing one day I told him what Lucy and I were planning and he said, "Yeas, that's a good idea. I've got a few clown bits which might help you with your act, and I'm sure Lucy would be great doing them."

"Thanks, Pepito, we would sure appreciate it."

We got a suite at the Coronado Hotel in San Diego and he spent two weeks working eight to ten hours a day with Lucy and me. He also converted a cello and a xylophone into great comic props— exactly like the ones he had used as part of his clown act. We used them both in our theater tour and later in the pilot film of *I Love Lucy*. They were two of the best routines Lucy ever did.

Bob Carroll, Jr., and Madelyn Pugh, who were writing her radio show with Jess Oppenheimer, wrote a short sketch for us. As it turned out, this was not the only thing they were going to write for us. By 1959 they had written 180 *I Love Lucy* half-hours, plus twelve hours of the *Lucy-Desi Comedy Hour,* and after that they wrote a number of *The Lucy Show* episodes, then many of the *Here's Lucy* shows. I tell them the next one they'll write for her will be *There Goes Lucy,* and then, I'm sure, *Here Comes Lucy Back*.

I wrote some lyrics for her to do with me on the second chorus of "Cuban Pete" and staged a wild rumba with which to finish that number. She was now ready to join our show.

The tour was arranged so that a true cross section of the country would see us. We appeared at the Roxy Theatre in New York, followed by theaters in Minneapolis, Omaha, San Francisco and others.

Of course she was sensational.

In the cello bit I would be on the stage doing a number and she, dressed in ill-fitting, broken-down white tie and tails and an old felt

I could have stayed home and been kept by my wife.

With the King Sisters in *Cuban Pete*, a "B-minus" picture.

It was just as if someone had plugged him in.

"What's the matter? Somebody hurt? Should we get a doctor?"

Leaving Our Lady of the Valley with Captain Ken Morgan and Ed Sedgwick.

The reception at the ranch: (left to right) Ed Sedgwick, Lolita, D.A., Lucy, Cleo, Ken.

"They call me Sally Sweet. I'm the Queen of Delancey Street."

hat, would come through the audience, carrying this cello down the center aisle. As the audience recognized her it created quite a commotion. I would pretend I didn't know what this commotion was all about and who was interrupting my show.

"What's going on out there? Please put the lights on."

She would then be spotted in the audience, asking, "Where is Dizzy Arnazy?" in a husky man's voice.

Then she would come onstage, look me up and down and say, "Are you Dizzy Arnazy?"

"Desi Arnaz," I would correct.

"That's what I said, Dizzy Arnazy."

Giving up, I would say, "Look, mister, what is it you want?"

"I want a job with your orchestra."

"Oh, are you a musician?" I asked.

"Yeah, that's right."

Then she would go into the band, starting to take the cello out of its case, climbing over music stands, hitting some of the guys in the head with the case as she was turning around and looking for a place to sit, until I had to go to her, saying, "Wait a minute! Wait a minute! Come back here!" And I would take her up front again.

She'd say, "What's the matter?"

"I have to see your credentials," I'd say.

She would then do a big take, look shocked and cross her arms over her bosom.

She is one of the greatest pantomimists in the world and a clown at heart. She had the routines Pepito had given her down pat. Every move she made, everything she did with the prop cello, while giving me an audition, got nothing but big yaks.

After the cello she played the xylophone, not as Lucy but as a seal, a seal playing the xylophone. Later in the show, during the second chorus of "Cuban Pete," she would come out with a "Frankie and Johnny" outfit, swinging a purse and singing, "They call me Sally Sweet/I'm the Queen of Delancey Street/When I start to dance, everything goes/Chick, chicky boom/Chick, chicky boom/Chick, chicky boom," and with the last "boom," she would do a big bump and knock the straw hat off my head. Then we would do the wild rumba dance to exit with.

This whole act, plus the short sketch that was written for us, and Pepito himself, eventually became the pilot show of *I Love Lucy*.

The tour was a tremendous success and convinced Lucy and me that the people liked us as a team, which meant more to us than whatever the executives of one network or another thought.

After the theater tour we came back to California. The orchestra and I were to open the first big nightclub in Palm Springs, The Chi Chi. Lucy was negotiating to star in Cecil B. DeMille's *The Greatest Show on Earth*.

We opened at The Chi Chi in October. Lucy came down and spent a couple of weeks with me. While I was there, Harry Ackerman, the head man for CBS on the West Coast, spoke to me about an idea Guy della Cioppa, his right-hand man in the radio department, had about a show to be called *Tropical Trip*. It was to be a musical quiz show with three contestants and the jackpot prize was a two-week vacation, all expenses paid, to a different country in Latin America each week.

He also explained to me that this was to be a "sustaining show," which meant they didn't have a sponsor yet, so the budget would be small. Sustaining shows are programs that the networks pay for themselves and use to fill certain time periods of the programming when they are not able to get a sponsor. They also use them to promote their big shows and to do public-service commercials, as for The March of Dimes, Heart Fund and Christmas Seals.

Mr. Ackerman told me that *Tropical Trip* was scheduled for Sunday afternoons, preceding Edgar Bergen and Charlie McCarthy, Jack Benny and all their other big guns on Sunday night. I wasn't particularly interested in his idea. I knew that by the time I paid for the band, the arrangements and the copyists, I wouldn't have much left.

I did like the *theme* of the show. It went hand in hand with President Roosevelt's Good Neighbor Policy of the early Forties, so ably assisted by the Rockefeller Foundation, but I could not afford to be as philanthropic as the Rockefellers. Fortunately, we had been doing pretty well until now.

Shortly after we finished at The Chi Chi, late in November of 1950, we returned to Ciro's in Hollywood. A couple of weeks later we found out Lucy was pregnant. This was by far the most important thing in our lives. Neither of us thought that this could be true, that she was really pregnant. But Dr. Joe Harris—his partner, Dr. Krone, was out of the country—said, "Yes, there's one on the way and you and Desi owe my partner a dinner at Chasen's."

I called Mr. Ackerman at CBS and asked him if he was still interested in our orchestra and myself doing the radio show Mr. della Cioppa had in mind; if he was, I would be pleased to come in and talk to them. He said he was, and we made an appointment.

I went in and finalized the deal to start doing *Tropical Trip* early in January, 1951. Mr. Ackerman was right. The budget was very small, but it did keep the band together and it kept me home. It also gave me a chance to build an addition to our Chatsworth house with my friend Earl Leverich, a professional builder. We were building a nursery, of course, with two bedrooms, a large bathroom, playroom and patio—the works. Earl made me nail every damn shingle on that roof.

Lucy at the same time was having some trouble with Harry Cohn at Columbia Pictures, where she was under contract, and still had one more film to make for them. Harry Cohn was one of the old-time pioneer movie moguls and a darn good picture maker. But he would always try to get the best of you.

Lucy was trying to get him to let her do *The Greatest Show on Earth* for Mr. DeMille, but she was not getting anyplace. Time and again she asked him, "Why won't you let me make this picture? You have loaned me out for lousy ones before, when it didn't matter."

Harry had to pay her $85,000 for that last film on her contract. I'm sure if he had asked Lucy to let him out of that commitment, she would have agreed in order to be able to do the DeMille picture. That was too simple for Harry. He wanted to outsmart her.

So he sent her a script called *The Magic Carpet*. It was a terrible script. It was the kind of thing that they wanted you to refuse to do, in order to break your contract. It was what they called a contract breaker.

She asked me to read this thing. I read it and said, "You would have to be crazy to do this thing."

"All I have to do to get the eighty-five thousand dollars," she said, "is appear. It only has a six-day schedule." (Even *Cuban Pete* had a twelve-day schedule.)

"I can't do the DeMille picture anymore because by the time Mr. DeMille is ready to go with *The Greatest Show on Earth* I'll be so big with your child that I won't be able to get away with it."

"What you're trying to tell me," I said, "is that you're going to go in there, don't tell anybody you're pregnant, do this crummy *Magic Carpet* picture, get your eighty-five thousand dollars and get the hell out of your Columbia contract."

"Why not?" she said.

"Yeah, why not?" I said. "The thing is so lousy I'm sure nobody will ever see it, so it can't do you much harm."

She was to play one of those harem girls, lying on a divan in a skimpy costume, while the slaves fed her grapes.

"Go ahead and do the goddamn thing."

She sent word to Columbia that she would be delighted to do this picture. Those harem girls are supposed to be a little plump, but Lucy was getting quite a bit plumper. The wardrobe girl couldn't figure out why they had to let out the costumes every day.

"Just tell them it's the Cuban dinners I cook for you."

She finished the picture for Columbia. Sam Katzman was the producer, a very nice man who used to do "B" pictures and serials, but since then he has done some very good films. He tried to do everything possible not to have Lucy do this picture. Lucy's salary of $85,000 was bigger than his whole budget.

"Why don't you let us rewrite it?" he asked. "I'm sure if we had a little more time we could make it much better for you."

But Lucy, knowing that she had to get it over with in a very short time, said, "Don't change a word. It's just beautiful. I like it the way it is."

After she finished the last scene in the picture she phoned Harry Cohn from the set and said, "Harry?"

"Yeah."

"This is Lucille Ball."

"What in hell do you want?"

"I just want you to be the first to know that Desi and I are going to have a baby."

To which Mr. Cohn answered, "Why, you bitch. You screwed me, didn't you? Why didn't you tell me before the picture?"

By now there was no chance for Lucy to do Mr. DeMille's picture, which was to be released by Paramount. DeMille's reaction to Lucy's having a baby was a little different from Mr. Cohn's. Lucy was very honest with him and told him the whole story about why she had done this lousy picture for Harry just to get her $85,000 and get out of her contract there.

I saw DeMille about a month afterward at a Hollywood affair. Mr. DeMille came up to me and said, "Congratulations, Mr. Arnaz. You are the only man who has ever screwed his wife, Cecil B. De-Mille, Paramount Pictures and Harry Cohn, all at the same time."

27

Shortly after we started doing *Tropical Trip,* William S. Paley, the head of CBS, agreed to do our television pilot show. He told his people, "I think the viewers might believe those two could be married. The audiences throughout the country really liked them working as a team on that theater tour they did, and besides, they have been married for ten years."

The first script was not written about Lucy and Ricky Ricardo. It was written about Lucille Ball and Desi Arnaz. It was a funny script and it was well written, but she was playing Lucille Ball, a successful movie actress, married to a Cuban orchestra leader who was also very successful. So we would really be playing ourselves in that script.

The fun in the script was about the trouble this couple had in trying to be together. I would be on the road most of the time and she would be working at the studio; or if I was working in a Hollywood nightclub, we would meet at 5:30 A.M. at the top of Coldwater Canyon, she going to the studio and I returning from the nightclub on the way home to bed. In other words, just like what was actually happening in our lives.

In addition to that, the first script had to do with our anniversary. We had carefully planned to spend it together quietly. We had been planning it for a long time before we found out that *Life* magazine was to do a cover story about us on that date. We received word at the last minute that a photographer and writer would be coming to the house to spend our anniversary with us, and this sort of loused up our planned celebration.

As I said, it was funny and well written, but I felt that the television audience would not identify themselves with this kind of a couple. They would think, "So they're going to louse up their anniversary. So what! They're going to get a cover on *Life* magazine. Why in hell are they so unhappy? That is a pretty good break!"

I am certain there are couples in our industry, whether in films or on the stage, who would get a kick out of that situation and could identify with it. But I have always been of the opinion that you should not do a show for the people who can afford to go to "21" in New York or to Dave Chasen's in Beverly Hills, but instead for those people who cannot go to such places, and that would be most Americans.

So we changed the format to a more down-to-earth situation. Instead of my part being that of Desi Arnaz, the successful orchestra leader, he became Ricky Ricardo, also an orchestra leader, but a struggling one, just trying to make it. We took Lucy completely out of show business and made her just a plain housewife who would have liked to get into show business, but had no talent at all.

In the second show—they were not in the pilot—we would have neighbors, Fred and Ethel Mertz. The episode would include all the problems that a husband and wife normally would have. Everybody understands those. They would also understand the relationship with neighbors, and the battle of the sexes—Lucy and Ethel versus Ricky and Fred.

That is how we eventually arrived at the *I Love Lucy* format.

Jess Oppenheimer, Bob Carroll, Jr., and Madelyn Pugh had seen our theater act, and they wrote the pilot script around it. We did it live at CBS Sunset and Gower headquarters in their large Studio A. In those days—1951—most shows were done that way. There was very little television on film, almost none.

A pilot is a production that is intended to show a network, possible sponsors and their advertising agencies what your format is and what you intend to do in the future with this kind of material. It is like an audition. The network takes this half-hour and goes to the various advertising agencies and shows them the kinescope, saying, "CBS likes this show and we are planning to make a series, starring Lucille Ball and Desi Arnaz in this kind of situation comedy."

We had also given CBS six or eight more story outlines which Jess, Bob and Madelyn had written so that they could tell the interested parties what would follow in other episodes.

The pilot went back to CBS in New York City and within forty-eight hours it was sold to Philip Morris. The Biow Company was the advertising agency. The price of each episode in the series would be $19,500, and we would make thirty-nine of them for that first season, 1951–1952, then Philip Morris would have the option either to continue the series for a second year or not. Today each episode would cost $100,000 or more, and you would make only twenty or twenty-two and fill the rest of the series with repeat shows.

The selling of our first pilot was the most thrilling experience. A network, a sponsor and a time period, Monday night at nine o'clock, all within two days. Unbelievable!

One month later I received a call from Mr. Milton Biow in New York. He asked me, "When will Lucy and you be moving to

New York to start the series?" That was a very shaking question.

Everything we had done, trying to work as a team, we had done in order to see if we could at last be together and stay home. And now in particular, when we were anxiously awaiting the arrival of our first child, this man was asking us when we were going to be in New York.

At the time I received that call from Mr. Biow, Lucy was in the last two months of her pregnancy. She used to waddle out of the house, as big as an elephant, look up at me and Earl on the roof and say, "Hurry up, you guys. This baby is not going to wait forever. Cut out the beer breaks."

"Don't worry, sweetheart, we'll make it."

When I told Mr. Biow that we had no intention of moving to New York to do the series, he countered with "You can't do the show in California. If you did, all we would get on the East Coast would be the kinescope and the quality of that is terrible."

There was no coaxial cable from the East Coast to the West Coast. What we got on the West Coast was a kinescope and the quality was terrible. On the East Coast, where all the big shows were done live, the quality, of course, was good. Now, thanks to the cable and the communication satellites, viewers get the picture live from anywhere in the world, and the quality is the same on either coast of the United States or in London, Japan or Argentina. Something I have never been able to figure out is how you can turn a knob on the set at home and watch what is happening as it happens, wherever it is happening. It is way beyond my comprehension. But then, I have never really believed that anybody got to the moon. The Houston Space Center worked it out somehow with Disney's animation department.

Mr. Biow continued, "There are more people looking at shows east of Chicago than in the rest of the entire country west of Chicago. I'm sure you understand that the sponsor wants the show to be seen at its best by the biggest audience. We will not accept the show being live from California, with only the kinescope coming to the East Coast."

I understood all right, but we did not want to move to New York. On the other hand, we certainly did not want to lose our sponsor.

There must be a way, I thought.

Then Someone from somewhere touched my shoulder and whispered, "Film."

That was it! Of course! We would do it on film! We would be

able to make as many prints as needed and the whole country would get the same top quality. The sponsor bought the film idea immediately. CBS didn't argue about it much, but they did say, "We like Lucy working in front of an audience. That's the way she does her radio show and she's a lot better with an audience than without one. If you do it on film, she will not be able to work in front of an audience and we do not want that."

I couldn't argue with them. They were right. She *is* much better in front of an audience.

So I said, "Well, why don't we do it on film in front of an audience?"

"What the hell is that?" they answered.

I didn't know what the hell "that" was either, but I had already said it, so I said it again.

"We'll do it on film in front of an audience, that's all."

"How do you do that?" they asked.

Nobody had done a situation comedy on film in front of an audience. I didn't have the slightest idea of how you would do that, either. But I thought, Live shows are done in front of an audience, so why not a filmed show?

There was one other question they wanted answered. "How much is that going to cost—to film it in front of an audience?"

Again, I didn't know. I figured we would have to stage it as a play and while doing it photograph it simultaneously with three or four 35-mm motion-picture cameras—I had promised top quality so 16 mm was out—and record it all at the same time in front of an audience. So, trying to sound as if I knew what I was talking about, I took a figure out of the air and told them, "At least five thousand dollars more, twenty-four thousand, five hundred dollars for each episode."

That price sounds ridiculously cheap today, but it was big, big money in those days. The negotiations went back and forth until Philip Morris agreed to go up two thousand dollars. CBS agreed to put up another two thousand as their contribution to the budget.

I'll never forget what came next. As I mentioned, I was doing *Tropical Trip* on CBS radio, when Don Sharpe, who was our agent at the time, came to a rehearsal and said, "I'm sure they'll let you do it the way you want, but you and Lucy will have to take a cut in salary."

"How much of a cut?" I asked.

"A thousand dollars a week. That will make up the five thousand dollars more for each show."

At that time, our deal was five thousand dollars per episode for both of us, plus 50 percent of the profits, if eventually there would be any profits. Being a long-shot player, I said, "Okay, Don, we'll take the thousand-dollar cut for the first thirty-nine shows, if you can get them to agree that we will then own all the shows of this year and all the shows of all future years, if any, one hundred percent."

We really were not gambling too much money. In our bracket, another $39,000 in income would mean that, after taxes, we could keep only $4,000, or possibly $5,000 at the most. In reality, we would be buying the other 50 percent of the *I Love Lucy* films for $5,000 or less. CBS agreed.

A few years later we sold the films back to them for $4,500,000. One of the times that trying to make a plus out of a minus (as my father did with the broken tiles) paid off—and what a payoff! The biggest jackpot of our lives!

I think the reason CBS agreed is because they did not think that filming the shows the way we wanted to do them was going to work. So, what the hell? they probably thought. Let them struggle for a few episodes and they'll soon be glad to come to New York and do them live. And, if their way happens to work out, so what?

Nobody was giving much thought to residuals in those days, or what a film library could be worth in the future. Therefore, I'm sure, they felt that giving away 50 percent ownership meant nothing anyway.

To be honest with you, we never dreamed it would either. I just knew we could do a better show on film. Lucy would be better photographed and whatever mistakes were made during the filming could be corrected by retakes.

In those days I had seen so many TV shows with such ridiculous mistakes in them that they actually ruined the story for you—like a corpse getting up and walking away while the camera was still photographing him. In a revue or variety show, those kinds of mistakes sometimes even add to the fun. But we were not doing those types of shows, we were doing situation comedy, which, to be funny and real, also has to be believable. So I knew that our final product on film had to be better than doing them live.

I also felt that a family sitting at home, watching a show, couldn't care less about how that show was mechanically done, live or on film. They would only be interested in watching a good show and being entertained by it.

By wanting to stay home to await the arrival of our first child, not lose our sponsor, and accommodate CBS's wishes to have Lucy work in front of an audience, I had concocted "that" way of doing it. And now my neck was stretched way out to there. I had made them all believe that I knew what I was talking about, when in reality I didn't have the first clue.

I told Lucy my dilemma and then added, "How about it, Red, do you have any thoughts or ideas?"

She said, "Well, it's going to be photographed on film, same as a motion picture—right?"

"Sí, Señora."

"Well, then, Señor, you better start by getting someone who knows how to photograph it."

"Thank you, Red, you just gave me my first clue."

28

I had met Karl Freund while Lucy was costarring with Red Skelton in *DuBarry Was a Lady* at MGM.

Mr. Freund was the director of photography for that film and a great artist. Neither Garbo nor Hepburn would make a picture without Karl. He was a big, fat, jolly man who waddled around all over the set carrying a Thermos full of martinis and giving orders in his thick German accent. I never saw him drunk though, and he was a kind and brilliant man. Everybody called him Papa.

He had won the coveted Academy Award for *The Good Earth*, which starred Luise Rainer and Paul Muni. He was also a very inventive man, which is the reason I thought of him first.

It was Karl who first successfully exploited the moving camera. He used dollies and cranes for the film *The Last Laugh,* starring Emil Jannings, which Papa photographed in Germany in 1924.

A *dolly* is a platform with four wheels, which fit on tracks, the camera mounted on the platform. The tracks are laid level to keep the camera from shaking.

Motion-picture studio floors used to be all wooden and not smooth at all. Even now a lot of them are still that way. On the dolly you can move the camera straight back or forward as need be. (Zoom lenses didn't make their appearance until the late Fifties.)

Before the invention of dollies a camera was placed on a tripod and remained stationary wherever you put it, and if you needed a closer shot or a different angle, you picked up the camera and moved it to the location needed for that.

A *crane* is also a platform, only larger and more solid, with bigger wheels on heavier tracks to be able to support the camera mounted on the crane, which you can raise or lower as you wish. There are small cranes which can only go up to ten feet, and there are others which can go up to twenty-five or thirty feet or more, depending on what kind of shot you are trying to film. Busby Berkeley almost went into orbit for some crane shots in those great musicals he directed for Warner Brothers.

In 1942 Papa also introduced his exposure meter, which tells you if the lighting you have is right for the type of film you are using. His exposure meter is the one that most directors of photography used and are still using.

He was also credited with the invention of the *process shot*. A process shot is a way to show a person driving in the mountains or flying a plane, without ever leaving the studio stage. This is done by having a big transparent screen on the stage. A few feet in back of that screen is a motion-picture projection machine, which projects the background you need, whether it be stationary or moving, for that scene on the screen. You have filmed the background earlier. In front of that screen you put the car and the people in it or the plane and its pilot and passengers. You then photograph the whole thing with a 35-mm motion-picture camera, which is placed facing the big screen and including whatever you put in front of it, which gives you the effect that the car is traveling or the plane is flying, or perhaps just that a group of people is standing and looking up at the Eiffel Tower in Paris, the ruins of Rome or the Great Wall of China.

Freund was the type of photographer I needed for "that" way of doing the *I Love Lucy* shows. At this point in time he was in Washington, D.C., working for the government in the Film Research and Development laboratory. I called Karl and told him what I wanted to do.

"I want to stage the show as a play, film it in continuity in front of an audience of perhaps three hundred people, using three thirty-five-millimeter cameras and recording the audience's laughter and reactions simultaneously with our dialogue, all cameras synchronized on one sound track so that we can cut from the master shot to a medium shot or to a close-up when we later edit the film."

"You cannot do it," he said. He wasn't a man of many words.

"Why, Papa?" I asked gently.

"It's impossible. You're asking me to use one camera to photograph the master shot, the full set with whoever is in it? Correct?"

"Correct."

"At the same time that the second camera is taking a medium shot, closer than the master and with only two, three or four people?"

"That's right."

"While the third camera is taking a close-up of Lucy or you or whoever?" he asked.

"Yes, sir."

"You cannot do it."

"Why not?"

"Because, my dear boy, you must light for the master shot one way, light for the medium shot another way and light for the close-ups in yet another way. You can't photograph all three angles at the same time and get any kind of good film quality. On top of that you want to do it in front of an audience."

"Well, I know that nobody has done it up to now, but I figured that if there was anybody in the world who could do it, it would be Karl Freund."

"That's very flattering."

"My God, Papa," I said, "you showed how to use a moving camera, you invented the light meter and the process shot and I understand you are now developing a tiny camera for the Army Medical Department, which a person can swallow and which takes a color-film picture on the way through the digestive process—the small intestine, the large intestine and the anus, as it comes out that other end. For such a genius, what I want you to do should be a pushover."

"Well, thanks for thinking that about me," he said, "but you know that Lucy's no chicken. You want her to look good, don't you?"

"Of course."

"Well, then, for her close-ups I would have to use special lighting, put a little gauze on the lens . . ."

I interrupted, "I don't know that end of it, Papa. You are the master at that."

I could feel I was getting to him.

He said, "Oh—well—now, thanks, but believe me, Desi, it would be very difficult. We would have to try and design a whole new way of lighting, and I still don't think . . ."

I almost had him.

"I don't care what you have to do, Papa," I said, "I'll get you whatever you need."

"When do we have to do this thing?" he asked.

Now I knew I had him.

"To meet our air date and be a few shows ahead in case anyone gets sick or something, we should be doing them just as soon as possible."

Finally he said he would come out and discuss it. Then he asked me, "Where are you going to do this?"

"What do you mean by that?"

"Where are you going to shoot it? You can't take three hundred people into a studio stage while they're filming. They won't let you. And I doubt if you could find a theater where you could build three or four sets across the stage, which you would have to do if you want good, solid, realistic sets and not that stuff they use on live TV, where you open a door and the whole wall shakes."

"That is a problem, isn't it?" I said. "I tell you what—when you come out here we'll look at different places, discuss all problems and then, if you still think it is beyond your capabilities, we'll forget it."

That was all he needed to hear. He was a proud man and rightly so.

Then I added, "By the way, Papa, there's one other thing I've got to tell you. I haven't any money."

Silence. Finally a flat reading: "You haven't any money?"

I knew he had been making fifteen hundred dollars a week at MGM, guaranteed for fifty-two weeks a year. In those days, hell, even today, that's a very top salary for a director of photography and he was worth every dollar.

"You have no money to pay me a salary?" he asked.

"Well I'll have to pay you basic union scale, of course."

"Basic union scale for Karl Freund?"

"Look, Papa, we don't have to publicize it. And if this works, I give you my word that within a year or much less you'll be making just as much as, if not more than, you were making at MGM. Besides, I know that if you are going to try to do this, you won't be doing it for the money. You will be doing it for the challenge."

"Okay, I come out and we talk and we look."

He came out. Papa was loaded, anyway. He could buy and sell Lucy and me three or four times. The money he had made out of the light meter alone, plus a lot of acreage in orange trees he owned in the San Fernando Valley, made him a man of considerable means. The challenge was what got him, and that's what I was counting on.

Karl and we looked at nightclubs, theaters, ballrooms, all kinds of locations, but we couldn't find one place that would serve his needs and ours.

Earl Carroll's restaurant and nightclub was large enough for the cameras and for Papa's new type of lighting, which he was already designing and building, but the stage was not quite large enough to put three or four sets side by side, which I knew, in some shows, we would need. The writers had already written several of them. Also, Earl Carroll's was shaped in such a way that only the ringsiders would be able to see the performers' expressions, and for our type of intimate situation-comedy stuff we wanted that audience, all of them, just as close as possible.

The other places presented the same problem or different ones that could not be overcome. *The Groucho Marx Show* was done in a small theater and filmed with multiple cameras in front of an audience. They used five cameras, placed at different strategic places where they remained stationary for the entire show, and by using different lenses in each camera they had a selection of five different angles, but Groucho used only one small set, in which he sat on a stool and talked to two contestants at a time who were standing next to him, and they both remained stationary also.

We couldn't do that. Our cameras would have to be on dollies and not only move back and forth but also sideways all over the floor space between our sets and the audience. The only problem with that was that there were no such camera dollies. The electronic television cameras were mounted on such dollies and were able to go in every direction, but they were not big enough or strong enough to support a 35-mm motion-picture sound camera, a camera operator and an assistant operator. I knew Papa had been looking into the problem and was confident he'd come up with something.

One night Lucy and I were in bed at our little ranch in Northridge. It was about two o'clock in the morning. I woke up suddenly, sat up, shook her and asked, "Where do they make pictures?"

Half asleep, she said, "Wha . . . wha . . . ?"

"Where do they make pictures?"

"What is this?" she asked. "You drunk or something?"

"No, I am not. Where do they make pictures?"

"At motion-picture studios, you silly Cuban. Where the hell else would they make pictures?"

"There's where we are going to make our show," I told her. "On a motion-picture sound stage."

"You cannot do it," she said.

"Why not?"

"They won't let you bring three hundred people inside a motion-picture sound stage."

"That's what Karl said, but there must be a way."

I started to look into it. Karl and Lucy were right. They would not allow us to bring an audience of three hundred people or even many fewer onto a motion-picture stage while we were filming. And they had all kinds of pretty good reasons and laws to prevent you. The fire department would not let you do it, the health-and-welfare department would not let you do it and, at some studios, even the zoning department would not let you do it.

I went to see the head of the fire department and he told me personally, "It's against our fire-prevention regulations to bring three hundred people into a movie-studio stage while filming. You can't do it."

"I know that," I said. "The reason I'm here is to ask you how I can do what I cannot do."

"I beg your pardon?"

"What would I have to do to a movie-studio sound stage to be able to film our show in front of an audience? The networks do some of their television shows in front of an audience. We did the pilot of *I Love Lucy* that way at CBS's Studio A in Hollywood."

"The network stages conformed to our regulations. I presume that if you had a movie-studio stage with the sprinkler system all over the ceiling and two good exit doors, at two different ends of one wall, leading to the main studio street, plus one big double exit door leading into a city street, we would allow you to do it, but the health-and-welfare department would have to approve the audience seating arrangement and sanitary facilities. And you better make sure that this movie-studio stage is adjacent to a city street in a part of town that would not conflict with the zoning department before you start doing all the things I told you our fire department would require."

"Okay, I'll check with those other governmental departments."

"There's one more thing," he said. "You'd have to have one or possibly two firemen on the premises every time you brought the audience in."

"All right," I said. "Would you mind putting all that down on paper?"

He then wrote me a letter saying that if we did this and that, and got approval of the other government departments, the fire department would okay it.

"Thank you very much. You have been very kind."

We looked at many studios and could have rented space at any of them. The motion-picture industry wasn't doing too well, and most of the sound stages were half or totally empty. We found the perfect one at General Service Studios' Stage 2.

It was long enough to be able to accommodate four or five sets side by side if needed and wide enough to allow for a backstage area, the depth of the sets, the cameras' floor space, the audience bleacher-type seating arrangement we had settled on, and the sound booth and electric controls above that. It was also adjacent to a city street.

The floors were awful but they were awful at every studio in town—made of wood and full of cracks and holes from the tracks, sets and heavy light stands that had been nailed to them and taken up again and again during all the years since the studios were built. So we knew we had to find some kind of floor that would serve our purpose. We would have to take up these old ones no matter where we went.

An interesting sidelight to this was that Stage 2 was where Shirley Temple made her first film, a ten-minute short subject.

The street this stage was adjacent to was a narrow one (Selma Avenue in Hollywood) and that's where our double-door exit would have to be. There were small family homes right across from it, so I thought we'd better check with the zoning department before making a rental deal and starting to tear out walls and put in sprinklers, new floors and so forth.

The head of the zoning department told me,"You were wise to check with us. That is a residential section, and any kind of a building at which an audience would gather—like your proposed theater stage—would not conform with that zoning."

"Why is that?"

"The people waiting to get in to see the show would be all over that block and there would be the noise of the music, laughter and applause during the filming of it, which would bother the homeowners, so you can't do it."

"That's what I was afraid you'd say. I went to the head of the fire department last week and he also told me the same thing, 'I cannot do it,' not for your same reasons, but because of their fire-prevention regulations. Then after I explained to him that this was a brand-new thing we were trying to do and that, if proven successful, it would help the film industry in this town, he gave me a list of things which I would have to do in order to comply with their rules and regulations. He also said that I should check with you people on the zoning and with the health-and-welfare department.

"Would it be all right with you if I go and talk to the people who either own or rent homes in that block to see if perhaps they would agree to an exception for this kind of an operation in their zoning?"

"Sure," he said, "if you get their approval, and get it in writing from everyone on that block, we'll go along with you."

I thanked him and went to talk to the people. I think there were six or eight homes in that block. I told them what Lucy and I wanted to do and that I was sure, if we soundproofed the wall adjacent to the street, they would not hear anything at all.

"You'll probably hear less than what you hear now when they're making a picture," I told them, "because that wall is not now sound-proofed." I also told them that we would have studio guards directing the audience, waiting to enter the stage, to stand in a single file against our studio wall to eliminate confusion on the street; and that if this new technique of filming a television show proved successful, we would need more space for offices. When and if that happened Desilu Productions would be more than willing to buy their property at a good and fair price, if they wished to sell. In the meantime, if they'd like to see the shows, I'd make sure that they and their families would have good reserved seats.

They all gave me their consent in writing and we overcame the zoning problem. The next year, Desilu bought all the homes in that block, which we converted into offices. The American Federation of Musicians owned the other two lots in that block, on which they built their Los Angeles Union offices.

We had accomplished quite a bit up until now, thanks to the understanding and cooperation of the different governmental departments in Los Angeles, to whom we will always be grateful, but there were still several little details to be taken care of before we could start doing I Love Lucy "that" way.

The first thing we had to do was to have a contract with General Service Studios so that we could start remodeling Stage 2 to comply with the regulations.

We went there and talked to Jimmy and George Nasser, who owned the place. Unfortunately for them, but fortunately for us, they were in a lot of trouble. They were either into bankruptcy or about to go into bankruptcy. The day I went there a guy from the bankruptcy department, or whatever you call it, was there looking over their assets.

I told the Nassers that we would like to make a long-term deal for that one stage and have options on other stages, plus offices, dressing rooms, whatever lighting equipment they had, cutting rooms, props and so forth. In other words, any and all equipment they had and the entire facilities of their studio would have to be available to us on a first-call basis.

They were happy to see us and said, "Sure, whatever you want, but we don't know that we can give you a contract because we are about to lose the place."

I asked them, "What would it take for you to hang on to it? How much money would you have to pay these people?"

They told me, "Fifty thousand dollars."

I went back to CBS, talked to Mr. Ackerman and told him the situation.

Mr. Ackerman said, "Well, you don't have much time."

We didn't. We would have to start filming no later than September 1 in order to have our show ready to be televised on October 15. The reconstruction job on Stage 2 wasn't going to be an overnight deal.

Mr. Ackerman said, "Okay, tell them they'll have the fifty thousand dollars."

"Will you call the Nassers?" I asked. "There is a man there who is about to take the studio away from them, but I'm sure if you call them and say that CBS is going to send them a check tomorrow morning, we'll be able to get the contract signed and get going."

The fifty thousand dollars would be an advance against the cost of remodeling the stage, which General Service Studios would have to assume, and also against the rental of space, equipment and facilities. By advancing the money we got the best rental and facility deal we could have gotten in any studio in Hollywood, but, what the hell, it also enabled Jimmy and George Nasser to hold on to their property.

CBS sent the check the following day. We signed the contract and started tearing that Stage 2 apart. I must say that Jimmy and George were a little wide-eyed when they saw us taking up the old wooden floor and cutting a big hole in their studio wall adjacent to the street so we could make the double-door exit.

We had found the perfect type of floor on the loading platform of the May Company department store in downtown Los Angeles. It was not cement but some kind of new composition, very smooth and level, able to support heavy weights; you could nail into it without its cracking; and if you had to repair an area, you could cut that spot, lift it out and pour some more composition in there, and after smoothing it over, you couldn't tell where it had been repaired.

Papa found a man who had been working on the kind of dolly we needed. We helped the man finish it and, after testing it, ordered three of them, which Desilu bought. We called them "crab dollies," as they could move as crabs do, in every direction.

The Desilu company was making progress; but, of far more importance, our vice-president gave birth to our lovely daughter, Lucie Desiree Arnaz, on July 17, 1951.

What a glorious day that was!

29

We had been so busy doing all these things we hadn't yet hired the actor and actress who were to play our neighbors.

The format of the series was to be pretty close to that in the pilot show, but Bob, Madelyn and Jess felt, and rightly so, that we should have another couple as our best friends and neighbors. As it turned out, they also became our landlords, which helped the fun even more.

The writers said, "It may be tiresome just to have Lucy and Ricky week after week. Also, the Lucy character needs someone to be her ally. The Ethel character should be the one she would talk into helping her with her wild plans and schemes, and even though Ethel many times would say, 'Oh, no, you're not going to get me into that deal,' Lucy would eventually connive or blackmail her into it."

They also felt that Ricky needed the counterpart of Ethel. That would be Fred, her husband, Ricky's ally in these battles of the sexes.

While we were trying to resolve all the physical, mechanical and bureaucratic problems, the writers had been busy writing the first few segments of the series, which we would have to start doing soon in order to meet our on-the-air schedule. So we had to find somebody—two somebodies—who fitted what those neighbors were supposed to be like.

I must say we were pretty lucky (all due respect to Philip Morris, who never allowed us to use that word while they were sponsoring our show) to find the two people we found to play Fred and Ethel Mertz.

Soon after this writers' conference and decision I got a call from William Frawley. I hadn't thought about him for the part, but somehow he knew about the series format and wanted to be considered for Fred. I had seen Frawley in many pictures with Bing Crosby, James Cagney, Pat O'Brien and other stars. He had been a top character actor for years but hadn't done anything lately.

"Thanks for calling, Mr. Frawley," I said. "I think you might be a possibility. Let me call you back."

After I hung up I kept seeing his puss and remembering how good he was at playing the kind of gruff character he usually played. The more I thought about it, the more I became convinced he was Fred Mertz.

I then checked with the CBS people, the sponsor and the advertising agency. They all said, "Yeah, we know what he has done in the past, but what has he done lately? Besides, he's an alcoholic. You'd be out of your mind to hire him. There are a lot of actors who are much more dependable and can play that part."

The more they kept tearing this guy apart, the more I liked the idea of hiring him, and the more I thought he would be perfect for Fred.

According to my contract as executive producer, I had complete creative control of the show. I knew I could land on my ass by doing the wrong thing, but I'd rather land on it by doing that than by having someone else talk me into doing something which would land me there anyway.

I made up my mind to hire Frawley, regardless of what they said. I made a date to meet him the next day at Nickodell's, a restaurant and bar on Melrose Avenue, right behind RKO Studios. We had a drink together and I told him that everybody was telling me he was an alcoholic, that he might not even show up, etc.

"Well, those bastards, those sonsabitches," he said. "They're always saying that about me. How the hell do they know, those bastards?"

"Look, I don't give a damn whether you drink or not. I like to drink myself and I'll drink you under the table anytime you'd like to give it a try, except during working hours. But Lucy and I have everything going on this project. She's given up her motion-picture career and I've given up my band business. If we fail, I don't want it to be because some character like you loused us up."

"Give us another drink here, will you?" he told the waiter.

"Now listen, Mr. Frawley . . ."

"Call me Bill."

"All right, Bill, I want you to know that I have given this thing a lot of thought. I have considered many good character actors for this part, especially Gale Gordon, who's very well-liked by the agencies and the networks."

"What can he do that I can't?" Bill asked.

"Nothing, it's what you do that he doesn't do that louses you up. But I am convinced that there is no one better in the whole world to play Fred Mertz than William Frawley."

The drinks arrived and he told the waiter this was his tab.

Then he turned to me and said, "All right, so what's your problem? William Frawley is now sitting next to you and willing to listen to the kind of proposition you are willing to offer him to make your show a success."

"Okay, Bill, I'll tell you what I'll do with you. The first time you are not able to do your job, I'll try to work around you for that day. The second time, I'll try to manage again. But if you do it three times, you are through, and I mean *through*, not only on our show, but you'll never work in this town again as long as you live. Is that fair enough?"

"All right, goddamn it, that's fair enough."

"After work, if you feel like coming to Nickodell's and splitting a bottle of whatever you like, I'll be happy to come and split it with you."

"Hey, waiter, what the hell is this, the Sahara Desert? We are thirsty. Okay, Cuban, we have a deal and we'll show all them bastards how wrong they are."

He never missed a day's work nor was he even a few minutes late during all the years he was with us.

Every time Lucy and I went to any city in the United States the first thing the people would ask us was "Where's Fred?"

He couldn't stand Ethel (Vivian Vance) though. "Where the hell did you find this bitch?" he would ask. "She can't sing worth a damn. You're going to have her sing again?"

"Bill, she's a hell of a good actress and Ethel Mertz, the part she's playing, is not supposed to sing good."

"Well, she bugs me," he said. "You know that dance routine she and I are supposed to do next week?"

"Yeah."

"Well, this silly broad tells the choreographer she doesn't think we'll be able to do it because I'll never be able to learn it. Like it was going to be a Fred Astaire and Ginger Rogers number or something.

All we are supposed to do in this thing is an old-fashioned soft-shoe routine. Well, for Crissakes, I was in vaudeville since I was five years old and I guarantee you I'll wind up teaching old fat-ass how to do the fucking thing."

Fortunately that same gruff quality of Bill's was perfect for the part of Fred. Another thing about Bill which used to tickle the hell out of me was that he wouldn't take a complete script home with him after the Monday reading and first rehearsal. He'd only take the pages where he'd find FRED: Only his lines. So sometimes he wouldn't understand the jokes. We would get to a joke and he would say to me, "This is not funny."

"What do you mean?" I'd ask. "It's not funny? You haven't read the five other pages where we have been building up to your entrance."

"What are you talking about?"

"You're just reading what *you* are supposed to say and we've been building up for you to come in and say, 'Hello, Ethel,' and get a big laugh."

"You think 'Hello, Ethel' is funny?"

"No, 'Hello, Ethel' is not funny, but we've been building up this situation in which Ethel is inside a costume, representing the last half of a horse, and as you come through the door, she is bending down and facing away from you. All you can see is the last half of this horse—the horse's ass is all you can see—and you say, 'Hello, Ethel' and *that* is funny."

"Oh, yes, that *is* funny!"

Bill's agent was Walter Meyers, a wonderful old guy who loved his client. He didn't handle many people but he usually kept them all working. Bill trusted him. Vivian Vance's agent was another cup of tea. He represented many big names in the business and was considered quite a power in negotiations, which we always seemed to be in with him.

Before the start of each new season he would come in and tell me that unless Vivian got a new contract with a considerable raise, he could not guarantee that she would stay in show business.

"She needs this kind of appreciation and incentive to prevent her from having a nervous breakdown."

He said that some years before she had hidden out on a New Mexico ranch for quite a while before anyone could talk her into going back to work.

We always managed to meet his terms and Vivian was worth everything she got.

Meyers would not come in and press for a new deal every year, but he would hear about the negotiations going on with Vivian's agent, and believing, rightly so, that Bill was as important to the show as she was, he would tell me that if Vivian was going to get a new contract and raise, he felt it was only fair I should, at that time, think about Bill also.

I would tell him, "Relax, Walter, don't worry about Bill. I'll handle his action for you. I promise you whatever Vivian gets, Bill gets."

He would stop me on the lot and ask, "How's she doing for the next season?"

"I'm getting killed!" I'd tell him.

"That good, huh?"

"Yeah, that good."

When we finally stopped doing *I Love Lucy,* Fred MacMurray signed Bill for *My Three Sons,* in which he played the same type of cantankerous character.

The sponsor of that show was an automobile company and Bill was given a car for his personal use. However, that presented a problem. Bill's past history included many traffic tickets, and finally he had his driver's license picked up, for driving under the influence, and was never able to get another one. A Yellow Cab driver became his buddy.

Desilu was filming the MacMurray show and I would always run into Bill on the lot. One day he stopped me and said, "Come with me, I want to show you my new car and chauffeur."

I went with him and met a very beautiful, sexy young doll—his chauffeur.

Bill had a heart attack and died on March 3, 1966. His services were held at the Good Samaritan Catholic Church on Sunset Boulevard in Hollywood. Fred MacMurray and I were paired as pallbearers at the front of the coffin. It was a very heavy coffin and a very hot day. Both of us were really sweating and struggling.

I looked across at MacMurray and said, "I know Bill is up there, looking down at us struggling with this goddamn coffin, sweating, breaking our backs, and I'll bet you he's laughing like hell."

I loved Bill and I know that the American people who viewed our shows loved him too.

30

October 15, the day of our television debut, was approaching by leaps and bounds. Our writers were turning out some wonderful scripts and we had cast Fred. But we still had a few things to do before we could start filming and meet that date.

I went to CBS and told Harry Ackerman I needed help. Did he know anyone who could become my production manager or my assistant producer or whatever you want to call it?

Harry said, "I think I know someone who may be just right for you. His name is Al Simon. I'll make a date for you to meet him."

Harry told me that Mr. Simon had been involved in some of the filming of *The Groucho Marx Show* and a few other small film ventures for television. I met Mr. Simon. He was a bright, young, enthusiastic, inventive and conscientious man. He also liked what we were trying to do.

After that first meeting I knew he was the kind of man who wouldn't be afraid to tackle anything. He became our production manager.

We had to get a director, a man who knew how to move those multiple cameras around and get the particular shots that were needed for each scene.

We figured our best bet would be someone who had done live television in front of an audience. The only difficulty the live television director would have with our system was he wouldn't be able to see what he was getting while he was getting it. We couldn't have monitors in the booth as they have in live television. He would have to work from the floor, look through the lenses for what he wanted for that particular shot, check it, mark it and give it to his camera coordinator.

We found this fellow in Marc Daniels, a young man who had done many good live television shows in New York. His camera coordinator was his wife, a very efficient young lady, and they worked well together.

For the sound we couldn't use anybody from the sound departments of picture studios because all they record, while they are filming, is the dialogue; and after that, in the dubbing room, they add the music, the sound effects and whatever else they need for background. We needed someone from radio to mix the dialogue, the audience reaction, the sound effects and the music simultaneously while filming in front of an audience. We finally wound up with Cam McCullough of Glen Glenn Sound.

One thing I didn't have to worry about was how the show was going to be photographed. I knew Papa had been working on that for quite a while, designing different kinds of lighting; and, by the time we were ready, he would be ready.

We needed a first assistant director. Again, we had to have a young man who would not be tied down to the old-fashioned Hollywood ideas of how to make motion pictures and who could adapt himself to our technique. We were fortunate to find James Paisley.

We had to have a film editor, and he had to be free of any preconceived ideas of how to edit this show.

Of course we needed a set designer, a set dresser and a musical director. I knew I couldn't be playing Ricky and in the middle of a scene give a downbeat for the music cue. We also needed an arranger, a lyricist, a music composer, a costume designer, a special-effects expert, a property man; wardrobe people, makeup people, hairdressers and a janitor.

The last one sounds like a small item, but the way we were trying to do our show, the janitor was very important. The new floors we were about to lay on Stage 2 at General Service had to be really clean and smooth for our cameras to move any way they had to move without any cigarette butts, matchsticks or what have you. It is unbelievable, the jump in the film when a camera rolls over a little matchstick. We got a hell of a guy, Lou Jacoby. Jacoby not only took care of that but he found himself a lot of other jobs. He made sure the water coolers were full every day, that we had doughnuts and coffee on the first day of rehearsal, that chairs were always handy for the cast. If I'd been standing around for a while, all of a sudden I would look around and Lou would be in back of me with a chair, saying, "Sit down, Boss." He was quite a guy!

Everybody on the crew had earphones in order to get the cues from the booth. One day Paisley, our assistant director, was giving Jacoby hell because there was a spot on the stage that had not been cleaned well enough. Jacoby turned to him and said, "How am I supposed to know what to do? I don't have any earphones." Our janitor, Jacoby, really proved that this had to be a team operation. Any one of these people I have mentioned had to do their job and if any one of them didn't the whole show would fall on its ass.

A few years later, when I produced a picture for MGM called *Forever, Darling,* Jacoby proved his worth again.

I had told Metro that our motion-picture company, Zanra, could make it for a million dollars if we could do it at our studio and not at MGM. Eddie Mannix, who was in charge of that department at MGM, didn't think I could.

We started *Forever, Darling* on a Monday. Mannix called me at eleven o'clock that morning.

"How are you doing?" he asked.

"I'm doing fine, Mr. Mannix. We're three days ahead of schedule."

"What the hell are you talking about? How could you be three days ahead of schedule? You only started shooting this morning."

"I know that, but we're three days ahead of schedule."

Mr. Mannix was a very wise man, so after a pause he said, "You sonofabitch Cuban, you shot the tests."

"Yes, sir."

What he meant was that in all preproduction budgets they had enough money for three days to test the clothes, the sets, the lighting, the makeup and the hair. I had Harold ("Lippy") Lipstein, an Academy Award winner, as director of photography.

"Do you need these three preproduction days to find out how Lucy's clothes will look against the sets, or what lighting you have to use on this film?"

"I don't need them," Lipstein answered.

"Then what are we doing them for?"

"That's the way we always do it."

"Look, Lippy," I said, "why don't we bring in the sound? That's all we need. We've got the actors, we've got the clothes, we've got the sets, and you've got the cameras and the lights. Why don't we shoot 'picture' in those three days, not just tests? In case something is not quite right and you are not satisfied with it, I promise you we'll retake it."

"That's fine with me," he said.

We made the picture for under a million dollars. After we finished, Mr. Mannix asked if I would mind coming over and having a meeting with him and his production people at MGM.

"Of course not, Mr. Mannix, anytime you want."

J. J. Cohn, his top production financial man for many years, was there, and a few other assistants.

Mr. Mannix said, "I know how you saved a lot of money by using those three days of tests to get a nice chunk of picture. I don't know why in hell we never thought of that. But there are a few other things I'd like to ask you about. They are kind of specific."

"Go ahead."

"When the bell rings and the stage doors are supposed to be closed before you start filming, who's in charge of that?"

"Lou Jacoby," I said, "he's in charge of that."

"Lou Jacoby."

"That's right."

"Okay. When you finish shooting on a set at the end of the day and you have to come back to that same set the next day, but by now that set is dusty and let's say there are some flowers in there and they look wilted, who is in charge of making that set just as clean and those flowers just as fresh as the day before?"

"Lou Jacoby, he's in charge of that."

"I see," glancing at J. J. Cohn. "You have water coolers on your stage so that the cast, the extras and the crew can have a drink of water?"

"Of course we do."

"Who's in charge of seeing that they are filled and in good working condition?"

"Jacoby does that."

"Uh huh. Say that you're on location and it's a very early call. You have coffee, doughnuts, sweet rolls and such things for the crew and the cast when they first arrive there, before they start to work?"

"Of course we do, Mr. Mannix."

"Who's in charge of seeing that all that stuff is there?"

"Jacoby."

Mr. Mannix then turned to J. J. Cohn and his assistants and said, "This whole meeting was to try to figure out how we could hold down our below-the-line costs the way Desi's company, Zanra, does. The answer is very simple. All we have to do is get Jacoby."

31

Meanwhile, back at the ranch, Mrs. A. was getting herself in shape for the very strenuous work that lay ahead of us and, at the same time, having a ball taking care of our little daughter, who was growing into a laughing, huggable, lovely child. Everything was so happy and peaceful and beautiful there. Even the plants and the trees seemed to be thriving. I hadn't tasted such delicious fruits and vegetables since I was a Cuban.

The only thing that wasn't working out too well was my livestock program. All those chickens and hens we had bought were now walking around on crutches. Lucy had named and made pets of all of them and when I suggested that a couple of those hens, simmered for four days, would make a good soup, she was horrified and called me a murderous monster.

On Christmas Eve in Cuba, we have a roast pig instead of the traditional turkey you have here. I had bought a little piglet a few months before the previous Christmas and fattened him up real nice, but by the time Christmas came around he had become "Little Sancho." So we had turkey.

The Duchess of Devonshire was still with us, getting bigger and fatter. If I had suggested butchering her, Lucy would have killed me.

I tried to get home as early as I could every evening from the studio, just to be able to hold my little girl in my lap in a rocking chair I had in the nursery. Lucy would keep her awake until I got home. She didn't think that it was important whether little Lucie got to bed at seven, eight, or nine o'clock, just as long as she got her rest.

She would have her all nice, clean and pretty for me in her bedclothes. I would hold little Lucie on my chest, with her cheek next to mine and rock her back and forth. When I did that she would coo and laugh and play with my ears, my nose and my lips, pull my hair and stick her finger in my eye.

I would have loved to have had more time to spend with her and Lucy at the ranch. But by now the element of time had become our biggest worry, especially since we had not yet found an Ethel.

It is difficult to figure out why we hadn't. The motion-picture business wasn't doing so well and there were certainly a lot of actresses available, but for some reason or other none of those we considered was acceptable. Some of them were not right to play Bill's wife, some Lucy did not like at all, others did not have any stage experience, which eliminated them right away. They had to be accustomed to working in front of an audience.

About a week before we had to start filming. Marc Daniels, our director, came to me and said he thought he had a really good possibilty for Ethel, Vivian Vance, whom he had known before in live television and on the stage, and she was now appearing at the La Jolla Playhouse.

The La Jolla Playhouse was a summer theater run by Mel Ferrer,

Gregory Peck and a few friends of theirs as an artistic endeavor, not really a commercial venture. I was anxious to see Miss Vance. For some reason or other I couldn't make it until Saturday night. Marc Daniels, Kenny Morgan, Don Sharpe and I drove to La Jolla to watch Miss Vance in *The Voice of the Turtle*.

Vivian was playing the very sarcastic bitch in that play. It was not what you would call typecasting for Ethel. Nevertheless, right after I saw her do the first scene, I knew we had found Ethel.

She was such a wonderful actress, so honest. Every line, every reaction, every move she made was just perfect. I couldn't wait to get backstage and talk to her. I'm sure Marc had called her before and explained what we were doing and what the part was. But I had never met the lady. After the show I went backstage, talked to her and signed her right there and then to play Ethel.

As we were driving back to Los Angeles—it was now early Sunday morning and we were to start rehearsing for the first *I Love Lucy* episode on the following Monday morning—lightning struck.

"Oh, my God, what have I done? Suppose Lucy doesn't like her? What the hell do I do then?"

I could have asked Miss Vance to come into the studio, read with us, meet Lucy and see how they got along, but I was so sure she was so right for the part of Ethel I just didn't think of anything else but signing her for it.

I got home early Sunday morning and told Lucy we had found the perfect actress for Ethel.

"Who?" she asked.

"Vivian Vance," I answered.

"Who the hell is she?"

"No one you would know. I saw her at the La Jolla Playhouse tonight and she's such a good actress, so honest in everything she does, that I'm sure she will be wonderful with you."

Fortunately, it was love at first sight. When they met Monday morning and we all sat down and read together, it was just perfect. Another time I was very lucky.

We could have never found anyone to play Ethel any better or even as well as Vivian Vance did. She was great in the part. She *was* Ethel, or maybe I should put it this way: she was such a good actress that she made herself *become* Ethel.

She was also very good in putting up with old Bill. She never felt any animosity toward him. She just figured he was an old poop and too much so to change his ways.

I read somewhere in one of Vivian's interviews about the casting of *I Love Lucy,* "Theoretically, our show consisted of three mis-casts and one case of perfect casting, Lucy. I had always played sophisticated 'other-woman' roles in musical comedies, Bill Frawley was a vaudevillian and Desi a bandleader."

I really can't argue too much with Vivian's opinion. Our casting was certainly not conforming to the norm, but maybe that is what made it good. All I know is that the chemistry which developed between those four characters—Lucy, Ethel, Fred and Ricky—was, I am sure, one of the reasons for the success of *I Love Lucy.*

Television is people and the television audience has to get to know these people and like them before they invite them into their homes week after week.

32

A lot of things had happened since Lucy and I decided to go on the theater tour to find out if the American people would like us working as a team, but now this was it! The bell at the starting gate was about to ring! This was the night we were to do our first show "that" way. We had done everything possible to try to make it a success.

We had gotten the best people we could to help us. Papa was ready, his cameramen were ready, Marc Daniels was ready, my orchestra was there on the stage playing under the direction of Wilbur Hatch, the sets looked great, everybody was in makeup, but there were a lot of nervous people around.

Nobody really knew if this system or technique, "that" way of doing our show, would really work, including me. We were loaded with CBS executives, agency executives and members of the press. There was a line going around the whole block with people waiting to get in. The ushers, whom we got from CBS every week, were making sure that everything was clean and putting down the cushions on the bleachers we had built.

Backstage, Lucy, Vivian, Bill and I were going over last-minute details with our director. I remember that the carpenters were still hammering away.

At this point a gentleman from the sanitation section of the health-and-welfare department wanted to talk to me. I excused myself from the meeting, went to see him and told him I was glad he could make it for our opening show.

"I don't think you can go on and do this show tonight," he said.

"What do you mean by that?"

"Well, according to our regulations, you have to have two bath-rooms, one for ladies and another for men, within a certain pre-scribed distance from where the audience is sitting. You have one for the men within that distance, but none for the ladies. I cannot allow that audience in unless you have both."

I called Kenny Morgan. "Would you go with this gentleman and see if you can find a bathroom acceptable to his department for the ladies to go to?"

I went back to the meeting with the writers, the cast and the rest of our group. A little while later this guy and Kenny came back and said they had found one.

"That's fine," I said. "Everything is all right then?"

"We don't know," said Kenny. "The only one the right distance from the audience is the bathroom in Lucy's dressing room."

Jess came up to us and asked, "What the hell are you guys talking about? We're about to go on and do our first show and you're looking for a *bathroom?*"

"That's right, Jess, we are supposed to supply a place for the ladies in our audience to be able to pee in, or at, in case they feel the urge to do so, and the only one which is the right distance from our audience, in order to comply with regulations of the sanitation section of the health-and-welfare department, is the bathroom in Lucy's dressing room."

Lucy spoke up. "That's no problem. Tell the ladies to be my guests."

I then asked the man if it would be all right *now* to let the audience come in to our little theater.

"Yeah, go ahead," he said.

"Thank you very much."

Jess then said to me, "Those people have been out there for twenty or thirty minutes longer than they were supposed to be, and we sure as hell don't want a grouchy, unhappy audience. They won't react well to our jokes, so why don't you go out there and warm them up?"

"What the hell does that mean, warm them up?"

"Oh, for Crissake," he said, "go out there, welcome them, make them feel at home, tell them about the technique we're using to film our shows, then tell them a few jokes to get them in the mood to laugh. After that, introduce the cast and we'll start filming."

"Okay, I'll give it a try."

I went out. The band was playing and the audience was coming in. I spotted Kenny taking care of all the executives (we were up to our ass with them) and the press. It was exciting. Opening night is always exciting and nerve-racking. This one, as far as I was concerned, even topped the New York opening of *Too Many Girls*. At least there all I had to worry about was my performance. Abbott had taken care of everything else.

Jacoby had cleaned, wiped, and I think he had even licked the floors. They literally glistened. Della Fox, never too calm at any time, was on the verge of collapse with trying to make sure of the right wardrobe changes for the right people for the right scene.

I welcomed the people. I explained to them what they were about to see, that we were doing a stage play which was going to be photographed at the same time. I told them not to worry about the cameras on the floor or the people who had to handle them, that I was sure the cameras, no matter what moves they had to make, would never interrupt or cover their line of vision. Then I thought I might as well make a joke out of it because there were times when the camera would get a little bit in their line of vision.

"I'll show you what I mean. Suppose I'm sitting there in this living-room set [I sat in a low chair] and the director tells the cameras to move in and take this shot."

As I was saying this I signaled to all three cameramen to move in, but move in close and around me. By the time they got there, the audience couldn't see me at all.

"You see what I mean? At no time will the cameras interrupt your line of vision."

That got a big laugh. I knew nothing that bad would happen during the show, but perhaps it was better to touch on it now than not to mention it at all. It worked out so well I used it in every show warm-up from then on.

"I was told to tell you a few funny stories to get you in the mood to laugh. I don't know many funny stories but there was an old vaude-villian with us for several weeks on our first theater tour. I heard this one so many times that I think I know it pretty good. Here's the way it goes:

"This beautiful seventeen-year-old girl was swimming around in a lake, late in the evening, when she heard a voice saying, 'Little girl, beautiful girl, come over here.' The girl looked around and could see no one. She said, 'Who's calling me? I see no one.' The voice again said, 'I'm over here on top of this rock.' The girl swam over to the rock and there was a little turtle sitting there.

"The young, beautiful girl said to the turtle, 'Are you the one who was calling me?' 'Yes, I was.' 'How come? You are a turtle and you can talk!' 'I was not always a turtle. I used to be an Army sergeant, but some witch put a curse on me and turned me into a turtle. The reason I called you over here is because you can help me.' The girl asked, 'How can I help you?' 'If you take me home with you and let me sleep in your bed under your pillow, by tomorrow morning I'll be an Army sergeant again.' 'I don't think I can do that.' 'Oh, please, you have to. I am so tired of being a turtle,' said the turtle. 'I just have to get back into the Army.' (Kind of a crazy turtle, I guess.) 'All right,' the young, beautiful girl said, 'I'll help you.' She took the little turtle home with her, took it to bed with her and let it stay there for the night.

"The next morning her mother came into the room. The young girl was late getting up to go to school. And there in the bed, lying right next to her daughter, was this very handsome six foot two Army sergeant.

"And, do you know, to this very day that little girl's mother doesn't believe the story about the turtle?"

After the turtle story I introduced the cast to the audience—Bill Frawley as Fred Mertz, Vivian Vance as Ethel and then, "Here's my favorite wife, the mother of my child, the vice-president of Desilu Productions—*I* am the president—my favorite redhead, the girl who plays Lucy, Lucille Ball!"

And in she came with her red hair flying, while the orchestra played the *I Love Lucy* theme, and, believe me, she is just as good as Hope or Jolson or Chevalier about taking over an audience. She went over and kissed Bill and Vivian, came to me and said, "How ya doing, you gorgeous Cuban?" and threw kisses to the audience. The whole atmosphere had a happy, carnival type of feeling.

Then the voice from the booth. "Please take your places for the first scene . . . cameras get ready . . . roll the sound . . . roll the film . . . now go on and do a good show for us tonight. Action!"

We were off and running—*I Love Lucy* was launched. How smoothly everything went that night, mechanically and performance-wise, was hard to believe. It all seemed effortless, which only goes to prove that it takes a lot of effort to make something look effortless.

The network executives, the sponsor, the advertising guys and the press were all very complimentary. We had a party on the stage right afterward and everybody was celebrating and drinking it up. But I still had no idea what we had in those cameras. We had to wait for the film to go to the lab and be processed before we knew what we had.

When I saw the film the following day I knew that Marc and everybody else had done a great job. I knew we had a show, a hell of a show, and that "that" way worked, and worked better than any other way that had been used before for a television comedy.

I took the first two shows we had filmed and showed them in a theater in Riverside, a town in Orange County, about forty miles from Los Angeles. I had made sure the picture playing there was a good one. I wanted a full house for the test. I wanted to see if the theater audience would react in the same spots as our audiences had reacted when we shot the shows. They reacted so much the same way that you could not hear our studio audience's laughter; the laughter of the audience in the theater in the same places covered it.

It was a good test. It convinced me that our system, besides accomplishing what CBS wanted—to have Lucy work in front of an audience—also showed us what kind of a show we had each week—funny, very funny. Or perhaps, if it wasn't either, we had time to fix whatever jokes or routines had not worked *before* it went over the network.

I don't think anybody can really tell what kind of laugh a line is going to get. You can sit in the projection room and say, "Put a little chuckle in there, a good laugh here," but there were so many routines in *I Love Lucy* which got long and big laughs that I would not have dared to put in. I would not have had the guts or the ego to do so. Another advantage to having a live audience was that the actors had to know their parts to a T and be *up* for it, and running through the action in continuity, we picked up spontaneity, which was then only found in live shows.

The postproduction on each one of these shows required four to five weeks before it was ready to ship. I was always working on eight or nine shows at a time, each one in a different stage of pre- or postproduction: the ideas of a new show coming up, the first draft of a script, the final draft of another, the show we were rehearsing and filming that week, the editing of another show, the integration of commercials in one or two others, the dubbing of another, and the composite print check of others.

Of all these different stages, the editing was taking much too much time. For a half-hour show, in those days, we edited the enter-

I never gave anyone
any trouble.

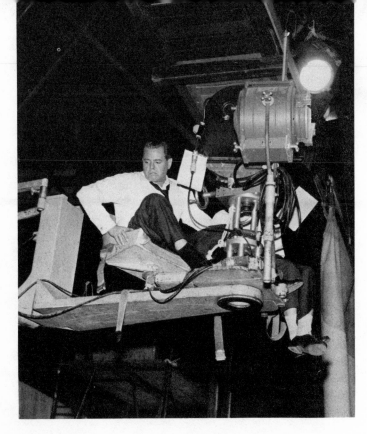

"Basic union scale for Karl Freund?"

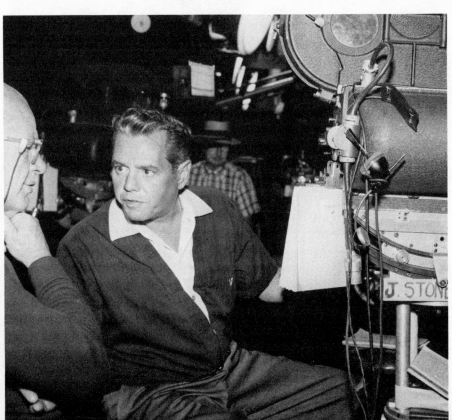

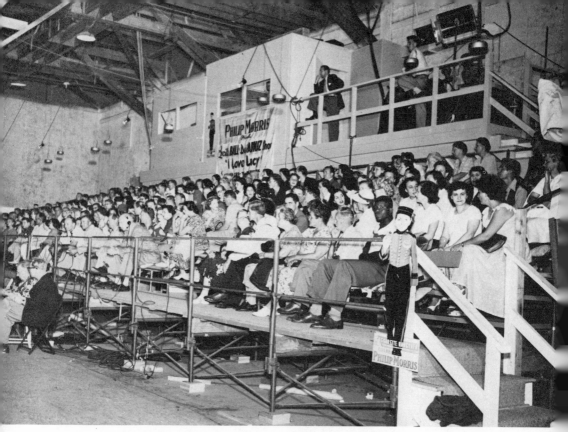

Our first studio audience. Harry Ackerman, with his foot on the railing (top center), seems a little worried.

"I was not always a turtle. I used to be an Army sergeant."

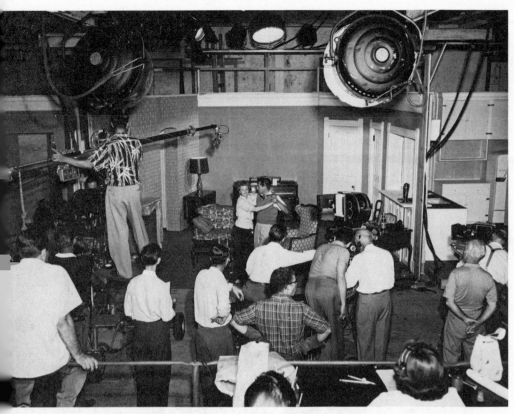

The cameras would never cover their line of vision.

And, of course, we could see the audience clearly.

Buster Keaton wanted us to settle down to serious comedy.

tainment part, meaning without commercials, credits and station breaks, to 24 minutes and 30 seconds. Today it's even less.

The networks, the local stations, the sponsors, the unions demanding credit for a hell of a lot more people, have cut the entertainment portion to 22 minutes and change. We usually filmed at least 29 or 30 minutes and many times went over that, which meant, if we were only using three cameras—the least we could use—we had to look at 90 to 100 minutes of film before starting to edit the show. That takes quite a while and by the time we ran Camera A all the way through, then Cameras B and C, we had forgotten what kind of angle we had on Camera A at the same place.

I found myself spending five, six, seven hours a day or night in the projection room with our film editor, Danny Cahn. The live television people looked at all the three angles simultaneously through their monitors. The motion-picture industry had the same old Moviolas, capable of running only one piece of film at a time.

I asked Al Simon, "Why can't we put three of these Moviolas together and synchronize them with one sound track so we can look at all three angles, go back with all three or with just one or two or whatever we have to do? It would save Danny and me three or four hours a day in the projection room."

Al found some guy who had worked for the people who made Moviolas, told him what we wanted and asked him if it was possible.

The man said, "I don't see why not."

He went to work on it and built this "thing," three Moviolas mounted on a cast-iron platform, with four legs and wheels. It also had four arms, three of them extending upward from the side of each Moviola and capable of holding a thousand-foot reel, the other one extending also upward and to the left side of all three and anchored to a piece of pipe, attached to the platform with an elbow, hooking another piece of pipe to hold the sound-track reel.

About a foot and a half below each Moviola screen were three more arms for the take-up reels of A, B and C cameras, and a fourth arm aligned with the sound reel for its take-up reel. All three film reels were synchronized with the sound reel.

Just below the platform were individual pedals for each of the four reels, in case you just wanted one camera to go back and/or hold, and one master pedal which controlled all four at the same time.

This contraption got to be known as "Desilu's four-headed Monster." It was sensational.

The guy who built it wanted to rent it to us. I said, "No, I don't want to rent it. I want to buy it."

Al said, "I'll cost us thirty-five hundred dollars."

"Okay, buy it."

Unbelievably, that was the only four-headed monster in town until the demands for it were so many we built the second one. That's one of the things that is hard to understand about Hollywood. They're still working with the same equipment D. W. Griffith used in *The Birth of a Nation*.

Playing Ricky at the same time was the least of my problems. After a while I could have phoned Ricky in.

I did have quite a problem with the budget of $24,500, which I had promised CBS. First of all, at that time we didn't have a big operation with an accounting department or a legal department. We were not yet departmentalized.

I'd get home at night, get out the bills, go over them and make out checks to pay them. And if some were for things we'd have to use every week, I would try to buy them instead of renting them. I didn't know that nonrecurrent expenses like the sprinkler system, the expense of rebuilding the stage and putting in the big doors, the seats on the stage, changing the surface of the floor, the crab dollies, the four-headed Monster and many others should be totaled and divided among all thirty-nine shows. That's the way it should be done, but all I did was pay each bill as I went along.

The result was that the first show cost in the vicinity of $95,000; the second $85,000; the third $75,000; and the fourth $60,000. Then I got a call from Harry Ackerman, the guy who had okayed the $50,000 loan to start the whole project. He had stuck his neck way out in recommending and approving this loan. The deal we had was for $24,500 *plus,* which meant that if we went over the budget we didn't have to pay, CBS did; and they were getting kind of nervous at this point. (They never gave me that kind of a deal again.)

By the fourth show we were somewhere in the neighborhood of $220,000 over budget. Harry said that the Doctor had called him. Everyone knew when they'd said "Doctor," they meant Frank Stanton, the chairman of the board of CBS.

Another executive at CBS was Howard Meighan, whose big project at the time was Television City, and he had wanted us to do the show live from there.

Harry told me, "Howard Meighan wants to bet Stanton fifty-thousand dollars that CBS will lose more than half a million dollars on the first year of *I Love Lucy*. What would you like me to tell the good Doctor?"

"Tell him I will take half the bet."

"You sound awful cocky."

"Yeah, well, I think you'll soon see things starting to drop. I've been charging everything as I went along and there are a lot of expenses here which are nonrecurring that I should have amortized over all thirty-nine shows." (I had just found out from our personal manager, Andrew Hickox, what the two words meant.)

We had been buying a lot of stuff which we could use over and over, without paying rental companies. Eventually we did some shows in the neighborhood of $15,000, others for $18,000, some for even $12,000. The thirty-nine shows went about $9,500 over budget for the lot. So instead of each costing $24,500, they each cost $24,750, which was right next door. That was fine with everybody. And why not? It was a bargain.

An American Research Bureau press release out of Washington, D.C., in early 1952, gives the reason in far more official and dramatic terms than I am capable of:

ARB Television Reports Reveal *I LOVE LUCY*
First TV Show in History to Reach 10 Million Homes

For the first time in the history of television, a regularly scheduled TV program has been seen in 10 million American homes. American Research Bureau Reports for April reveal the Monday night comedy show *I Love Lucy* reached 10,600,000 homes on April 7. In announcing the figure ARB Director James W. Seiler said this is a "first" for the industry and a milestone in television viewing.

The program, presented on CBS Monday nights from 9 to 9:30, stars the husband and wife team of Lucille Ball and Desi Arnaz. In addition to breaking the 10-million mark, *I Love Lucy* was the top program in the nation in April with a rating of 63.2, and it was the first-ranking show in practically every major city. The program is released in 62 of the 64 television markets, but actually is within range of viewers in all 64 areas.

ARB Director Seiler also pointed out that while the program reached 10,600,000 homes, there was an average of 2.9 viewers watching on each television set. This means, he said, that the show was seen by 30,740,000 individuals—nearly a fifth of the nation's population. Of these, a compilation of ARB diary figures shows 32% or 9,836,800 were men, 44% or 13,525,000 were women, and 24% or 7,377,600 were children.

I Love Lucy made its TV debut this season and was rated for the first time in November. The ARB report for that month shows it reached 5,050,000 homes, had 50 outlets and a rating of 38.5—the 16th most popular program in the nation. In December it jumped to 7th place on the ARB rating list; in January and February it was 5th, and in March it became the second-ranking program in the nation.

A summary of ARB figures from the six reports covering *I Love Lucy* shows the program has increased its rating 24.7 points in the period, has more than doubled the number of homes it reaches and has added 17 million viewers to its audience.

4/30/52

I have always wondered what the 0.9 viewer looked like.

33

We were about to begin filming our second season, early in 1952, when Lucy came to me and said, 'Hey, Father, I've got news for you. I'm pregnant again."

We were so happy we couldn't believe it. For ten years we had wanted children so much and all we were able to get were cats, dogs, bees, old chickens and The Duchess of Devonshire, and here it was nine months after our beautiful girl was born and Lucy was pregnant again.

After we calmed down, I said, "Jesus, I better tell Jess Oppenheimer about it." I arranged a meeting with him and told him there was a situation we had to think about.

"What's that?" he asked.

"Lucy's pregnant again."

"Oh, my God," he said, "what are we going to do?"

I laughed and said, "What do you mean, what are we going to do? She's going to have a baby. Whatever there was to be done about it, Lucy and I have already done it."

"Yeah, but what about the show?" he asked. "You know how big she gets. There's no way we can hide it for more than a couple of months at the most."

"I know. So how about Lucy Ricardo having a baby as part of our shows this year?"

"They'll never let you do that," he answered.

"Why won't they? And who are 'they'?"

"You know—the sponsor, the network, the advertising agency."

"Well, I don't see why not," I said. "What's wrong with Lucy Ricardo having a baby? Lucy and Ricky are married. She's pregnant.

There is no way we can hide that fact from the audience. We have already signed the contracts. This is the number-one show on the air. There is only one way to do it—Lucy Ricardo will have a baby."

"It'd be a hell of a gimmick," said Jess, "if they would let you do it."

I called the Biow agency and told them the situation. They said, "There's no way you can do that. You cannot show a pregnant woman on television."

I called CBS. They had the same answer, and so did the Philip Morris people. No matter how much I argued that Lucy and Ricky were married, that it was a natural thing for them to have a child, "What the hell could be wrong with that?"

They wouldn't agree to it. They wanted us to do the shows without showing she was pregnant.

They asked, "Can you hide her behind chairs or something or other?"

"There ain't no way I can hide Lucy's pregnancy. By the time fall comes around she'll be as big as the Goodyear blimp. And I still don't see what is so wrong if she has a baby in the show as Lucy Ricardo."

Well, I couldn't get anywhere.

They finally said, "Can you just do one or two shows about it?"

"No, it cannot be done that way. We need at least eight or ten shows to do them honestly and well, and have any kind of continuity in the series. First, she has to tell Ricky she's going to have a baby. Lucy and Ricky, in our story life, have been married for more than ten years without having a child, so that has to be great news in the Ricardo household and we couldn't do it justice without doing one whole show just about that. Then, even though we will cover the last six months of her pregnancy in eight or ten shows, we certainly could not make them fun and sentimental and honest and real in much less than at least eight shows."

Mr. Alfred Lyons, chairman of the board at Philip Morris, was not in the United States. He was in England. A wonderful, wise old gent, he had always been very kind to us and also very understanding.

He had visited the ranch in Chatsworth shortly after he bought our show. When he first met Lucy at our house she was not feeling too well. As he came into the bedroom, Lucy was propped up in bed, wearing a lovely bed jacket, reading a book and smoking a Chesterfield, a fact she could not hide because there was a whole carton of Chesterfields staring at Mr. Lyons from the night table next to her. He took it very gracefully and after the how-do-you do's and how-do-you-feel's and hope-you're-on-your-feet-soon's, he said, "That's a very funny joke."

"What?" asked Lucy.

"Putting the carton of Chesterfields on your night table."

"Oh, my God!" said Lucy.

As we walked out of the room, he told me, "Look, if she must smoke Chesterfields, make sure you put them inside a Philip Morris package and inside a Philip Morris carton."

We did this for some time, until one day I told our propman not to switch them and see if she would notice. She didn't. We didn't switch them anymore.

I decided to write a letter to Mr. Lyons and explain the whole situation about Lucy being pregnant and how I wanted to treat that in the show, how all these people were against it, including his own Philip Morris people, his advertising agency and the network.

> Mr. Lyons, I guess it all comes down to you. You are the man who is paying the money for this show and I guess I will have to do whatever you decide. There's only one thing I want to make certain that you understand. We have given you the number-one show in the country and, up till now, the creative decisions have been in our hands. Your people are now telling us we cannot do this, so the only thing I want from you, if you agree with them, is that you must inform them that we will not accept them telling us what not to do unless, in the future, they will also tell us what to do.
>
> At that point, and if this is your decision, we will cease to be responsible to you for the show being the number-one show on television, and you will have to look to your people, to the network and to the Biow Agency for that responsibility.
>
> Thank you very much for all you have done for us in the past.
> Sincerely yours.

About a week after I sent the letter, all arguments about the "pregnant" shows stopped. Nobody was squawking anymore about whether there should only be two shows or no shows or eight shows or whatever. I figured Mr. Lyons must have done something, but I wasn't about to find out what. The fact that the opposition had stopped was good enough for me.

A couple of years later I was in New York and, as usual, went to Mr. Lyons' office just to say hello to him and thank him again for all his trust and cooperation in the past. As I was leaving, I was stopped at the door by his secretary, the lady who had been with the old man for thirty or forty years, and with whom I had a very good relationship.

She asked, "Did you ever wonder why all the arguments stopped when you wanted to do those shows about Lucy being pregnant and everybody was against it?"

"Yes, I sure did. I figured Mr. Lyons must have said something to somebody, but I wasn't about to ask too many questions and maybe create some other problems. Let good enough alone, you know."

"I have a memo here I want to show you," she said, "but don't you ever tell anybody I showed it to you."

The memo, sent from England, read: "To whom it may concern: Don't fuck around with the Cuban! Signed, A.L."

I almost fell to the floor. What a great old man he was!

After the opposition to the "baby" shows stopped, we got together with Jess, Bob and Madelyn and laid out what we all thought should be done, how we should introduce it, and how many shows we should do. We finally decided that in the first show Lucy should find out she was pregnant and tell Ricky about it. In the eighth show he would take her to the hospital and the baby would be born.

In between, we could do shows about Lucy having cravings for strange combinations of food, like chocolate ice cream, sardines and pickles, mixed together. Ricky would develop sympathetic labor pains and order the same horrible mixture, and other humorous things common to pregnancies, like Lucy not being able to get out of an easy chair or tie her own shoes. An obvious one was that Ricky should not talk to the baby, so he or she would not be handicapped by his accent.

If we needed a break or two from the pregnancy shows, or if we needed to extend the period of time to make the birth of the Ricardo baby coincide as close as possible with the actual birth of the Arnaz baby, we would use repeats of past shows as if we were reminiscing about what had happened. One short scene would be sufficient to lead us into each repeat.

One thing in our favor for the timing was that Lucie, our first child, was born by Caesarean operation. It wasn't supposed to be that way, but at the last minute Dr. Joe Harris found the child had turned the wrong way, and he didn't want to take a chance.

She was a nice big baby and he was very glad he decided to operate, because Lucy was about two weeks overdue. If we had lost that second child after losing the first, it would have been such a tragedy I don't think we could have taken it.

Every day of my life when I think of this gorgeous daughter of ours, I bless Dr. Harris and thank God.

Lucy, having had a Caesarean, would also have to have her next child by Caesarean. Knowing this, we asked Dr. Harris when he thought the baby would be born. He said it would be sometime in January of 1953. It was then sometime in August. We started counting back from the middle of January and decided that on one show in October of 1952 Lucy would tell Ricky that she was pregnant.

We didn't have to go week by week. In the writing we could say it was the next day or the next month.

We figured that, with eight shows about the baby and perhaps one, two or three repeats, we could cover the rest of the pregnancy leading to the birth of the Ricardo child and come pretty close to the birth of our own child.

And that's the way it was all laid out.

One other thing we wanted to make sure of was that we didn't do or say anything that would offend our television audience in any way whatsoever. So I called Cardinal James McIntyre, who was our top man out here. I also called Rabbi Edgar Magnin and the Protestant leader concerned with television, Rev. Clifton Moore of the Hollywood Presbyterian Church. I explained to each of them what we were doing and asked them to assign someone to be with us during this entire period to read the scripts, come to the rehearsals and see the filming.

They graciously agreed. We had a Catholic priest, Monsignor Joseph Devlin of St. Vincent's Catholic Church and head of the Catholic Legion of Decency; Rabbi Alfred Wolf, of the Wilshire Temple, representing the Jewish faith; and Mr. Moore himself. They were with us four days a week to see the rehearsals and filming. They used to have lunch and dinner together and became very good friends.

They never objected to anything. As a matter of fact, we had the word "pregnant" in one of the shows and the CBS censor would not let us say it, but the rabbi, the minister and the priest said, "Well, what's wrong with 'pregnant'? That's what it is."

I met with them and said, "Look, what's the difference? What else can we say?"

"Expecting," all three advised.

"Okay, we'll use 'expecting.' I'll probably get a laugh with that because I can't pronounce 'expecting' too well. It will probably come out 'specting' and Lucy will then be able to imitate my way of saying it. 'Yeah, like he says, I'm 'specting.' "

It is hard to believe in this day and age that CBS or anyone else could have been prudish about the word pregnant. Today they not only use the word but also show you how to get into that condition.

I didn't want Lucy to work beyond her fifth month of pregnancy, which would be in October, more than three months before the birth of our child.

We knew the child was going to be born sometime in January. That meant the last show had to be done at least three or four months before that.

By this time I had checked again with Dr. Harris and he had told me the second week in January.

So we had to film the show about Lucy Ricardo having the baby not later than the first of October, and then Lucy Arnaz could go home and wait for the birth of our child.

The next question was, Is it going to be a boy or a girl? As far as the show was concerned, we had to decide this three and a half months before the baby was actually born.

I asked Dr. Harris, "Can you tell me what it's going to be?"

"I can tell you it's going to be a boy or a girl."

"Yeah, but I've got to film the show in the next couple of weeks."

"You're a gambler," he said. "It's a fifty–fifty shot."

"Well, Joe, I've already discussed this with Lucy and we have agreed the Ricardos should have a boy, regardless of what the Arnazes have. We are thinking of our daughter, who has never been in the show. She wasn't even born when we started. So if the Ricardos have a boy, and we get an actor to play the part, our daughter will understand that he's only a member of the Ricardos' make-believe family and that she and the newborn baby are the only real members of the Arnaz family. It's all settled. Lucy Ricardo's child is going to be a boy, regardless of what Lucy Ball Arnaz gives birth to."

A couple of weeks after that we started rehearsing the eighth show in which little Ricky would be born. The writers had really outdone themselves for that one. The routine of rehearsing and timing how Ethel, Fred and Ricky would act when Lucy would tell us it was time to take her to the hospital, and how our very well-planned and -timed procedure fell apart when the actual time came, has always been one of my favorites.

In the hospital scene when Ricky was shown the baby and was told "It's a boy," he fainted beautifully. I hope Ricky appreciates that I got a hell of a bump on my head doing that full-figure backward fall to portray his faint.

You probably couldn't see my tears through that crazy makeup and headdress of a tribal Indian chief that I had on, but my eyes were full. I was thinking that in ten or twelve weeks I would be in a real maternity ward waiting to hear our baby had been born and was healthy. Of course, I was really praying our baby would be a boy, but not for the sake of the show.

I was the only male of the Arnaz family in my generation. Both of my father's brothers had girls, and, as I mentioned before, the family was a very old family. If I didn't have a son, that would be the end of the Arnaz name. So, of course, I was extremely interested in having a son, and this was my last chance because, after this one, Lucy could not have another child. The doctor had already said, "She's not that young anymore and two Caesareans are enough. Another one would be dangerous."

I'll be the first to admit that Lucy Arnaz having a baby boy at 8:30 A.M. on Monday, the nineteenth of January, 1953, and Lucy Ricardo having a baby boy that same night on CBS was the most unbelievable piece of timing I know of. But, as Dr. Harris said, "It was a fifty–fifty shot."

One of the reasons it happened on the same day was that Dr. Harris always performed his Caesareans on Monday, unless there was an emergency of some kind. He had told me that if the baby cooperated and continued making the progress he was making, on Monday, January 19, he should be ready to make his debut and join the world.

All we had to do, to have the eighth show televised the same Monday, was to use two repeats of previous, nonbaby shows on Christmas Eve and New Year's Eve.

A tremendous amount of lucky breaks and a hell of a lot of hardworking and dedicated people helped us to accomplish this. As the shows about the Ricardos' going to have a baby started to be shown on television, they created the most incredible interest all over the world, and it kept building up. When it was announced that the Arnaz baby would, in all probability, be born the same day, reporters from all over the world and every wire service in the United States and Latin America descended upon me. They all wanted to be with me in the fathers' waiting room at the hospital. Of course it was impossible to accommodate all of them. I asked them to pick one guy to represent the wire services and the newspapers and only he would be with me in the fathers' waiting room.

Lucy went to surgery at eight o'clock in the morning. James Bacon of the Associated Press, who is now writing a syndicated column appearing in the *Los Angeles Herald-Examiner,* was the one picked to be in the fathers' waiting room with me. It was a small room right next to the delivery room, where the surgery was being done. There was only a swinging door between me and Lucy, but they wouldn't let me go inside and be with her.

All the doctors, the nurses, everyone else who was in that room with Lucy had been looking at the shows and knew the Ricardos' baby was going to be born that same evening on television, and that it would be a boy.

Simultaneously, Jim and I heard a loud baby cry and a happy choir of voices sing out, "It's a boy!"

Bacon took off like a rocket, shouting "Congratulations!" Later on he told me that within ninety seconds the news was on Japanese radio. News services all over the world were standing by during the surgery.

"It's a boy!" I wish I had a recording of it, but I really don't need it—I can hear it today.

The national ratings on *I Love Lucy* the night the baby was born were the highest ever on television. Front pages carried the story that over two million more people saw our show that night than watched General Eisenhower being inaugurated as President of the United States the following day. I will never forget when Desi was nine or ten years old and he was spending a weekend with me in Palm Springs. We happened to run into General Eisenhower, who was about to tee off at El Dorado Country Club. The General looked up while we were watching and waiting to tee off after him, and then he asked me, "Is this the little fellow who knocked me off the front pages the day before I was inaugurated?"

"Yes, sir, General, that's him."

General Eisenhower seemed to get a kick out of meeting Desi, and afterward in the clubhouse bought him a banana split. Desi has never forgotten that day.

The year 1953 seemed to be bringing us nothing but blessings, success, honors and wealth.

Less than a month after Desi was born, Lucy and I signed with MGM to costar in *The Long, Long Trailer* for $250,000. A studio spokesman said it was the most expensive deal ever made in MGM history.

It was a pleasure dealing with Benny Thau again and getting that kind of dough. He accused me of holding them up for so much because I was still mad at the studio for hiring Montalban.

So I made him a deal. "I'll tell you what, Benny. If the picture doesn't gross as much as *Father of the Bride* in the United States, we will give you back twenty-five thousand dollars, but if it grosses more you will pay us fifty thousand dollars more." He jumped at that.

Father of the Bride had grossed more than any other MGM comedy up to that time.

I said, "Put it in the contract."

About a year a half later, when most of the box-office receipts were in, we received a check for the additional $50,000, making the total $300,000, which tripled the combined salaries we had received for a whole year when we were under contract to MGM previously.

During the same week we signed an agreement to continue producing *I Love Lucy* for two more years. It was the largest single television contract ever negotiated. It provided for a cost to Philip Morris of $8 million, out of which CBS would get $3 million for their nine-to-nine-thirty Monday-night time period, and Desilu $5 million for the production.

In that same February my Columbia record of "I Love Lucy," flip side "There's a Brand New Baby at Our House" (which I wrote with Eddie Maxwell) was in the first five of the best-selling records in the country. I also made the list of the Ten Best Dressed Men in the United States, with such dandies as President Eisenhower, former President Harry S. Truman, Rex Harrison, Ezio Pinza, and Danny Kaye.

The National Academy of Television Arts and Sciences gave Lucy an Emmy for the Best Comedienne of 1952, and both of us an Emmy for Best Situation Comedy.

The New York Times commented on February 5: "With Lucille Ball's baby and Ike in as scheduled, the American situation can now be said to be well in hand."

Of course, the most important thing of all was that we now had our daughter, our son, and two people couldn't have been more in love or happier than we were.

Then the shit hit the fan.

34

I was playing poker at Irving Briskin's house in Del Mar when I got a phone call from Ken Morgan, telling me that Walter Winchell had just made a comment on his radio show in one of his "blind" items: "The top television comedienne has been confronted with her membership in the Communist Party!"

It was Sunday, September 6.

That was not a "blind" item to me. It had 20-20 vision as far as I was concerned. I knew immediately he meant Lucy. I knew the whole story about Grandpa and how Lucy and her mother and brother Fred had been investigated and, after they had answered a lot of questions, how they had been cleared. Nevertheless, Fred had lost a job in an airplane factory in Kansas on account of some rumors about his investigation and he had had to go to the FBI to get a security clearance before he could get another job in any defense plant.

And just two days before Winchell's broadcast, Lucy had again met with William Wheeler, an investigator for the House Un-American Activities Committee. Donald Jackson, the Representative from Santa Monica, California, was the head of that one.

I was very familiar with the transcript of that interrogation, which the Committee was kind enough to let me read. So I knew that she was not guilty of anything, but in those days the climate was bad for even the smallest innuendos. Joe McCarthy and his Senate hearings were like witch-hunts. He even accused General George C. Marshall of having Communist leanings.

Larry Parks, who did such a great job portraying Jolson in the film *The Jolson Story* and again in *Jolson Sings Again,* had his motion-picture career ended in the United States because he got scared and at first said he had never been a member of the Party but later admitted that he had been. And even though being a member was not a crime, and he wasn't convicted of anything else, nobody would give him a job after that.

So when Kenny filled me in on the Winchell broadcast, I told him, "I'm driving into town right now. You meet me at the house in Chatsworth and bring Howard Strickling."

I was driving the 130 miles or so from Del Mar to the ranch when it hit me that history was repeating itself in an ironic sort of way. Twenty years before I had been playing poker at Jack Cendoya's house in Santiago when I got a phone call from my uncle, telling me that a bunch of Communists (Bolsheviks in those days) were on their way to ransack our house and asking me to get my mother the hell out of there. It occurred to me that I should either stop playing poker or disconnect the phone while doing so.

Howard Strickling was the vice-president in charge of public relations for MGM Studios, for which we had just completed filming *The Long, Long Trailer,* which hadn't been released yet.

I got home about 2 A.M. and Kenny, Howard and Lucy were waiting for me.

After a little discussion, Howard, who stuttered pretty badly and who had already been briefed by Kenny, said, "Well, m-m-maybe W-W-Winchell doesn't mean L-L-Lucy. M-M-Maybe he m-m-means Imogene C-C-Coca."

Lucy said pluckily, "I resent that, Howard. Everyone knows that *I'm* the top comedienne!"

"I wish you wouldn't brag at this time," I told her.

Then I turned to Howard and said, "Now look, Lucy has been investigated and she has been cleared. She did have a registration card she signed in nineteen thirty-six, but it expired in nineteen thirty-eight. She didn't know what the hell she signed. Here, read the transcript of the last meeting with the Committee investigator, two days ago."

TESTIMONY OF SEPTEMBER 4, 1953

After Miss Ball stated that she was appearing voluntarily and after she told how she got her start as a film actress at $50 or $75 a week in Hollywood, the testimony, in part, was as follows:

MR. WHEELER: When did you first register to vote?

MISS BALL: I guess the first time I ever did was in '36.

MR. WHEELER: I would like to hand you a photostatic copy of a voter's registration and ask you if that is your signature.

MISS BALL: That looks like my handwriting.

MR. WHEELER: You will note that the party that you intended to affiliate with at that time was the Communist Party.

MISS BALL: In '36?

MR. WHEELER: Yes.

MISS BALL: I guess so.

MR. WHEELER: You did register to vote then as a Communist or intending to vote the Communist ticket?

MISS BALL: Yes.

MR. WHEELER: Would you go into detail and explain the background, the reason you voted or registered to vote as a Communist or person who intended to affiliate with the Communist Party?

MISS BALL: It was our grandfather, Fred C. Hunt. He just wanted us to, and we just did something to please him. I didn't intend to vote that way. As I recall, I didn't. My grandfather started years ago —he was a Socialist as long as I can remember. He is the only father we ever knew, my grandfather. My father died when I was tiny, before my brother was born. He was my brother's only father. All through his life he had been a Socialist, as far back as Eugene V. Debs, and he was in sympathy with the working man as long as I have known and he took the *Daily Worker*. It never meant much to us, because he was so radical on the subject that he pressed his point a little too much, actually, probably, during our childhood, because he finally got over our heads and we didn't do anything but consider it a nuisance, but as a dad, and he got into his seventies, and it became so vital to him that the world must be right twenty-four hours a day, all over it, and he was trying his damnedest to do the best he could for everybody and especially the working man; that is, from the garbage man, the maid in the kitchen, the studio worker, the factory worker. He never lost a chance to do what he considered bettering their positions. Sometimes it got a little ridiculous because *my* position in the so-called capitalist world was pretty good and it was a little hard to reconcile the two. We didn't argue with him very much because he had had a couple of strokes and if he got overly excited, why, he would have another one. So finally there came a point where my brother was twenty-one, and he was going to see that Freddie registered to help the working man, which was, in his idea then, the Communist Party. At that time it wasn't a thing to hide behind doors, to be a member of the Party.

MR. WHEELER: He considered the Communist Party a working man's party?

MISS BALL: That is all I ever heard. I never heard my grandfather use the word "Communist." He always talked about the working man and read the *Daily Worker*. He got very confused in his latter years, when Russia and—who got together?—Russia and Germany?

MR. WHEELER: That's right.

That period I remember well and I'm glad Lucy finally got it right about who got together with whom. But it is a fact that Grandpa was very confused. When Kenny volunteered to go into the Army in 1942, and I was unable to join the Navy and was drafted in 1943, he was very upset and kept questioning us about who the hell was allied with whom. Were we with Germany and Russia, and, if so, against whom? We explained to him that Germany and Russia were no longer friends and that our allies were Russia, England and France, and our enemies were Germany, Italy and Japan. He was by then pretty old and I know we all felt sorry for him.

MR. WHEELER: Have you ever been a member of the Communist Party?

MISS BALL: Not to my knowledge.

MR. WHEELER: Have you ever been asked to become a member of the Communist Party?

MISS BALL: No.

MR. WHEELER: Did you ever attend any meetings that you later discovered were Communist Party meetings?

MISS BALL: No.

MR. WHEELER: Do you know whether or not any meetings were ever held in your home at 1344 North Ogden Drive?

MISS BALL: No, I know nothing of that. I don't believe it is true.

MR. WHEELER: How old were you in 1936?

MISS BALL: I am 42 now; 24.

This was 1953 so she was forty-two, but that means she was twenty-five in 1936, not twenty-four. Mathematics was not her best subject.

MR. WHEELER: I would like to introduce the affidavit of registration No. 847584. This affidavit of registration is signed by Lucille Ball and dated the nineteenth of March, 1936. Have you ever known an individual by the name of Emil Freed?

MISS BALL: I never heard the name before, to my knowledge, as I recall.

MR. WHEELER: Are you aware that you were a member of the Central Committee of the Communist Party for the year 1936?

MISS BALL: Was I aware before you told me, you mean?

MR. WHEELER: Yes.

MISS BALL: No.

MR. WHEELER: Well, I would like to hand you a document entitled "Appointment of Members of the State Central Committee Meeting at Sacramento in the year of 1936." It is stamped "Communist Party," and this document discloses that Emil Freed was a delegate by nomination to the State Central Committee of the Communist Party for that year. And he appointed three individuals as delegates. Those appointments, according to the document, are Jacob Berger, 822 North Orange Drive, Fred Hunt, 1344 North Ogden Drive, and Lucille Ball, 1344 North Ogden Drive.

MISS BALL: I don't know Emil Freed. I never heard of Emil Freed, and if Emil Freed appointed me as a delegate to the State Central Committee it was done without my knowledge or consent.

MR. WHEELER: Do you know who could be responsible for your name appearing on this document?

MISS BALL: Possibly my grandfather, Fred C. Hunt.

Lucy had called her grandpa Fred C. Hunt since the year she received a Christmas card from him signed "Fred C. Hunt."

MR. WHEELER: I assume you did not attend the meeting of the State Central Committee at Sacramento.

MISS BALL: I didn't even know there was one. I still don't know what it means.

MR. WHEELER: I would like to refer to the report of the un-American activities in California for the year 1943, and refer to page 127 of that document, which is a portion of an affidavit by Rena M. Vale. In this affidavit she has admitted she was one time a member of the Communist Party and she is discussing how she became a member:

"That within a few days after my third application to join the Communist Party was made, I received a notice to attend a meeting on North Ogden Drive, Hollywood; although it was a typed, unsigned note, merely requesting my presence at the address at 8 o'clock in the evening on a given day, I knew it was the long-awaited notice to attend Communist Party new members classes.

"That on arrival at this address I found several others present; an elderly man informed us that we were the guests of the screen actress, Lucille Ball, and showed us various objects to establish that fact, and stated she was glad to loan her home for a Communist Party new members class." Do you have any knowledge of any meetings held in your home, Miss Ball?

MISS BALL: None whatsoever.

MR. WHEELER: Are you acquainted with Rena Vale?

MISS BALL: I never heard the name before in my life.

MR. WHEELER: Do you know whether or not your grandfather, Fred Hunt, held meetings at the home?

MISS BALL: Not to our knowledge ever.

Either Rena Vale was lying to make herself a big shot, or Grandpa did hold those meetings and her mother and Fred were afraid to tell Lucy.

MR. WHEELER: I also have a photostatic copy of an Affidavit of Registration for the year 1936 for Mrs. Desiree E. Ball, and it discloses that she also registered to vote as a person who intended to affiliate with the Communist Party on the twelfth day of June, 1936. What relation is Desiree Ball to you?

MISS BALL: My mother.

MR. WHEELER: Do you know whether or not she was ever a member of the Communist Party?

MISS BALL: Not to my knowledge.

MR. WHEELER: I have a second photostat here, a voter's registration, signed by Fred E. Hunt, who also intended to affiliate with the Communist Party.

MISS BALL: Fred C. Hunt.

MR. WHEELER: Fred C. Hunt, rather. This document is dated the twelfth day of June, 1936, and also shows he changed the vote to Democrat 11-18-40.

That's when he got pissed off at the Russians for becoming Nazi allies.

> MR. WHEELER: The Affidavit of Registration discloses you voted in the primary for the year 1938 . . . the Affidavit of Registration on the reverse side discloses that you signed two petitions for the year 1936, the Freed nominating petition for the 57th Assembly District, or, rather, it is a sponsor certificate. This document was also obtained from the files of the Secretary of State and I will introduce it in the record as Ball Exhibit No. 3. I would like to refer to the second page of this document, under line 23, and there appears the signature of Lucille Ball, 1344 Ogden Drive, and occupation, artist. It is dated 6-16-36. Is that your signature [indicating]?
> MISS BALL: I would say it was.
> MR. WHEELER: Do you recall signing the document?
> MISS BALL: It is something I signed without looking at it, or if I looked at it, it didn't seem like a big thing at the time.

That would be exactly like Lucy. She signed hundreds of documents that I gave her without looking any further than my signature. If I had signed them, she would automatically sign under me. These included the $8 million Philip Morris contract and the $989,642.69 income tax bill from Uncle Sam in 1957.

> MR. WHEELER: Are you familiar with the words or the phrase "Criminal Syndicalism"?
> MISS BALL: No, but it is pretty. What does it mean?

You cannot help but love her for that remark. I know I did. I'm sure she was frightened but she could still keep her sense of humor.

> MR. WHEELER: The Communists were taken to court and tried for criminal syndicalism, and . . .
> MISS BALL: And I signed something else?
> MR. WHEELER: . . . you signed this petition to take the Criminal Syndicalism Act off the statutes of the State of California.
> MISS BALL: I did? May I see the signature?
> MR. WHEELER: Unfortunately they have been destroyed, those particular petitions.
> MISS BALL: By whom?
> MR. WHEELER: They are retained for a few years, under law, and they can be destroyed.
> MISS BALL: Was this the same time we were being Nice-to-Daddy week?

What a lovely, honest question.

> MR. WHEELER: It was in the year 1936.

MISS BALL: I imagine that petition ties up with the Un-American Activities committee business, constitutional rights they are all standing up for now. Is that what it means?

MR. WHEELER: Well, it means more or less like this: "An act defining criminal syndicalism and sabotage, proscribing certain acts and methods in connection therewith and in pursuance thereof and providing penalties and punishments therefore."

No wonder she didn't know what the hell he was talking about.

MISS BALL: Well, anyway, I don't know what it means.

MR. WHEELER: You were previously contacted by myself, an investigator for the House Committee on Un-American Activities?

MISS BALL: Yes.

MR. WHEELER: You recall the date as April 3, 1952?

MISS BALL: Yes.

And how she recalled that date, and so did I. That's why we were both so surprised when she was called again this time, plus the Winchell item and the *Herald-Express* picking it up. There was something phony and intentionally malicious about the whole second interview. The Committee knew the whole story in 1952.

MR. WHEELER: Well, your name is mentioned in the Daily People's World, the issue of 10-26-47, page 1, columns 5 and 6, as one of the high personalities who were sponsoring or a member of the Committee of the First Amendment. That committee was formed here in Hollywood to oppose the congressional hearings in 1947.

MISS BALL: Fine. Then I have no knowledge of signing it.

This had to do with the Hollywood Unfriendly Ten. She never knowingly did anything, pro or con, about that. The subject was discussed in our house many times and her interest in the case was nil. Of course I had seen what a well-organized and distorted propaganda campaign could do, as it did in Cuba. However, I felt that most of the Unfriendly Ten were just pawns of the pros.

MR. WHEELER: Do you have anything in addition you would like to add for the record?

MISS BALL: I have never done anything for Communists, to my knowledge, at any time. I have never contributed money or attended a meeting or even had anything to do with people connected with it, if to my knowledge they were. I am not a Communist now. I never have been. I never wanted to be. Nothing in the world could ever change my mind. At no time in my life have I ever been in sympathy with anything that even faintly resembled it. He was always opposed [indicating me] to how my grandfather felt about any other way this country should be run. I thought things were just fine the way they were.

It sounds a little weak and silly and corny now, but at the time it was very important because we knew we weren't going to have Daddy with us very long. If it made him happy it was important at the time. But I was always conscious of the fact I could go just so far to make him happy. I tried not to go any farther. In those days that was not a big, terrible thing to do. It was almost as terrible to be a Republican in those days.

Well, honey, today is even worse.

MISS BALL: I have never been too civic-minded and certainly never political-minded in my life.

Not true! She could have also said that if it hadn't been for her help we could have never gotten the few people we did get to have dinner with President Truman and the First Lady in 1948. She could also have said that the first time in her life she voted in a general election, and knowing exactly what she was doing, was when we both voted for General Eisenhower in 1952.

MR. WHEELER: I have no further questions. Thank you for your cooperation.

35

While reading parts of the transcript that night after the Winchell broadcast, Howard Strickling laughed at some of Lucy's answers and her stories about Grandpa. He also advised us to ignore Winchell's broadcast and to keep quiet about the whole thing. He was sure it would just blow away.

When you look at it in retrospect and hindsight (as they say in Washington), you realize that Howard was not the only one who has ever thought this way.

President Nixon, referring to Watergate, told John Mitchell on the telephone, according to the tape transcripts, "This thing is just one of those side issues and a month from now everybody will look back and wonder what all the shouting was about."

I honestly didn't share Howard's confidence that this was the best way to handle the situation. I wanted everything out in the open, and as soon as possible. I knew the members of the Un-American Activities Committee could not accuse Lucy of any intentional wrong-doing, and had even thanked her for her honest answers and coop-eration in clearing this whole matter. But one of them must have leaked the fact of the second interrogation to Winchell in the hope of bring-ing the House Committee front-page publicity, which up until now had been hogged by the McCarthy Senate group.

To spare Lucy and her family any further embarrassment, I went along with Strickling's advice. And it began to look as though he'd been right. Nothing broke in the papers Monday, Tuesday, Wednesday or Thursday. We rehearsed our show as usual. Howard called me Thursday night, very happy that no one had picked up Winchell's "blind" item, and he was by now convinced nobody would and the whole thing would just die a natural death. I thanked him for the call and told him I hoped he was right.

That hope didn't last long.

Next morning it had just begun to get light, and Lucy and I were in bed, sleeping, when I awoke to see a guy with a camera, just outside the big window in our bedroom. I went outside and grabbed the photographer by the neck.

"What in hell do you think you're doing with that camera out there?" I yelled at him.

There was a reporter with him who told me, "Sorry, sir, but we have orders from the paper to interview Lucy."

"What paper and who ordered you?" I demanded to know.

"The *Herald-Express* and the city editor, Agness M. Under-wood."

He showed me his credentials and said, "The paper has a photo-static copy of an affidavit showing Miss Ball had registered in nine-teen thirty-six as a voter, intending to affiliate with the Communist Party."

I told them to come in. I got Aggie Underwood on the phone and told her that Lucy would talk to nobody. Then I told her to tell these characters to get the hell off the ranch. I handed the phone to the reporter and he got his orders to leave. They had been covering a fire near us and had called in to the paper, at which time they were given orders to see Lucy.

Unlike that of Larry Parks, my reaction was the extreme op-posite of getting scared. I got so goddamn mad thinking how ironic this was. One of the reasons our family lost all we had in the Revolu-tion of '33 was because *my father* had been the first man *to put a*

Bolshevik in jail. Now here we were, twenty years later, and it looked like we might blow the whole goddamn Desilu empire and all we had, because *my wife was being called a Communist.*

I couldn't get Aggie to hold the story until she could talk to Congressman Donald Jackson. Before noon they came out with an extra. On the front page the sonsabitches had printed a four-inch banner, in red ink yet, LUCILLE BALL A RED.

The card Lucy had signed, and which they had gotten a photostatic copy of, said on the side, "CANCELLED," and under it the date 12-30-38. The *Herald-Express* printed it on the front page with the word CANCELLED actually cut out from the document. Their vicious distortion of that card was a pretty good example of lousy yellow journalism.

I am glad to say most newspapers that carried the story not only did not cut out CANCELLED, but carried a caption underneath, saying, "Note the cancellation at left."

And in all fairness to the Hearst people, a couple of days later one of the Hearst boys called and was very apologetic. He told me that he had established some pretty strong new rules and had fired a couple of people on account of that distortion.

When we got to the studio and saw the extra, I picked up the telephone and called J. Edgar Hoover in Washington, D.C. I knew Mr. Hoover because he came to Del Mar every summer to have a checkup at Scripps Clinic and then he'd go to the races in the afternoon. I got him on the phone right away and told him what had happened and what the *Herald-Express* headline was. Then I asked, "I want to know, Mr. Hoover, do you have anything against Lucy, does the FBI have any case against her, any proof of wrongdoing? Because what I understand about this, the only thing I know of, is that her grandfather, about seventeen years ago, had her sign this goddamn card, and I want to know what else you've got, if anything."

"Absolutely nothing! She's one hundred percent clear as far as we are concerned," he said.

"Thank you very much, Mr. Hoover."

I then called Dr. Frank Stanton at CBS in New York. "Doctor, there is a horrible headline on the front page of the Los Angeles *Herald-Express* this morning."

I told him what it said and that, of course, it would probably be in newspapers all over the country by now. I also told him I had just finished talking to J. Edgar Hoover and what Hoover had said.

"How do you feel about it?" asked Frank.

"Frank, I am so goddamn mad I'm going to fight like I've never fought before. This is so ridiculous. It is a terrible thing for anyone to say about Lucy. She couldn't care less about politics. She hasn't even been able to understand the nineteen thirty-three Revolution in Cuba and what happened to our family.

"I have explained it to her a hundred times and she says, 'splain it again.' I wish somebody would 'splain' to me how this Senator Mc-Carthy and this other group, the Un-American Activities Committee, can get away with all this shit. But we are not going to get scared. What happened to Larry Parks is not going to happen to her. I guarantee you that!"

I also told him that I hadn't talked to Philip Morris yet, so I didn't know what their reaction would be, but if they got scared and wanted to pull off the show next Monday, I wanted the time spot.

"I want nine to nine-thirty P.M. next Monday on all the same stations that carry *I Love Lucy* and any others you can get, if there are any that don't.

"Whatever it costs, Desilu will pay. Lucy and I will go on the air and tell the story about Grandpa and all the goddamn things Lucy had to go through. We have got to let the American people know what this is all about. She is not going to be crucified by malicious insinuations, distorted facts, and/or false accusations. Besides, Lucy and I telling all the stories about Grandpa could be our funniest show."

"Okay, okay, Cuban. If Philip Morris pulls out, you want nine to nine-thirty next Monday night?"

"Yes, sir!"

"Do you know how much that costs?"

"About thirty thousand. Right?"

"Yeah, that's about it."

"If we need it, can we have it?"

"I hope you don't need it, but if you do you got it, and I guarantee you I'll be watching. It'll be very interesting to see what you do with it. Tell Lucy we are behind you both a hundred percent. I'll tell Paley about it. Anything else you want, just pick up the phone and call Bill or me."

Then I called Alfred Lyons, chairman of the board of Philip Morris, and told him that I had talked to Hoover, that I had talked to Stanton, and that if Philip Morris got nervous, we were going to take over the half-hour.

"Mr. Lyons, I have to know whether you are going to put *I Love Lucy* on the air next Monday night, or whether you are not going to put it on the air next Monday night, and I have to know it now! I must warn you to be prepared for some lousy headlines today, but maybe by tomorrow or the day after they'll tell our side of the story."

"That's a tough decision to make," he said, "with the climate like it is throughout the country and everything."

"Yes, sir, I am very much aware of the climate, and if you want to pull out I can't blame you too much and I'm sure Lucy won't either."

"No, young man, I ain't pulling out," said the nice old bastard. "Let's go get some good headlines!"

Those were the first three calls I made that day. I had tried to get Winchell the night Kenny told me what he had said on his broadcast about the top comedienne, but I couldn't get him on the telephone. I talked to Sherman Billingsley at the Stork Club in New York and told him, "Sherman, Walter had this goddamn item on the air and he may not know it, but he has created a hell of a lot of problems for Lucy and me, and he should know better. I'm sure he knows the true story. He's a friend of J. Edgar Hoover, so all he has to do is pick up the phone and call Mr. Hoover."

Lucy couldn't stop crying. She could not believe the lousy headline and was ashamed that people could think she was a "Communist spy."

I said to her, "Now look, Red," which made her give out with a big wail.

"Oh, Christ, now listen to me. The American people are not going to pass judgment on you until they hear your story. I am trying right now to get Jackson on the phone to hold a press conference."

"Who's he?" she asked.

"He's *el hijo de la madre del cabron* [translation deleted] committee and I am sure one of those members leaked the story about the interrogation. So now, goddamn it, he had better have a press conference and give out the full story. Tell the people how you have been cleared by them and the FBI and everybody else. I'm sure he will. He knows that every wire service, every television station and every newsreel camera will be there covering that press conference. He won't pass the chance to become a big man by clearing you publicly. What the hell else can he do? You ain't guilty of nothing."

"You are not guilty of anything," she corrected.

"Never mind my fucking English. I've just had a call from Hedda Hopper. I told her that the only thing red about you is your hair, and even that is not legitimate."

"You 'dint'!" she said.

When she started making fun of my accent I knew she was feeling better.

"What about the show tonight? Suppose the audience starts boo-ing or something?"

"Don't worry about that, sweetheart. We are going to do the show tonight and we are going to do it in front of the audience and nobody is going to boo you."

She wasn't the only one worrying about that. The CBS people, even some of my own Desilu people, had the same worry. But I felt that to suddenly cancel the audience would be an indication of weakness, perhaps even of guilt.

Lucy agreed and we decided not only to have an audience, but also representatives of the press to report on the audience reaction.

Jackson called me about 1 P.M. and said, "I understand you're pretty upset."

"You're goddamn right I'm pretty upset," I said. "Did your secretary tell you about the press conference for you and your committee?"

"Statler Hotel, six P.M.?"

"That's correct. I want a statement from you and your committee that you have absolutely nothing against Lucille Ball, which is exactly the truth."

"I don't know if I can get the committee together in time for the six o'clock conference."

"Well, you better get them together, because either you are going to be there, or I am going to be there."

"Let me call you back in a while. Look, I don't know how this thing came about. We have nothing against Lucy."

"Yeah. But you've got to say that."

"Let me see how many of these guys I can get hold of."

At three-thirty or four o'clock, he called back and said, "Okay, I've got enough."

"Do you want us at the press conference?" I asked.

"No. I'll be there."

I didn't ask him what he was going to say. I just said, "Thank you very much."

I then called Jim Bacon at the Associated Press, the guy who was with me when Desi was born, and said, "Jim, Jackson is going to have a press conference."

"Yeah. We heard about it," he said.

"I want you to be there and I want you to call me the minute this thing is over. I must know what he said, what the result of the press conference was, because that will be just before I go in front of the audience to do the warm-up for the show."

I know that this was one of the most miserable days Lucy ever had in her life. But she came, rehearsed, kept going and had the show in good shape.

Just before I went out in front to do the warm-up, to a full audience and about fifty reporters, Ken Morgan called me to the backstage phone. It was Jim Bacon, who said, "Okay. The press conference is over. You'll be having nothing but beautiful headlines tomorrow morning."

"What did he say?" I asked, and got Lucy to listen.

"He cleared her a hundred percent," Jim answered, "no question about it. We all love Lucy kind of stuff."

"Beautiful!"

We still had those people out there to contend with. All they knew was what they had read during the day, and what they had read during the day was pretty bad.

I gave Lucy a big kiss and told her, "Come out swinging!"

I went out front and said, "Ladies and gentlemen, I know that you have read a lot of bad headlines about my wife today. I came from Cuba, but during my years in the United States Army I became an American citizen, and one of the things I admire about this country is that you are considered innocent until you are proven guilty.

"Up to now, you have only read what people have said about Lucy, but you have not had a chance to read our answer to those accusations. So I will ask you to only do one thing tonight, and that is to reserve your judgment until you read the newspapers tomorrow, where our story will be. In the meantime, I hope you can enjoy the show under these trying circumstances."

Then I introduced Fred and Ethel.

"And now the girl to whom I've been married for thirteen years and who, I know, is as American as J. Edgar Hoover, President Eisenhower or Barney Baruch, my favorite wife, the mother of my children, the vice-president of Desilu Productions—I am the president—my favorite redhead—even *that* is not legitimate. The girl who plays Lucy—Lucille Ball!"

It was an unbelievably emotional moment for everyone who was on that stage. The audience stood up, applauded and shouted, "We love you, Lucy." Bill and Vivian were crying, the orchestra was playing our *I Love Lucy* theme song, the cameramen, the electricians, the whole crew were all shouting, applauding, crying, laughing.

I took a peek at where the reporters were seated and they were all making notes like crazy about the happy pandemonium which was going on. Their photographer and ours, Buddy Graybill, had bulbs flashing in every direction.

Lucy stood there sobbing and laughing and thanking everybody. She hugged Vivian and Bill and me and then went up into the audience, hugged and kissed her mother, and her brother, and my mother, and the writers, and the newspaper people, and Kenny and Cleo, and most of the people in the audience whom she could get to or who got to her.

How the hell she ever got hold of herself and went on to do one of the finest performances of her life, after all this, only proves what a tremendous actress this girl is.

The next day the headlines were all about the Committee clearing her 100 percent, with Jackson saying, "We, too, love Lucy." And stories about our audience reaction the night before. Hedda Hopper, also on the front page of the *Times,* quoted me with "The only thing red about her is her hair and even that is not legitimate." Even the *Herald-Express* report of it was fairly accurate.

Sunday noon we had a press conference at our ranch in Northridge. The newspaper guys wanted to hear our part of the story, in person.

I asked our neighbor Bill Henry of the *Los Angeles Times* to conduct the press conference. We had a nice layout around the pool with food, booze, and soft drinks.

They all had the full transcript, which we had insisted Jackson make public, and also Emil Freed's statement to the press which had appeared that Saturday morning, confirming Lucy's testimony that she had never met him. (I had been trying to locate Mr. Freed since I first read the transcript.)

It said, "I have never met Miss Ball."

He also stated that his recollection of the appointments to the Central Committee, seventeen years ago, was that they came from persons who gathered signatures for him.

By now all the press people had concluded that this whole thing had just been a lot of unjustified and unfair publicity for Lucy. They asked a lot of questions, most of them about Grandpa, and we told them a lot of the stories.

At the end, Dan Jenkins, who was western editor of *TV Guide* and also had been television editor of the *Hollywood Reporter,* got up and said, "Ladies and gentlemen of the press. I think perhaps you will agree with me that we all owe Lucy an apology."

They all clapped and she cried again.

When you go through something like this you find out who your friends are. We found out in the Cuban Revolution. The first guys who came to the house, even before the good headlines on Saturday, were our neighbors in the Valley: Lou Costello, Lionel Barrymore, and Jack Oakie. Mr. Barrymore came in his wheelchair.

During the press conference on Sunday, Larry Parks rang at the front door and asked the maid to see us. He had never been to our house before. I went to the door and he had a large bouquet of red roses for Lucy.

I thanked him very much for his thoughtful gesture and mentioned that we were in the midst of a large press conference and, as diplomatically as I could, I told him to get lost. I explained it wouldn't do him or Lucy any good to have a story about Larry Parks bringing Lucy red roses at that particular "period in time." Some sonofabitch would accuse them of belonging to the same cell.

Larry, who had suffered enough from some of this same bad publicity and who has always been a perfect gentleman, understood. I really felt like a shit but I didn't dare to take the chance.

That same Sunday evening, Walter Winchell began his weekly radio broadcast with: "Mr. and Mrs. America, and all the ships at sea: During this past week, Donald Jackson, Chairman of the House Un-American Activities Committee, and all its members cleared Lucy a hundred percent, and so did J. Edgar Hoover and the FBI, plus every newspaper in America and, tonight, Mr. Lincoln is drying his tears for making her go through this."

"This" was started only a week ago by him and his "blind" item.

On Monday the fourteenth, most newspapers in the country published the transcript of Lucy's testimony, Emil Freed's statement, and very favorable stories about the press conference at our ranch.

There was also a story in most of them about the fact that there would be many chairmen of many multimillion-dollar corporations anxiously awaiting the Neilsen, Trendex and other overnight local and national ratings of our show that evening.

Sitting closest to their television sets, with a telephone in their laps awaiting the results of those different rating polls, would be William S. Paley, CBS chairman, Alfred Lyons of Philip Morris, Milton Biow of the Biow Company and Louis B. Mayer of MGM. L.B. was not the chairman but nobody ever paid any attention to who the chairman of that board was anyway, as long as L.B. was alive.

Needless to say, the president and chairman of the board of directors of Desilu Productions would be fighting for the phone with his gorgeous redheaded vice-president the minute it rang.

And ring it did, loud and clear, shortly after midnight. How the

Madelyn and Bob could always break me up.

And so could Vivian and Bill.

In this episode we were doing a little dance number to impress Dore Schary and somehow we managed to fall in the pool.

Lucy finds a live celebrity (Bill Holden) at the Brown Derby.

Lucy finds uranium in one of the *Lucy-Desi Comedy Hours* with Fred MacMurray.

With Tallulah Bankhead in Lucy-Desi episode
the night we bought RKO Studios.

hell they get those "overnights" that fast I'll never know. Our time spot was 9 P.M. across the nation. The results were indeed very satisfying. *I Love Lucy* was still number one, by a comfortable margin.

The headlines on Tuesday the fifteenth all commented on that fact. The *Los Angeles Times,* for example, read: "Everybody Still Loves Lucy."

Two weeks later we received an invitation from the President and Mrs. Eisenhower to be their guests at the White House on November 26. Subsequently, Dr. Stanton informed us that November 26 was the President's birthday and that he, the President, had expressed a desire to have us perform at his party that evening, and to please bring Fred and Ethel with us.

The day before going to Washington Lucy received the B'nai B'rith award for "Woman of the Year." It was the first time that award had been presented to an actress.

The President and Mamie and their VIP guests gave us a wonderful welcome, laughed all through our antics with gusto and, at the end, gave us the most resounding and warm standing ovation we had ever received.

After the show two of the White House's impressive pages came backstage and asked us to follow them. "The President and the First Lady request the pleasure of your company at their table."

God bless America!

36

Why was *I Love Lucy* successful?

Everybody wanted us to dissect that question and come up with an answer, a foolproof formula. Well, unfortunately, making a television show, or any show, is not like making Coca-Cola or Bacardí rum. Not that those companies do not deserve a lot of credit for finding great formulas, but once they found the ingredients they never changed them. They just kept repeating them and always came up with the same product. The human element in our business prevents us from finding a successful formula every time. But once in a while we stumble into one.

The way we filmed our shows—the Desilu technique, as it came to be known—proved to be the best way to do television comedies.

The chemistry which ignited at the first meeting of Lucy and Vivian, and the rapport and understanding Bill and I had, was somehow naturally transferred to the characters of Lucy and Ethel, and Ricky and Fred. No one, including me, could have visualized that it would turn out so perfectly.

I am sure there have been occasions when you had a great time at a party for no particularly obvious reason. Why did you? The chemistry, the mixture of the people there made it fun.

The basic elements of our format, dealing with the institution of marriage with its day-to-day trials and tribulations of husband and wife, and their involvement with neighbors and friends, have a universal theme understood by young and old, particularly on television, where it is seen by the whole family sitting at home.

We didn't have an exclusive or monopoly in the humor inherent in that format. It is as old as the theater itself, but the way our writers treated those basic elements, with their God-given gift of superb understanding of farce, was what made the difference.

They began every script with a logical and credible premise, laying the groundwork, the motivation for the wild antics that would follow. The Ricardos and the Mertzes' involvement always dealt with basic and real human emotions like love, jealousy, greed, hate or fear. The same ones that other neighbors, everywhere, had at one time or another experienced.

Therefore it was easy for our viewers to identify with the characters in our show, who were believable. The situations they got into were credible and, we hoped, funny. If they weren't, we were in trouble.

This reminds me of a story about Greer Garson and Jimmie Durante. Miss Garson was at the very height of her brilliant and distinguished career in motion pictures, having just completed *Mrs. Miniver* at Metro-Goldwyn-Mayer, and was to appear as a special guest on Durante's very successful NBC radio show. She graciously insisted on going to Jimmie's house for the first reading of the script.

As she arrived, Durante came down the stairs from his second-floor bedroom, dressed immaculately and, of course, with his old broken-down felt hat on his head. Jimmie does not think he is properly and fully dressed without his hat. It also enabled him to take it off and salute Miss Garson in his most gentlemanly manner.

They read the script, and after she had finished reading the sketch she was to do with Jimmie, Miss Garson asked, "These are the jokes?"

DURANTE: Yes, ma'am, those are them.

GARSON: I see—and they are the ones we are supposed to get laughs with?

DURANTE: That's right, ma'am.

GARSON: What if nobody laughs?

DURANTE: Well, then we'll all be in the *terlet*.

Normally, Jim would have said, "We'll all be in the shithouse," but he was doing his best to be as polite as possible in front of Mrs. Miniver.

At times we were criticized for doing too much slapstick. I don't believe in *mild* comedy, and neither does Lucy. That's the kind the audience is just supposed to smile at. We like them to laugh out loud. Nothing makes anyone feel better than a good hearty laugh. It is good therapy, spiritually and physically.

Our type of comedy did get pretty wild at times. That is why setting up the reasons for getting to those antics had to be fundamentally solid. There is a very thin line between the honest and believable physical comedy routines and the "just trying to be funny" routines. But you better know where that line is and tread it carefully.

None of us who worked on the planning and production of *I Love Lucy* would claim we were geniuses who knew from the start what we had to have for the show to be a success. But when you look back in hindsight and retrospect, as the man said, it seems to me that certain ingredients were essential.

We did have some rules from the very beginning: basic good taste, moral values, never do a joke if that joke, no matter how funny and what a big laugh it could get, would in any way offend even a small segment of our viewers. This eliminated jokes about physical defects, like harelip, nervous twitch and crazy-people jokes, and Polish, Jewish, black, Mexican, Japanese, Chinese and other ethnic jokes.

The only ones close to an ethnic joke were the ones about Ricky's accent, and of course those were in the category of making fun of yourself, which is fine. But even those did not work too well if anybody but Lucy used them. When Fred and Ethel made fun of Ricky's accent, they didn't get a laugh. Interesting, isn't it?

Ricky could be distressed by Lucy's shenanigans, which at times seemed would bring catastrophic results. That was natural, and the audience knew he had a reason. But, and that was a big *but,* he should never get *real* mad at her, or *mad* mad as the writers called it. He should only get *funny* mad, exasperated, as you would with a naughty child. On the other hand, I did not want Ricky to lose believability in those instances and look silly; but if he showed any kind of mean-ness, audiences would resent it and we'd lose the humor of the fight.

It was the most difficult problem I faced while playing Ricky. It helped when I overemphasized the acceptable Latin use of hands and arms when I was excited. It was also handy to let my eyes pop out of their sockets. Most of all, the rat-tat-tat-tat parade of Spanish words helped me tread that thin line between *funny* mad and *mad* mad.

Today, twenty-four years later, kids come up to me. "Hey, Ricky, say *'Mira que tene . . .'* how do you say it?"

"Miraquetienecosalamujeresta."

"That's it! That's it!"

Making the show look as real as possible was mandatory and an area in which I would not compromise. A vase of flowers which is supposed to look fresh, fragrant and alive in a scene should be fresh, fragrant and alive, not phony and droopy. A prop, an appliance, any-thing that Lucy or Ricky, Fred or Ethel had to work with, had to be real and functional. Our kitchens, refrigerators, sinks, washing ma-chines, ovens, coffee pots, toasters, radios, TV sets were all practical. When the script called for Lucy and Ethel to make their first loaf of bread, that loaf of bread had to turn out gigantic and look like a monster trying to reach out for them as it started to grow out of the oven.

I told James Paisley, our first assistant director, that I wanted it to be real bread, not made out of papier-mâché or rubber and painted to look like a real loaf. Jim had to make hundreds of calls to find a bakery that would attempt this job. Some didn't have a large enough oven and others were afraid the weight of an eight-foot loaf would break down the oven. He finally found one willing to try it. We had to have two loaves, one as a stand-in, each to weigh three hundred pounds.

After our show close to three hundred people in our audience came down from their seats to the Tropicana set, where Ricky worked. We had set up tables with a few gallons of jam, jellies and butter, and everybody enjoyed a piece of our good bread and took the rest of their slice home. Each slice was two inches thick and two feet square.

A single prop that does not look real to an audience can louse you up. The same is true of the smallest flaw in setting up the motiva-tion in a story line. The audience will be thinking of the prop or the flaw and miss the joke coming up.

The best way to fix a flaw, a weak spot, in the story line is for one of the characters in the show to bring it out in the open. Fred might say to Ricky, "That doesn't make any sense." Ricky would then explain to Fred how and why it makes sense, and as Fred said, "Oh, I see," the audience would also be saying, "Oh, I see."

The story of the two tunas is a good example of how hard we tried for reality. Part of this episode had to do with a seventy-five dollar bet which Lucy and Ethel made with Fred and Ricky about who would catch the biggest fish the following day. The girls were to use one boat and the boys another. We established that in the first scene.

The second scene starts as the door to the Ricardos' apartment opens and Lucy and Ethel come in, carrying a sixty-pound tuna. Ethel is squawking about how ridiculous it is to spend so much money on a tuna. Lucy is trying to justify doing it by telling Ethel the man said they may not run tomorrow. "Do you want to lose seventy-five dollars? Come on, let's hide it." They put it in the tub in our bathroom.

The scene continues as the door of the Mertzes' apartment opens and Ricky and Fred come in, carrying another sixty-pound tuna. The exchange of dialogue is almost the same, Fred saying what Ethel said and Ricky using the same justification Lucy did. When Ricky ends with "Do you want to lose seventy-five dollars?" Fred immediately says, "Where can we hide it?" And of course they hide it in the tub of the Mertz bathroom.

Ricky goes back to his apartment and Ethel to hers.

As Ricky is getting ready to take a bath, Lucy calls Ethel and tells her to hurry up there, they have to move the tuna, and that she will stall Ricky until they do so.

"But I was just going to take a bath," says Ethel.

"Never mind," says Lucy, "you can take one later. Hurry!"

During that exchange on the phone Fred comes through the Ricardo's kitchen and tells Ricky Ethel is about to take a bath and they both hurry down the back-door stairs.

The girls then take their tuna to the Mertzes' apartment and hide it in their bathtub. Fred and Ricky take their tuna and hide it in the Ricardos' bathtub.

This type of near-miss is very much in the style of French farce, only in French farce the near-misses are between husbands and lovers, not between tunas.

The same routine with variations kept going on several times, and everyone was going crazy trying to figure out how the goddamn tunas kept showing up at the same place they had just taken them from. Fred says to Ricky, "Maybe they swim upstream like the salmon do."

Finally, while trying to hide our tunas in a different place and the girls trying to do the same, the men, carrying a sixty-pound tuna, backed into the girls in the hallway, and of course they were also carrying their tuna.

We had a great prop department and they had made two perfect-looking sixty-pound rubber tunas, and I'm sure our television viewers would have thought they were real tunas.

We used them during the first three days of rehearsal, and as we carried them from one place to another, we were doing pretty well pretending they were real sixty-pound tunas. But we *knew* they were not, and I was sure our studio audience would also know. No matter how well our prop department had made them, they just weren't going to work well enough.

Having fished since I can't remember when, I knew that our actions and reactions in this particular routine would be 1000 percent better if we were handling slimy, slippery, unscaled, smelly, *real* sixty-pound tunas.

At the end of our last day of rehearsal we always had a dress rehearsal. Afterward there would be a meeting in my office. That meeting would include the writers, Bob and Madelyn and Jess; our director at that time, Bill Asher; Karl Freund; our assistant director, Jack Aldworth (we had promoted Paisley to production manager); Lucy, Fred and Ethel; the wardrobe lady, Della Fox; the propman, Jerry Miggins; our script girl, Dorothy; the special-effects man. Anyone who had something to do with the writing, performance, sound, action and photography of the show had to be there.

Each one of us would bring up whatever problems we might have in our own department, no matter how insignificant, as we reviewed the script page by page.

When we got to the tunas I addressed Jack Aldworth. "Jack, I want you to get me two sixty-pound tunas exactly alike—same species, uncleaned and unscaled—and I want them here in time for the camera rehearsals at one o'clock tomorrow afternoon." I then turned to Lucy with my next note. "Do you think the dress that you wear in . . ." At that point I heard Jack clear his throat and I saw him raise his hand.

"What is it, Jack?"

"I just wanted to make sure I understood you correctly, sir. Did you say you wanted me to get two real sixty-pound tunas, uncleaned and unscaled, and you want them here tomorrow afternoon at one o'clock?"

"That's right, Jack."

I turned back to Lucy. "Well, what do you think about—" Jack's hand was up again.

"What is it now, Jack? You have to go to the bathroom?"

"No, sir," he answered. He always addressed everybody as "sir," whether it was I or the janitor. "Sir, if I'm going to have to find those tunas I think I should be excused from the rest of this meeting and get going."

"You're right—get going."

We finished our meeting. Those things usually lasted anywhere from an hour and a half to three or three and a half hours.

The next day, shortly before noon, Jack came into my office and asked, "Will you come over to our stage and see if they're all right?"

I'll be damned if he didn't have two tunas, same species, same size, same sixty-pound weight, and caught the day before. They were still fresh. Each one of them was wrapped in towels inside of what looked like little coffins with dry ice in them. I thanked him very much and asked him where he got them.

"Well," he said, "I called all the sport-fishing companies and canneries, but none of them had any such size tunas around here. One guy told me that perhaps in the canneries around the Bay area in San Francisco, or north of there, I might have better luck. I located the owner of one of those canneries and told him what I wanted. The man told me where he was and how to get there, and that he would have one hundred and twenty pounds of tuna all packed and ready.

"I told him that was not what I wanted. 'I want two tunas, sixty pounds each, freshly caught, uncleaned and unscaled, and they have to look alike.' The man started to hang up on me. I stopped him. He asked if I was some kind of a nut. I then explained to him why I wanted them and who they were for.

"He told me he was a fan of the *Lucy* show, never missed one of them, and that only such a crazy group as ours would be looking for twin tunas at two o'clock in the morning.

"He then told me he would get the tunas, to bring some kind of a container or box large enough to carry them back to Los Angeles, and he would give me some dry ice to keep them fresh.

"At three o'clock in the morning I flew to San Francisco. Everything there was closed. I couldn't find any box or container or anything in which to put the tunas. As I was walking around trying to think what to do next, I saw a light in front of a funeral parlor, with a sign on the front which said OPEN. That's when I thought of the little baby coffins.

"I went in and asked the fellow in charge if he had two cheap baby coffins for sale. He also thought I was some kind of nut or practical joker. I asked him if I could use the phone, that I had to call a cannery and would pay him for the call. He told me, 'Go ahead,' but he stayed on my heels.

"I got the owner of the cannery on the phone. The funeral-parlor fellow could not quite believe the conversation he was hearing about two tunas and whether these coffins would be long and wide enough for them. The cannery man said they would be just right.

"I chartered a small plane, put the two baby coffins in it and flew to the cannery. We put dry ice in the coffins, wrapped the tunas in towels, laid them on top of the ice, and then all three of us flew back to San Francisco, took the next plane to Los Angeles, and here we are!"

I was laughing so much I was crying. That is what I call a real first assistant director with a great amount of ingenuity. And that is why Jack also became a production manager for several Desilu shows and, in later years, production manager for some of the biggest-budget motion pictures in the industry.

By the way, our script girl, Dorothy, one of the best, was Jack's wife, with the same dedication to her work as he.

Having those real tunas made that show a lot funnier than it would have been with the rubber ones. They were almost impossible to handle, and by the time we did the show we sure as hell didn't have to pretend they were gamy—they were. It was worth all the trouble and expense.

We used many of our personal life experiences as the basis for some of our scripts—the eternal struggle, for example, about hot and cold between Lucy and me at home. She would open all the windows in our house because she likes it cold, and I would follow a few minutes later, closing them all, because I like it hot.

The chickens at our Desilu ranch in Chatsworth, which Lucy would never allow me to kill and eat, laid eggs that cost us about $4.50 apiece. Our writers used that in one of the shows. When Lucy and Ricky and the Mertzes moved to the country, Lucy and Ethel decided they would save money on their grocery bill by buying a few chickens and hens, and the same thing happened. Fred and Ricky told the girls to get rid of them, as I had told Lucy in Chatsworth.

To develop the story further, the writers had Lucy concoct a scheme to be able to keep them. She and Ethel would buy four dozen eggs at the store and put them under the hens, then the next day they would take Fred and Ricky to the chicken coops and say, "Look at those eggs! These are really good hardworking hens. We told you it would pay off."

The show featured a number Lucy and Ricky were to do at a PTA benefit for Little Ricky's school. It was a tango with a fancy ending in which Ricky threw Lucy away from him, then grabbed her hand, spun her back, crushing her against his chest, and then, grabbing a handful of hair, threw her head back and kissed her. One of the early scenes in the show was their first rehearsal of this number.

The plot thickened and Lucy's scheme was nearing disaster as Ricky, who wasn't too happy about the way that rehearsal had gone, came home much earlier than usual, almost catching Lucy red-handed with the two dozen eggs still inside their cardboard box. As he was taking off his hat and coat he called out, "Lucy?"

"Yes, dear," she answered from the kitchen, frantically trying to figure out where to hide the eggs. As she heard Ricky coming toward the kitchen, she hid them inside her blouse and buttoned down a street coat she had over it.

Ricky came in and said, "Come on, we gotta rehearse."

"Rehearse? Rehearse what, dear?"

"The tango—I'm not too happy with the way that finish is going."

"Now?" she asked. "We have to rehearse the finish of the tango now?"

"Yeah, right now. Just the ending, that's all. When I spin you back and crush you against my chest, I have to do it more forcefully, the way the Argentinian apaches do it."

This is an instance where telegraphing a joke is good. The audience is anticipating disaster. We didn't let them down.

As we got to the finish of the tango I threw her away as far as I could and then grabbed her and spun her back, really crushing her against my chest. I didn't follow up by grabbing her hair and kissing her for the finish. I just stood there, looking at her and wondering what I had heard and felt happening inside her coat.

This is the type of situation Lucy is so great at. There's no comedienne in the business who can come close to her. She knows the audience knows what is happening to her, and she can milk their reaction for as long as she wants.

She first looked at Ricky with a silly little smile on that pitiful-looking face, the big blue eyes dancing from Ricky to the audience and back to Ricky, as if claiming innocence. She then looked squirmishly at her bosom and daintily pulled her blouse away from it, looked back at Ricky with the same silly smile, shook her torso and her waist a little bit, letting the audience know the broken eggs were finding their way down her body.

When she thought the audience laughter might be easing up a bit, she shook her left leg and foot, which told them the eggs had completed their downward tour and were now all over her, bringing up the laughter louder and bigger than before.

Our editor and sound cutter timed that laugh and recorded it as the longest one we'd ever gotten. This is a perfect example of why an audience is so important. I would never have had the guts to dub in that big a laugh. Some other shows were filmed without an audience and the laughs were put in later. They always sounded phony to me. That's why all our comedy shows were done in front of an audience.

It is kind of amusing when, at the end of *All in the Family*, which I love, and some other comedy shows, they proudly show you a large sign—"TAPED IN FRONT OF AN AUDIENCE."

Lucy is such a perfectionist she insisted on never using the eggs inside her blouse during rehearsals. She didn't want to know or anticipate the feeling of two dozen eggs breaking against her body. She used them only when we actually filmed the scene.

In shows that called for Lucy to satirize something that she had never done before, like the one about getting a job in a pizza parlor, the comedic values depended on how well she satirized the way they twirl the dough around and flip it up in the air as they are molding it.

She spent many hours at a pizza parlor after our rehearsals until she could handle that dough as well as the pizza maker. That, of course, is the only way. You have to know how to do it right before you can satirize it.

When we made *The Long, Long Trailer* I had to drive it all over the country, up and down mountains, tear down a carport at her family's home in the story. I had to learn how to drive that big thing right before I could make it do all the things that it should not do.

When Lucy did the seal bit on the stage and in our pilot, she learned how to play the xylophone as a seal would play it, her mouth squeezing different sizes of old-fashioned automobile horns.

Nothing was too hard for her, and she never squawked about the extra work and longer hours. When the writers asked her if she thought she could play "Glowworm, Glow," on a saxophone, she told them, "Give me a week." At the end of the week she could. We could've had Lucy *fake* playing the xylophone and the sax, while someone off-camera did it, but it wouldn't have been as funny as Lucy struggling to do it well herself.

Another thing that helped in the planinng, production and execution of our show was that everyone involved in the creative end had the same objective—pure entertainment, unencumbered with messages. Some people called it superficial, with no literary or intellectual values—only escapism. Okay, but I see nothing wrong with a show that is just that.

We always had in mind the guy who has worked eight or ten hours a day driving a truck or a taxi, or putting down bricks and mortar, or fixing facuets, or driving nails, or sitting at a desk, or whatever his job is. When he gets home at night, kicks off his shoes, puts his feet up on a chair, opens a cold can of beer and, by turning his television set on, has a half-hour of just laughs and relaxation, I'm all for it.

I think it is very important to allow him to escape, for a while at least, from all the goddamn worries and struggles of our everyday life. Television should not be ashamed but proud to help him do so. The real intellectuals also like to escape once in a while from their world of intellect.

Charles Young, a brilliant young man who has done a great job as chancellor of UCLA, when asked about entertainment in general, said: "I like entertainment, especially television. I don't care to watch deep, involved movies or television programs that hit me over the head with education and information. I like light entertainment. My attitude on entertainment is—down with messages."

Now, if you happen to come up with a television show, a play or a movie that is good entertainment, and which at the same time delivers a message without knocking people on the top of the head with it, that's fine and dandy. One of our most loyal fans and friends, who wrote to us often about how much he enjoyed relaxing and looking at our show, who said that he wouldn't miss it for anything, was our brilliant senior statesman Barney Baruch. Another was the publisher of the *Chicago Tribune,* Colonel Robert R. McCormick. Hedda Hopper told us that all conversation ceased at the colonel's home at nine o'clock Monday night and didn't start again until he had seen *I Love Lucy*.

As far as messages were concerned, even though we never tried to deliver any, once in a while one sneaked through to someone. One fellow wrote: "Dear Ricky, I want you to know I thought my wife was a real nut and was about to divorce her. But after looking at your shows, she began to look pretty normal. Thank you for saving our marriage."

One of Dad's philosophical beliefs, "There must be a way,"

helped in some instances when I had a problem with the *Lucy* show. For some inexplicable reason one show was two and a half minutes short. Most of the time we were too long and had a hell of a tough time cutting the show down to the twenty-four minutes and thirty seconds we had to deliver to the network. I can't remember any other instance in which we were short.

It was another one of those shows in which Lucy and Ethel had talked Ricky into appearing at a benefit for some women's club or something. It would have been very easy to fill the two and a half minutes by having Ricky sing another song at that function, but I felt Ricky had sung enough on that show and I wanted to see if there wasn't a better way to fix it. The obvious way would be to get just any kind of an act to do two and a half minutes as part of the show Lucy and Ethel were putting on, which in our story was not supposed to be a big, professional, theatrical smash anyway.

I decided to try to get the best two and a half goddamn minutes in the business. I told Lucy what I had in mind.

She said, "There ain't no way you are going to get Sam Goldwyn to give you a two-and-a-half-minute film clip of Frank Sinatra singing one of the top songs from *Guys and Dolls*. The picture hasn't even opened yet."

"I don't know," I told her. "It might be pretty darn good publicity for the picture. Besides, Mr. Goldwyn is the guy who first brought you out to Hollywood as a Goldwyn Girl, and he has always remained a real good friend of yours. As a matter of fact, every time he sees me, he is very complimentary about our decision to do our shows on film. Besides, all he can say is no. I'm going to try."

I called Mr. Goldwyn on the telephone and said, "Mr. Goldwyn, this is Desi Arnaz."

"Oh yeah, yeah—you're the fellow married to Lucille Ball."

"That's right, Mr. Goldwyn. I've met you a couple of times."

"Yeah, yeah—you're the fellow who bought that studio where you're doing film for television. I like your show very much. I see it every week."

"Thank you very much, Mr. Goldwyn."

"What can I do for you?"

"Well, I'm two and a half minutes short on this particular *Lucy* show which we have already done, and thinking about her being a Goldwyn Girl when she first came to Hollywood . . ."

"Yeah, I brought her out here. I remember that."

"Well, Mr. Goldwyn, I thought perhaps I could get some film from you to fill in this two and a half minutes."

"Oh, sure, but I'll tell you what," he said, "I'll do better than that. I will come over to your studio there and I will talk on your television show with Lucy about when she came out here as a Goldwyn Girl."

"I see. Well, Mr. Goldwyn, uh—uh—thank you very much—but we can't do that."

"Why not can we do that?" he asked.

"Well—Lucy's not Lucille."

"Lucy's not Lucille?"

"No, sir, Lucille was the girl who came out here as a Goldwyn Girl, but that's not the Lucy in our show."

"It's the same girl, isn't it? I mean, the girl who is there with you in *I Love Lucy?* That is the girl I brought out here as a Goldwyn Girl. Right?"

"Yes, sir, it is the same girl. But it would make no sense for Mr. Goldwyn to talk to the girl on *I Love Lucy* about the time she was a Goldwyn Girl, because that was not Lucy, that was Lucille."

"It was not Lucy, it was Lucille. But it is the same girl."

"I'm afraid I'm not explaining it too well. Let's see, the girl you brought to Hollywood as a Goldwyn Girl was Lucille. The girl, in our show, is pretending—"

He cut in, "To be Lucille. *Now* I got it."

"No, no, Mr. Goldwyn, Lucille is pretending to be Lucy."

I should have expected that my trying to explain anything to Mr. Goldwyn over the phone wasn't going to be easy. Even when face to face we couldn't understand each other too well.

Then Mr. Goldwyn said, "I really don't know what it is you want and I have to hang up, but whatever it is—you got it."

Fifteen minutes later, Mr. Goldwyn's secretary called Johnny Aitchison, my secretary, and said, "Mr. Aitchison, my boss just gave your boss something. We would like to find out what it is so we can send it over."

About a year later I saw Frank and he said, "How the hell did I wind up in *I Love Lucy* singing a song from *Guys and Dolls?*"

"It's a long story, Frank. Why don't you ask Mr. Goldwyn?"

The New York Times Magazine did a whole article about the same question: Why was *I Love Lucy* successful?

They asked me, "If you had to divide the credit between the writers, the directors and the cast, how would you do it?"

"I would give Lucy ninety percent and divide the other ten percent among the rest of us."

The show was being televised in many countries all over the world, so *The New York Times Magazine* interviewed and quoted people from different countries. It was interesting to see what some of them to say.

A British anthropologist who was making a study about what "sends" the American people, had come to watch how we rehearsed and filmed the show. His opinion of what made the show a success: "Lucy and Ricky and their friends, Ethel and Fred, are the typical American middle-class in a typical American middle-class environment, but with a significant difference—instead of sitting around waiting for things to happen, they *make* things happen. They and their audience are so alike, the audience comes to believe that it is 'it' that makes things happen—pure mass hypnosis, or if I may say so, twaddle, but awfully clever, hmmm?"

A visiting French actor explained his addiction to the show in this manner: "It has the reality of 'l'amour,' or as you say, sex. While it is possible to believe that other husband and wife comedy teams share the same bedroom, it is not possible to believe that they do so with pleasure. Lucy and Ricky skirmish in the daytime so they can 'reconcile' at night."

I agree with the Frenchman. The lack of romance and sex does not help any show. I think our audience could visualize Lucy and Ricky going to bed together and enjoying it.

I got a fan letter addressed to Ricky from a guy who said, "Lucy must be pretty good in the hay for you to put up with all the crazy things she does."

The *Times Magazine* also interviewed an American sociopsychologist who belonged to the school that maintains that the American woman dominates the American man and despises him for letting her do it. He said, "The extraordinary appeal of the *Lucy* show is based upon its ability to assume two guilt factors, deep in the American subconscious: A) The American woman is in despair over the state to which she has reduced the man. Therefore, she thanks Heaven that in the Ricardo house at least Ricky's the boss and Lucy knows it and the American woman knows it and that makes all of them, together, glad, for the duration of the show anyway. [This one didn't know how right he was!] B) Somewhere in the background of most Americans there is a foreign-born relative whose alien accent embarrassed them and they're sorry for it now. But Ricky speaks with a foreign accent, yet everybody respects him. By sharing their respect for Ricky, the audience appeases its conscience."

What do you know!

The magazine continued: "An otherwise articulate matron, who's proud of her enslavement to the *Lucy* show, clarifies its hold on her thus: 'I don't know. I just love Lucy, I love Lucy—my husband doesn't.' "

The *Times* interviewer then said to me, "Just one more question. Do you think that *I Love Lucy* is so successful because you have continually done the best show on television?"

"No, I don't think so. I think it is because we have continually never done a bad one."

37

When *I Love Lucy* became the number-one television show in the nation during the 1951–1952 season, I began to get inquiries from stars and producers about whether or not our company would be willing and able to film their shows, if and when they went on television, in the same manner we filmed *I Love Lucy*. The first one to come and talk to me about that possibility was Eve Arden, whom I had known from the picture business and who was a good friend of Lucy's.

She was the star of a radio show for CBS, a very successful and popular one, *Our Miss Brooks*. Eve said that CBS had approached her about adapting the show for television, as they had intended to do with Lucy and *My Favorite Husband*, and that she had told them she would do it if they agreed to have it done the way we were doing *I Love Lucy*.

Eve then asked me if we could and would and I said, "I don't see why not. We've got the equipment, cameras, sound and electrical crews we use only two days a week, Thursday and Friday, and film Friday nights. Tuesday and Wednesday we rehearse without them. You could use them on those days and shoot Wednesday nights. We would have to fix up another audience stage but that's not too big a deal now."

I had never thought about the production and filming of other stars' shows, but I didn't see why we shouldn't do it. I knew the crews would be happy with the extra work. What I didn't know was what a big can of beans I was opening.

The networks weren't particularly happy to see this trend of television shows wanting to go on film and kept promoting the idea that live was better than film. But there was no way that CBS could tell that to Eve when their number-one show was on film.

The reason they were against film was that they knew that the more shows done on film instead of live, the more power and control they would lose. If a show was live, independent local television stations wanting that show had to become an affiliate of the network that was televising it. The network would then feed it to them over the cable, if the cable reached them, or it would send them a kinescope of it. But with film, the local independent stations could make direct deals with the producers. That's how syndication started.

Film was much better for the artist and the creative talent, because if their show was a success at the end of a few years, even if they'd had to make a deal with the networks—be partners with them —they would still own a very nice chunk of that valuable film library, which is the only way that the stars and the "created by" people ever made some real money out of television. A live show, once telecast, was gone forever, and nobody ever got another cent out of it.

We started producing and filming *Our Miss Brooks* for Eve Arden's company and CBS in 1952. We were also doing some commercials for General Foods and Philip Morris.

Before we started that 1952–1953 season, CBS negotiated a new deal with Desilu. I guess that, even though they hadn't lost anything on the 1951–1952 season, they got a little shook up when the first few shows cost so much, but as I explained there was a reason for that. Nevertheless, they decided that they would never again give us a cost-plus contract. The new deal was that we would receive a flat sum. I think it was $28,500 or $30,000 for each of the thirty new episodes, and half of that for each of nine repeats, which was quite a large sum in those days.

CBS also bought 25 percent of Desilu Productions for one million dollars. At about the same time I organized another company, under which umbrella we would produce motion pictures and rent equipment. We called it Zanra. Lucy and I owned 80 percent of the stock, and the other 20 percent was distributed among our key people, then no more than five or six, our children and our mothers.

Desilu sold all the equpiment which we had been buying during the original season of *I Love Lucy,* such as the lights Karl had designed and built, the crab dollies, the four-headed Monster, the props, the portable dressing rooms and bleachers, at cost to Zanra. It was a way our key people could make some extra money. Someday they could sell their stock in Zanra on a capital-gain basis, and the harder they worked to make Zanra a successful and financially solid corporation, the more their stock would be worth.

Zanra in turn rented that equipment to Desilu Productions, not only for *I Love Lucy* but also for *Our Miss Brooks* and for the commercials which we were filming. This caused a little controversy.

I was having lunch with Paley and Spencer Harrison, CBS lawyer and head of business affairs, in New York while we were finalizing the new contract for the *Lucy* shows, the sale of 25 percent of our stock to them and the *Our Miss Brooks* deal. Spencer told Mr. Paley that I was giving them a screwing. He said that the equipment we had bought with the *I Love Lucy* budget was now being rented back to them. Paley asked me if that was true and I answered, "Yes, it is true to a certain extent. When CBS negotiated our new contract, no more cost-plus basis but a flat sum, I claimed that all the equipment we had bought during the first year of producing *I Love Lucy* should by rights belong to Desilu because it was part of the budget of *I Love Lucy*. That was discussed at length and finally accepted by CBS. We inserted a clause in the contract to that effect."

"That's true," Spencer said, "but that contract was signed before we gave you a deal to produce and film *Brooks,* which is owned by CBS, with Arden receiving a percentage of profits, and in which Desilu has no percentage or ownership."

"I don't see what that has to do with Zanra's rental business, Mr. Harrison. Zanra owns the equipment and rents it to Desilu for *Lucy, Brooks* or whatever. I guess *Brooks* could rent it from some other rental company in Hollywood if Desilu was not producing and filming it. And if there was another rental company that had the same kind of equipment needed to do it like *Lucy,* which is what I understand Miss Arden wants."

"What are you charging *Brooks* for the rental of the different things you bought?" Mr. Paley asked.

"I'm not charging anything. Zanra charges Desilu and Desilu charges its productions the same as, if not less than, what they would have to pay if they could rent it from another rental company, which they can't, because there is—"

Paley finished it: "No other rental company that has that equipment."

"That's right," I said.

Paley then asked me, "How much of Arnaz spelled backward do the Arnazes own?"

"Eighty percent."

"Who owns the rest?"

"We gave ten percent to our department heads as an incentive, and ten percent to our children and our mothers. Why? Do you want to buy some of Zanra's stock?"

"No, no, I'm involved in enough deals with you as of now."

Then he turned to Spencer and said, "I don't see that Chico has done anything wrong. It is Zanra's equipment and they can rent to whomever they want. If he screwed anybody it was the people who negotiated all the details of the new *Lucy* contract, but it seems to me he screwed them fair and square."

"Thank you, Mr. Paley."

I'm sure Spencer knew I was right. He has always been a very honest man and, while trying to get the best deal he could for CBS, a very fair negotiator. He was just trying to see if there was any room to renegotiate in front of the boss, and Paley was needling him for having been outnegotiated.

The end result of all this was that buying that equipment as we went along in the first year, instead of renting it, turned out to be a pretty good deal. The four-headed Monster alone grossed over $300,-000 in rental fees for Zanra before it got too old and had to be put to rest.

In 1953 we moved to Motion Picture Center. General Service did not have enough stages that could be converted to accommodate an audience. At Motion Picture Center they had six, all adjacent to a city street, and eventually Desilu remodeled and converted all of them to theater-audience stages.

Besides the *Lucy* and *Brooks* shows, which we would continue to do, we had been contracted to film thirty-six episodes of Loretta Young's *Letter to Loretta*, thirty *Danny Thomas Shows,* thirty *Ray Bolger Shows* and four of the *Jack Benny Shows* they wanted to try in our system.

That was also the year we filmed *The Long, Long Trailer* at MGM. During the filming of the picture I was able to recruit two hardworking, sharp, and very capable young men into our company. One was the first assistant director to Vincente Minnelli, Jerry Thorpe. I had been watching him, working as Minnelli's first assistant, and had been very impressed with the way he directed all the extras, the care and attention he gave to even the most minor details so that every scene was set and ready for Mr. Minnelli, normally even before Vincente was ready to film it. I figured he would be the kind of young person we were looking for to train in this new Desilu technique. The older, established directors were scared to death of it.

I told Jerry, "You'll start as the first assistant director on *I Love Lucy* and just stick right behind my back while we're rehearsing, while we're setting the cameras, while I go to the cutting room—wherever I go—and when *you* think you are ready to try your hand at directing one of these shows, you tell me."

"That's fair enough," said Jerry, "but I would like to take my second assistant, he's a great help to me."

"Is that Aldworth?"

"Yes."

"Fine, he'll start in his same capacity with you."

That was Jack Aldworth, whom you have already met in the tuna incident.

Another young man who came over to Desilu that same year was Martin Leeds, who had been the head of business affairs for CBS on the West Coast. This sonofabitch had given me so much trouble, arguing about the CBS money we were spending on *I Love Lucy* during the year we were on a cost-plus basis, you'd think it was his own. I mean, this character would squawk about a $3.50 cleaning bill. I figured it would be better to have him fighting on my side.

In the early part of 1953, Frank Sinatra agreed to do a pilot for us called *Downbeat,* which we hopefully would sell as a series for the fall. It was a story about a singer who had a small combo in New York and who would always get mixed up with broads and gangsters and all kinds of different intrigues in his struggle for success and often just plain survival. It was a kind of melodrama with generous portions of music and humor. Frank liked it very much. That was much before *Guy and Dolls* and at the time his career wasn't doing too well. Even his agents had told him they did not wish to represent him anymore and had torn up his contract, which was a lousy and ungrateful thing to do to a guy who had made millions for them. They forgot that once a champion, always a champion.

Sinatra, who had been such a tremendous hit, a national craze, all of a sudden couldn't get arrested. I had always thought that Frank was a hell of a good actor. In his singing he proved that. He just doesn't sing a song, he acts out a poem to music, and his phrasing gives the words in each sentence the right meaning, whether it is that of a tender caress or a brash rebuke.

We were about ready to go with the pilot when Frank came to my office at General Service and told me that he had gotten this part in *From Here to Eternity,* which he really wanted and had worked hard to get. He was anxious to do it and thought it would be a tremendous break for him. But being the kind of guy he is, he wanted to know how much we had invested in the development of the pilot and if he could reimburse us for it or perhaps do it later.

I told him, "Forget it, Frank. What the hell, we can do a television series some other time. We'll just let this thing sleep in the files for a while and see what happens."

I was very happy to see what happened.

38

Nineteen fifty-three had been quite a busy little year. The best thing that happened was that Desi was born and the worst was that goddamn ridiculous but frightening episode with the House Un-American Activities Committee.

For the 1954–55 television season we also produced and filmed two other wholly owned Desilu comedies. One was the pilot which went on the following season of *Those Whiting Girls,* starring Margaret and her sister, Barbara, and Mabel Albertson, and featuring Jerry Paris, whom we later gave a chance to direct. He did so well that he directed many hit shows for Desilu and today is one of the top directors in the business, with more offers than he can accept.

The other one starred June Havoc, as a woman lawyer in *Willy.* A young, skinny, shy, strange-looking kid started his television career playing a few bits in that show. Today he is not so skinny and shy anymore, and his looks I thought strange are now considered fashionable. He is one of the best and most successful producers of film for television, not only series but movies of the week—Aaron Spelling.

During that same season, in partnership with Parke Levy, and eventually CBS too, we produced and filmed *December Bride,* starring Spring Byington. I had nothing to do with initiating the negotiations for that partnership. It was fortunately dumped in my lap.

Parke Levy, the creator and writer of *December Bride,* which had been a very successful show on radio for years, owned 50 percent of the show. CBS owned the other 50 percent. The network wanted to transfer it to television as they had done with *Our Miss Brooks,* but they did not want Spring Byington in the role she had played on radio.

Parke, a brilliant writer and creator of radio shows, did not

With our neighbor in Chatsworth, Bill Henry of the *Los Angeles Times*.

Lucie's first birthday.

Grandpa supervises Desi's first haircut.

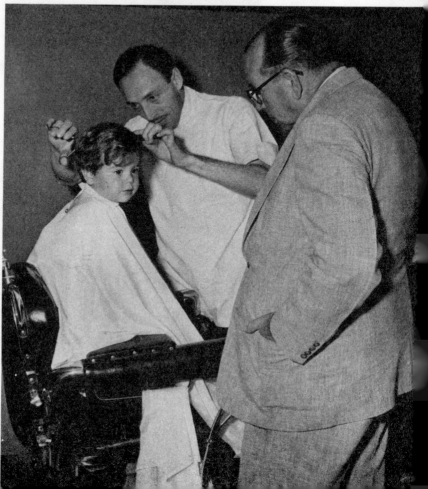

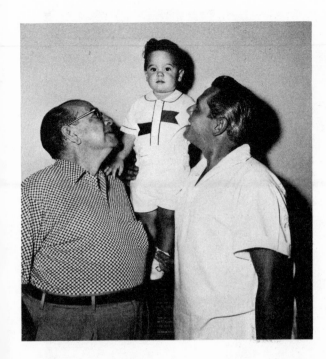

Desiderio II with Desi, Jr. and Desi, Sr.

At least the adults were willing to pose for this family portrait.

Lucie, Desi, and Little Ricky.

The Desilu company picnic, which started out with fifteen couples and a dozen children in 1952. At the last one I attended in 1962, we had approximately 250 couples and perhaps a thousand children.

We had to take over an entire park.

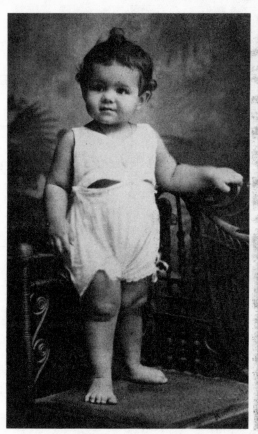

The photographs of the president and vice-president of Desilu that were in my office at RKO Gower.

This was not just an ordinary kiss.

want to do it without Spring Byington. The option that CBS had, to do it on television, was coming to an end and the controversy continued to exist. I learned all about this when Parke came to see me and explained the situation.

He then asked me, "Would you do it with Spring Byington?"

"Sure, I think she'd be great in it," I told him. "I don't know why CBS doesn't want to do it with her."

"Good," Parke said. "I'll let you know what happens."

About a month later he came back to my office at Motion Picture Center and told me that CBS had not exercised their option and that he now owned *December Bride* 100 percent.

I asked him, "What would Desilu's position be if we financed the pilot?"

"The same position that CBS had. You'll own fifty percent of the show and I'll own fifty percent."

During that month, between Parke's visits, I read all the radio scripts they had done and listened to many of the tapes. They did the radio show in front of an audience just as Lucy had done *My Favorite Husband,* and that was another big reason Parke had come to see me. He wanted it done the same way as *I Love Lucy* and our other comedies. Desilu was still the only company filming shows with multiple cameras, in front of an audience.

The material I read and/or listened to was very good and got big laughs from the studio audience. I was convinced that if we were able to cast the young daughter and son-in-law of Spring, and their neighbors, the show would be a hit. Even if Parke didn't write any new episodes for television (which, of course, owning 50 percent, he would) the material from radio could be easily adapted.

I told Parke, "Okay, you've got a deal."

This was the first time I put up our own money for a pilot show. Desilu was not a public company yet. I told Lucy the deal I had made with Parke and asked her what she thought.

"You handle the deals. I play Lucy," she said. "Besides, you've already made it, haven't you?"

"Yeah . . . but why do you think CBS did not want to do it with Spring?" I asked her.

"I don't know, but I think you and Parke were right. She'll be great in it. Film is nothing new to her. And since when do you care what a network did or did not want to do?"

"We are putting up our own money to produce and film the pilot. CBS dropped their option and gave up fifty percent ownership in the property because they didn't want to do it with Spring, and

ABC doesn't have enough outlets yet, so if we don't sell it to NBC, we could lose a lot of money."

"Look, Cuban, don't bother me with your gruesome business problems. Just make sure to come up with a hit."

"Thanks."

We adapted the radio show for television and were able to cast it just right: Frances Rafferty, a beautiful redhead who had done some pictures at MGM, as the daughter; Dean Miller, a young, handsome guy who could do sophisticated comedy (a la Cary Grant) as the son-in-law; Verna Felton, a top radio and motion-picture comedienne as the next-door confidante; and one of the best character actors and comedians in the business, Harry Morgan, as the neighbor.

Jerry Thorpe had done a fine job as the first assistant director on *Lucy,* while at the same time watching carefully every angle of our technique. I had a tough time even going to the bathroom without Jerry looking over my shoulder. It was almost a year after joining us when he told me, "Boss, I think I'm ready to direct when you need me."

This proved how conscientious he was. Most young men trying to move up the ladder of their career would have watched how we did it for a few weeks and then said they were ready. I gave Jerry his first directorial assignment on the pilot of *December Bride.* He did a fine technical job and, even more important, Parke, the cast and the crew respected his ability and enjoyed working with him. He made them work really hard but they all had fun on the set, which, believe me, shows up on the screen, particularly when doing comedy.

Our studio audience reaction was great and we all felt we had a hit. Spring could not understand why the CBS people were not around. She told me Mr. Paley never failed to send her flowers at the beginning of each radio season and presents for Christmas with a note saying that her radio show was one of his favorites and how glad he was to have it on the network.

I did not want to tell Spring why they weren't around but I learned a very important piece of information. As it happens so many times in those big companies, Mr. Paley may not have known they had dropped their option. His subordinates could have considered it too small a thing to bother him with.

General Foods saw the pilot, liked it and wanted it as a series on CBS. I told them I didn't know about CBS, but if they wanted to show it to them to make sure Mr. Paley was at the screening. They did. Paley saw it and, still in the projection room, congratulated all his men.

"I'm so glad we did this as a television show. It has always been one of my favorite CBS partly owned properties."

There was a lot of feet shuffling, nervous coughs and scared looks among his executives, but they had to tell him.

"Well . . . uh . . . uh . . . Mr. Paley, we don't own a piece of the television show," someone finally said.

"What do you mean? We owned fifty percent of that show since its inception, and it has always been one of our top-rated radio shows."

"Yes, sir, but CBS didn't make it into a television show."

"Why didn't we and who did?"

"Desi did."

"Desi? Spencer was right. How did he screw us this time?"

"Well, it's a long story," they told him.

He didn't wait to hear it. He got up, went to his office and called me immediately.

"Chico, you are a crook."

"Now hold on, Chief. What are you talking about?"

"You stole *December Bride* from me."

"I did no such thing. I'll tell you exactly what happened. Parke Levy came to my office and told me that CBS had let the option lapse because someone there didn't want Spring Byington to play the part she did on radio."

"Who the hell was that stupid sonofabitch?" he asked. "Spring is great in the pilot."

"That's what I thought she would be, so we went ahead and did it with our own money. In return Parke gave Desilu fifty percent ownership, which, as I understood, was what CBS originally had."

"You understood right. I'm sorry I called you a crook. It's a hell of a good show, Chico. I'd like to see it on CBS."

"Do you want to get back in?" I asked.

"How?"

"Give me nine-thirty Monday night, following *I Love Lucy,* and you got twenty-five percent. Maybe we can talk Parke out of a few more percentage points, but he has already given some to a couple of other writers and I think some to Spring. Even so, the worst that can happen is you got half of what I got."

"Do you think the rest of the episodes in the series will be as good as the pilot?"

"As good or better, Chief, and this thing can go on as long as you want it to. We've got a million ways to go."

"Okay," he said, "you got nine-thirty Monday night and I got half of what I had. I blew twenty-five percent when some ignoramus dropped the option without telling me about it."

"Well, maybe this ignoramus wouldn't have done it as well as we did."

"You're probably right, Chico. Does Spring know we dropped the option and why?"

"No, Chief, neither Parke nor I ever told her anything."

"Good, I'll send her some flowers right away and tell her I loved the pilot and how happy we all are she is going to be on our network in such a good time spot."

December Bride stayed on CBS for five years, always in the Top Ten. It was our second most successful comedy series.

Besides the ones already mentioned, we were still filming *Our Miss Brooks, Danny Thomas, Ray Bolger, The Lineup,* a new CBS show, and three Jimmy Durante specials for NBC.

All in all, Desilu would do 229 half-hour shows that year, the equivalent of about eighty motion pictures.

At that time we were still renting space at Motion Picture Center. Joe Justman and his partners owned it. They were all in the vegetable business. It seems I keep running into these vegetable people. Joe had told me when we first made the rental deal that if Desilu wanted to own Motion Picture Center or just buy control of it, he was sure most of his partners would be willing to sell us the stock.

It was a nice little studio, and with the right planning and hard work it could be run without a big overhead. But in 1953 I wasn't thinking about buying a studio.

Toward the end of 1954 Joe told me that they had a buyer for Motion Picture Center, but he could not tell me who that was.

On a lovely Saturday morning, during the first week of 1955, I was playing golf at the Thunderbird Country Club in Palm Springs when I received a call from Kenny Morgan, who said, "Irving Briskin is trying to get in touch with you. He told me that Harry Cohn has just about finalized a deal for Columbia to buy Motion Picture Center and that you should not worry about it. Mr. Cohn promises that Desilu would still have the stages you have been using for as long as you want."

That scared the hell out of me! Harry Cohn was a man I admired at times, but I knew he was absolutely ruthless in business. If Desilu was dependent on him for its life, it could be a short one. I was certain that if he at any time needed our stages we would be out in the street looking for another place.

I called Joe Justman immediately and made an appointment for lunch on Sunday at our ranch. I then called Art Manella, our tax attorney, a brilliant young man who used to work for the Internal Revenue Service.

I told him, "Art, we have a very serious situation. I have just found out that Harry Cohn is about to buy Motion Picture Center. I cannot trust Mr. Cohn and what Columbia could do to us. Joe Justman is coming to Chatsworth tomorrow for lunch and I want you to come and be prepared to stay until we own fifty-one percent of Motion Picture Center."

We talked from noon until eight o'clock that night before we had all the details worked out.

Joe then got up and said, "I have to go and see this one guy who represents my partners and as soon as I get his okay I'll be back."

He left.

"How ya doing with the deal?" Lucy asked me.

"Well, we've worked out the details," I told her, "but he has to check it out with one other fellow."

"Aha! I wish you luck but I'm sure Mr. Cohn already has Justman in his pocket."

"I don't know, honey. Joe seems to be a decent kind of man and he promised he would definitely be back. He thinks he can work it out."

An hour went by, two hours went by, three hours went by and we still hadn't heard from Joe.

"I told you," said Lucy, "there just ain't no way you can fight with Harry Cohn without getting screwed."

Art and I were beginning to think she was right when I saw the lights of a car, driving up the road to our ranch.

We had control of Motion Picture Center!

39

In May of 1955, Lucy and I had to say good-bye to our ranch in Chatsworth. It was not a happy moment. San Fernando Valley's tremendous growth and the traffic congestion it created made it impractical to commute. A whole new era began when we sold the Desilu Ranchito. From now on we had to be practical.

prac' ti.cal—from *prossein,* to do, to work, designed for use,
utilitarian, as a *practical* dress, exhibited in, or ob-
tained through a *practical* way of living, and in
distinction from *ideal.*

I hate the word and its meaning.

A couple of months before moving to 1000 North Roxbury,
Beverly Hills, Lucy and I had a long talk about our future. I told her,
"We have two alternatives. We can sell four years of the *I Love Lucy*
shows we have done for Philip Morris for at least three million dollars,
I'm sure. After we give Uncle Sam his cut, we'll invest the rest safely
and conservatively, which should bring us at least one hundred and
fifty thousand dollars a year in income, without touching the capital.

"After we finish *Forever, Darling* [which we were about to start]
and you'd want to do a special or another picture once in a while, you
could. If you didn't feel like it, you wouldn't have to do anything. I
would still have to run Desilu, produce our other shows and supervise
the ones we'd film for others, but without having to also spend fifty
hours a week just on *I Love Lucy.* It would be a breeze.

"And now that we have two wonderful children, after waiting
all these years, it'd be a shame not to be able to spend more time with
them, enjoy watching them grow. Desi will be two and a half and
Lucie four this summer. We could teach them to fish, ride a horse, and
I could take all of you to Cuba to meet your thousands of relatives.
What do you think?"

"You said we had two alternatives. What is the other one?" she
asked.

"I hate to even consider it. We must get to be as big as MGM,
Twentieth Century-Fox, Warner Brothers, Paramount, Columbia or
any of the other big studios. That means hiring a lot more people, top
creative people, if I can get them, to help carry the load, and rent or
buy a bigger studio. Motion Picture Center doesn't even have a back
lot or the facilities we would need to compete, on an equal footing,
with the big giants. They are all coming into television now and I'm
beginning to feel the pressure when I go to Madison Avenue to try to
sell a show."

The advertising agencies and sponsors, even the networks, were
anxious to get these giants of the motion-picture business to give them
bigger production values, as if that would have anything to do with
the success of a television show. Big panoramic scenes and large,
fabulous sets with lots of people don't mean a goddamn thing on
television, which is a very intimate medium. The format, the people in

that format and their human involvement are what make or break a show.

I Love Lucy, The Honeymooners, Dick Van Dyke and Mary Tyler Moore, Ann Sothern's *Private Secretary,* Danny Thomas's *Make Room for Daddy,* Spring Byington's *December Bride,* Eve Arden, Gale Gordon and Richard Crenna's *Our Miss Brooks,* Walter Brennan's *The Real McCoys,* and other big hits had only two or three small sets and four or five people. And the same thing is true of the big hits of today: *All in the Family, Maude, The Carol Burnett Show, Sanford and Son, Chico and the Man, The Mary Tyler Moore Show, Rhoda* and others.

Even those who televise sports events have learned that when they pull their cameras back to show the entire field of play or even just the two teams lining up against each other, as in football, those shots are only good for a few seconds to establish where they are and what the formation is, but from then on they stay pretty much with the medium and close-up shots.

In baseball, that centerfield camera with a zoom lens shoots just the back of the pitcher, the batter, the catcher and the umpire, and the reverse of that shot from the umpire's back to the pitcher, and those two shots are the ones that are used most, plus plenty of individual closeups. Until the television screen becomes 8 feet by 6 feet, occupying a big chunk of one of the walls in your home (it will happen in the future), this will be true.

But in those days some of the people I had to deal with on Madison Avenue thought the bigger the studio, the more production values they could get, the better their show would be. So even though I didn't relish the idea of getting any bigger—we were too goddamn big already—I knew that in comparison to MGM, Twentieth Century-Fox, etc., we were just a nice little company, and unfortunately there is no such thing as a nice little company surviving anymore. You don't see many individually owned grocery stores or the little drugstore on the corner that Joe used to run. They're all gone. Big Fish eats them all up.

Lucy asked me, "If we quit after we sell our shows, what happens to the people who have been working with us?"

"Well, let me tell you a story. During our first three years I stole a few people from CBS, like Ed Holly, Martin Leeds, Bernie Weitzman and others. Paley did not like that at all and made me give him my word that I would not raid CBS for any more of their personnel. I kept my word to Mr. Paley, but not too long after that some of his people started flirting with some of our personnel. So when we signed the contract to do at least two more years of *I Love Lucy* for Philip Morris, I inserted a clause which forbade CBS from stealing any Desilu personnel. So don't worry about them. Our people are the top people in the business. Before we lock up the place, they'll have as good or better jobs, either at CBS or someplace else."

"I don't want to quit," she said.

"Okay, then we'll just have to get bigger or lose the whole ball of wax."

I knew Paley did not want us to stop making the *I Love Lucy* shows and had General Foods standing in the wings to pick up the sponsor's tab.

Lucy had already told me her choice from the two alternatives we had. So Desilu made a new deal with CBS. We would do 26 more *Lucy* shows for the 1955–1956 season and 26 more for the following year. At the same time CBS agreed to buy our ownership in 179 *I Love Lucy* shows, which would be the total at the end of the 1956–1957 season, for $4,500,000 in cash, plus a minimum guarantee of three CBS shows to be filmed and produced by Desilu in each of the next two years. We also sold them our ownership in *December Bride* for $500,000.

At the same time Lucy and I got one million dollars for our exclusivity as performers for CBS during the next ten years. We needed the money to get bigger.

During the 1955–1956 and 1956–1957 seasons Desilu's output of filmed shows for television totaled 691 half-hours, without counting our pilots. Included in this figure were the new 52 *Lucy,* 30 more *Brooks,* 60 *Danny Thomas,* 74 *Lineup,* 61 *December Bride,* 13 *Durante* specials, 26 *Those Whiting Girls,* 26 of a new Desilu show, *It's Always Jan,* starring Janis Paige, 39 *Whirlybirds,* 39 *Sheriff of Cochise,* also Desilu shows, plus 13 *My Favorite Husband* for CBS (which was the third time around for this property: first, Lucy on radio; second, CBS did it live with Joan Caulfield, which didn't work out; third, filmed in our technique with Vanessa Brown, which was sold but lasted only thirteen weeks. I guess the property needed Lucy).

Besides those, we filmed 25 *Red Skelton,* 38 *Jim Bowie,* 26 *The Brothers,* 39 *Wire Service,* 15 *Du Pont Cavalcade,* three *The Betty White Show* and the CBS pilot of *The Real McCoys* with Walter Brennan.

"Little Ricky," as a three-year-old young man, made his debut on the first fall show of 1956. A lot of people still think Desi was Little Ricky, but Desi was never in the show. The reason for that, as I've already mentioned, was that we didn't want his sister watching her brother in the show and wondering why she wasn't in it.

When we first showed the baby in 1953, we had to get twins. At that early age babies are not allowed to be photographed for more than thirty seconds at a time.

Jim Paisley went over ten thousand birth certificates to find the right pair of twins. For this season of 1956 we wanted Little Ricky to be a little older so we could do more things with him, instead of just having him lie in a crib.

Horace Heidt, the orchestra leader, had a television show where amateur talent appeared. One night Lucy and I saw a young kid playing the drums in that show. Almost in unison we said, "Migawd, that's Little Ricky!" Keith Thibodeaux, from Lafayette, Louisiana, was great on the drums and could not have been more than three years old. I talked to his father that same night, he brought his son to Hollywood, we auditioned him, I tried a couple of drum numbers with him, he looked as if he could be my son, and the fact that Ricky played the drums and this kid could also play the drums gave us a perfect setup.

For billing purposes we changed his name to Richard Keith and he became Little Ricky. Richard was almost two years older than Desi but didn't look it. One of the reasons Desi got interested in music and playing the drums was that he wanted to do everything Little Ricky did in the show, and they became really good friends.

Keith, as Desi always calls him, stayed at our house all the time. During the weekends and our summer hiatus he'd come to Palm Springs or Del Mar with us. Desi and Keith got to be like brothers. They grew up together. I taught Lucie, Keith and Desi how to swim, ride horses, handle boats and fish expertly. All three of them had landed marlin and sailfish before they were seven years old.

Lucy became Keith's acting coach and looked after his appearance, wardrobe, schooling, etc. It was as if we had three children instead of two.

Keith's father, a very nice young man, came with him and stayed part of every year to work in our public-relations department under Ken Morgan. In that way he could always be close to Keith at the studio; and whenever he liked and was able to, he'd join us on weekends and vacations.

I'm glad to say that to this very day Desi, Lucie and Keith remain the best of friends.

At the end of that 1956–1957 season I went to New York, met

with Paley and told him I wanted to stop doing the half-hour *Lucy* shows and just do a few hours as specials.

"What are you talking about?" he said. "You're the number-one show on television. You can't quit now."

"Now look, Chief, we've been on for six years. I think that now is the time to go to some hour specials, then in a year or two I'm sure Lucy will come back and do another half-hour series, maybe with Vivian. We can call it *The Lucy Show,* or something like that. I promise you I'll start working with the writers right away and develop a good format for her. As a matter of fact, I already have an option on a book by Irene Kampen, *Life Without George,* which I think would make a good series for her. It will be good for Lucy to quit doing the half-hour series while *I Love Lucy* is still number one, and then, when she comes back and does a new half-hour series, I'm sure she'll go right to the top again. This way she'll be a tremendously valuable property for you, for as many years as you want, but I just can't go on doing everything I'm doing running Desilu and still be in front of the cameras on a weekly series, playing Ricky and producing the shows."

It was getting pretty rough. I had to supervise all of our own shows, our commercial tie-ups with dozens of manufacturers, the business end of Desilu, our own personal investments and the creation, development and sales of new pilots. In order to sell our pilots I had to guarantee they would be done in the same Desilu quality by top producers, writers and directors, but no matter whom I got to do these things—and we always had the very best people we could get— Madison Avenue would still hold me personally responsible for their success or failure. Failure is the most terrible thing in our business. When we fail, the whole world knows it. When a Fuller Brush man fails, does the whole world know it? That's why we keep breaking our ass not to.

I was working much too hard. My health was beginning to deteriorate. I knew something would have to give.

About a year before I had gone to see Dr. Marcus Rabwin, a brilliant physician, chief surgeon at Cedars of Lebanon Hospital and a very dear friend. I had met Dr. Rabwin and his wife, Marcella, through Lucy, who had been a friend of theirs for many years. Marcella and Marc are part of that very small group you can really call friends. Marcella had been David O. Selznick's executive assistant for many years and I learned a lot from her about how David took care of the preproduction, writing, casting, planning, execution and postproduction of not only *Gone With the Wind* but of all his other films.

Lucy and I had been their guests at Del Mar. When I went to see Marc, I told him I was afraid I was not going to be able to keep up the pace.

"I'm at the studio at seven or seven-thirty A.M., don't get home until after dinner, then I have a lot of paper work to take care of. I hardly ever see my children unless it's just before they go to school and, if I'm lucky, during some weekends. I'm all tied up in a knot most of the time and in order to untie it and keep going I'm beginning to drink too much at times."

He gave me a complete checkup. He told me that I should cut down on the work load, that my colon was full of diverticula, and continuous pressure and tension would make it worse.

A few years later he had to operate on me for diverticulitis. By then it was so bad I had to have a colostomy for over a year.

Marc knew how much I loved the ocean and recommended that I rent a house at the beach in Del Mar.

"Get away from the studio the minute you finish filming that week's *Lucy* show. Have somebody drive you to the beach and stay there until Monday morning. Have Lucy and the children join you there for Saturday and Sunday and don't even think about the business. During the summer take six or eight weeks off, and even if they offer you the entire CBS network to come back to work during those weeks, tell them to stick it."

It was wonderful advice and it helped a lot, at least for a while.

Paley finally agreed that for the 1957–58 season we would only do five specials, keeping the same format, same cast of Lucy and Ricky, Fred and Ethel and Little Ricky, and we would get top stars to be guests of ours. We had Ann Sothern, Cesar Romero, Rudy Vallee and Hedda Hopper for the first one and, for the other four, Betty Grable and Harry James, Fred MacMurray and his wife, June Haver, Fernando Lamas and Tallulah Bankhead. The Ford Motor Company agreed to sponsor the specials.

Bob and Madelyn came up with what we thought would make a great first *Lucy-Desi Comedy Hour*. Bob Schiller and Bob Weiskopf, now writing a lot of the *Maude* scripts, worked with them on the script. We had gotten the two Bobs a few years before when Jess Oppenheimer left us to go to NBC.

This first *Lucy-Desi Comedy Hour* was a flashback about how Lucy met Ricky. Ann Sothern and Lucy played two secretaries going to Havana for their vacation. Rudy Vallee was on the same boat, and when they arrived in Havana they were met by these two Cubans who had a horse and buggy carriage and made their living hustling the tourists. The two Cubans were Cesar Romero and myself.

Hedda Hopper was in the first scene, interviewing Lucy about our sixteen years of married life, and when she asked Lucy how she met Ricky, she started telling her and we did a flashback to that time. *Lucy Goes to Havana* was the title.

We had a lot of music and dancing in the show. Barrie Chase, the girl who danced with Fred Astaire later on, and two other girls did a number with Cesar and me in the show.

The script was beautifully written and it played great. Even though it was an hour, we still did it in front of an audience. We had to use two stages because we had a lot of sets. During the intermission we had coffee, doughnuts and cake for the audience. We made it a big party, everybody enjoyed it and everything worked out perfectly, except that we were much too long. After we had finished editing we wound up with an hour and fifteen minutes.

I got a call from Paley. He knew we had done the show and he wanted to know how the first hour came out. Remember that he was against going into hours to start out with.

I told him, "Chief, it's the best thing we've ever done."

"I'm glad to hear it, because we're going to have full-page ads in a lot of papers to kick off the start of the next season."

"Well, it's just great. There's only one little problem."

"What's that?"

"We got an hour and fifteen minutes."

"That's no problem," said Paley. "Cut it down to an hour."

"I tried to do that; it doesn't work."

"What do you mean?"

"I'll ruin it if I cut it down to an hour."

"All right, we'll make your opening show an hour and a half, and the rest will be an hour."

"I tried that too, but it also louses it up. It slows it down here and there. What we've got is a great hour and fifteen minutes."

"Now, Chico, let me explain something to you. Television has fifteen-minute shows, half-hour shows, hour shows, sometimes even an hour-and-a-half or two-hour shows, but it does not have any such thing as an hour-and-fifteen-minute show."

"Well, that's what we've got. Why can't we get fifteen more minutes from whoever follows us?"

"You know who will follow you this season?"

"No, I don't know what the layout is for next year."

"Right after your hour special comes *The United States Steel Hour.*"

"So tell them to give us fifteen minutes of their time."

"You want me to call United States Steel and tell them to give you fifteen minutes of their time! You're out of your mind. That's one of our biggest customers."

"I know that, but if they've got the same show as they had last year, it's not a very good show. It wouldn't hurt them any if they had only a forty-five-minute show that week."

"I see. You want me to call United States Steel, tell them they've got such a lousy show it wouldn't hurt them any if they gave you fifteen minutes of their time. There is no way that the guy who is making them pay so much money—me—for that particular time spot could tell that to them."

"Would you mind if I called them?"

"No, you do whatever you want, just be sure you keep me out of it."

I found out who was in charge of television at United States Steel and told him my problem. Actually, I had a pretty good idea in mind. I knew they hadn't been getting any rating with their show, which wasn't a good program.

So I said to the man, "Look, this show we're doing is the first special Lucy and I have done. We have been number one for six years, doing the half-hour *Lucy* series. This will be the premiere of the specials. The only trouble is that I've got an hour and fifteen minutes instead of an hour. Paley thinks I'm out of my mind to bother you, but I thought that perhaps it would be very good for you also, and it would solve my problem."

"How's that?"

"Well, your show is not doing very good."

"You can say that again."

"It wouldn't hurt you if that particular week's show is only forty-five minutes. It might even make it a little better, or fifteen minutes less bad."

He was laughing like hell. I guess they were fed up with the goddamn show anyway.

"Yeah, well, keep going," he said.

"You give me fifteen minutes from the front of your show. Instead of you going on at ten o'clock, you go on at ten-fifteen. At the end of our show, at ten-fourteen exactly, I will come on, in person, as Desi Arnaz, not as Ricky, and thank *The United States Steel Hour* for allowing Lucy and me to cut into your time period, tell the audience we have seen your show and it is one of the best dramatic shows we have ever seen and to make sure to stay tuned for it. I know we're going to have a big audience. Even out of curiosity they'll want to see what Lucy and I and the rest of our group are going to do in an hour and fifteen minutes. Besides that, when we finish, all the other shows will already be fifteen minutes old. So the viewers might as well stick where they are. I know you've got to double your rating that night."

"Who pays for those fifteen minutes we are going to give up?"

"Our sponsor, the Ford Motor Company."

"You got yourself a deal."

I then asked him, "Would you please call Mr. Paley and tell him that, because if I call him he won't believe me."

"I'll call him right now," he said.

An hour later Paley called me back. "I'm going to give up on you, Chico. You're going on the air with an hour-and-fifteen-minute show."

That was the only hour-and-fifteen-minute show that has ever been on television—before or since. And *The United Steel Hour* did double its rating.

The season standings announced that all five of our specials were in the Top Ten, three of them occupying first, second and third place. But, most important of all, I got a new Thunderbird, the original one, now a classic, for introducing it on one of those specials.

40

In September, 1957, I received a call from Dan O'Shea, who had been the head of David Selznick's distribution company and one of David's right-hand people. I had gotten to know Dan very well during the time he was with CBS, after David passed away. He was now supervising General Tires' interests in their RKO properties.

He said, "Desi, General Tires wants to sell the RKO Studios."

General Tires had bought RKO from Howard Hughes. At the time they bought it they were looking for diversification. Tom O'Neal, young son of the founder of the tire company, thought that one good way to diversify was to go into the motion-picture business. So they bought RKO from Howard Hughes and put Bill Dozier in as head of the studio.

Their timing was wrong. The picture business was going through a very bad time. The net result was that they made ten pictures and lost ten million dollars. So the elder O'Neal called his son and said, "Look, I believe in diversification as much as you do, but this is ridiculous. Get rid of those motion-picture studios and get rid of them NOW!"

Dan also told me that they had to finalize the deal in this fiscal year because of a tax situation—they had to take a capital loss to offset a capital gain.

"I don't think we have a prayer of handling that deal, Dan," I told him. "We still owe money on Motion Picture Center, the little studio we bought."

"Well, I thought I'd let you know first," he said. "I think it's quite a good deal."

"What do they want for the studios?" I asked.

"For RKO Gower and RKO Culver and everything inside of them—all the equipment, the cameras, the sets, the props, office furniture, all the physical assets, everything except unproduced scripts and stories and finished films—they want $6,500,000. And *that's* a bargain. Desi. The real estate alone is worth more than that."

I called Howard Hughes, whom I had met when he used to come to Ciro's, and told him about General Tires wanting to sell the studios.

"What do they want for them?" he asked.

"Six million five hundred thousand dollars," I told him.

"Grab it! Even if you tear them down and make them into parking lots, you've gotta make money."

The real estate they owned at Melrose and Gower and the Culver City property added up to sixty-five acres of prime land in the heart of Hollywood and in the center of Culver City. The Gower lot covered more than twelve acres, right next to the cemetery which I once drove into with Richard. The RKO Culver lot was just a few blocks from Metro, facing Washington Boulevard, the main street of Culver City, and where Selznick Studios were when David made *Gone With the Wind*. The back lot at Culver was forty acres or so, and had everything we would ever need in our get-bigger plan.

Nevertheless, no matter what a big bargain it was, if you haven't the money to swing the deal, you haven't the money to swing the deal. That's why the saying, "It takes money to make money." When a good opportunity comes and you have the money, you can grab it. We had some money, but after paying Uncle Sam the taxes in the *Lucy* sale and paying off the note on the shares for Motion Picture Center, we didn't have nearly enough.

Anyway, after Hughes said it was good, I called Argyle Nelson into my office. He had been with us for five years and was now vice-president of Desilu in charge of production, and before that had been vice-president of RKO, also in charge of production, for thirteen years. So he knew those studios. He knew what was inside of them and what was on those back lots, as he knew the palm of his hand.

I told him about the deal and Argy said, "Boy, if you can swing it, it'd be great!"

I called O'Shea and said, "Danny, could you give me twenty-four hours before you put this deal on the market? Have you told anybody else about it?"

"No, I told you first and nobody else."

"You haven't told Paley about it?" I asked.

"No, because I don't think he wants any part of buying a studio."

"Okay, give me twenty-four hours. If you put it on the market now, I'll be competing with Jules Stein [MCA had not bought Universal yet, so they did not have a studio], Harry Cohn and all the big shots, and I wouldn't have a prayer, but I promise you in twenty-four hours I'll say yes or no."

"Okay, you got twenty-four hours."

Dan also said they wanted $2 million down and ten years to pay the rest and that General Tires would carry their own mortgage at 5½ or 6 percent.

I picked up the phone, called the main office of the Bank of America and asked for the same man who had handled the loan that had allowed us to buy control of Motion Picture Center.

"Hello, this is Desi Arnaz. I want to ask you if I could borrow two million dollars, and I need the money not later than tomorrow noon."

There was dead silence at the other end of the line. I didn't know if the guy had hung up or had left the room or what.

"Hello, hello," I said. "Are you still there?"

"Yeah, yeah, I'm still here all right. Would you mind telling me why you want two million by tomorrow noon, and what you are going to do with it?"

I told him the deal and he said, "You got the two million. Whom do we send the check to?"

"Wait a minute . . . wait a minute."

That was too darn easy. I had just picked up the phone and

called the guy on a long, long shot. The worst he could have said was no, but the minute I finished telling him why I wanted the $2 million, and without any further discussion or anything, he said, "You got it." I began to worry.

I told him, "Don't start writing nothing until I call you back."

I then called O'Shea. "Dan, I think I may have a chance to swing this deal, but it's not going to be easy. How about making it six million, instead of six and a half?"

"Desi, I gave you twenty-four hours without putting it on the market. Now you're going to start negotiating with me and you are going to blow the whole thing."

"There must be some area for negotiation, I'm having a tough time with the bank. They just loaned me money for Motion Picture Center and they think I'm crazy, buying another two studios."

Incidentally, I had already called Paley and asked him if he wanted one-half of this deal. "I don't want any part of brick and mortar," he said. "You buy them and we'll rent space from you."

He could have had one-half ownership in both the RKO Studios for a little over $3 million. A few years later he bought Republic Studios for $11 million, which was not as good as either one of the RKO Studios. But that's life.

Dan said, "Okay, this is it, six million three hundred fifty thousand dollars, and your deadline is midnight."

I called the bank back. "I can get the deal for six million, three hundred fifty thousand dollars and I think I could get it down even further."

The bank warned me, "Don't push it too much. It was a hell of a deal at six point five."

We were doing the hour shows at that time. Our guest star that week was Tallulah Bankhead. During the intermission I went to my office, which was right across from the stage where we did our shows. It was about 9 P.M.

Dan and I had been talking back and forth all day. I had asked him for all the stock footage to be thrown into the deal. I knew there was about a million feet of film Orson Welles had shot in Brazil which had never been seen. There was, of course, many more millions of stock footage RKO had accumulated over the years.

The *Lucy-Desi* episode we were doing was a show within a show of an old Shakespearean play. I was dressed as an English lord, with a plumed hat, breeches and stuff. At nine o'clock I called O'Shea and told him I would give them $6,150,000.

"I think you just blew it," he said, "but I'll present your offer and call you right back."

I waited with my silly Shakespearean costume and plumed hat —we still had to do the second act. Lucy came in and said, "Come on, what are you doing? We are waiting for you."

Just then the phone rang. It was Dan, who said, "You got it."

I told him, "You will receive a two million certified check from the Bank of America tomorrow."

Lucy asked, "What the hell was that all about?"

"We just bought RKO Studios."

"We did *what?*"

"We bought RKO Studios."

I hadn't told her anything about the negotiations; she was having enough trouble with Miss Bankhead on the show. Tallulah was half-crocked all through that whole week of rehearsals and would never give us a good rehearsal. Lucy, being the perfectionist she is, hates that. So I didn't want to give her any more problems with business deals.

When she finally digested what I had said, she repeated, *"We bought RKO?"*

"Yeah, we bought RKO Gower, where we used to work, and RKO Culver, where Selznick made *Gone With the Wind.*"

"I know where Selznick made *Gone With the Wind,*" she said. "but have we enough money to buy them?"

"No, but we bought 'em. I think it's a hell of a deal and the Bank of America thinks it's a hell of a deal and they will send General Tires two million tomorrow morning, as our down payment. So don't worry about it. Come on, let's go and do the second act."

After the show we spent the whole night sitting up and talking. She wanted me to fill her in on all the details. I told her all I had done, that I had talked with Howard Hughes and with the bank, and I included all the details of the back-and-forth negotiations with Dan O'Shea.

I also told her, "Look, honey, I know the cemetery has been dying to buy RKO Gower because they are running out of space to put the stiffs in, so if worse comes to worst, we'll get our money out of it by selling it to them. Besides, don't forget our talk a couple of years ago. Either we quit or get bigger. You opted for bigger. Well, this was the opportunity to do so."

About a month and a half later I got a call from Dan O'Shea. "Desi, we can't take the check for two million."

"What do you mean?"

"We haven't cashed it yet. We can't."

"It's no good . . . Bank of America?"

"Oh, it's good all right, but for tax reasons we can't take that much money down this year. The most we can take is five hundred thousand dollars."

"Well, tear up the two million check and I'll tell the bank to send you a check for five hundred thousand dollars."

"But if it's only five hundred thousand dollars down, Desi, we have to go back to six million, five hundred thousand, the original sale price."

"Like hell we will. We made a deal for six-one-five-zero. You wanted two million down and you've got it in your pocket. I couldn't care less what Mr. General Tires can or cannot do with his two-million check. He can cash it, tear it up or wipe his ass with it, but the sale price is not going to change."

"That's exactly what I told them you were going to say."

"Good try, Danny."

That, of course, was an unbelievable break. One and a half million for ten years at 6 percent is $900,000. We actually bought the place for almost a million dollars less.

By acquiring RKO Gower and RKO Culver, plus control of Motion Picture Center, we now had thirty-five stages, plus a back lot of more than forty acres—the biggest motion-picture and television facility in the world. We named them Desilu Gower and Desilu Culver, and Motion Picture Center became Desilu Cahuenga. MGM, Twentieth Century-Fox, or any of the other "giants" could not even come close to us. We didn't get as big . . . we got the biggest.

We were now in a position to do outdoor shows on our big back lot. *Whirlybirds, Sheriff of Cochise, Walter Winchell File, Official Detective, The Texan, U.S. Marshal, Grand Jury, The Man Nobody Knows* (the basis of *Mission Impossible*), *Kraft Mystery Theatre* and others were all filmed there. We also had enough stages and other facilities to add a few more comedies to our Desilu film library. *This Is Alice, The Ann Sothern Show, Guestward Ho, Harrigan and Son* and *Fair Exchange* (the first weekly comedy hour) were some of them.

In early 1958 I prepared a presentation of the *Desilu Playhouse*, an hour weekly show which I would host. We didn't make a pilot, just a rundown on the type of stories we would do. Some of them would be drama, some, adventure and some mystery, all designed for family viewing, and a *Lucy-Desi Comedy Hour* every third or fourth week of the series, intended for the 1958–1959 season.

At that time Westinghouse had a show called *Studio One* which wasn't doing too well. I decided this was our best sponsor possibility, went to Pittsburgh and presented our program to Mark Cresap, Jr., the president of Westinghouse. He was quite a guy, reminded me a hell of a lot of Mike Todd. I had been very fond of Mike and always remembered him telling me, "You know, Cuban, you and I have been broke many times, but we've never been poor."

After my presentation Mr. Cresap said, "What's the budget?"

"Twelve million dollars," I answered.

"That's double our budget."

"Yes, I know, but what are you getting with *Studio One?*"

They were only getting a rating of 11 or 12 at that time, which was very bad.

"This is too big for me to approve on my own. It's quite a jump from six to twelve. I will have to take it to the board of directors."

"Do you want to sell it to the board of directors?" I asked him.

"Yeah, I think it's a great idea. What would you tell the board of directors if you were me and wanted to get this thing approved?"

"Well, I would tell them that we would double your ratings."

I had no doubt that we would double the ratings. It wasn't that much to double.

Then he said, "What would you tell them about our sales?"

"Tell them we'll double your sales."

"You've got a lot more guts than I've got," he said. "What happens if I get approval of this contract and you don't do what you said you would?"

"Very simple. I'll just go back to Cuba."

"Don't go without calling me," he said. "I'll have to go with you."

He did present it to the board of directors and they approved it. The next day Mr. Cresap took me to a warehouse, as big as the biggest RKO sound stage, which was filled from floor to ceiling and from wall to wall with radio and television sets, and with just a very small, narrow passage to walk through the place.

While he was showing me around, I said, "You've got a lot of television and radio sets."

"That's right, and I would like to give a dance here on New Year's Eve for our employees."

It was then April. In those days you didn't work that far ahead for the next television season, so I was selling what would go on the air in October, and he wanted all those sets sold and out of there before the end of the year.

"I got your message," I said.

I came back to California with the biggest contract ever negotiated for television. It called for 41 *Desilu Playhouses,* one *Lucy Special*, two *Desi Specials* and eight more *Lucy-Desi Comedy Hours* for the next two years.

I told Lucy about it and she was elated. The more she has to perform, the more she likes it. Then I couldn't wait to tell the writers. But to my surprise, Bob and Madelyn said they were not going to write any more of the *Lucy-Desi Comedy Hours.*

I said, "I don't want to really be aware of what you said just now. I'm going to fix myself a stiff drink, then I will come back and you tell me I heard wrong."

I came back and asked, "Now what is it you wanted to tell me."

"We're dried out," they told me. "We just cannot write anymore for the Lucy character."

That was quite a shock. We had them under contract for five years, but what could I do? I couldn't take a whip and say to a pair of comedy writers, "That's too bad you're dried out for the Lucy character, you have a contract, so you sit down and write and write funny, goddamnit."

All they would have to say is that they didn't feel funny, so there was no real way to make them do it. Those writers' contracts only work for the writers. They're not good for the production company.

I was, and still am, extremely fond of Bob and Madelyn and I could understand that they had been writing the Lucy character for seven years with Jess and then with Schiller and Weiskopf. Madelyn had gotten married to Quinn Martin, one of our sound cutters, and they had just had their first baby, so I figured she wanted to stay home and take care of the baby. Bob, who was single, hadn't been away for a while and I knew how he loved to go to Italy every few months or so. Besides, I couldn't force them.

"Okay, Madelyn, you want to go home and take care of your baby, and Bob, I guess you want to go to Italy and fuck some Italian broads. So there's nothing I can do. And much as I hate not to have you here for the new hour shows, I know both of you deserve a vacation. The company will pay for your trip to Italy, Bob, and build a nice nursery in your house, Madelyn. That's the least we can do as a bonus for the great work you've done for us. Whenever you feel like coming back to work, you let me know."

They both said, "Wait a minute, Cuban. We know you. You're getting us hooked by buying the trip and building a nursery. You want to make us feel obligated to you."

"How can you say such a thing?" I asked. "I'm just trying to show you our appreciation."

"Bullshit!" they said. "We want you to know we might not come back to work for five years."

"*Que será, será*. Whatever you want."

They did leave, and now I was faced with doing the first *Desi-Luci Comedy Hour,* which would open the season for our new *Westinghouse-Desilu Playhouse,* without any of the original writers.

I remembered Everett Freeman from my old days at MGM, a top comedy screenplay writer. I called him, and he said he would come over and kick a few ideas around. I think he suggested doing a show about Lucy going to Mexico with border crossing problems and, to top it all, getting involved in a bullfight.

"That sounds like a helluva good idea, Everett," I said.

The two Bobs, Schiller and Weiskopf, and Everett went to work and wrote *Lucy Goes to Mexico,* which opened the first season of the *Westinghouse-Desilu Playhouse.* Our guest star, and what a guest star, was Maurice Chevalier. It turned out great.

Bob and Madelyn were back at their desks before the *Lucy Goes to Mexico* script was filmed, and they stayed to write the *Lucy Specials* and the other seven *Lucy-Desi Comedy Hours* with the two Bobs. Madelyn's baby's nursery was built right next to her office. She wanted to be able to bring him to the studio while she was working.

In those shows we had such stars as Milton Berle, Red Skelton, Danny Thomas, Ida Lupino and Howard Duff, Paul Douglas and Bob Cummings. The last one was with the late Ernie Kovacs and his wife, Edie Adams.

During the years we did the half-hours, we were also fortunate to get motion picture stars who had never even appeared on television, such as John Wayne, Bill Holden, Rock Hudson, Richard Widmark, Harpo Marx and Cornel Wilde.

We couldn't have paid the regular salaries of any of the stars mentioned above. They did them because they liked the shows, and I am sure that almost all of them donated their salaries (whatever was in our budget for a guest, which was much less than they would normally get) to their favorite charity. I thanked them all one more time.

I also thanked Everett Freeman *mucho mucho* for taking a leave from his MGM chores and helping us come up with such a great show.

After that my main concern was to do a good hour show every week for Westinghouse, whether or not any of them had the potential of being a pilot (a spinoff, as they are called) for a weekly series. We did do a few which were both—a good hour show for the *Playhouse* and a possibility for a series. Rod Serling's *Twilight Zone* and *The Untouchables* were the two most prominent ones.

Ray Stark and his partner, Eliot Hyman, owned all the Warner Brothers properties, including finished pictures. Ray's mother-in-law was Fanny Brice, whom Barbra Streisand portrayed in *Funny Girl* and *Funny Lady*. Ray and Eliot were about to split their partnership and Ray asked me, "Would you like to buy all these Warner Brothers properties?"

There was no way we could handle *that* whole deal, but there were some properties in that package I would have liked to have for the *Desilu Playhouses*.

One of them was *The Untouchables,* a book Eliot Ness wrote with Oscar Fraley, a well-known sportswriter, but which Warners had never developed.

I told Ray, "I would like to buy a couple of things out of that package, but we haven't got enough money to buy the entire package."

We were already pretty much in hock to the bank for RKO.

He said, "We don't want to sell anything out of the package because that would weaken it." This I could understand.

I told Bernie Weitzman of our legal department to find out what was the status of *The Untouchables* book. Bernie reported that Ray Stark and Eliot Hyman had an option on the property for about six more months.

"Stay on top of it. If they drop it, I want it."

Bernie called the literary agent in New York and the minute the six-month option lapsed, we owned it.

It was an exciting book. I turned it over to Bert Granet, who was then my right-hand man in charge of developing dramatic things for the *Playhouse*. I told Bert I wanted to do the book as a two-parter. The first hour would be when Eliot Ness was knocking hell out of the Capone empire in Chicago while Capone was in jail. The second would start when Capone got out of jail, building up to what was going to happen then to Mr. Ness.

It was all in the book, written beautifully by Mr. Ness and Mr. Fraley. Bert got Paul Monash, a brilliant writer who is now at Twentieth Century-Fox, doing a lot of successful pictures and television shows. When I got the first draft from Monash, *The Untouchables* had become a psychological study of what made gangsters be gangsters, which was not what I wanted. I wanted plain cops and robbers.

I'll never forget the first meeting I had with Mr. Monash. "Paul, what the hell are you doing with this thing? I waited quite a while to get this book, finally got it, and now you give me a psychological study of gangsterism."

"Well, that's what your man told me to do," he answered.

I knew Mr. Monash was a very good writer, so I said, "Well, I'm sorry, Paul, I guess Bert misunderstood me. I want cops and robbers."

"I agree with you a hundred percent," said Monash. "That is what it should be, and I'll have it back to you in two weeks, just like you want it."

If it hadn't come back that way, I was going to use the book as the script for the film. It was good enough to shoot from. But Mr. Monash came back a couple of weeks later and it was exactly what I wanted. Granet left for Europe, took his vacation; he didn't want any part of it.

The executive vice-president of Desilu at the time, Martin Leeds, thought I was trying to break our company. In that day and age, you didn't spend $200,000 for an hour, that was a hell of a lot of money; and for two *Untouchables* hours about Capone, I was going to spend close to a half-million dollars, more than double the budget for the two hours.

Having gone to high school and been such good friends with Sonny Capone, I knew damn well, even though I hadn't seen or heard from Sonny for many years, that I was going to get a call from him.

I told my secretary, Johnny Aitchison, "You're going to get a call from Sonny Capone. I want to talk to him."

The day the story broke in the papers that we had bought the book and were going to do two hours for the *Desilu Playhouse* about Capone, I got a call from Sonny.

"Why you? Why did *you* have to do it?" he asked.

Why did I have to do it? Desilu was about to become a public company on December 3, 1958, which meant I had to think about the best way to serve our stockholders. It was a book I knew somebody was going to do. It had to make a great two hours, with the possibility of becoming a hell of a series. We were also producing and filming it, so that a year after the television exposure we could put the two hours together and release them as *The Scarface Mob* in theaters around the world.

"Sonny, if I don't do it," I said, "somebody else is going to do it, and maybe it's better that I'm going to do it."

We didn't treat Capone too roughly. There were certain things we left out altogether. One was the story about the dinner in which Capone allegedly killed someone with a baseball bat. We never showed that one on *The Untouchables*.

But I couldn't get to first base with Sonny. He didn't talk to me for five or six years after that. He and his family even started a suit against Desilu Productions and Desi Arnaz personally, which they lost.

My first choice to play Eliot Ness was Van Heflin, who turned it down. My second choice was Van Johnson, perhaps for sentimental reasons. To play the role of Eliot Ness I did not want the obvious cop type. I wanted more of an Alan Ladd type.

Van wasn't doing a goddamn thing at the time and was tickled pink when he got the job.

I was in Palm Springs on a Saturday night. Ken Morgan was with me when I got a call from Evie Johnson. She had been married to Keenan Wynn and was now married to Van.

Van was to get ten thousand dollars, a good price for television even in today's market, but Evie, who was handling his whole career at the time, said, "I understand you're going to show one hour one week, and one hour the following week, so Van should get twenty thousand dollars."

We were to start shooting Monday morning. It was Saturday night, and the first scene we were going to film Monday morning was the one in which Eliot Ness took a truck, busted into a brewery with his men and proceeded to tear it apart. We had five cameras and five crews already on call, plus electricians, extras, etc.—about 150 union people—and you can't cancel a call on a weekend.

Evie knew this, so she was putting a gun in my back. "Either give him twenty thousand dollars," she said, "or he won't be there Monday morning."

That is the wrong thing to do to me. There ain't no way I'm going to go for blackmail.

"Evie," I said, "you know what you can do with Van, don't you?"

"What are you going to do Monday morning?" she asked.

"That's my problem, isn't it? Good-bye."

I called Argyle Nelson, our vice-president in charge of production, and told him what had happened.

"You are out of your mind," he said. "Pay him the twenty thousand dollars. It's going to cost you one hundred and fifty thousand dollars if you don't shoot on Monday."

"Maybe it will, Argy, but I am not going to kiss this lady's ass."

Then I started looking through *The Academy Directory,* a book with names and pictures of all the actors. After making lots of notes, eliminating some, considering others, I finally settled on Bob Stack. Up to this point he was mostly known as the guy who first kissed Deanna Durbin. But I knew he had the looks and the quality I was looking for, the Alan Ladd kind of quality and the same even-toned performance.

I didn't know Bob very well. I didn't go around socially with the group he and his wife did. I started trying to locate him by phone. At two o'clock in the morning—by now it was Sunday—I found him at Chasen's and told him about the two-parter we were doing for the *Westinghouse Desilu Playhouse.*

I also told him, "Van Heflin was my first choice to play Ness, but he turned it down. Then Van Johnson, who was all set, is now out. I am telling you this because the papers, particularly the trades, may make something out of you being a third choice, but don't let that make you turn it down, because I think this could be the best *Desilu Playhouse.* For the two hours you'll get ten thousand dollars, and if it goes to a series, seventy-five hundred dollars per episode, plus fifteen percent of the profits, which I will give you in Desilu stock."

Bob didn't really need the money. He comes from a very wealthy family. He listened to all of this, probably thinking, Why in hell is this guy calling me at Chasen's at two o'clock in the morning with this deal?

I continued, "Do me a favor and go home now. By the time you get there the scripts for the two hours will be waiting for you; read them and call be back at this number. I'll stay up until I hear from you."

He called back about two and a half or three hours later and said, "I read both of them. They're great. When are you planning to start filming it?"

"Tomorrow morning."

"Tomorrow morning?"

"Nine A.M. tomorrow morning."

"You've got to be kidding."

"Wait a minute. You like the shows, right?"

"Yeah, I like them."

"Do you take my word for the financial arrangements?"

"Yeah, I'll take your word."

We had no time for lawyers or contracts or anything.

I said, "Thank you. Now go back to bed. At six tonight I'll have the wardrobe man over at your house to fit everything to your satisfaction, and tomorrow, Monday, report to Desilu Culver makeup department at eight A.M." Which he did without signing a contract or anything.

Because of our long association I still told Paley what new shows Desilu was presenting as network series for the fall. This particular year I told him we had *The Texan* with Rory Calhoun, *The Ann Sothern Show* and *The Untouchables*.

He said, *"The Ann Sothern Show* and *The Texan* sound like something we can use, but I'll have to pass on *The Untouchables."*

"I think you're making a mistake, Chief. I think *The Untouchables* may turn out to be the best of the three. We're doing two hours of that property on the *Westinghouse Desilu Playhouse* on your network."

"Yes," he said, "but what the hell are you going to do after you do Capone?"

"Don't you know how many crooks you had in this country? We can go on forever telling the stories about all the gangsters."

"Well, Chico, there is another problem. Paramount is doing a pilot for us about gangsters."

Mr. Paley had a policy. If Desilu was doing a show about gangsterism or some other subject for CBS, he would not deal with another independent producer about that same type of show. His policy had worked in our favor previously.

"I didn't know Paramount was doing such a pilot," I said, "and it's too bad, because I think ours is going to be a hell of a lot better than theirs."

"Well, I've got to pass," said Mr. Paley.

The first *Westinghouse Desilu Playhouse, Lucy Goes to Mexico,* with Maurice Chevalier, went on CBS October 13, 1958.

The following week I began my chores as host of our other *Playhouses* by introducing Pier Angeli in *Bernadette,* based on the book by Margaret Blanton. That show got great ratings and marvelous critical acclaim.

When the first hour about Capone went on the air, I got a call from ABC, who asked, "How is next week's show?"

"Next week's show is better than this week's show and it'll top the first-hour ratings." Which it sure did.

The morning after the second hour went on, ABC called again, and we had a deal for the *Untouchables* series—thirty-two hours guaranteed, which was unheard of in those days.

Some people claim those wonderful old cars of the Twenties were the big stars of the show, but we shouldn't forget that Quinn Martin, whom we had promoted from sound cutter to producer, and Phil Carlson, who directed the two-parter, did a fine job. The cast— Neville Brand as Capone, Bruce Gordon as Frank Nitti, Bill Williams, Jerry Paris, Paul Picerni, Nick Georgiadi and Abel Fernandez as Eliot's group of Untouchables, Pat Crowley as Eliot's wife and Barbara Nichols as the stripper—were all great and would continue their roles in the series. The only one we couldn't get to stay with the series was Keenan Wynn. So we killed him off in the second hour.

I had a tough time getting ABC *and* Lucy to accept Winchell as the narrator. Walter was involved in a multimillion-dollar suit against ABC and Lucy had never forgiven him for the "blind" item that brought back all the Communist bullshit. But I had creative control and felt sure that Walter's narration would provide an authenticity which was extremely important to the show.

I told Lucy, "Look, honey, this is business, so let bygones be bygones." And ABC could not tell me how, who or why.

The Untouchables was soon in the Top Five of all series, and became the most successful dramatic show Desilu ever developed, produced and filmed for television. *The Scarface Mob* made a hell of a profit when released in theaters around the world.

Bob Stack eventually made $750,000, capital gain, out of his deal and also received an Emmy Award. He deserved them both. He worked hard, the best worker we had, and *The Untouchables* was not an easy show to do.

Bert Granet came back from Europe after we had sold it as a series, and did a fine job on the rest of our *Playhouses*. And Martin Leeds shut up for a while.

I went back to Pittsburgh in March of the following year. Mr. Cresap was at the airport and as I came down the ramp, he greeted me with "We gave the dance."

The Untouchables is still being shown on television in this year of 1975, as a daily syndicated show. Don Freeman, TV-radio editor of the *San Diego Union,* wrote:

Just about the best source to spot once-unknowns who later achieved substantial reputations are the repeats of *The Untouchables,* wherein Eliot Ness stalked the mob guys in Prohibition-era Chicago.

The series originally ran from 1959 through '63, with Walter Winchell's crackling voice supplying the narration. You can spot in villainous roles such actors as Peter Falk of *Columbo,* Mike Connors of *Mannix,* Jack Klugman of *The Odd Couple,* and Telly Savalas, now the peerless *Kojak,* snarling in true hoodlum fashion. Playing either gangsters or government agents are such people as Lee Marvin, Robert Redford, Charles Bronson, Cliff Robertson, Ricardo Montalban, Frank Gorshin.

In fact, it's become a game now for sharp-eyed followers of *The Untouchables* to pick out familiar faces who were then listed somewhere deep in the supporting casts.

41

A year later, Leonard Goldenson, president of ABC, and his two top executives, Tom Moore and Jim Aubrey, came to our house in Beverly Hills. We showed them *The Fountain of Youth,* which Orson Welles had done with Desilu a few years before, but which had not sold as a series.

I told them, "It's too bad this didn't sell. I thought it was a great format. You can tell an hour-and-a-half story in a half-hour."

When I made my deal with Orson for the pilot, I was trying to develop an anthology series which would include *The Fountain of Youth* (about Ponce de Leon discovering eternal youth) and the kind of stories Edgar Allan Poe is famous for, like "The Pit and the Pendulum."

Most of the anthologies on television opened with the host sitting in his library and taking a book off the shelf. They all seemed to use the same kind of setting. Hitchcock did his hosting differently and better than anybody else, but that was a few years later.

I told Orson about this and how I would like to use the host. "If we could accomplish the effect of you, as the host, in front of the television set in the viewer's living room, telling them what is happening or about to happen behind you, it would be much more intimate and you wouldn't have to be in the same set all the time. What do you think?"

Orson is one of the most brilliant men I have ever met in our business, and I was very pleased when he said, "That's great and I'm sure we can do it."

He continued with "Who do you have in your art department?"

"Claudio Guzman is a real sharp young Chilean," I answered, "and he would try anything." Claudio later became one of our best directors.

We used still pictures and "hold frames," and a lot of the stuff they think is so new today. If we wanted to show a guy making a successful play for a girl, we would use four still pictures: he looking, she looking, he winking, she winking, hold frame. It was almost a comic-strip technique and hadn't been used on television.

Hubbell Robinson was then head of programming for CBS in New York. He saw the pilot and called me. "This is the greatest pilot I have ever seen. It is the only innovation I've seen in television in years. Tell Orson it's brilliant. . . ."

I knew Hubbell well enough to know there must be a "but" coming. So I was listening to all the nice, pleasant things he was saying and waiting for it.

Finally it came: *"But . . .will the average viewer understand it?"*

"You understood it, didn't you, Hubbell?"

After a long pause he said, "Was that intended to be a nasty crack?"

"No, not a nasty crack. Who are you to be so different from the average American audience? Who am I? The heir to the Spanish throne? Why wouldn't the average viewer understand it?"

The show was given a time spot on CBS. General Foods wanted to buy it, but then they began to have trouble with Orson about whether he was going to do thirty-eight weeks, thirty weeks or what. It's kind of hard to pin Orson down. Everybody got scared and the show never went on the air as a series.

When the ABC brass had visited us at our Beverly Hills home Lucy had given them a lovely dinner, after which they saw the pilot. A few months later I read that ABC had signed Orson Welles to develop a project for them, and that Orson was to do it in Italy. ABC didn't even have the courtesy to call me. Desilu had been left out of this new deal.

I called Jim Aubrey. "I hope you are going to lose a bundle

with Orson. In fact, I know you will because he doesn't care how much of the Establishment's money he spends."

Before signing our deal with him for *The Fountain of Youth*, I told him, "Orson, I know that you are partly responsible for breaking RKO Studios. You went to Brazil to do a picture, shot a million feet of film and never made the picture, and you couldn't have cared less. But I am not RKO. This is my 'Babalu' money, so don't you fuck around with it."

I never had any trouble with Orson and, as Hubbell said, he did a brilliant job.

Sometime after I had talked to Aubrey, we were supposed to meet in Hollywood about an *Untouchables* problem with the Italian League or something. Instead, he called me and said, "I won't be able to be there for our meeting."

"Oh? Well, that's all right," I said. "What's the matter?"

"I have to go to Italy."

"You have to go to Italy, huh?" And I started to laugh. "I wondered how soon it would be before you had to go to Italy."

I knew Orson had been in Italy for more than three months, shooting film for the ABC project.

"You're terrible, you goddamn Cuban. You know why I'm going to Italy, don't you?"

"Of course, Mr. Aubrey. How much has Orson spent already?"

"Over two hundred thousand dollars and we haven't seen one fucking foot of film yet."

"Serves you right."

Jim went to Italy. About three weeks later he came back and we met.

"What happened in Italy?" I asked him.

"Can you believe this?" Jim said. "He wouldn't even see me."

The Fountain of Youth went on *Colgate Theatre* as one of four of our unsold pilots for a one-time exposure and won the Peabody Award. It was the only unsold pilot ever to win the then most coveted award in television.

Mr. Tutt, another pilot we were unable to sell, also went on *Colgate*. It was based on the Arthur Train stories in the *Saturday Evening Post*, and it starred Walter Brennan. The reason the brains of Madison Avenue gave me for not buying this one was "Who wants to see a show about lawyers?"

The third one in that group, *The Country Doctor*, starred Charles Coburn. The brains gave me the same reason as the one they gave me for *Mr. Tutt,* except this time they picked on another profession: "Who wants to see a show about doctors?"

The different reasons why some of these pilots were not sold would not be complete without the reason we were given about *The Wildcatters,* starring Charles Bronson.

I'm sure most everybody knows that Charlie is now one of the three or four top leading men in the world, the only one I know who has been offered $2 million to do one picture.

The brains turned down *The Wildcatters* because Charlie Bronson wasn't good-looking enough to be a leading man!

There were other pilots we did not sell because they were just no good. One of them was so bad that after I ran the rough cut, my film editor, Bud Molin, asked me, "Don't you have any notes for me?"

I answered him, "Yes, just one—burn it."

I had not let such failures discourage me. The fact that my judgment had been bad in selecting material, or the execution of the material, or the casting, or whatever else that had contributed to their not turning out the way I thought they would was something I had learned to accept. It's part of the game. But when we made certain products and considered them some of our best, and they didn't sell, not because Madison Avenue told us they were no good, but because of some idiotic reasons, then it really became frustrating.

In 1950 and for the next few years, television was still a baby— a new form of entertainment—and of course we had our problems but we also had the wonderful opportunity to innovate, to try new approaches and different types of shows. No one thought he had all the answers.

There was no score written; we all played it by ear. But now "they"—the "brains"—knew all the answers, or thought they knew all the answers. "Full of opinions and void of knowledge," Pascal said when referring to some people in power. Originality scared the hell out of them and no one has ever made it big in show business by not being original.

After *I Love Lucy,* situation comedies came out by the dozens. After *Dragnet,* they all wanted police shows. After Uncle Miltie's *Texaco Hour* and Arthur Godfrey's *Talent Scouts,* variety shows; and after *Playhouse 90,* dramatic anthologies.

But even worse than the pilot situation, the economics of the television business began to get ridiculously bad. I put the blame for that squarely on all the major motion-picture studios. When they finally decided to enter television, they would sell a series for much less than they knew it would cost them, just in order to sell it.

Their annual stockholders' reports would look better if they could say that they had two or three series on television. The loss their company was incurring by doing so was easily covered by manipulating the books. They could charge more to a motion-picture cost and less to a television series. They could claim a lesser profit in the selling of their old pictures, their film library, in which they had no residuals to pay, and use that money to cover some of the losses of their television series.

We couldn't do that. We had no backlog of motion pictures. I knew we were fighting a losing battle when a pilot we sold as a series had to be successful for at least three years before we could get a decent syndication deal, and then, perhaps, we might break even. Why go to all that work and take all those chances and have all that money tied up for three, four or five years, just in the hope of getting even? We were even before we made the pilot.

The big studios didn't care. They were losing their asses, but it kept the price of their stock on the market at a decent figure, which was their main concern. They did that for quite a while until they started running out of their film backlog and had no room to manipulate. When that happened, most of those companies went broke and their stock wasn't worth the paper it was printed on. The big boys helped keep up the market price, and the officers and directors knew what they were doing and when to get out. I don't know one of them who lost a nickel. They had the control to insure their own future, and they didn't give a damn about the little guy, the small stockholder.

In July of 1959, as president of Desilu, in my annual report, I announced the gross of our fiscal year just ended, $20,400,000, as compared to a gross of $4,600,000 in 1954. But the company had realized a profit of only $250,000 for the year. That is about 1¼ percent of the gross. We could have done better by putting our money in a savings account. And sometimes people wonder why I got fed up with the whole business.

I wanted to sell. I wanted to sell then more than ever. And we could have sold. MGM made us a fine offer. Clint Murchison, one of the richest men in the world, made us an even better one. He wanted to create something like the General Motors of televison. Those Texas boys think very big. The reason they made us the offers was because they knew that our book value was a true book value and our report of profit and loss was a true report. Our book value was backed by cash, real estate, hundreds of thousands of dollars of the best and newest equipment, many other solid physical assets, and a pretty goddamn good television film library for the future. It was not a value arrived at by phony or possible revenues or so-called receivables which would never be received.

Our book value was even better than the price of our shares indicated at the time. If we'd sold at 14 or 15, which we could have gotten, everybody who wanted to get out would have gotten out in fine shape. Most of our stockholders had bought at 10, the price at which our shares went on the market. But again, I am sorry to say, my partner did not want to sell.

Perhaps her attitude would have been different if our personal lives had been different. When I look back on our marriage now and ask myself what went wrong, I think that one of the problems was that we were both working too hard and were together too much—all day and all night. Little arguments became big arguments. There was really no chance to be away from each other and let things cool off. It was really ironic. For the first ten years of our married life we had both worked like hell trying to solve the problem of being separated too much.

I was still very much in love with Lucy and I felt that she was in love with me. But in a little different way. She had fallen in love with me the way I was, for whatever I was, whatever good was in me or whatever bad, whatever it all added up to, and she accepted me for that. The combination of good and bad, strength and weakness. But by this time, because of the prominence we had achieved by being in front of the public all the time, she wanted me to be a little better, to show no faults at all. I don't think a man can change that late in life.

Since I was very young I have always worked hard at whatever I have had to do. The hours and energy required to do a good job, whatever that job was, meant absolutely nothing to me, and I have also played hard at whatever games I was playing, disregarding what people thought or said.

It's true that this is a lot easier to do when you are not known by the whole world. But when I got to be known I still didn't give a damn about what people thought or said. The one thing I have never been able to do is work and play concurrently and in moderation, whatever that means. I guess I have a lot of company though—Alcoholics Anonymous for the drinkers, Weight Watchers for the fat ones, Cigarettes Anonymous for the smoker. And considering all the action,

Sex Anonymous may be next. If they are all successful we could become a pretty dull group of skinny, sober, thumb-sucking virgins. I guess if I had learned the meaning of moderation and had been able to practice it, the Desilu monster we had created and our marriage might not have been so hard to cope with.

As a producer of television shows, Desilu had two big problems. One: we were doing too many of them. Two: there were not enough hours in the day. For quality—and that was all I was interested in selling—we needed time and people who cared enough to use it well. I cared enough but I didn't have enough time. I think you can say the same thing about all American television. There is too much of it and not enough time to do it.

I had always been a drinking man. Lucy knew that. The first night we went out after that rehearsal of *Too Many Girls* at RKO, we both got bombed and had a ball. But now she was resenting it. As president of three studios and all that bullshit, I should be more dignified.

One night we were invited to go to a party at Dean Martin's house. It was to be a big Hollywood party with a tent, entertainment and orchestra, and it was black tie, of course. I had worked hard and fast all day to get home early and not have to go to the studio the following day. I showered, shaved and put my tuxedo on. Lucy looked lovely in a new evening gown. As we got into our chauffeur-driven limousine, I told her, "Lucy, you look like a doll. I'm going to have the best-looking date at the party."

She turned to me and said, "Are we going to be the last ones to leave the party again?"

Well, that kind of loused up that evening.

I said, "For Crissakes, Lucy, we haven't even left the fucking driveway yet and you're worrying about whether we're going to be the last ones to leave the party. I've got to be the last one to leave the party now. There ain't no way I can miss. You know, in Cuba, when we have a party and it doesn't wind up with everybody having breakfast the next morning, we consider it a lousy party. And now, if I'm having fun and want to stay a little longer than the other people, you consider me an asshole."

The more frustrating and impractical this whole business became, the more difficult my job became. The more our love life deteriorated, the more we fought, the less sex we had. The more unhappy we were, the more I worked, and the more I drank.

The trouble is that drinking intensifies all your pressures and all your needs. At this point I hadn't slept in the master bedroom for almost a year. I was sleeping in a bed I had in my dressing room. So I began to fill my needs elsewhere. And so did she.

The vicious cycle continued. The more we fought, the less sex we had, the more seeking others, the more jealousy, the more separations, the more drinking, which led right back to more fights, less sex and more seeking others, etc., etc., etc. The cycle was soon completed. Add to this the herculean effort we had to make to maintain the imaginary bliss of Lucy and Ricky, and our lives became a nightmare.

42

Right after that stockholders' meeting in July, I went to Miami. I wanted to talk to my dad. As I arrived at Dad's home in Coral Gables, I was pleasantly surprised to see Alfonso Menencier, our old conga friend from Santiago, who was just leaving.

After warm greetings I asked him, "How do you like it here?"

Mr. Menencier answered, "It's a beautiful country, but before I came to Florida, the only time I noticed I was black was when I took a bath."

After my dad told him, "Don't forget, we're expecting you for dinner tonight," we sat down quietly in his study and I explained to him everything that was happening.

Dad sad, "Jesus, I thought that everything was going great for you. Why haven't you said anything?"

"I didn't want to worry you. I thought that maybe I could handle things myself, but unfortunately I have reached the point now that I don't know what the hell to do."

"Remember what I always told you, when you're not sure?"

"I know, I read your letter before I flew here."

Dad said, "You kept it all this time?"

"It is now hanging in the president's office at Desilu Gower, broken glass and all."

"Why didn't you get it fixed?"

"I wanted to keep it just like Bombalé found it."

This is it, in its entirety.

March, 1933

Dear Desi,

Well, pardner, you are now sixteen, and in my book that means you are no longer a child; you are a man.

You will get your driver's license and you will drive your own car. A note of warning about driving, particularly about driving on the road that lies before you—the one we all have to travel—the road of life.

It is very much like the road from Santiago to El Cobre. There are stretches that are so smooth and beautiful that they take your breath away, and then there are others that are so ugly and rough that you wish you had never gotten on the damn thing, and you wonder if you will ever get through.

Somewhere along the way, you will get into a particularly bad spot that presents a very difficult problem, and you may not know exactly what to do. When that happens, I'd advise you not to do anything. Examine the situation first. Turn it upside down and sideways as many times as you have to. But, then, when you have finally made up your mind, do not let anything or anybody stop you. If there is a mountain in your way, go through it.

Sometimes you will make it; sometimes you will not. But, if you are honest and thorough in your decision, you will learn something either way. We should learn as much from our mistakes as we do from our successes.

And when you do come up with a minus, try to convert it into a plus. You will be surprised how many times it will work. Use a setback as a stepping stone to better times ahead.

And don't be afraid to make mistakes; we all do. Nobody bats five hundred. Even if you did, that means you were wrong half of the time. But don't worry about it. Don't be ashamed of it. Because that is the way it is. That is life.

Remember, good things do not come easy, and you will have your share of woe—the road is lined with pitfalls. But you will make it, if when you fail you try and try again. Persevere. Keep swinging. And don't forget that the Man upstairs is always there, and all of us need His help. And no matter how unworthy you think yourself of it, don't be afraid to ask Him for it.

Good luck, son.

Love,

Dad

I sent this same letter almost word for word to my son on his sixteenth birthday. And he has it framed and hung in his room.

"What about the children?" Dad asked.

"Yeah, that's it. What about the children? I love them more than anything in the world. There is nothing I wouldn't do for their happiness. Lucie was eight last July. Desi will be seven in January. And they are very much aware of what's going on. So I don't think this is doing them any good either. But Lucy and I can't keep living together this way, ruining our lives just to accumulate more and more of those values some people think are so important—fame, power and money."

"One thing for sure," Dad said, "fame, power and money will never cure a crippled love life."

"It's crippled, all right. We haven't slept together for about a year."

"I'm sorry to hear all this, especially of course about your private life. And I'm very surprised to hear you say you don't like your business. I thought you liked what you are doing."

"I'm sorry too, Dad, and it's not that I don't like the business. I just don't like the direction the business has taken and my role in it. It has ceased to be fun. The things that I liked about it—the things I did best, finding an idea for a new show, working with the writers, producing and directing, the things that got me where I am—are the things that I can no longer do, now that I am there."

"That sounds like double-talk," Dad said.

"It isn't double-talk. At the beginning, learning about all the facets of the business was not easy. It was a challenge, but I thrived on the long hours I spent to meet that challenge, and when we started to grow with it it was very rewarding. I tried to get just so big and no bigger but circumstances prevented that. Now we are the biggest television company in the world and I hate every goddamn minute I have to spend trying to keep it so. I was happier cleaning birdcages and chasing rats."

Dad said, "Well, at least you have half of your problems solved."

"How do you mean that?"

"You know what's making you unhappy—you hate your business, and your home life is miserable. I read someplace that 'there is no greater delight than to be conscious of sincerity and self-examination.' What would you really like to be able to do?" he asked.

"I would like to be able to buy a truckful of shit if I felt like it, without worrying about what Lucy and Madison Avenue were going to say about it."

At least that got a big laugh out of Dad before he said, "You better get out of the public eye before you go around buying too many truckfuls of shit."

I told him a story about the Mexican fellow I go fishing with in Baja. I would tell Argyle Nelson, our production chief, "Argy, I'm going to be gone for two weeks. I'm going to get lost. The only time I want you to call me is if anything happens to Lucy or to my kids or to my mother or to my dad. So if the three studios burn down, don't call me, call the insurance company."

I'd go down there, rent a boat and go fishing with this Mexican fellow whenever I could steal a couple of weeks, which wasn't very often. We would fill the boat with bait, food and booze, and wherever we happened to be at the end of the day, we'd stay, whether it was a village or just an empty beach. For two weeks we'd fish and eat and drink, and if we'd found a couple of girls to take with us, we'd screw—wiping everything else out of my mind. Of course, eventually the two weeks were over and I'd have to come back to work.

The first time it happened, the Mexican said, "Why do you have to go back?"

"I gotta go back to work."

"Why?" he said.

"What do you mean, why? I got to go back to work. That's why."

"Didn't you have a good time down here?"

"Of course I had a good time down here. You know that. We had a ball."

"So why do you have to go back?"

"You silly, stupid Mexican, don't you understand I gotta go back to work?"

"Why?"

"I gotta go back to work to make enough money so that next year, or as soon as I can, I can come down here again and spend another two weeks with you."

"I'm here all the time," he said.

"You know, Dad, I think that Mexican was right."

"Well, he wasn't too far wrong but unfortunately we can't all do that."

"I know, but he's got something there. Most of us knock our fucking brains out most of the year just so we can enjoy ourselves for a couple of weeks now and then."

My dad said, "You wouldn't be happy being there all the time."

"Don't bet on it."

"What would you really want to do if you could do it? After you bought the truckful of shit, that is."

"Well, I can't do much right now. Lucy and I have to keep working together, at least until we fulfill our obligation to Westinghouse. After that I would like to get rid of all the studios and from then on just concentrate on one project at a time, whether it's a television show, a stage play, a movie or what have you. And I would very much love to have a happy home life."

He said, "Remember what I said? Don't do anything until you're sure of what you want to do."

"I know, and when I decide to do it, go through the mountain."

"Right. The only trouble with you is that you've got a tendency to go through too many mountains at the same time."

"You're right, Dad."

I came back to California. Sometime during November of that year, 1959, Lucy had just left my office after some other goddamn argument. There was a water fountain on the second floor of the administration building, to the right of my office, just before you go downstairs. I followed her and as she stopped to have a drink, I told her, "Lucy, I want a divorce."

She looked up at me, and those big blue eyes can express many emotions, the desire to kill not being the least of them.

"I just can't take it anymore. Perhaps if we had just done *I Love Lucy* and we had stayed at Chatsworth and I hadn't gotten involved in so many projects, this wouldn't have happened. But I cannot do everything I have to do here, and I don't see how the hell you can either while our personal lives are so miserable."

She didn't even answer. She just turned her back to me and left.

When I got home that night, she said, "You meant what you said?"

"Yes, I'm very sorry, but I did. I cannot keep on living this way."

Her temper got the best of her. "Why don't you die then? That would be a better solution, better for the children, better for everybody."

"I'm sorry, but dying is not on my immediate schedule."

"I'll tell you something, you bastard . . . you cheat . . . you drunken bum . . . I got enough on you to hang you. By the time I get through with you you'll be as broke as when you got here. You goddamn spic . . . you . . . you wetback!"

That would be something for a Cuban to be. The Straits of Florida are quite a bit wider than the Rio Grande.

I went to my dressing room, where I had a little cardboard box in my dresser in which I kept a lot of stuff like old cuff links, chains, broken watches. I'm the type who never throws anything away.

I was about to light a cigarette when she came at me with a dueling pistol, pointed it at my face and pulled the trigger. I lit my cigarette on its flame and then showed her the bottom of the little cardboard box. A man's name, a telephone number and a New York address were written on it. Her blush must have been the blushiest blush since Fawn told Bambi she was pregnant.

I told her, "Look, I know you didn't mean everything you said, but for the sake of the children let's try to make this as amicable as possible. We'll get a good lawyer for you and you'll be the one to sue for divorce. We will have no trouble arriving at a fair financial settlement and all that other stuff, but please, don't ever threaten me again."

We never lived together under the same roof after that night.

Before the end of the year, we had to do the last *Lucy-Desi Comedy Hour* for the *Westinghouse Desilu Playhouse*. The late Ernie Kovacs and his wife, Edie Adams, were to be our guests, and I would direct it. Not because I wanted to; I would have rather had one of our other directors do it, but they were all busy. Between our own series and the ones we did for others, Desilu would be responsible for twenty-six different television series that year.

Doing that last *Lucy-Desi Comedy Hour* was not easy. We knew it was the last time we would be Lucy and Ricky. As fate would have it, the very last scene in that story called for a long clinch and a kiss-and-make-up ending. As we got to it, we looked at each other, embraced and kissed. This was not just an ordinary kiss for a scene in a show. It was a kiss that would wrap up twenty years of love and friendship, triumphs and failures, ecstasy and sex, jealousy and regrets, heartbreaks and laughter . . . and tears. The only thing we were not able to hide was the tears.

After the kiss we just stood there looking at each other and licking the salt.

Then Lucy said, "You're supposed to say 'cut.' "

"I know. Cut, goddamn it!"

I Love Lucy was never just a title.

Epilogue

When I was first asked to write this book, I thought to myself, "Write a book? I don't even like to write letters."

I thought about it for quite a while, and the more I thought about it the more I convinced myself I wouldn't even know how to start. There was only one thing that made me try, and that was the memory of my father and his wonderful attitude whenever he was faced with a seemingly insurmountable problem—*there must be a way!*

I want to thank all the people mentioned in this book who were kind and generous and understanding and who gave me a hand along the way. I know there are many others who, either inadvertently or for lack of space or memory on my part, were not included.

I want to thank the United States of America and her people. I cannot think of another country in the world in which a young man of sixteen, broke and unable to speak the language, could have been given the chances to accomplish what I did, or the welcome, *cariño*, praise and honor which were given me.

I want to thank my father, without whose advice, honesty, down-to-earth common sense I could not have made it, and, of course, my mother, who still lives with me, for her understanding, her class, her never-wavering trust in God's justice and compassion, and her inexhaustible well of love for me and my friends and my children.

I want to thank my wife, Edie, who came into my life at a time when my life was at its lowest ebb and seemed hopeless, and by giving me her love, made me see hope again.

I want to thank Lucie and Desi for their friendship and for being who they are today in spite of all my mistakes, and for being able to handle and overcome all the confusion and sorrow Lucy and I saddled them with.

As for Lucy herself, all I can say is that I loved her very much and, in my own and perhaps peculiar way, I will always love her. We spent twenty years together; many happy moments and many unhappy moments came and went during that time. It is a precious God-given gift that I mostly remember the happy ones. I hope she was given the same gift.

The success of *I Love Lucy* is something that only happens once in a lifetime, if you are fortunate enough to have it happen at all.

If we hadn't done anything else but bring that half hour of fun, pleasure, and relaxation to most of the world, a world in such dire need of even that short a time-out from its problems and sorrows, we should be content. But we did more. With God's help we also created Lucie and Desi.

Acknowledgments

A dialogue between the two fishes of Pisces about the title, one swimming north and the other swimming south:

NORTHBOUND: What are you going to call it?

SOUTHBOUND: I am going to call it *A Book.*

NORTHBOUND: [*in disbelief*] *A Book?* Why?

SOUTHBOUND: What am I writing with?

NORTHBOUND: A pencil.

SOUTHBOUND: Why do you call it a pencil?

NORTHBOUND: Because that's what it is.

SOUTHBOUND: Okay. What am I writing with this pencil?

NORTHBOUND: You are writing a book.

SOUTHBOUND: Right! So what should I call it? *A Pencil?*

Howard Cady, Senior Editor of William Morrow and Company, liked the title and presented it to his leader, Larry Hughes, President of Morrow, who said, "I have always liked simplicity and nothing could be simpler than calling a book *A Book.*"

Howard finally got me started by coming out to Del Mar, where I now live when I'm not in Las Cruces, and by spending a week—day and night—listening to me talk into a tape machine, recollecting what had happened during my oftentimes hectic life.

I did not want a ghostwriter. Not that I thought I could do it better, but I knew that I could not use flowery language and large, many-syllabled words because I don't know them. I knew I would have to write it my way, with my own not too good knowledge of the English language.

Ken Morgan, our former head of Public Relations at Desilu, left his other interests and came back to work with me on the book. He was indispensable in helping me with research, digging up all the Desilu records, newspaper accounts, and photographs. I wanted to make sure that what I wrote was accurate.

Kenny turned out to be the only one who could decipher my accent on the tapes and understand my scribbled notes on the re-writes, so he had to type all of it before turning it over to Morrow in some kind of book form. During the two years I wrote and rewrote *A Book,* Kenny became the world's fastest two-fingered typist. Finally Louise Fisher retyped the whole manuscript for us.

Marvin Moss, my agent, was the one who started the ball rolling by going to Howard Cady and suggesting the book.

Madelyn and Bob, our *Lucy* writers; Ed Holly, one of our vice-presidents and secretary and treasurer at Desilu; James Paisley, our former assistant director; Jerry Thorpe and many others from the *Lucy* era helped a lot to refresh my memory. And Lucy herself would bring up things I had forgotten or wanted to forget.

There is no need to mention what a great help Howard Cady was with the editing. He is very honest and explicit in his comments and criticisms, at times brutally so, and that is exactly the type of person I love to work with.

To all of them—*muchas gracias!*